The Nature of Fascism

Roger Griffin

London and New York

First published in Great Britain in 1991
by Pinter Publishers Limited

First published in paperback 1993
by Routledge
11 New Fetter Lane, London EC4P 4EE

Simultaneously published in the USA and Canada
by Routledge
29 West 35th Street, New York, NY 10001

Reprinted 1994, 1996

© 1991 Roger Griffin

Typeset by Florencetype Ltd, Stoodleigh, Devon
Printed and bound in Great Britain by
Biddles Ltd, Guildford and King's Lynn

British Library Cataloguing in Publication Data
A catalogue record for this book is available from the
British Library

Library of Congress Cataloguing in Publication Data
A catalogue record for this book is available from the Library
of Congress

ISBN 0–415–09661–8

Contents

Preface   v

Preface to the Paperback Edition   viii

Preface to the 1996 Printing   xii

Acknowledgements   xvi

1. The 'Nature' of Generic Fascism   1

2. A New Ideal Type of Generic Fascism   26

3. Italian Fascism   56

4. German Fascism   85

5. Abortive Fascist Movements in Inter-war Europe   116

6. Non-European and Post-war Fascisms   146

7. The Psycho-historical Bases of Generic Fascism   182

8. Socio-political Determinants of Fascism's Success   208

   Postscript   237

   Glossary   238

   Index   242

For Mariella

Preface

There are moments when from above the horizon of the mind a new constellation dazzles the eyes of all those who cannot find inner peace, an annunciation and storm-siren betokening a turning point in world history, just as it once did for the kings from the East. From this point on the surrounding stars are engulfed in a fiery blaze, idols shatter into shards of clay, and everything that has taken shape hitherto is melted down in a thousand furnaces to be cast into new values.

The epiphany to which the German Ernst Jünger was alluding here on the first page of his novel, *Battle as Inner Experience*, was bound up with his personal experience of front-line combat during the First World War. However, his words express a central component of all revolutionary sentiment: that privileged moment when frustration and despair in the contemporary state of human affairs are suddenly transfigured into the visionary sense of an imminent metamorphosis, a new world.

There is no need to be a modern Nostradamus to predict that all societies which operate the Judaeo–Christian scheme of historical time will, as the year 2000 approaches, be rife with speculations about the immediate fate of the world. Prophets of doom will vie with utopian futurologists in announcing competing visions of decadence and renewal as our *fin de siècle* gives way to the third millennium, a prospect laden with mythic force even for 'modern' minds. The collective sense of an historical watershed can only be reinforced by a number of major transformations in the perceived and objective structures of world society: the rise of fundamentalist, separatist and tribal nationalisms; the overthrow or dissolution of oppressive state communisms through revolutionary and gradualist democratic movements; the proposal of a 'new world order' safeguarded by a United Nations which finally lives up to the visionary ideals which led to its foundation; the growing realization of how imminent ecological catastrophe might be, and the efforts to transform a suicidal and biocidal modern civilization into an indefinitely sustainable framework for all terrestrial life, including that of our own species. To say that humanity is at a crossroads may for once not be a piece of ethnocentric rhetoric.

At such a time it may well be asked if an investigation into 'the nature of fascism' can really justify the intellectual, publishing and paper resources expended on it. After all, if by 'fascism' we mean Fascism and Nazism and movements which sought to emulate them, it comprehensively failed in its bid to lay the foundations of a post-liberal society immune from the evils which it attributed to liberalism and socialism, despite the horrendously destructive persecutions and wars it unleashed. The New Order in which nations would be refounded on 'healthy' principles and the New Man who would inhabit it remained a chimera. In the immediate aftermath of the Second World War it was only too natural that the human sciences devoted considerable resources to explaining the meteoric trajectory traced by Nazism and Fascism before they both burnt out and to investigating kindred movements which had not achieved power but were symptoms of the same international crisis. Half a century on, in an age dominated by dreams, not of the reborn national community but the international one, does a preoccupation with the definition and dynamics of fascism have any direct 'relevance' except as a contribution to a well-established sub-discipline of history already overflowing with data and theories?

It is one of the premises underlying this book that it is precisely in the turbulent social and ideological climate of the late twentieth century that the dynamics of fascism and the place it occupies in the unfolding of modern history can best be understood by the non-fascist. Fascism was no freak display of anti-modernism or of social pathological processes in the special paths of development followed by a few nation-states. Its raw materials were such forces as militarism, racism, charismatic leadership, populist nationalism, fears that the nation or civilization as a whole was being undermined by the forces of decadence, deep anxiety about the modern age and longings for a new era to begin, all of which are active ingredients in contemporary history. What made it possible for these ingredients to be forged together into popular, and even mass movements in the inter-war period and for two of them, Fascism and Nazism, eventually to erect a new type of single party state, was an extraordinary conjuncture of acute socio-political tensions resulting directly or indirectly from the First World War and the Russian Revolution. Fascism is thus very much a child of the twentieth century. At a time when ethnic nationalisms are displaying increasing virulence, and even the most dispassionate armchair politician or contemporary historian is torn between premonitions of cataclysm and hopes of a new dawn, it makes smaller demands on the 'historical imagination' to understand the perverse mythic logic which underlies the fascist project of destroying the old order so that the nation can be created anew.

Hopefully it will be shown that when the elusive 'fascist minimum' is defined strictly in terms of the reborn nation and the post-liberal society which will supposedly underpin it, the resulting ideal type is not only more concise and 'elegant' than those formulated to date but provides new insights into the dynamics of individual fascist movements. Clearly, a book on the 'nature of fascism' written on this basis will be an exercise in the applied history of ideas. As such it will pay the scantiest attention to the myriad events in which each fascist movement is enmeshed or the particular socio-political and economic factors which facilitate or inhibit its success, but will instead focus on the core ideology of fascism. Given the vast range of diverse phenomena in which this ideology manifests itself, the text which results will necessarily be short on detail and original research but long on theorizing and judgments based on secondary sources.

Considerations of space preclude all but the most fleeting allusions to the extensive primary sources of fascist ideology subsumed within the analysis this book offers, especially in Chapters 3 to 6. (Incidentally, all translations of quotations or passages taken from books published in languages other than English are my own.) The result is a book which as far as its register and format are concerned, addresses itself primarily to undergraduates, non-academic researchers and to sixth-form or high school teachers, as well as to postgraduates and (more hesitantly) experts working in this field. Obviously these represent two quite different constituencies of readers. The first will clearly need to avail themselves of secondary works on some of the phenom-ena which I treat so schematically, as well as of 'rival' generic theories, if they are to gain an adequate grasp of specific aspects of the many issues I touch on and a rounded view of the debate as a whole. I trust that the abundant (but far from exhaustive) bibliographical references to (mainly English-language) sources will be helpful to this end. The second group will be acutely aware of the contentiousness of the theory I develop and the considerable simplifications and omissions which its exposition has necessit-ated. I would be very grateful, both for my own research purposes and for the sake of improving any revised edition that might be contemplated, if readers of either category would write to me personally care of the Humanities Department of Oxford Polytechnic to point out sections of the argument which are confusing or obscure, to put me right on particularly disturbing empirical gaffes and lapses or to point out material which might corroborate or refine my thesis on fascism but of which I seem to be oblivious.

In the case of Fascism and Nazism, the only two fascisms to have formed a government autonomously as a result of a successful (and partly 'legal') assault on state power, I have integrated my analysis into an historical overview of their evolution from movement to regime. This is for the benefit both of the general reader new to the subject and of those experts familiar with one but not the other. To bring out the structural kinship in the political ecology and geology of the many more highly disparate varieties of fascisms which in one way or another remained abortive revolutionary movements, Chapters 5 and 6 provide satellite photos, or artist's im-pressions, of vast areas of fascist terrain, parts of which may be well trodden by some readers on the ground but completely new to others. My aim throughout has not been to offer a 'potted history' of fascism but rather to throw into relief the high degree of cohesion which 'structurally' underlies the extraordinary surface heterogeneity of its ideology and at the same time to identify the veins of regularity which run through the apparent chaos of the fates which befall its various manifestations. Such a book clearly runs the risk of being neither the fish of a general reader nor the fowl of a specialist text, but I hope that all those fascinated by the enigma of fascism will find that, like the curate's egg, it is at least edible in parts.

Roger Griffin
Oxford, February 1991

Preface to the Paperback Edition

Eighteen months have passed since I wrote the first preface to *The Nature of Fascism*. The fact that a new one to a paperback edition is being written at all testifies to the favourable reaction that a number of eminent specialists in fascist studies have had to the basic approach which it adopts to the ideological dynamics of fascism, notably Ian Kershaw, Paul Mazgaj, George Mosse, Stanley Payne, Richard Thurlow and Zeev Sternhell. I thank them all for the confidence which they have shown in the book, which in no small measure helped to convince commissioning editors at Routledge that it merited a wider circulation. However, their comments, along with feedback from students at Oxford Polytechnic, have made me only too aware of various aspects of the text which could have been improved. Naturally, minor errors which slipped through the last proof-reading process have been corrected as far as was possible without upsetting the printers. However, some potential sources of difficulty or confusion have been pointed out which are intrinsic to the way the book was conceived and thus are not so easily dealt with. I am pleased to take this opportunity to alert the reader to them early on.

Firstly, it is in the nature of a book about the 'nature of fascism' that the tone is overwhelmingly theoretical at the outset, for it cannot avoid taking stock of the intense and convoluted academic debate that has grown up around this issue before explaining the essential features of the 'new' approach. For better or for worse, I also decided to go into the methodological premises behind this approach in some detail. As a result, parts of the first two chapters are certainly demanding for undergraduates who have never wrestled with basic concepts in the human sciences before, or with the heated academic controversies they can generate. This is particularly true if the events associated with the word 'fascism' do not already inspire in the reader a mixture of horror and fascination, and if the acute lack of consensus among experts about it has not generated in advance some of the intellectual curiosity and frustration which this book sets out to placate.

A further consequence of the book's bias towards political theory rather than history is that it contains a number of words some students (in the widest sense of the term) will find off-putting, not to say 'jargonous'. I have added a short glossary to this edition to cater for those unfamiliar with some of the key terms which may pose problems, but I would suggest to those who find that the whole style of exposition initially seems to erect more barricades to understanding the subject than it tears down, that they should seriously consider the following option: they skip from the end of the section 'The Continuing Search for a Consensus Definition' of fascism at the bottom of page 8 directly to its 'discursive definition' on page 44, availing themselves of the glossary where necessary. They can then take a rain-check on the invitation to return to the rest of Chapters 1 and 2 if sufficiently intrigued by the deeper implications of terms such as 'ideology', 'ideal type', 'ultra-nationalism' and 'palingenetic'.

Secondly, some basic implications of my theory of fascism may tend to get obscured in the attempt to treat the subject as comprehensively as possible in such a small book. It boils down to the assertion that fascism is best defined as a revolutionary form of nationalism, one which sets out to be a political, social and ethical revolution, welding the 'people' into a dynamic national community under new elites infused with new heroic values. The core myth which inspires this project is that only a populist, trans-class movement of purifying, cathartic national rebirth (palingenesis) can stem the tide of decadence. While on this point it is worth stressing that, though this book give scant attention to the social basis of fascism, the theory which it elaborates is entirely consistent with the detailed empirical research which has accumulated demonstrating that no fascist movement has recruited its followers exclusively from a particular social grouping, let alone from a single 'class' (cf. pp.222–4).

Another important inference from this premise is that the whole thrust of the fascist revolutionary programme is anti-conservative, though not in the same way that it is anti-liberal or anti-Marxist. Like modern conservatives (and here I am referring to illiberal conservatives rather than liberal ones), many fascists celebrate the virtues of the nation, the family, hierarchy, (state) law and (natural) order, discipline and patriotism. In inter-war Europe, when illiberal conservatism was still such a powerful force, fascists therefore often found themselves allied with its upholders against common enemies perceived as undermining these institutions and values, even if at bottom fascism has always been bent on revolutionizing their content in ways which would eventually transform, marginalize or sweep away conservative elites (cf. pp.49–50).

A further matter to be clarified relates to my identification of 'ultra-nationalism' as a definitional component of fascism. Some would argue that I use the term in a way which obscures the distinction between nationalism and racism, especially biological racism of the sort so central to Nazism. Against this I would argue that illiberal nationalism ('ultra-nationalism') is a force which always has recourse to some mythical component to create an artificial sense of common destiny and identity, and that 'purity of the blood' is simply one of them. Thus an obsession with racial history and eugenics merely indicates that a particular *variety* of ultra-nationalism is at work rather than its contradiction. What is more important to stress in this context is that fascist ultra-nationalism does not *necessarily* preclude alliances with other nations as long as they are perceived as experiencing their own parallel process of 'awakening' (palingenesis), thus becoming kindred spirits rather than enemies (what I call 'universalist' fascism – see p.49). It is thus quite consistent with the way fascism is defined here if the concept of a 'Europe of nations' has become increasingly important to fascist ideology since 1945 (see p.171).

Other central features of my argument which might not emerge sufficiently clearly on a first reading are that: i) fascism is a relatively original, coherent and homogeneous ideology in terms *not* of its doctrine or surface rationalization, but of its core *myth* of national rebirth; ii) Nazism proves to be an outstanding specimen of generic fascism once it is analysed in terms of this core myth; iii) fascism was not interred within Hitler's bunker in 1945 but continues to inspire both theorists and activists down to the present day; iv) far from being mere imitations of inter-war variants, some neo-fascisms represent original syntheses of ideas.

The upshot of this argument is that, while fascism's potential for creating a *regime* may be safely regarded as extinguished with the defeat of the Axis powers in the Second World War, as a *political ideology* capable of spawning new movements it should be treated as a permanent feature of modern political culture. Indeed, it may suddenly appear on the stage of contemporary history dressed up in strikingly new doctrinal clothes, and is liable to undergo a headline-grabbing 'resurgence' whenever objective conditions of social, economic or political crisis in an established nation-state awaken a generalized longing to transform 'decadence' into 'rebirth' (as events in South Africa, the former Eastern bloc and the new Germany have amply borne out since this book was first published). Moreover, its current potency as a self-renewing source of organized racial hatred is deeply bound up both socio-politically and psychologically with the growing virulence of ethnic nationalism, tribalism, separatism and xenophobia all over the world. Seen in this light, fascism underlines yet again (as if history had not sated us with examples already) how easily the 'healthy' human need for transcendence and belonging can be perverted into pathological forms of social and political energy even, or rather especially, in the 'modern world'.

Finally, though the book defines fascism in terms of its generic 'core myth', the myth of the nation rising phoenix-like from the ashes of decadence, there was only space for tantalizing snippets from primary sources to illustrate the type of political thought this vision generates. Oxford University Press have recently commissioned an anthology of passages selected from a wide range of primary and secondary sources relating to fascism which will be published in their *Oxford Readers* series, thus filling the 'regrettable lacuna' referred to on page 20. But to give the flavour of fascist discourse and so prepare the reader for the somewhat abstract theory expounded in Chapter 2, it may be useful to offer a 'free sample'. It is taken from *The Political Soldier*, a lengthy pamphlet written in the late 1980s by the British fascist Derek Holland and produced in English, Swedish, German and Portuguese to be circulated among a 'select' readership in Europe and the United States, and to act as an ideological manual for his own revolutionary faction (see p.174). With their constant stress on the mission of 'true' nationalists to combat decline and decadence (here expressed in both national and pan-European terms profoundly influenced by Julius Evola, see p.169), such passages epitomize a purging, *palingenetic* brand of *ultra-nationalistic* political myth which goes well beyond conservative longings in the call for a New Order:

> If we are to have a redeeming National Revolution, that will act as a cleansing fire of purification, we must go beneath the surface, we must go to the heart of the matter: the New Man that will build the New Social Order must of necessity appear before the National Revolution because the Builder must precede in time and space the Building which he has undertaken to construct . . . If the British Family of Nations is to survive the double headed axe of Capitalism and Marxism, those who would defend this family must act now. . . . But if the glorification of Thought, unconnected to objective reality – daily life, real life – is a gross error resulting in political impotence, so too is the glorification of Action. The Fascists are perhaps the best example of this aberration: faced with a world of sterility and immobility, the call to pure action is indeed tempting. To feel the heart pound once again, to feel the blood coursing through the arteries of our European culture is highly attractive. But if we truly love Europe, we must not be blindly impetuous. . . . As the modern world goes up in flames, we who would be Political Soldiers, are called upon to found a sacred brotherhood dedicated to the redemption of our People, and to the salvation of the European Motherland.

Such nebulous utopianism would not be worth analysing by political scientists if the activists it inspires (for whom it is not a utopia but a 'vision of the world') did not continue to foment racial hatred and orchestrate political violence in contemporary society. Nor would the aberrant ideology it embodies be of much concern to historians if it were not a blood relation of Nazism, which a mere two generations ago used the state power it had seized to carry out 'purification' on a mass scale in the bid to realize its structurally identical *Weltanschauung*, one which also called for a 'national revolution' and a 'New Man'.

Roger Griffin
Oxford, August 1992

Preface to the 1996 Printing

Since I wrote the Preface to the paperback edition, fascist movements have doggedly survived within the political cultures of the Westernized world, retaining enough vitality to make the most of localized socio-political crises whenever they get the chance. This they have sometimes done to dramatic effect. In the early 1990s the world's media attention was regularly grabbed by the AWB's attempt to abort the birth of a genuinely liberal South Africa and by the wave of murderous violence directed against 'foreigners' by neo-Nazis in the new Germany. The surprise election of a British National Party local councillor to a ward in East London in 1993 was soon followed by what was widely taken to be a far more ominous sign of the times: the emergence of the ultra-nationalist Zhirinovsky as a serious contender to presidential power in Russia against the background of rising chauvinist fervour. Then Italy's 1994 general election caused considerable dismay abroad when it resulted in the inclusion of some 'post-Fascists' from the MSI's new incarnation, the National Alliance, in the first coalition government of the 'Second Republic'. A year later the Oklahoma bombing alerted the American public to the seriousness with which some fellow-citizens take paranoid fantasies of a coming showdown between the Aryan and non-Aryan 'races', even in a period of relative stability. Meanwhile the globalization of contacts and of information-sharing between fascists of every complexion has been given a major boost thanks to the wonders of the Internet. Fascism thus stubbornly remains an issue of concern to political scientists and the guardians of democracy alike.

However, fears that a generalized resurgence of fascism will lead to a Fourth Reich in Germany, or a single-party state in Russia, Italy or the USA remain groundless, not to say hysterical. Ironically, they give credence to the fascists' own chronic misjudgment of the strength of their cause and the imminence of their revolution. The democratization of South Africa has gone ahead, while in Germany neo-Nazi violence has abated and the electoral fortunes of crypto-fascist parties have declined (though not before the country's once generous asylum laws were repealed). In Britain the lone BNP councillor was ousted the next time round, while Zhirinovsky made a pathetic showing in Russia's 1995 general elections. The subsequent Italian elections (1996) produced a centre-left government so that electoral fascism had to simmer on the back-burner once more, while America's neo-Nazi militias began to be vigorously hounded by their own mythic arch-enemy, the Federal government. As for the Internet, there is no more likelihood of a surfer being converted to fascism than to any other of the myriad world-views, obsessions and fetishes on offer. The threats to global democratization come not from fascism, but from other, yet more virulent forms of fanaticism: fanaticism fed by longings for an ethnically separate or religiously pure state, from authoritarian regimes where countervailing forces have been crushed or cultural minorities are persecuted, from 'modernized' tribal wars. More insidious dangers to humanity are posed by contaminated versions of liberal democracy, especially when they operate under the cover of a myth of progress which blinds the world's power brokers to the long-term side-effects of the late twentieth century's dual crisis: the demographic explosion in the South combined with escalating man-made dysfunctions in every sphere of the ecosystem.

In fact, post-war fascism continues to confirm the scenario suggested in Chapter 8 of this book, namely that it is condemned by structural conditions to remain a constantly evolving but highly marginalized force, a shadow of its former self. But if fascism itself is not undergoing a general resurgence, fascist studies are. The last few years have seen the appearance in English of fresh overviews of generic fascism from such established figures as Eatwell (1995), Laqueur (1995) and Payne (1996), not to mention numerous sophisticated monographs and essays on particular aspects of it: for example, our understanding of Italian fascism has been enriched by Adamson (1993), Sternhell (1994) and Ferraresi (1995). My own contribution includes the documentary reader promised in the last preface (Griffin, 1995a), a chapter on post-war fascism's failure to achieve power (Griffin, 1996a) and on the relationship between fascism and the theatre (Griffin, 1996b), as well as articles on Eurofascism (Griffin, 1993), fascism and modernity (Griffin, 1994), fascist art (1995b, 1996c) and the 'post-fascism' of the Alleanza Nazionale (Griffin, 1996d). The cultural policies of generic fascism will be the subject of a monograph *Culture under Fascism* to be published by Macmillan, while another reader, this time devoted entirely to theories of fascism, will be brought out by Edward Arnold.

What I hoped to achieve when I wrote this book was to offer a concise definition of fascism which, however cryptic initially, would come to establish itself as more heuristically useful to fellow researchers than earlier ones (see p.12). Ideally its value was to have two aspects: it would allow the study of discrete fascist phenomena to proceed without undue methodological and definitional agonizing of the sort to which I have had to resort in the first two chapters; it would also illuminate the generic ideological dynamics and structural preconditions of fascism which would make individual manifestations of it more intelligible. Five years after its first publication there are some signs that the definition expounded here may actually be starting to fulfil this brief, as when it informs the conceptual framework for a study of the British National Party (Copsey, 1994), of A.K. Chesterton (Baker, 1996) or of the Irish Blueshirts (Cronin, 1997), or persuades experts to make 'national rebirth' central to their characterization of fascism (Ignazi, 1994; Eatwell, 1995; Payne, 1996). There is even the prospect that, as the centrality of the rebirth myth to all revolutionary aspirations becomes more fully appreciated, the term 'palingenetic' may yet become a household tool of political scientific analysis!

Ultimately, though, no theory can do justice to the complexity of the phenomenon it sets out to account for. Those who feel strongly that my definition caricatures, plays down or leaves out of the account important aspects of fascism are quite right. Such distortion and simplification is in the nature of every model or thesis in the human sciences. At bottom they are but 'essays' in the original sense of the word: an attempt to take stock of what we know so that we and others can see things more clearly. And as T.S. Eliot said, 'Ours is only the trying. The rest is not our business'.

Roger Griffin
Oxford, 1996

References

Adamson, W., 1993. *Avant-garde Florence. From Modernism to Fascism*, Harvard University Press, Cambridge, Massachusetts.

Baker, D., 1996. *Ideology of Obsession: A.K. Chesterton and British Fascism*, Tauris, London.

Copsey, N., 1994. Fascism: the ideology of the British National Movement, *Politics*, Vol.14, No.3, pp.101–8.

Cronin, M., 1997. *The Blueshirts and Irish Politics*, Cork University Press, Cork.

Eatwell, R., 1995. *Fascism: A History*, Chatto & Windus, London.

Ferraresi, F., 1995. *Minacce alla democrazia*, Feltrinelli, Milan.

Griffin, R., 1993. Europe for the Europeans: the fascist vision of the new Europe, Humanities Research Centre Occasional Paper, No.1, Oxford Brookes University.

Griffin, R., 1994. Modernity under the New Order: the fascist project for managing the future, Thamesman Publications, School of Business, Oxford Brookes University.

Griffin, R., 1995a. *Fascism*, Oxford University Press, Oxford.

Griffin, R., 1995b. Romantic twilight or post-modernist dawn?, *Oxford Art Journal*, Vol.18, No.2.

Griffin, R., 1996a. British Fascism: the ugly duckling, in Michael Cronin (ed.), *The Failure of British Fascism*, Macmillan, London.

Griffin, R., 1996b. Staging the nation's rebirth, in G. Berghaus (ed.), *Fascism and Theatre*, Berghahn, Oxford.

Griffin, R., 1996c. Totalitarian art and the nemesis of modernity, *Oxford Art Journal*, Vol.19, No.2.

Griffin, R., 1996d. The post-fascism of the Alleanza Nazionale: a case-study in ideological morphology, *Journal of Political Ideologies*, Vol.1, No.2, pp.123–45.

Ignazi, P., 1994. *L'Estrema destra in Italia*, il Mulino, Bologna.

Laqueur, W., 1994. *Fascism: Past, Present, Future*, Oxford University Press, New York.

Payne, S.G., 1996. *A History of Fascism 1914–1945*, University College London Press, London.

Sternhell, Z., with M. Sznajder and M. Asheri, 1994. *The Birth of Fascist Ideology*, Princeton University Press, Princeton, New Jersey.

Acknowledgements

I would like to thank the British Academy for a timely 'small personal research grant' which enabled me to call on the invaluable services of William Goodall to make primary and secondary sources in Portuguese accessible. There are also a number of persons without whose encouragement at crucial moments this book and the D.Phil research on which it draws would not have seen the light of day (but who naturally cannot be held responsible for any of the conclusions I have reached). I am particularly indebted in this respect to Cyprian Blamires, Detlef Mühlberger, Peter Pulzer, Herminio Martins, Ian Kershaw, Roger Eatwell, Iain Stevenson, John Pollard, Martin Blinkhorn, and Stein Larsen. Thanks are due also to the Humanities Department of Oxford Brookes University (formerly Oxford Polytechnic) which has been very supportive throughout this venture. A very special role has also been played by my English family at Forest Green and my Italian family at Campomorone.

1 The 'Nature' of Generic Fascism

The 'Conundrum' of Fascism

'Although enormous amounts of research time and mental energy have been put into the study of it . . . fascism has stubbornly remained the great conundrum for students of the twentieth century' (Robinson, 1981, p.1). Such is the welter of divergent opinion surrounding the term that it is almost *de rigueur* to open contributions to the debate on fascism with some such observation. Indeed, one of the few uncontroversial statements that can be made about fascism is that it was the name given to the political force headed by Mussolini between March 1919 and April 1945 and which became the official ideological basis of a dictatorial regime established in Italy by him between 1925 and 1943. The word fascism here, however, is the anglicized form of the Italian proper name *fascismo* (henceforth to be referred to as 'Fascism'). To apply it to phenomena outside Italy is to change the status of the word: it becomes a generic term. The use of fascism in this sense (for which we will always use the lower case) is documented by the *Oxford English Dictionary* as having already established itself in English as early as 1923 when *The Contemporary Review* made a comment on the political situation in the Weimar Republic which, given Hitler's accession to power a decade later, is laden with tragic irony: 'Fascism in Germany will never be more than one of several factors.' As the inter-war period unfolded the term was soon subject to a process which one historian has described as 'inflation' (Huizinga, 1956, pp.295–6), which, as we all know, inevitably leads to devaluation. In the case of words this means that they are used to embrace more and more phenomena and so progressively lose their discriminating power: the 'blanket term' or 'conceptual hold-all' is born.

When political movements such as Valois's *Faisceau* or Mosley's British Union of Fascists appropriated the word as a badge of honour it showed that some political activists at least were convinced that Mussolini's dictatorship was to be emulated as the manifestation of a positive new force in modern politics, one not confined to the Italian peninsula but supra-national, and hence 'generic'. But it was opponents of this force who were mainly responsible for its depreciation. By the mid-thirties the word had gained wide currency within the left as a pejorative term for any movement or regime bent on destroying Marxism and representative government, so that most of Europe could be seen as threatened by 'fascism' in one form or another. The concrete support Franco was given by Mussolini and Hitler made it far from hysterical to conceive the Spanish Civil War as a conflict between fascism and democracy, especially for the thousands of volunteers from abroad prepared to sacrifice their lives to defend the Republic.

Since the Second World War was easily seen as a show-down between 'fascist' and 'anti-fascist' forces, the term has predictably been passed on to post-war generations as an emotionally charged word of condemnation for any political regime or action perceived as oppressive, authoritarian or elitist. Few would blame the Chinese students encamped in Peking in June 1989 or the Romanian citizens in the streets of Bucharest and Timisoara six months later when they denounced the 'fascism' of the state power which resorted to ruthless brutality against them on the pretext of defending Communism. It was less understandable when practically on the anniversary of the Tienanmen Square massacre, Romania's democratically elected president, Ion Iliesco claimed anti-government demonstrations were the work of 'fascists' and sent in miners to do the work of repression once performed by the *Securitate*. Meanwhile, in colloquial usage the term has been distorted out of all recognition. It raises few eyebrows nowadays to hear an officious bureaucrat or an overbearing 'phallocrat' being called by their victims 'a bit of a fascist', to read an article in *The Face* (September 1990, no. 24) exposing 'fashion fascism', or to hear radical anti-smokers being referred to as 'health fascists'. Obviously this book is not proposing counter-inflationary measures to remedy the situation at the level of common speech: given the relative impotence of academics to affect the evolution of the spoken language, this would not only be unrealistic, but also patronizing, not to say 'fascist' in intent (which shows how contagious this loose usage is!).

What makes a book like this potentially 'relevant' as a contribution to the human sciences, however, is that the word has suffered an unacceptable loss of precision within academic circles as well. An example is the word 'ecofascist'. It sounds perhaps like an embittered taunt directed at manufacturers who claim that 'Man' has a natural right to exploit the planet's resources irrespective of the ecological consequences. Quite the reverse: it is a technical term used in environmental studies for 'dark' Greens who propose that the state should be empowered to take Draconian interventionist measures to solve ecological problems (Pepper, 1985). At this point the term's inflation seems to have spread like a semantic virus, contaminating even the social sciences where key words are supposed to operate under controlled conditions.

Historically, if not morally, some of the blame for eroding fascism's lexical value must be placed at the door of Marxist theoreticians. In November 1922, only weeks after Mussolini's March on Rome, the Fourth Congress of the Communist International held in Moscow debated how Fascism was to be explained within a Marxist–Leninist perspective. One interpretation which resulted predictably saw it as an essentially reactionary movement which had been forced into existence when the attempted proletarian revolution of the so-called 'red biennium' (1919–20) threatened the bourgeois-liberal order (see Bordiga, 1922; and especially Togliatti, 1970). Like colonialism, imperialism and the First World War before it, Fascism was thus accommodated without too much soul-searching (or 'self-criticism') within the teleological scheme of revolutionary socialism which predicted the imminent collapse of capitalism. As new forms of openly anti-Bolshevik military dictatorships sprouted up like baleful toadstools in the very countries where the weakness of liberalism had raised hopes of communist breakthroughs, they were automatically identified as new permutations of Fascism (that is as fascism) by hard-line Marxists. These even came to brand as 'social fascists' their historical kith and kin, the social democrats, whose reformism was regarded as a betrayal of the revolutionary class struggle in which all 'true' socialists were meant to engage, one consequence of which was that left-wing opposition to Nazism in the last years of Weimar was tragically split. In this way both the generic and the inflated use of the term was to become established in left-wing academic usage well before the outbreak of the Second World War. Generally, for the extreme left, the theoretical analysis of fascism pursued in the quiet of the library has largely corroborated the gut reaction to it experienced in the heat of battle: it is counter-revolution by the forces of capitalism in league with the vestiges of feudalism.

As long as the Iron Curtain stood, social scientists behind it remained advocates of the timeless laws of dialectical materialism. They therefore continued to carry out their analyses broadly in line with Dimitroff's assertion at the Seventh Congress of the Comintern in 1935 which had characterized fascism as 'the most open terroristic dictatorship of the most reactionary, most chauvinist and most imperialist elements of finance capital' (Dimitroff, 1982, p.50). This definition is repeated word for word in the 1980 edition of the *Philosophical Dictionary* published by Moscow's Progress Editions. Just what an indiscriminate term it became on the basis of such a definition can be gleaned from the wide-ranging survey of fascist studies carried out by two East German academics (Eichholtz and Gossweiler, 1980, p.234) in which the British National Front sits in the same category as the Monday Club and the National Association for Freedom, both of which may be on the far right of the spectrum of parliamentary politics but have no revolutionary plans to overthrow liberal democracy as such.

Since Lenin was only one of countless revisionists intent on adapting Marx's theories to the particular historical conditions of their country, it is hardly surprising if some highly nuanced Marxist interpretations of fascism came into being outside the hegemony of the Comintern even before the Second World War. The most significant of these were the elaborations of Marx's concept of Bonapartism by Thalheimer and Bauer, and the sophisticated explanatory model of Fascism which Gramsci constructed on the basis of his concept of ideological hegemony and of Lenin's theory of a 'Prussian' path to capitalism, both of which influenced post-war Marxist theorists. By the 1980s, crude equations of fascism with monopoly capitalism (for example Guerin, 1973) had become largely a thing of the past outside the East bloc (see Poulantzas, 1974; Botz, 1976; Dülffer, 1976;

Bottomore and Goode, 1978; Davis, 1979). In addition over the years some valuable information has emerged by the application of 'sophisticated' Marxist analysis (even by some non-Marxists) to such topics as the collusion between fascism and big business or middle class interests (for an overview of this and other economic aspects of the fascist debate see Milward, 1979).

However, the tendency to reduce fascism to an aggressive form of capitalism always lurks when Marxists approach the subject, and the historian of what was then the GDR, Petzold, speaks for even the most 'unvulgar' of his comrades when he reaffirms Horkheimer's 1939 dictum according to which 'whosoever refuses to speak of capitalism should equally be silent on the subject of fascism' (Petzold, 1983, p.viii). By assuming fascism to be an essentially anti-proletarian force, they play down its antagonism to the ethos of *laissez-faire* economics, consumerist materialism and the bourgeoisie, and are unable to take seriously its claim to be the negation of nineteenth-century liberalism rather than its perpetuation in a different guise. More seriously, they are reluctant to grant it any autonomous revolutionary thrust as a new ideological force. It will be interesting to see how long it takes before the democratic movements in former Warsaw Pact countries, which in 1989 began repudiating communism and embracing elements of capitalist economics along with pluralist political institutions, lead to the waning of Leninist and Stalinist influence in the fascist studies carried out in their universities. Western Marxists could eventually find themselves in an untenably reactionary position *vis-à-vis* their reformed Eastern colleagues. (For an excellent overview of Marxist theories of fascism and Nazism see Kershaw, 1985, pp.24–6, 43–50.)

The Continuing Search for a Consensus Definition

In the academic 'Free World' where market forces prevail as much in intellectual as in commercial matters, the concept of a generic fascism has suffered not only from inflation, but from a process which is equally damaging for the precision and usefulness of a concept. To stay within the register of commercial English we might call it 'diversification'. Each academic who has turned his or her mind to defining the term has tended to give it distinct connotations. At one extreme there are those who treat fascism as little more than a twentieth-century radicalization of the extreme right which came into being as an anti-liberal tradition in European thought in the wake of 1789. This is implied by the series 'Roots of the Right', in which the ultra-conservative de Maistre (McClellan, 1970) and the Fascist Mussolini (Lyttleton, 1973) are forced into uneasy cohabitation (cf. Rogger and Weber, 1966; Rees, 1985; and Ó Maoláin, 1987 for a similar blurring of the demarcation line).

Then there are scholars who see fascism as an essentially new force, distinct from the radical right and, moreover, a major factor in contemporary history both within Europe and outside it (for example – in quite different ways – Moore, 1966; Gregor, 1969). Another interpretation sees it

as a phenomenon restricted to inter-war Europe but with a signifi
distinction between the ideologically motivated Nazi and more opportuni
tic Fascist variants (Weber, 1964). Alternatively, there are those who treat it
as an international phenomenon which found its most complete 'paradigma-
tic' expression in Nazism and Fascism (for example O'Sullivan, 1983;
Organski, 1968), or Nazism alone (for example Hayes, 1973; and most
Marxists). This latter position conflicts head-on with the conviction that
there is unquestionably a family of generic fascisms but that Nazism is too
different (too 'biologically' racist) to be included as a member of it (for
example Sternhell, 1979 and 1987; cf. again Gregor, 1969, pp.xiii–iv, who
comes to a similar conclusion via a different route). Students and academic
specialists alike thus find they have strayed into a conceptual labyrinth
whenever their research intersects with fascist studies. Scores of self-
appointed Ariadnes dangle threads temptingly in front of their faces showing them the way out, but each route leads to a different exit, or, as often as
not, to another point in the maze. So many conflicting assessments are in
circulation that there have been several attempts to provide guides to them as
well, though each inevitably has its own emphasis on how the debate can be
broken into different schools of thought (such 'paradigms of paradigms' are
offered by Nolte, 1967; Gregor, 1974; Kitchen, 1976; De Felice, 1977;
Carsten, 1979; Hagtvet and Kühnl, 1980; Payne, 1980; Revelli, 1981).

As a result, all the major questions pertaining to one of the most powerful
historical forces to have shaped modern history in the first half of the
twentieth century are still wide open: are Italian Fascism and Nazism related
and if so how, and are they part of a wider phenomenon? If there is a generic
fascism, is it one confined to Europe, or has it a global dimension? For
example, was there a Russian (Rogger and Weber, 1966), South American
(Hennessy, 1979), or Japanese fascism (Kasza, 1984; Payne, 1984)? Does the
'age of fascism' extend beyond 1945? Nolte (1965, p.401), Trevor-Roper
(1968, p.18) and Payne (1980) imply it did not, and the whole issue of neo-
fascism is largely ignored by the standard anthologies of essays on fascism
(for example Woolf, 1968; Laqueur, 1969; Mosse, 1979). What is the relationship between fascism and conservatism, the radical right, totalitarianism, modernization, nationalism, racism, socialism, capitalism,
imperialism? Is it to be associated with a special stage in the evolution of the
nation-state (for example Moore, 1966; Gregor, 1979), psychological predisposition (Reich, 1946; Fromm, 1960; Theweleit, 1987 and 1989) or social
grouping? In the latter case was it a middle class or a mass movement
(contrast Lipset, 1960 with Mühlberger, 1987)?

Then again, did fascism, if its generic existence is accepted, have a 'real'
ideology, or is it right to say that it had 'the form of an ideology but without
the specific content'? (Scruton, 1982, p.169; cf. Schüddekopf, 1973, p.18)? If
it *had* a specific content, was this a 'positive' one (as variously suggested by
Gregor, 1969; Sternhell, 1979; or Mosse, 1979, ch.1) or basically negative,
making fascism at bottom an 'anti-phenomenon' definable primarily in terms
of what it opposed rather than what it stood for (cf. the different emphasis
given to the anti-dimension by Nolte, 1969; Linz, 1979; Payne, 1980; Billig,
1989)? De Felice and Ledeen (1976) go so far as to suggest that fascism had

a 'negative common denominator, that is a series of things which fascisms refute', but question whether they shared anything in terms of positive goals. Taking this argument to its logical conclusion, was fascism ultimately a revolutionary form of 'nihilism', as Rauschning postulated about Nazism, or just plain 'evil', as the repeat of a Channel 4 documentary series of that title was still insisting on British television in the autumn of 1990?

As an example of the divergence of opinions (by no means the most extreme which could have been chosen) it is instructive to compare the approach to fascism of two of its most famous contemporary theorists, the Israeli scholar Zeev Sternhell and the American Stanley Payne, both non-Marxists. Sternhell has written detailed studies of francophone fascism (1973, 1978, 1983), as well as contributing a major article on fascist ideology (1979) and supplying a generic definition for *The Blackwell Encyclopedia of Political Thought* (Miller, 1987) – one which inevitably conflicts with those proffered by Paul Wilkinson and myself in two companion volumes on political institutions (Bogdanor, 1987) and social thought (Outhwaite and Bottomore, 1992) respectively. The contentious nature of the fascist debate at the highest level of scholarship is well illustrated by Sternhell's short survey of the course it had taken up to the mid-seventies (1979, pp.385–98), especially the space he devotes to a courteous but damning critique of one of the best known (but least used) theories of generic fascism, the one formulated on 'phenomenological' principles by Ernst Nolte (1965). What distinguishes Sternhell's own approach is his belief that: (i) the student of fascism should look to various movements at work in inter-war France in order to construct a paradigm of its ideological make-up undistorted by being implemented as the basis of a regime; (ii) fascist ideology represents a fairly coherent synthesis of two major currents of modern political thought, anti-materialist socialism and nationalism; (iii) the central thrust of this synthesis is that it makes possible a third way between liberalism and communism which is neither 'right' nor 'left'; (iv) it is thus a movement in political ideas peculiar to the twentieth century with its own intellectual and historical roots and rationale (he ascribes particular importance to the *fin-de-siècle* revolt against positivism, especially among such thinkers as Nietzsche, Sorel, Barrès and Michels); (v) while several inter-war movements fit the pattern he has discerned, Nazism is too different (for example 'biologically' racist) to be associated with it.

Paradoxically, though Sternhell is often cited as an authority in his field, and his meticulous studies of three generations of radical right thought in France demonstrate the fertility of his approach, his definition of fascism has generated more polemic than consensus. Among the objections which have been raised to his theory are that (i) it creates a rigid dichotomy which causes thinkers in inter-war France to be classified as either 'democratic' or 'fascist', thus ignoring the existence of, for example, a powerful current of political Catholicism which sought to forge a viable alternative to liberalism, communism *and* fascism (see Conway, 1990, p.1); (ii) it applies the history of ideas to fascism in a way which takes insufficient account of the unique sociological and national preconditions of its different permutations, of its bias towards action rather than theory and of its practical consequences (see Pinto, 1986). The reader will have to judge whether the 'ideocentric' premises of my own approach have lured me into making similar errors.

In terms of consumer 'demand', the most successful paradigm of generic fascism is apparently that supplied by Stanley Payne, the author of a major work on the Spanish Falange (1961) and numerous contributions to fascist studies. His 'typological definition' of fascism is presented in a book which goes on to demonstrate its considerable taxonomic value in categorizing ultra-right movements in the inter-war period. Since its publication, it has been cited by several scholars as the most useful approach to date, if only in a spirit of *faute de mieux* (for example Kasza, 1984; Cullen, 1986; van der Wusten, 1987; Botz, 1987). It consists of a restatement of the 'anti-dimension' of fascism (which has greatly impressed anti-fascists), followed by a synthetic description of 'ideology and goals' and 'style and organization'. Together these three sets of criteria are offered as a sort of check-list, specific enough to distinguish between fascist and non-fascist movements (which include the conservative and radical right) but still flexible enough to accommodate a number of movements other than those of Mussolini or Hitler. For example the Falange is pin-pointed as a genuinely fascist element within Franco's radical right (that is non-fascist) regime. Significantly, Nazism emerges as a prime specimen of fascism, *pace* Sternhell.

Payne's definition convincingly articulates much prevailing 'common sense' among non-Marxists on the nature of fascism. Its weakness is not only that the elaborate tripartite 'typology' is somewhat cumbersome as a conceptual framework but that it marks out fascism as a genus of political energy which is unique in apparently requiring its self-professed ideological goals to be supplemented by its 'style' and 'negations' before they can serve as an adequate basis for a definition. It is not surprising, therefore, that one scholar should regard its increasing adoption as a symptom of 'resignation' (Eley, 1983), while another who uses it nevertheless begins his article by saying that 'the academic search for some workable definition of fascism that embraces the various manifestations of this phenomenon will be a long one' (Cullen, 1986). The limited success of Payne's typology to provide an adequate degree of consensus among academics working on fascism is reflected too in the convoluted passage in which Richard Thurlow, an expert on British fascism, deals with the problem of delimiting his subject, and which at one point offers a tautological 'operational definition' of fascism embracing all those movements 'which called themselves fascist' (Thurlow, 1987, pp.xv-xvii). It should not raise eyebrows, then, if the American scholar, Robert Soucy, after more than two decades of outstanding work on French fascism, can still use it in a loose way which draws the charge from a colleague that he seriously confuses basic issues (Watson, 1988, reviewing Soucy, 1986).

Given the prevailing state of confusion, it is equally understandable to come across the extreme scepticism of the American scholar, Gilbert Allardyce, who exhorts his colleagues to dispense with the term altogether. He asserts dogmatically that 'fascism is not a generic concept', and then, somewhat tautologically, that 'the word *fascismo* has no meaning outside Italy' (Allardyce, 1979, p.370), even if Oswald Mosley for one obviously thought it did when he formed his British Union of Fascists. The whole *raison d'être* of the present book thus vanishes with a wave of a lexicographical magic wand. No wonder if a note of despair occasionally creeps into academic contributions to the debate, as when Paul Preston (1985, p.46) remarks 'the study of fascism becomes every year a more daunting and bewildering task' (cf. Woolf, 1968, ch.1; Schüddekopf, 1973, pp. 16–24; Larsen *et al.*, 1980, p.19). Even in the most recent literature on the subject scholars still feel the need to draw attention to the continuing disagreement over what its salient features were (for example Billig, 1989, p.147).

If readers are tempted to feel that such a lack of agreement on the semantics of a political concept is irrelevant to the so-called 'real world' outside academia, then they should consider the problems faced by the EEC's 1985 Committee of Inquiry into the Rise of Fascism and Racism in Europe as its members tried to establish precisely what they were meant to investigate. They picked their way laboriously through the brambles of conflicting theories and assertions offered by numerous books and expert witnesses and at the end of the day resorted to a working definition which comes across as more of an implicit reassertion of EEC liberalism than a characterization of fascism:

> A nationalistic attitude essentially hostile to the principles of democracy, to the rule of law and to the fundamental rights and freedoms, as well as the irrational exaltation of a particular community, in relation to which people outside it are systematically excluded. (Evrigenis, 1986, Part A, pp.17–8).

Not surprisingly, the committee were unable to clarify the precise relationship of modern fascism to racism on the basis of such a model.

An outsider might think that the rampant inflation and prolific diversification of the term is no more than an extreme example of the problem of using language to describe any experiential reality, as in the quip: 'I can't describe an elephant, but I know one when I see it.' But it has more in common with the elephant described in an ancient parable (Shah, 1979, p.84) which is brought for the first time to a remote Indian village where all the inhabitants are blind. When the local sages are invited to examine it, each one creates a completely false picture by imagining the whole animal from the part they happen to have grasped initially (a tusk, a foot, an ear). As a result each of their theories cannot be reconciled with any other. There is a tendency for this to happen with the key words of all intellectual debates; however, in the case of 'fascism' there is not even a consensus about whether there is a unique genus of animal in the menagerie of political phenomena to merit a distinctive name. Some experts feel that the discipline has in fact been dealing with the mutation of a more familiar creature such as a water-buffalo or rhinoceros or that it was a one-off 'freak' rather than a new species.

Fascism as an Ideal Type

We spoke earlier of the dilemma faced by someone who is drawn sufficiently into the semantics of the debate over fascism to feel frustrated by the maze of conflicting definitional pathways to follow and the dead ends they often run into eventually. Clearly a book entitled 'the nature of fascism' must offer its own map to enable readers to extricate themselves from methodological issues in order to concentrate on the particularity of social and historical events. The clue to finding a 'way out' of the fascist debate is to recognize that any new theory of fascism must take full account of how the existing maze of diverging definitions first came into being.

One elegant explanation for the tendency towards inflation and diversification of all social scientific terms is to consider them to be 'ideal types'. Indeed, the 'conundrum' which fascism poses is largely solved once the deeper implications of the expression are appreciated. The term 'ideal type' was coined by Max Weber as a result of his sustained methodological musings on the special status acquired by any generic concept which is made central to the investigation of processes and events concerning human beings. Once it is applied to phenomena outside Italy, 'fascism' is just such a concept. The starting point for appreciating Weber's approach is to accept one of its basic premises, namely that before human consciousness acts upon the world to derive the meaning and values which form the fabric of experiential reality, it consists of a 'meaningless infinity' of phenomena (quoted in Burger, 1976, p.80 – since Weber's own methodological theories are scattered through his voluminous writings, I recommend Burger's detailed reconstruction of how he conceived the 'ideal type' for a fuller and more scholarly exposition of what follows). To perceive or know anything at all, the mind needs a filter capable of drastically editing this infinity, much in the way a camera needs a lens before it will photograph anything recognizable. A total autobiography or biography of just one individual, for example, would be far longer than Proust's multi-volume fictional reconstruction of his life even if it were 'only' to take into account most of what she or he had ever said or done. Such an undertaking would pose literally infinite problems if it attempted to recreate the countless psychological, cultural, social, political and historical realities which that life embodied or impinged upon.

How much more superhuman, then, in absolute terms is the task undertaken by the most elementary history book, namely to give an account of episodes which involve the interaction of hundreds, thousands or even millions of lives, not to mention the 'impersonal' (that is structural and collective) forces which affected them, whether socio-economic or politico-cultural. Just as some stars are revealed by powerful telescopes to be entire galaxies made up of millions of stars, so individual historical events consist on closer inspection of countless interacting personal and supra-personal systems of 'facts'. Each of these dissolves into yet smaller or even larger patterns of phenomena as research moves up and down the scales of time and 'event horizons' shift. When reconstituted as historiography, then, the seamless web of history is woven in fibres which are highly synthetic (and, as gender historians rightly point out, have till recently been largely *man*-made). It is language-based thought which organizes complex constellations of data into a single entity by means of a verbal expression which allows the imagination to 'get hold of' them (the original meaning of the verb 'conceive') and so investigate them. In the social sciences the single concept, the 'it', under investigation, is nearly always a collective pronoun, subsuming a myriad realities.

Singularities such as 'the Renaissance', 'the French Revolution' or 'the democratization of the Eastern bloc' are thus code words for entities which have to be consciously or not 'modelled' in the mind to reduce them to manageable proportions for the purpose of investigation. Once the subject becomes renaissances, revolutions or democratization 'in general', then insights can only be generated about them if the individual episodes or events embraced by such terms are shorn of the countless elements which make them unique, and we concentrate instead on the common properties, the shared patterns which make them case studies in a recurring 'genus' or type of phenomena. For Weber it is precisely those concepts or linguistic models in the human sciences which allow disparate singularities of the external world to be conceptualized as a single entity and explored which he designated 'ideal types'. The homogeneous 'type' is 'ideal' because it does not exist empirically but only at the level of abstraction in an intellectual world stripped of the heterogeneity and (for the investigator of regularities and causal patterns) 'messiness' of real phenomena. Its relationship to reality is analogous to that of the caricature to the subject. Weber himself implied this in the following definition:

> An ideal type is formed by the one-sided exaggeration (*Steigerung*) of one or several viewpoints and by the combination of a great many single phenomena (*Einzelerscheinungen*) existing diffusely and discretely, more or less present and occasionally absent, which are compatible with those one-sidedly empha-sized viewpoints, into an internally consistent thought-picture (*Gedanken-bild*). In its conceptual purity this thought-picture cannot be found empirically anywhere in reality, it is a utopia. (Burger, 1976, pp.127–8)

In other words, the power that an ideal type gives the researcher to exercise conceptual control over aspects of external reality derives from a piece of 'sleight-of-mind' jointly performed by language, the discursive intellect and the social scientific imagination. The image it creates is an illusion (a 'utopia'), though not one created in the world of fantasy alone, but based on or inferred from the 'real world' of human affairs. Only in this way can concepts such as 'modernization' or 'class' conjure up a discrete and con-stant pattern or genus of human reality to be defined and studied in its different permutations. Such a genus exists as an internally consistent whole only 'on paper'. In external reality the regular pattern of human phenomena it posits is present only incompletely and is inextricably bound up with vast areas of phenomena which have been censured out (whether consciously or not) and whose inclusion would make it unmanageable as a concept (and hence useless for the purposes of scientific research). Since the ideal type does not correspond to an objective entity, any number of different ones can be devised appropriate to the 'same' phenomena, depending on the re-searcher's point of view. Weber's own example of the proliferation of ideal types of a given phenomenon (and hence the infinite regress of any ultimate definition of it) was one central to his own research interests: capitalism.

It is possible, or rather it must be accepted that several, indeed in each case very numerous utopias (e.g. of capitalism) of this sort can be worked out, of which none is like another, of which none ever can be observed in empirical reality as the actually existing organization of the [capitalistic] society, but each of which, however, claims that it is a representation of the 'idea' of capitalistic culture. Each of these can claim this in so far as each has actually taken certain features of our culture, which are significant in their particularity, from reality and brought them together into a unified ideal picture. (Quoted in Burger, 1976, p.129)

The immediate inference to be drawn from this way of approaching conceptualization in the social sciences is that no definition of any key generic term used in them can be 'true' in the descriptive sense, but only *useful*. In other words, applied consciously as an ideal type, it allows valuable research to be carried out into particular issues on which empirically sound methods can be brought to bear. Ideal types are misused if they are treated as *definitive* taxonomic categories, for their value is purely 'heuristic': they serve not to describe or explain facts as such but to provide tentative conceptual frameworks with which significant patterns of facts can be identified, causal relationships investigated and phenomena classified. Similarly, there can be no 'objective' use of a generic term: the impression of objectivity (an illusion, if 'objective' is taken to mean 'value free') is generated when enough people tacitly accept the ideal-typical interpretation placed on it to the point of creating a community in which everybody means more or less the same thing by it.

The implications of Weber's theory for this, and for *any* book on fascism are far-reaching. First, the various positions which have emerged concerning the definition of fascism since the 1920s have all been competing ideal types, a fraction of the number that could potentially be formulated. The fact that they are so many but only partially, if at all, reconcilable is consistent with what must be expected to happen when generations of theoreticians attempt to get to the bottom of any historical phenomenon. It is all the more predictable when the phenomenon in question is associated with an intense period of political transformations and destruction on an unprecedented scale, events completely at odds with the confident vision of human progress which dominated liberal societies up to the First World War. Moreover, they occurred when both information technology and the human sciences had advanced to a point unthinkable even a hundred years before, thus leaving a documentation of gargantuan proportions just at a time when more professionals were on hand than ever before to study them.

Therefore, if the divergence of opinion about the term 'fascist' is even more acute than that concerning other key political ideologies, whether older ones such as 'nationalism' or newer ones such as 'terrorism', it says little about the intractable nature of the phenomenon itself. What it does speak volumes for is the sheer amount of attention it has attracted both within and outside the social sciences, attention which has inevitably militated against the emergence of a high degree of consensus about the most suitable ideal type to use. An exception is constituted by pre-1989

Marxists, whose broad agreement on the materialist conception of history ensured a fair measure of overlap on basics, if by no means total uniformity in actual interpretation. Even this pocket of 'objectivity' (that is interpersonal subjectivity) in fascist studies is likely to break down further with the new stage in the crisis of Marxism as an all-embracing social science which is almost certain to ensue from the collapse of a number of regimes purporting to be based on it. Nor will any amount of effort or research resolve the lack of consensus: in fact it can only tend to make it more acute because as new historical perspectives emerge with the unfolding of contemporary events, as new paradigms come to be employed in the social sciences and as researchers make empirical advances and creative leaps in their investigations of fascism in its concrete manifestations, so the term 'fascism' itself will be turned into any number of new ideal types.

The fact that fascism is to be approached from this methodological perspective has been explicitly recognized in some recent scholarship, as when Kershaw talks of 'the need of a generic "ideal type" of fascism' (1985, p.150 – cf. Payne 1980; Herf, 1984; Kasza, 1984; Robinson, 1981; Cullen, 1986; van den Wusten, 1987; Botz, 1987). It is also implicit in the way many experts deliberately resort to the construction of a 'model' of fascism in order to investigate it (for example Hayes, 1973; O'Sullivan, 1983; Eccleshall *et al.*, 1984), and in Kater's call for fascism to be 'defined more clearly vis-à-vis the other concepts that abound' such as authoritarianism (1988). One of the clearest acknowledgments of the central role played by 'idealizing abstraction' in any definition of fascism is to be found in Zeev Sternhell's introduction to his *Ni droite ni gauche*, where he states 'It is *up to the researcher* to discern the common denominator, the fascist "minimum", that is shared not only by the different political movements and ideologies which claim to be fascist, but also by those which reject the description yet nevertheless belong to the same family' (Sternhell, 1983, p. 18; my emphasis).

A book such as this can therefore never hope to resolve the debate over fascism. What it can do, though, is offer a consciously constructed ideal type of fascism which sets out to be more heuristically useful to academic research than existing ones.

The 'Nature' of Fascism

Now that our ruminations on basic methodological issues have been aired we are in a position to be more precise about the way the problems of defining fascism will be approached in this book. The main premises are:

(i)   The term 'fascism' has come into being because of an intuitive recognition that a new genus of revolutionary politics entered European history with the establishment of Fascism in Italy. The currency it subsequently gained as a political category registered the underlying affinity which Mussolini's revolutionary form of politics was sensed to have with a growing number of other political movements and ideologies in the inter-war period.

(ii) Used generically, the term 'fascism' cannot be given an absolute definition by social scientists because it is an ideal type. Nevertheless, it is still capable of

serving as a valuable heuristic and taxonomic device within the hum.
ences, if a broad consensus could be achieved about what that ideal type:
be.

(iii)   Outside Marxist social science even a working consensus concerning
          appropriate model has not materialized, resulting in a bewildering variety
          conflicting definitions and theories about the nature of fascism.
(iv)   The time is ripe in the social sciences for a new theory of the fascist minimum,
          especially if, when reduced to its bare essentials, the resulting definition is
          more economical and 'elegant' than previous ones.

The aim of what follows, then, is to offer a new ideal type of fascism with
which to identify what constitutes its 'family' trait in response to recurrent
appeals for a more satisfactory definition than is currently available. Some of
the specifications which this new ideal type should satisfy are that it should:

(i)   identify a common core of fascist phenomena which can be treated as its
          definitional minimum, while allowing for the profound differences which exist
          between the Fascism which took power in Italy and all other movements
          subsequently associated with it;
(ii)   clarify how fascism relates to a number of other social scientific terms which
          abound in fascist scholarship, the most obvious being 'the right', 'conserva-
          tism' and 'totalitarianism' (others which will occur in the course of the analysis
          are 'cultural pessimism', 'nihilism', 'anti-modernism', 'millenarianism', 'politi-
          cal religion', 'revolution');
(iii)   complement as far as possible what has been established by existing historical
          scholarship about the dynamics of particular movements and regimes which it
          identifies as members of the family of generic fascism;
(iv)   represent an advance on existing ideal types in terms of succinctness and
          manageability (even if the new definition based on it will in the first instance
          require considerable elaboration and 'unpacking' because of its unfamiliarity).

The assumption on which the construction of this ideal type will proceed
is that fascism is broadly on a par with such concepts as 'liberalism',
'socialism', 'conservatism' or 'nationalism' (not that the semantic problems
these pose are by any means identical). All such concepts refer just as much
to political thought as to the behaviour, events and institutions to which this
thought gives rise. Yet within the social sciences this has not inhibited
researchers from defining such generic ideological terms primarily in respect
of what their 'carriers' believed in, rather than the concrete phenomena
which their beliefs brought about (for example, see the definitions given in
Scruton, 1982). I propose to approach fascism in like manner, namely as a
political force definable ideal-typically in terms of its generic ideological
core, even if one scholar has commented that such an approach is 'temporarily out of fashion' (Preston, 1985, p.48).

I do not wish to deny the validity of empirical investigations of fascism
which attach central importance either to (i) its characteristic 'style' of
political activity as expressed in rallies, paramilitary violence, uniforms,
symbols, leader cult (an aspect stressed even by an intellectual historian
such as O'Sullivan, 1983), or to (ii) typical structures which it aimed to
produce in fulfilment of its theory (such as youth organizations, corporative economic institutions, a single-party 'totalitarian' state etc.) or which it

ended up creating in practice, such as a terror apparatus, a propaganda machine, a leader cult (see for example Hayes, 1973). Certainly, its 'negations' must also be taken into account (as by Nolte, 1965). I do however question the heuristic value of using such criteria as the basis of ideal types of generic fascism, even when all three are ingeniously woven into a composite 'typological definition' by Payne (1980).

All political ideologies when put into practice engender a certain style of political behaviour: one only has to think of the display of 'aesthetic politics' made by liberalism at the state opening of the British Parliament or in American presidential primaries. Similarly, when the liberal ideal of society is given institutional form it also generates characteristic constitutional, legal and economic structures (for example representative assemblies, independent judiciaries, stock exchanges), yet these are not taken as the starting point for defining liberalism. In any case, what might be considered a typically fascist structure, such as a secret police, might be created by any authoritarian regime (see Kertzer, 1988), while any number of political forces can found youth organizations, thus blurring distinctions rather than sharpening them if either are taken as definitional criteria. As for the value of concentrating on fascism's 'anti-' dimension, I find this particularly unhelpful and misleading. Liberalism is anti-despotism, and Marxism is (or was) anti-capitalist, which merely demonstrates that every ideology rejects certain values as a corollary of what it stands *for*. It thus seems desirable to attempt a definition of fascism primarily in terms of its 'positive' ideological axioms, from which its characteristic style, structures and negations follow.

Clearly, the attempt to define fascism in terms of its 'positive' ideology is open to a number of objections in principle. For example:

(i)   to search for a minimal definition of fascism based on its ideology is to lose sight of the material socio-economic conditions and objective political context which formed the preconditions for the genesis and structure of its particular manifestations;

(ii)   fascism never had any major theorists to rank with Locke or Marx, hence to concentrate on its ideology is to impose an artificially homogeneous intellectual coherence on a rag-bag of third-hand ideas and specious rationalizations. It is especially perverse to try to do so, given that the rhetoric of fascism openly attacked party-political programmes, celebrated violence and irrational values, and justified the systematic use of state terrorism;

(iii) approaching fascism primarily in terms of political theory and the history of ideas is misleading because it detracts attention from concrete events which constitute the real 'nature of fascism' and moreover euphemizes the immense human suffering caused when nebulous fascist ideals and policies become translated into gruesome political realities.

The danger of generating misleading impressions about the nature of fascism when taking its thought seriously is indeed grave, as is illustrated by the example set by several scholars who have made it central to their definition before me (for example Nolte, 1965; Gregor, 1969; Sternhell, 1986). It should therefore help forestall a number of misunderstandings if we establish at some length the concept of ideology which will inform this book.

'Ideology' in the Context of Generic Fascism

Predictably, the term ideology is no less contentious a word than fascism, being in the last analysis yet another particularly protean and inflated ideal type. Useful overviews of its complex semantic history have been given by Plamenatz (1970), Hall (1978) and Rossi-Landi (1990), while Hamilton (1987) has made an interesting attempt at a counter-inflationary definition. As for the way it will be used here, it has already been made clear that fascism is not being analysed from a Marxist point of view. A corollary is that several 'vulgar' Marxist assumptions about ideology do not apply here, particularly ones suggesting that (i) it is extensively determined by the socio-economic infrastructure, (ii) is rooted in 'false consciousness' and (iii) results in the 'mystification' of an essentially anti-socialist, and hence untenable, political system. More 'sophisticated' Marxist axioms which do have a bearing on our study of fascism relate to the insight that ideologies do not emanate from individual minds. Rather they are to be conceived as being 'passively' inherited in a historically determined situation by individuals who then modify them 'actively' in the process which Giddens (1976; 1984) calls 'structuration', that is in turn an integral part of 'social reproduction'. In other words, just as light behaves *both* as a wave *and* as a beam, ideology is simultaneously individual *and* supra-individual, depending on how it is being investigated. It exists at the point of conjuncture where individual consciousness, intention and rationalization of behaviour interact with the external 'supra-personal' forces which condition human existence.

Elaborating this approach, the following premises are implicit in the way ideology is conceived in the present investigation of the 'nature of fascism' (several of these points will be implicitly taken up and explored further both in the next chapter which unveils our own new model of fascism and in Chapters 7 and 8 which investigate its causes):

(i)   *Ideology embraces any expression of human thought*, whether verbal, symbolic or behavioural when considered in terms of its role in legitimating or challenging all or part of a particular economic, social, political and cultural order (cf. Eccleshall *et al.*, 1984).

(ii) *Ideology can assume a reactionary, progressive or revolutionary aspect*, according to whether it acts in a given situation as (a) a conformist, conservative, hegemonic force, (b) an idealistic, reforming, but 'systemic' force or (c) a utopian, subversive, 'extra-systemic' one (this trichotomy seems more appropriate than the usual dichotomy between 'conservative' and 'revolutionary' suggested in Mannheim, 1960; Rossi-Landi, 1990). In all three aspects the corollary of an ideology's positive ideals will be the rejection of those with which these conflict, so that all ideologies have an 'anti-' dimension (cf. Seliger, 1976).

(iii) *The utopia of an ideology can never be fully realized in practice*, for it is in the transition from the 'ideal' postulated in its revolutionary aspect to the 'reality' it generates as the basis of a regime (that is in its hegemonic aspect) that falls the shadow of which T.S. Eliot spoke in 'The Hollow Men' (a point implicit in Mannheim, 1960). As a result, each new system tends to create new social tensions, inequalities, tyrannies and forms of inhumanity which had not been anticipated in the ideology which it invokes in its legitimation (which is not to say that all systems are equal in the degree of human misery or happiness they generate).

(iv)   *Ideologies are lived out as truths*, being perceived as ideologies only when observed with critical detachment from outside. Their carriers experience them 'from within' as an integral part of their world-view and associate them with normality, common sense, reasonableness, convictions, self-evident facts. As such, ideologies embrace both the spoken and unspoken assumptions which ensure that all behaviour and actions 'make sense' subjectively to their protagonists (that is, ideologies have a normative function without which life and all activity is experienced as absurd).

(v)   *An ideology is intrinsically irrational*, for even if it claims to be rational in its self-legitimation and is articulated by some of its carriers or reconstituted by those studying it with a high degree of theoretical coherence, it owes its power to inspire action and provide a sense of reality to the fact that it is rooted in pre-verbal, subconscious feelings and affective drives (cf. Rossi-Landi, 1990).

(vi)   *There are many levels of commitment to an ideology*, ranging from the intensity of the activists, leadership and ideologues of a movement at the heart of its propagation to the more passive or pragmatic 'fellow travellers' at the periphery with no deep or lasting involvement with it. The contents of an ideology will become more nuanced and sophisticated towards a movement's activist core and more simplistic and crudely propagandistic towards the periphery (cf. Billig, 1978, chs 4–6, who distinguishes an ideology's 'depth' from its 'surface', and Thurlow, 1987, p. 146 who uses the terms 'esoteric' and 'exoteric' in a similar sense).

(vii)   *Commitment to an ideology is largely determined by self-interest*, as long as this phrase is taken to refer not only to narrow materialist egotism and immediate issues of survival, but also to complex psychological needs and irrational drives which may express themselves even in forms of 'selfless' idealism or the urge for 'self-transcendence' (cf. Koestler, 1967). Thus individuals gravitate towards a particular ideology on the basis of a largely subliminal 'elective affinity' with it (cf. Weber, 1948, pp. 284–5), both material and psychological. It is worth pointing out that in a modern pluralistic society it will be rare for the lives of even the most fanatical ideologues to be conditioned exclusively by one ideology, others coming into play in particular compartments of their existence.

(viii)   *Ideologies are not homogeneous at a lived level*, for every individual will rationalize them in a unique way, emphasize different aspects of the cluster of values and policies which they propound and have a personal elective affinity with them. This leads to the existence of highly nuanced and even conflicting intuitions and conceptions as to what an ideology's salient principles are and how best to implement them (what Billig, 1988, calls its 'dilemmatic' property).

(ix)   *Ideologies are not located in individuals as such* and can never be incarnated in, or fully expounded by, any one ideologue (cf. Mannheim, 1960, pp. 189–90; Sewel, 1985, p.61) for they exist in their entirety only at a collective, 'transpersonal' level. On this level they act as structural forces in conditioning people's lives and shaping historical events on a par with social, economic and political structures and in interaction with them. *As such neither their currency nor their impact on history can ever be explained in terms of ideas alone*, but only as an integral aspect of the particular historical context in which they exist.

(x) *Each ideology can be defined ideal-typically in terms of a core of values and perceptions of history* (cf. Freeden, 1986, pp.4–5, who uses 'core' in this sense; similarly Connolly, 1974, p.14, talks about a 'cluster' of axioms). This core underlies its vision of the ideal society, its evaluation of the present one and, if the perceived discrepancy is too great, its strategy for improving or transforming it (cf. Eccleshall, 1984, ch.1). A generic ideology is one in which a number of distinct political movements or regimes can be shown to share the same (ideally-typically constructed) ideological core.

These ten attributes of ideology can be synthesized into a definition on the following lines:

Ideology is a set of beliefs, values and goals considered in terms of their implications for the maintenance of the socio-political status quo (where ideology will tend to act as a conservative, reactionary force), for its improvement (where it becomes a reformist, gradualist force) or for its overthrow and replacement by an alternative order (where it will exhibit its utopian, revolutionary dimension). The socio-historical system created in the name of an ideology will always represent a travesty of the ideal society envisaged by those committed to it in its utopian, revolutionary aspect.

As a supra-personal structure an ideology can be pictured as a dynamic interaction of moral and political convictions, rejections of opposing values, and nuanced but converging visions of an ideal order of society and the policies to achieve it, all of which are capable of formulation at a high level of theoretical analysis. However, the extraordinary normative power of ideology, which is manifested historically in its ability to serve as the rationale of behaviour, the basis of social cohesion, the legitimation of a particular political regime and the inspiration of revolutionary action, is rooted in sub-rational and pre-verbal layers of consciousness within the individual and may express itself in a wide variety of both verbal and non-verbal cultural phenomena.

All ideologies may seem rational and coherent when articulated by a major theorist or reconstructed by an outside observer. However, they will tend to exhibit considerable heterogeneity at a 'lived' level, since all individuals will embody them in a partial and incomplete way as a function both of their unique social situation and of the specific psychological and material interests which condition their personal 'elective affinity' with it. There will also be notable differences in the level of affective commitment and theoretical self-consciousness on which individuals act as its 'carriers'. While rooted in human consciousness, ideologies do not originate or operate solely in the mind but both shape and are shaped by the cultural, social, economic and political structures which create the preconditions for the influence they exert on human behaviour and historical processes.

Each particular ideology can be ideal-typically defined in terms of an underlying core of values and goals which inform various policies and tactics, while a generic ideology is one whose core values and goals have expressed themselves in a variety of distinct, or even apparently conflicting surface manifestations.

This way of conceiving ideology acts as a built-in safeguard against (i) ignoring the crucial role played by non-ideological factors and structures in conditioning both fascism's emergence and success; (ii) reducing fascism to

rld-view of a single individual; (iii) homogenizing into simplistic
:tual formulas the diverse and sometimes conflicting ideological cur-
which made up individual fascisms. It is also consistent with it that
n can be defined primarily in terms of its 'positive' ideological goals
for the overthrow of existing society and the creation of a new order *as
formulated by its own thinkers and propagandists*, despite the notorious
absence of major systematizers to rank with the pioneers of liberal or
socialist thought. Furthermore, the extreme irrationality of fascism or the
radical differences between its promises as the creed of a revolutionary
movement and the realities to which it gives rise as the orthodoxy of a
regime, far from being 'awkward' to reconcile with our theory, become to a
large extent predictable by it.

Thus the first two objections we earlier raised rhetorically to our own way
of approaching fascism have been met. To forestall the third possible charge
to which this approach is open, namely of treating fascism at a level of
analysis and synthesis which is so abstract as to be dehumanizing, it is
necessary to spell out a major implication of the recognition that generic
fascism is an ideal type. Whenever 'idealizing abstraction' sets to work on
singularities so as to be able to treat them as case studies in a genus of
phenomena, it produces a picture of them which is more like an X-ray than a
photograph: the skeleton is thrown into relief while the surface features so
vital to a person's physical individuality become little more than shadows or
disappear entirely. Though this book will be concentrating on the genus
'fascism', this is not to deny that every movement ideal-typically categorized
as such is also unique. Not only will it comprise ideologies, policies,
personalities, structures and a style all peculiar to it, but it must operate in
and interact with its own historical context. Every manifestation of fascism
is thus both atypical and typical, according to whether it is being investigated in its uniqueness (that is in the 'idiographic' register in which historians specialize) or in terms of what makes it symptomatic of the genus.

To take a striking example, let us consider National Socialism. The
personality of its leader, the success of its drive to take over the instruments
of state power, the virulence of its anti-Semitism, the scale of its territorial
ambitions and the ruthlessness with which they were pursued are just some
of the features which make Nazism 'stand out from' other ultra-right
movements in inter-war Europe. None the less, if its unique characteristics
can be shown to be concrete permutations of what has been identified ideal-
typically as the common structural core of fascism, then Nazism is still, for
taxonomic purposes, fascist. It is at this structural 'nomothetic' level that
political and social science generally operate. Even so, to have demonstrated
how Nazism exhibits an aspect of the 'nature of fascism' can be no more
than a small contribution to revealing the 'nature of Nazism'.

Though this may seem obvious enough there is always the danger that
once Nazism or any other movement, is analyzed as an example of 'generic
fascism' the insights gained will be construed in a reductionist spirit, as if
the 'structural core' was all that mattered, rather like a doctor becoming
more interested in the illness than the patient. When this perverse perspective is applied, the millions of human beings who suffered or who died in

the most atrocious circumstances as the result of Nazism's uniqueness, risk becoming the mere epiphenomena of a 'deeper' reality. Let me categorically dissociate this book, then, from any implication that to identify those phenomena which 'fit' an ideal type in some measure is to suggest that their particular features and the experiential realities associated with them are being consigned to a kind of limbo of accidence or irrelevance. Human lives are not lived 'structurally', nor even 'historically', and any readers who risk losing sight of this fact while studying fascism are well advised to read an autobiographical account of just one person's experiences of what it could mean in human terms: Primo Levi's magnificent *If This is a Man* (1987).

The concepts to which intellectuals resort in order to 'grasp' human realities should never be allowed to imply the primacy of theory over lived experience. Instead, theories should always remain subordinate to the task of understanding and explaining the 'real' phenomena for which they were originally created. To take the example of Nazism once more, the heuristic function of applying to it an ideal type of the term 'fascism' is fulfilled only if certain aspects of its uniqueness and of concrete realities associated with it are illuminated by categorizing it as such. Otherwise it is a vain intellectual game which betrays the humanistic purpose which all research into social realities should serve. As long as these points are kept in mind there should be no psychological barrier to reconciling the unity (homogeneity) of different fascisms which exists at a structural level with the extreme contrasts (heterogeneity) which separate them at a historiographical level or to being constantly aware of the human realities subsumed in generalizations and causal models.

The Scope of this Book

Now that some of the methodological spadework has been completed, it should be clear that the approach we have adopted considerably narrows the scope of what this book will have to say about fascism's 'nature'. For one thing, there is clearly no question of it revealing the 'essence' of fascism. Fascism has already been demonized quite enough into a suprahuman force at the level of popular mythology (consider for example works on the 'occultist' basis of Nazism: for example Brennan, 1974; Pauwels and Bergier, 1972; for a corrective see Goodrick-Clarke, 1985) without the waters being muddied even further by an academic work with 'essentialist' implications. Even if the metaphorical power of language may sometimes mean that the ideological core which forms the basis of our ideal type is being treated like a 'matrix' generating historical realities from some occult a-temporal realm, the reader should never forget that it is the result of 'idealizing abstraction'. It is the result of consciously elaborating, formulating and systematizing a pattern 'seen' by me at a largely intuitive or unconscious level, only one of the many patterns which other researchers might 'read into' putative fascist phenomena when studied for analogies and parallels (nomothetically) rather than in their particularity (idiographically). Thus no attempt will be made to 'prove' the existence of the common ideological core we have invented (in the etymological sense of discovered and constructed).Instead it will be set out concisely at the beginning of Chapter 2 as a *fait accompli* of my earlier empirical investigation into the subject, and in particular into the original writings of scores of ideologues of different putative fascist movements.

It might be added at this point that a regrettable lacuna in this text is an appendix providing extensive and wide-ranging samples of fascist ideology, both inter- and post-war, to illustrate the highly nuanced and varied permutations that the same core of ideas can generate. An excellent prototype of this was provided for inter-war European fascism in a pioneering book on comparative fascism by Eugen Weber (1964), but to my knowledge nothing of its kind yet exists for post-war fascism. Until the situation is remedied, the reader is urged to consult original sources where possible as an integral part of any foray into fascist studies, a task which soon rewards the effort for those concerned to understand its unique ideological dynamics (and also provides a valuable empirical test of the interpretation of them which I am offering here).

A consequence of the emphasis on common ideological components is that the political, economic and sociological preconditions or bases of individual fascist movements which did not achieve power will be referred to only peripherally, if at all. Chapters 7 and 8 will consider how the ideal type constructed in this book correlates to existing research into the various levels of the causes of fascism as a generic phenomenon, but the causes, or 'aetiology', of specific fascisms, however important in other contexts, are not my primary concern. All I would say at this point is that the model of fascism expounded here anticipates that the social base of generic fascism, and even of one of its particular manifestations, will be far from homogeneous in terms of class, status, occupation, age group, or psychological type. Nor will it be associated with any particular stage in 'nation-building' or socio-economic 'development' (modernization), except in so far as it is structurally related to specific consequences of secularization and pluralism.

It also follows from the approach adopted that this book makes no claim to provide an inventory of all the forms fascism has taken, and that especially in the post-war period there are any number of groupings which I do not even name, since their existence adds nothing to the argument I am developing. In any case such labour would not only be Herculean but superfluous, since an excellent survey of world-wide inter-war fascism exists already (Payne, 1980) as well as a comprehensive world directory of the contemporary radical right (Ó Maoláin, 1987).

The approach adopted in this book similarly precludes any attempt to demonstrate the nature of fascism through reconstructing the history of the many discrete movements which comprise it. Such an exercise would rapidly degenerate into a series of potted histories culled from the many admirable monographs already in existence which are devoted to the fascism of individual countries, thus swelling the volume inordinately without throwing any light on the genus 'fascism'. The Italian historian Tasca is often quoted by those who believe that generic fascism is not susceptible to definition and that scholars should concentrate their energies on reconstructing its history. It is worth noting, however, that after his famous statement that 'for us to define Fascism is to write its history', he went on to add that any account of *generic fascism* must be based on 'common properties susceptible of being incorporated into a general definition' (quoted in Lyttleton, 1979, p.82), precisely what we have set out to provide. Historiographical detail is thus avoided on principle in the treatment of particular fascisms as quite incompatible with the length and scope of this book. The two exceptions to this principle are Fascism and Nazism, which merit special treatment because, as the only two fascist movements autonomously to 'seize' power, they provide important case studies in the all-important transition from revolutionary force to regime. It should be noted that the narrative information I build into my analysis is intended to help *non-experts* get their bearings on the ocean of particular events which constitutes the history of both, events fraught with complexity and controversy at every critical point. Experts are asked to bear with the writer for the all-too obvious signs of compression in the synopses given and to remember that the central aim of the two chapters is to highlight those aspects of Fascism and Nazism which assume particular relevance in the light of the theory I am developing. All other permutations of fascism will be dealt with in a highly condensed fashion, sometimes in a single sentence. I am confident that readers using this book at undergraduate level will be sufficiently interested in their subject, not to say academically 'street-wise', to realize that familiarity with 'competing' theories of fascism as well as knowledge of representative forms of it culled from other secondary sources are both *essential* if the elaborate theory and rudimentary background which I offer here is to be of any value at all in essay work or research.

If the 'nature of fascism' is not being investigated primarily in terms of its aetiology or, to stay within the medical register, individual case histories, and makes no attempt to be a comprehensive classification of all known forms it has taken (i.e. its 'nosology'), it could be said that this book does hope to offer fresh insights into its 'diagnostics'. Having established in Chapter 2 our ideal type of fascism, the four chapters which follow aim to build up a picture of the wide range of permutations in which that genus has manifested itself. Chapters 3 and 4 will deal with Fascism and Nazism respectively, Chapter 5 with other (abortive) inter-war fascisms in Europe and 6 with non-European and post-war fascisms. What should emerge cumulatively is how the same genus of political energy has acted as a remarkably protean force in the twentieth century, endowed as it is with an ideological core which can draw on the most varied and contradictory cultural components. At the same time, not only should the essentially utopian and unrealizable nature of its ideological goals (even when implemented by an authoritarian regime) become increasingly apparent, but also its fundamental impotence to do more than exert the most marginal influence on mainstream politics, except in the freak circumstances which prevailed in two nations in the inter-war period in Italy and Germany.

Readers of whatever category may well feel an understandable sense of disenchantment now that the highly circumscribed scope of this book has been made clear and the title 'unpacked'. It makes no claim to reveal an occult essence underlying fascism, to supply an absolute definition of it, to provide an exhaustive *catalogue raisonné* of phenomena embraced by the term or to survey the principal secondary sources dealing with it. I have written this book not with the Olympian perspective of an acknowledged expert ensconced in a private belvedere at the peak of his career, but as a relative newcomer to the subject bivouacked precariously some way up one of its unclimbed but scree-strewn slopes. In short, the truths in which this book deals are exploratory, tentative and light years removed from the mythical world of absolutes aspired to by the fascist mentality, for which doubt was a symptom of decadence.

Despite being consciously partial and necessarily incomplete, this book aims to convince those for whom fascism is still a bewildering conundrum that a distinctive ideology, one unleashing considerable affective energy in those who accepted its internal logic, underlies what could so easily be dismissed as fanatical ravings or cynical propaganda. Those content with their own ideal type of fascism will see for themselves whether this approach adds anything to what they already know. The new one merely sets out to offer a conceptual net to catch a particularly slippery and voracious genus of political fish. As an oriental proverb suggests, 'once you have caught the fish, throw away the net'.

References

Allardyce, G., 1979. What fascism is not: thoughts on the deflation of a concept, *The American History Review*, Vol.84, No.2.

Beetham, D., 1983. *Marxists in Face on Fascism*, Manchester University Press, Manchester.

Billig, M., 1978. *Fascists: A Social-psychological View of the National Front*, Harcourt Brace Jovanovich, London, New York.

Billig, M., *et al.*, 1988. *Ideological Dilemmas: A Social Psychology of Everyday Thinking*, Sage, London.

Billig, M., 1989. The extreme right: continuities in anti-Semitic conspiracy theory in post-war Europe, in R. Eatwell and N. O'Sullivan, (eds), *The Nature of the Right: American and European Politics and Political Thought Since 1789*, Pinter, London.

Bogdanor, V., (ed.), 1987. *The Blackwell Encyclopedia of Political Institutions*, Basil Blackwell, Oxford.

Bordiga, A., 1922. *Relazione del PCd'I al IV Congresso dell'Internazionale Comunista (novembre 1922)*, reprinted 1976, Israka, Milan.

Bottomore, T. and Goode, P., 1978. *Austro-Marxism*, Oxford University Press, Oxford.

Botz, G., 1976. Austro-Marxist interpretations of fascism, *Journal of Contemporary History*, Vol.11, No.4.

Botz, G., 1987. 'Austria', in D. Mühlberger (ed.), *The Social Basis of European Fascist Movements*, Croom Helm, London.

Brennan, J.H., 1974. *Occult Reich*, Futura, London.

Burger, T., 1976. *Max Weber's Theory of Concept Formation, History, Laws, and Ideal Types*, Duke University Press, Durham, North Carolina.

Carsten, F.L., 1979. Interpretations of fascism, in W. Laqueur, (ed.) *Fascism: A Reader's Guide*, The Penguin Press, Harmondsworth.

Connolly, W.E., 1976. *The Terms of Political Discourse*, Heath, Lexiton, Massachusetts.

Conway, M., 1990. Building the Christian city: Catholics and politics in inter-war francophone

Belgium, *Past and Present*, No.128.
Cullen, S.M., 1986. Leaders and martyrs: Codreanu, Mosley and José Antonio, *History*, Vol.71.
Davis, J. (ed.), 1979. *Gramsci and Italy's Passive Revolution*, Croom Helm, London.
De Felice, R., 1977. *Interpretations of Fascism* (trans. by Brenda Huff Everest), Harvard University Press, Cambridge, Massachusetts.
De Felice, R. and Ledeen, M., 1976. *Fascism: an Informal Introduction to its Theory and Practice*, Transaction, New Brunswick, New Jersey.
Dimitroff, G., 1982. *Gegen Faschismus und Krieg. Ausgewählte Reden und Schriften*, Reclam, Leipzig.
Dülffer, J., 1976. Bonapartism, fascism and national socialism, *Journal of Contemporary History*, Vol.11, No.4.
Eccleshall, R., Geoghegan, V., Jay, R., Wilford, R., 1984. *Political Ideologies*, Hutchinson, London.
Eichholtz, D. and Gossweiler, K., (eds) 1980. *Faschismusforschung. Positionen, Probleme, Polemik*, Pahl-Rugenstein Verlag, Cologne.
Eley, G., 1983. What produces fascism: preindustrial traditions or a crisis of the capitalist state?, *Politics and Society*, Vol.12, No.1.
Evrigenis, D. (ed.), 1986. *European Parliament Working Documents: Report Drawn Up on Behalf of the Committee of Inquiry into the Rise of Fascism and Racism*, report no. 2–160/85 (2 vols), European Parliament, Strasbourg.
Freeden, M., 1986. *Liberalism Divided*, Oxford University Press, Oxford.
Fromm, E., 1960. *Fear of Freedom*, Routledge & Kegan Paul, London.
Giddens, A., 1976. *New Rules of Sociological Method: A Positive Critique of Interpretative Sociology*, Hutchinson, London.
Giddens, A., 1984. *The Constitution of Society*, Polity Press, Cambridge.
Goodrick-Clarke, N., 1985. *The Occult Roots of Nazism*, The Aquarian Press, Wellingborough.
Gregor, A.J., 1969. *The Ideology of Fascism: The Rationale of Totalitarianism*, Free Press, New York.
Gregor, A.J., 1974. *Theories of Fascism*, General Learning Press, Morristown, New Jersey.
Gregor, A.J., 1979. *Italian Fascism and Developmental Dictatorship*, Princeton University Press, Princeton, New Jersey.
Guerin, D., 1973. *Fascism and Big Business*, Monad Press, New York.
Hagtvet, B. and Kühnl, R., 1980. Contemporary approaches to fascism: a survey of paradigms, in S.U. Larsen, B. Hagtvet, J.P. Myklebust (eds), *Who Were the Fascists*, Universitetsforlaget, Oslo.
Hall, S., 1978. The hinterland of science: ideology and the sociology of knowledge, in University of Birmingham, Centre for Cultural Studies, *On Ideology*, Hutchinson, London.
Hamilton, M.B., 1987. The elements of the concept ideology, *Political Studies*, Vol.35, No.1.
Hayes, P., 1973. *Fascism*, George Allen & Unwin, London.
Hennessy, A., 1979. Fascism and populism in Latin America, in W. Laqueur (ed.), *Fascism: A Reader's Guide*, The Penguin Press, Harmondsworth.
Herf, J., 1984. *Reactionary Modernism*, Cambridge University Press, London.
Huizinga, J., 1956. Historical conceptualization, in F. Stern, (ed.), *Varieties of History*, World Publishing Company, New York.
Kasza, G.J., 1984. Fascism from below? A comparative perspective on the Japanese right 1931–1936, *Journal of Contemporary History*, Vol.19, No.4.
Kater, M.H., 1988. Book review, *German History*, Vol.6, No.1.
Kershaw, I., 1985. *The Nazi Dictatorship*, Edward Arnold, London.
Kertzer, D.I., 1988. *Ritual, Politics and Power*, Yale University Press, New Haven, Connecticut.
Kitchen, M., 1976. *Fascism*, Macmillan, London.
Koestler, A., 1967. *The Ghost in the Machine*, Pan Books, London.
Kuhn, T.S., 1970. *The Structure of Scientific Revolutions*, University of Chicago Press, Chicago.
Laqueur, W. (ed.), 1969. *Fascism: A Reader's Guide*, The Penguin Press, Harmondsworth.
Larsen, S.U., Hagtvet, B., Myklebust, J.P. (eds), 1980. *Who Were the Fascists: Social Roots of European Fascism*, Universitetsforlaget, Oslo.
Levi, P., 1987. *If this is a Man*, Sphere, London.

Linz, J.J., 1979. Some notes towards the comparative study of fascism, in W. Laqueur, (ed.), *Fascism: A Reader's Guide*, The Penguin Press, Harmondsworth.

Lipset, S.M., 1960. 'Fascism' – Left, right and centre, in *Political Man*, William Heinemann, London.

Lyttleton, A. (ed.), 1973. *Italian Fascisms from Pareto to Gentile*, Jonathan Cape, London.

Lyttleton, A., 1979. Italian fascism, in W. Laqueur (ed.), *Fascism: A Reader's Guide*. The Penguin Press, Harmondsworth.

Mannheim, K., 1960. *Ideology and Utopia* (trans. by L. Wirth and E. Shils), Routledge & Kegan Paul, London.

Maritain, J., 1936. *Humanisme intégral*, Montaigne, Paris.

McClelland, J.S., 1970. *The French Right from De Maistre to Maurras*, Jonathan Cape. London.

Miller, D. (ed.), 1987. *The Blackwell Encyclopedia of Political Thought*, Basil Blackwell, Oxford.

Milward, A.S., 1979. Fascism and the economy, in W. Laqueur (ed.) *Fascism: A Reader's Guide*, The Penguin Press, Harmondsworth.

Moore, B., 1966. *The Social Origins of Dictatorship and Democracy*, Beacon Press, Boston.

Mosse, G.L., 1979. Towards a general theory of fascism, in G.L. Mosse (ed.), *International Fascism*, Sage Publications, London.

Mühlberger, D., 1987. Germany, in D. Mühlberger (ed.), *The Social Basis of European Fascism*, Croom Helm, London.

Nolte, E., 1967. *Theorien über den Faschismus*, Kiepenhauer und Witsch, Cologne.

Nolte, E., 1965. *Three Faces of Fascism: Action Française, Italian Fascism, National Socialism*, Weidenfeld & Nicolson, London.

Nolte, E., 1967. *Theorien über den Faschismus*, Kiepenhauer und Witsch, Cologne.

Ó Maoláin, C., 1987. *The Radical Right: A World Directory*, Longman, London.

O'Sullivan, N.K., 1983. *Fascism*, J.M. Dent & Sons, London.

Organski, A.F.K., 1968. Fascism and Modernization, in S. Woolf (ed.), *The Nature of Fascism*, Weidenfeld & Nicolson, London.

Outhwaite, W. and Bottomore, T. (ed.), 1992. *The Blackwell Dictionary of Twentieth-Century Social Thought*, Basil Blackwell, Oxford.

Pauwels, L. and Bergier, J., 1972. *Le matin des magiciens*, Gallimard, Paris.

Payne, S.G., 1961. *Falange. A History of Spanish Fascism*, Stanford University Press, Stanford.

Payne, S.G., 1980. *Fascism: Comparison and Definition*, University of Wisconsin Press, Madison, Wisconsin.

Payne, S.G., 1984. Fascism, Nazism, Japanism, *The International History Review*, Vol.6, No.2.

Pepper, D., 1985. *The Roots of Modern Environmentalism*, Croom Helm, London.

Petzold, J., 1983. *Die Demagogie des Hitler-Faschismus*, Röderberg-Verlag, Frankfurt-on-Main.

Pinto, A.C., 1986. Fascist ideology revisited: Zeev Sternhell and his critics, *European History Quarterly*, Vol.16.

Plamenatz, J., 1970. *Ideology*, Macmillan, London.

Poulantzas, N., 1974. *Fascism and Dictatorship*, NLB, London.

Preston, P., 1985, Reading history: fascism, *History Today*, Vol.35, September.

Rauschning, H., 1938. *Die Revolution des Nihilismus*, Europa Verlag, Zürich, New York.

Rees, P., 1985. *Fascism and Pre-fascism in Europe 1890–1945. A Bibliography of the Extreme Right*, 2 Vols, Harvester Press, Sussex.

Reich, W., 1946. *The Mass Psychology of Fascism* (trans. by Theodor P. Wolfe), Orgone Institute, New York.

Revelli, M., 1981. *Fascismo: teorie e interpretazioni*, in N. Trafaglia (ed.), *Il mondo contemporaneo*, Vol.2, Storia d'Europa, ch.4, La Nuova Italia, Florence.

Robinson, R.A.H., 1981. *Fascism In Europe*, The Historical Association, London.

Rogger, H. and Weber, E. (eds), 1966. *The European Right*, University of California Press, Berkeley, California.

Rossi-Landi, F., 1990. *Ideology*, Oxford University Press, Oxford.

Schüddekopf, O-E., 1973. *Fascism*, Weidenfeld & Nicolson, London.

Scruton, R., 1982. *A Dictionary of Political Thought*, Pan Books, London.

Seliger, M., 1976. *Ideology and Politics*, George Allen & Unwin, London.

Sewel, W.H., 1985. Ideologies and social revolutions: reflections on the French case, *Journal of Modern History*, Vol.57, No.1.

Shah, I., 1979. *World Tales*, Allen Lane/Kestrel, London.

Soucy, R.J., 1986. *French Fascism: The First Wave, 1924–33*, Yale University Press, New Haven and London.

Sternhell, Z., 1972. *Barrès et le nationalisme français*, Armand Colin, Paris.

Sternhell, Z., 1973. National socialism and antisemitism: the case of Maurice Barrès, *Journal of Contemporary History*, Vol.8, No.4.

Sternhell, Z., 1978. *La Droite révolutionnaire, 1885–1914*, Editions du Seuil, Paris.

Sternhell, Z., 1979. Fascist ideology, in W. Laqueur, *Fascism: A Reader's Guide*, The Penguin Press, Harmondsworth.

Sternhell, Z., 1983. *Ni droite ni gauche. L'idéologie fasciste en France*, Editions du Seuil, Paris. English edition 1986. *Neither Right nor Left: Fascist Ideology in France*, (trans. by D. Maisel), University of California Press, Berkeley and Los Angeles.

Sternhell, Z., 1987. Fascism, in D. Miller (ed.), *The Blackwell Encyclopedia of Political Thought*, Basil Blackwell, Oxford.

Theweleit, K., 1987. *Male Fantasies*, Vol. 1: *Women, Floods, Bodies, History*, Polity Press, Oxford.

Theweleit, K., 1989. *Male Fantasies*, Vol. 2: *Male Bodies: Psychoanalyzing the White Terror*, Polity Press, Oxford.

Thurlow, R., 1987. *Fascism in Britain: A History 1918–85*, Basil Blackwell, Oxford.

Togliatti, P., 1970. *Lezioni sul fascismo*, Editori Riuniti, Rome.

Trevor-Roper, H.R. 1968. The phenomenon of fascism, in S.J. Woolf (ed.), *European Fascism*, Weidenfeld & Nicolson, London.

Turner Jr, H.A., 1975. Fascism and modernization, in H.A. Turner Jr. (ed.), *Reappraisals of Fascism*, Franklin Watts, New York.

Watson, D.R., 1988. Book review, *History*, Vol.73, No.236.

Weber, E., 1964. *Varieties of Fascism*, Van Nostrand, New York.

Weber, M., 1948. *From Max Weber*, Routledge & Kegan Paul, London.

Woolf, S.J., 1968. Introduction, in S.J. Woolf (ed.), *European Fascism*, Weidenfeld & Nicolson, London.

Wusten, H. van der, 1987. The low countries, in D. Mühlberger (ed.), *The Social Basis of European Fascist Movements*, Croom Helm, London.

2 A New Ideal Type of Generic Fascism

A Concise Definition of Fascism

Since this book has so far done little more than emphasize the lack of consensus over the term 'fascism' and establish certain methodological premises, then it is high time we set out our own stall. We propose to do so by offering a concise definition, the major implications of which for the understanding of the nature of fascism will then be discursively 'unpacked' in the course of the chapter:

> Fascism is a genus of political ideology whose mythic core in its various permutations is a palingenetic form of populist ultra-nationalism.

The following exegesis of this as yet cryptic characterization of generic fascism falls into four sections: (i) implications of the assertion that it is 'a political ideology' containing a 'mythic core'; (ii) explanations of the key definitional components of this core: 'palingenetic' and 'populist ultra-nationalism', and of their repercussions for fascism's viability as a political ideology; (iii) an extended definition of fascism; (iv) conclusions to be drawn from the new ideal type for several recurring questions concerning the 'nature of fascism'.

Fascism as a Political Ideology

Generic Ideological Features of Fascism

A number of fascism's features can be anticipated *a priori* on the basis of the ten generic attributes of ideologies we identified in the last chapter:

(i)   The values and world-view which fascism embodies will be expressed not only in theoretical writings, speeches, propaganda and songs but in the semiotic language of rallies, symbols, uniforms: in short, the whole style of its politics.

(ii) Fascism will exhibit a utopian revolutionary aspect when attempting to overthrow the existing order but proceed to assume a reactionary, oppressive one if ever installed in power, even if some idealists will constantly seek to 'reform' it by narrowing the gap between the theory and the practice.

(iii) The utopia which fascism seeks to implement will never be realized in practice, only a travesty of it.

(iv) No matter how 'propagandistic' fascist thought will appear to those who do not sympathize with its underlying world-view, its most committed activists and supporters will find in it an outlet for idealism and self-sacrifice.

(v) Despite rationalizations of the fascist world-view by appeals to histori- cal, cultural, religious or scientific 'facts', its affective power is rooted in irrational drives and mythical assumptions.

(vi) Commitment to fascism can exist on varying levels of emotional intensity and active support and its ideas will express themselves in various degrees of sophistication or simplification.

(vii) Genuine (as opposed to feigned or tactical) support for fascism stems in each individual case from a largely subliminal elective affinity to it based on material and psychological interests.

(viii) Though a fascist movement may appear a cohesive ideological commu- nity and present itself as such, on closer inspection its support will prove to derive from a myriad personal motivations for joining it and idiosyncratic conceptions of the movement's goals.

(ix) Fascist ideology and the impact it achieves as the basis of a movement is not reducible to the theories and policies of any one ideologue or leader, for it acts as a transpersonal historical structure whose emerg- ence and success are conditioned by its interaction with other struc- tures both ideological and non-ideological.

(x) Generic fascism is definable ideal-typically in terms of a cluster of values and goals common to all its various permutations, in other words its ideological core.

Clearly this approach to fascism anticipates that extensive ideological heterogeneity will exist between different examples of it, and even within the same movement, as well as allowing for considerable complexity as far as its sociological base and the motivations of its supporters are concerned. Both these points will be developed further in the course of the book. For the moment it is important to elaborate on the notion that generic fascism has a homogeneous ideological or mythic core.

The Mythic Core of Political Ideologies

The core of an ideology can be conceived as the fundamental political myth which mobilizes its activists and supporters. The term 'political myth' in this context does not refer merely to specific historical myths exploited to legitimate policies (that is, in the sense explored by Tudor, 1972). Rather it denotes the irrational mainspring of *all* ideologies irrespective of their surface rationality or apparent 'common sense'. As Namier observed, 'to treat [political] ideas as the offspring of pure reason would be to assign them a parentage about as mythological as that of Pallas Athene. What matters most is the underlying emotions, the music, to which ideas are a mere libretto, often of very inferior quality' (quoted in Soucy, 1979, p.268).

A number of theorists have recognized that the roots of ideology lie in irrational forces (for example Pareto), but the symbolic father-figure of the theory adopted here is Georges Sorel, at least as far as his specialized use of the term 'myth' is concerned. Sorel concluded that what gives any religious or political creed its power to inspire revolutionary transformations in history are its core myths, namely those simple visionary principles:

> which enclose with them all the strongest inclinations of a people, of a party or a class, inclinations which recur to the mind with the insistence of instincts in all the circumstances of life; and which give an aspect of complete reality to the hopes of immediate action in which . . . men can reform their desires, passions and mental activity. (Sorel, 1961, p.125)

He cites as examples the belief in the imminent return of Christ which sustained Christians throughout the early history of the Church, the 'many Utopias' which inspired the French revolutionaries of 1789, and Mazzini's 'mad chimera' of a united Italian people which played a crucial role in the risorgimento. The major historical upheavals associated with such myths underline the fact that in each case it 'must be judged as a means of acting on the present; any attempt to discuss how far it can be taken literally as future history is devoid of sense. *It is the myth in its entirety which is important*: its parts are only of interest in so far as they bring out the main idea'. It was on this basis that Sorel attached such significance to the weapon of the general strike in the arsenal of socialist thought. Despite, or rather because of, its utopian nature, this concept effectively supplied to anarcho-syndicalists 'the *myth* in which Socialism is wholly comprised; i.e. a body of images capable of evoking all the sentiments which correspond to the different manifestations of the war undertaken by Socialism against modern society' (ibid. p.127; see also Roth, 1980).

We propose to use 'mythic' to refer to the inspirational, revolutionary power which an ideology can exert whatever its apparent rationality or practicality (as opposed to 'mythical' which connotes imaginary or fictitious), bringing it close to the way 'utopia' is used by some social scientists (for example Goodwin and Taylor, 1982; Lasky, 1976; Kumar, 1987). Once the affective driving force of fascism is conceived in terms of its 'mythic core', the type of ideology involved ceases to be the exclusive concern of the intellectual historian or political scientist. It raises social anthropological issues about the central role of belief systems and their corresponding ritual, not only in providing cohesion and stability to existing society (the 'structural-functionalist' view), but also in rationalizing ephemeral collective movements of extreme violence, including those bent on overthrowing society when it is perceived to be in crisis and replacing it by a new order (the Sorelian view). As this book sets out to demonstrate, it is this latter revolutionary aspect of myth, fully recognized by some social scientists (for example Reszler, 1981), which is crucial to the dynamics of fascism and which can be usefully made central to a definition of it.

The Secular Orientation of Political Ideologies

It should be noted that fascism has been consistently referred to in terms of *political* ideology and *political* myth. Once it is accepted that both the conservative and transforming power of *every* ideology resides in its mythic dimension, whether the society on which it operates is a 'traditional' or a 'modern' one, then it becomes important to differentiate between religious and political ideologies. Otherwise, the Crusades and the Italian *risorgimento* come to be subsumed within the same category of historical event which most would agree is not taxonomically helpful. Unlike a religious ideology, which affirms the primacy of the metaphysical over the secular, a political ideology derives its legitimation not from a tradition of revelation, whether oral or written, but from a cosmology which conceives the maintenance or transformation of society as dependant on human agency operating in unidimensional historical time. In other words, it does not allow for the possibility that suprahuman powers can permanently or periodically intervene in human affairs or that the present dispensation of history can give way to one governed by different laws in accordance with a preordained divine or metaphysical scheme of things.

The existence of a hybrid of these two distinct types of ideology, the 'political religion', has been postulated by several scholars, notably Voegelin (1938, 1952, 1968) and Sironneau (1982). Though their application of this ideal type has suggested some interesting structural affinities shared by millenaristic religion and certain revolutionary political ideologies, to postulate a direct historical or psychological relationship remains speculative to say the least. I question the heuristic value of treating any predominantly secular movement as if it is essentially the projection of religious or metaphysical speculation concerning the end of secular time on to a future located within the historical process. In particular, I part company with Voegelin when he sees the 'essence of modernity' (that is secular myths of progress) as the secularization of 'gnostic' concepts of transcendence (1952, p.126). While the taxonomic boundaries at issue here have not yet been satisfactorily drawn by the human sciences, it is highly debatable whether political cosmologies can be equated with religious ones, or even be seen simply as their travesties, without losing sight of important distinctions.

Especially in the contemporary world where religious fundamentalism is becoming a major political force, it is important not to confuse prevalently secular political movements, even those which claim to uphold traditional religious values, with politically militant forms of an organized and revealed religion which base themselves on an unbroken tradition of exegesis, ritual and hierarchic spiritual authority. Since these reassert the primacy of revealed faith over the secular forces which are eroding it, the basic thrust of this latter type of movement (for which the term 'political religion' seems quite appropriate) is thus restorationist in intent, at least morally and spiritually. This is true even if the impact of the modern world (that is its civil and military technology, communications networks and global socioeconomic systems) means that any state created by a political religion is now bound in practice to be radically different from the one in which the orthodoxy which it claims to represent first emerged. The various initiatives of 'political Catholicism' in inter-war Europe (see Conway, 1990; Buchanan and Conway, 1996), the politics of the American 'Bible Belt', and the proliferating contemporary movements, parties and regimes based on fundamentalist interpretations of Islam, Hinduism and Sikhism are examples of this distinctive type of ideological force. Thus when structural affinities *are* discernible between the cosmology of an established religious or mystic sect and the philosophy of history of an organized political movement, then it is more fruitful to attribute it to an archetype which can inform both spheres of human mythopoeia, than to see the political ideology as a derivation or travesty of the religious one. It should also be pointed out that it is unforgivably Euro- or 'North'-centric to equate 'religious' with Judeo-Christian, so that anything reminiscent of its highly particular rectilinear philosophy of history becomes treated as a vestige of religion *tout court*.

Certainly there has been no shortage of political movements in modern (Western) history which legitimate themselves by seeking to identify their policies and attacks on opponents with the moral convictions held by believers of a particular faith. The central role of Judaism in Zionism, the Anglicanism of Ulster Loyalists, the Catholicism invoked by nineteenth-century French conservatives such as De Bonald, as well as by several ultra-right movements which we will touch on later (for example *Action Française*, *Rex*, the Arrow Cross, Ustasha), not to mention the strong Orthodox Christian component in the thinking of the Iron Guard, all suggest that another hybrid concept, such as 'religious politics', might be a useful taxonomic sub-category of 'political ideology'. In such cases religious precepts are invoked without the official sanction of the hierarchs of the faith in question, and in such a way as to assert the primacy, not of the spiritual but of the political, not of metaphysical agency but of human agency. In other words, the hallmark of religious politics can be seen to lie in the way secular policies and tactics are extensively rationalized in ostensibly religious terms, but in an essentially heretical, even blasphemous, spirit from the point of view of established orthodoxy. Its legitimacy in combating perceived enemies or pursuing revolutionary goals thus depends largely on the credibility and dynamism (charisma) of the leadership and the religious and intellectual confusions of those who become its followers.

Fascism as a Political Ideology, not a Political Religion

The reason for dwelling on the need to distinguish between political and religious ideology is the readiness which a number of scholars have shown to treat fascism as a form of 'political religion'. Both Voegelin and Sironneau see Nazism as an outstanding example of it, and this assumption is reflected in a number of monographs (for example Pois, 1986, who talks of a National Socialist 'religion of nature'). The approach has also been recently applied to Fascism by E. Gentile (1990), who analyses it as a 'lay religion'. Closely related concepts applied especially to Nazism are 'millenarianism', 'chiliasm' or 'eschatology' (for example Mannheim, 1960; Billig, 1978, p.103; Smith, 1979, p.46; Rhodes, 1980), which mean that its vision of a new order is being directly compared to the vision of a New Heaven and a New Earth which St. John described in the Book of Revelation as following on the *eschaton* or Last Days. Voegelin, for example, analyses the vision of history underlying modern totalitarianism in general and Nazism in particular in terms of the 'immanentization of the *eschaton*', (1952, p.120; cf. chs.4,5,6 passim), and talks of Hitler's 'millennial prophecy' (ibid. p.113). Those who see fascism as a modern form of millenarianism often bracket it in this respect with Marxism (for example Voegelin, 1952, 1968; Sironneau, 1982), a tendency popularized by the pioneering research into genuine (that is, religious) millenarianism produced by Cohn (1970). Yet this is to ignore the ease with which even so secularized and 'rational' an ideology as liberalism can acquire a quasi-religious 'millenaristic' dimension when it inspires revolutionary change (a point to which we will return in our discussion of 'palingenetic' myth). Incidentally, Voegelin seems oblivious of the (quasi-mystic) teleological myth of history which he has concocted in order to see modern totalitarianism as 'the journey's end of the Gnostic search for a civil theology' (1952, p.163), or in applying the term 'gnostic mass movements' not just to Marxism, communism, fascism and national socialism, but also to 'progressivism, positivism and psychoanalysis' (1968, p.83).

This abuse of religious concepts has parallels with the uncritical application to fascism of other terms taken from comparative mysticism such as 'sacred time' or shamanism (for example Rogger and Weber, 1966, ch.1; Mosse, 1980, pp.69, 166). It is not uncommon to find this latter line of reasoning backed up by references to Mircea Eliade which is somewhat ironic since, before achieving an international reputation for his academic works on comparative religion and mysticism, Eliade was an apologist for Romanian fascism (see Jesi, 1979, pp.38–50) and has continued to influence Italian neo-fascism (cf. Evola, 1972, pp.139–40; Guerra and Revelli, 1983, p.428) as well as being a patron of GRECE, the think-tank of an important French school of neo-fascism. While this perhaps gives his extensive post-war analyses of sacred and profane time a profound bearing on the mythic dynamics of fascism, it should be noted that he himself does not endorse the notion that modern political ideologies are 'religions' or even 'secular religions' (whatever they are), but suggests that both satisfy a need to combat mythless and hence meaningless time, 'the terror of history' (see below, pp.189–90).

One advantage of using the phrase 'political myth' to refer to the fascist revolutionary struggle to change society is that it draws attention to its irrational dynamics without creating the impression that we are dealing with a throw-back to an earlier type of political energy somehow out of place in the 'modern age'. On the other hand, once the wearers of Brown or Black Shirts are discussed in the same language used to refer to the Anabaptists of sixteenth-century Münster, fascism is turned into an essentially atavistic phenomenon which has mysteriously resurfaced from the depths in the modern age like some dormant Kraken from another age. This is particularly misleading in the case of Nazism, for while some of fascism's manifestations have taken the form of 'religious politics' (for example in Romania, Spain, Belgium, Brazil and South Africa), Nazism was certainly not one of them in the strict taxonomic sense we have tried to establish. Though the Third Reich deliberately used Christian trappings in its ritual, symbolism and language, at the level of ideology mainstream Nazism was intensely anti-Christian, except for individual followers, such as Dinter, who was eventually ousted from the party for his insistence on the centrality to Nazism of a 'Germanic' Christianity. Indeed, the regime itself viewed the Protestant and Catholic Churches quite rightly as a potential threat, and much (though by no means all) official ritual and imagery alluded specifically to pagan (and hence anti-Christian) myth. Nor are there any grounds to regard its goal of creating a 'Third Reich' as a direct descendant of the twelfth-century mystic Joachim of Flora's triadic scheme of history as several writers have implied (for example Mosse, 1980, p.165; Voegelin, 1952, p.113; cf. Sandoz, 1981, pp.109–11). Even if Joachim helped imbue the phrase with mythic connotations which lingered on in the political speculation of the German radical right well into the twentieth century (particularly in Moeller van den Bruck, 1923), its influence on mainstream Nazi usage has been greatly exaggerated. We will return to this topic when we consider the psycho-historical bases of fascism in Chapter 7.

The Mythic Core of Generic Fascism

The deeper implications of the first part of our definition should now be clear. By defining fascism as a genus of political ideology we resist the temptation to treat it as a modern form of millenarianism or a revivalist cult, and locate it firmly among the political forces which constitute a modern secularizing society. We also know in advance that it will exhibit considerable heterogeneity and complexity when the various concrete realities in which it manifested itself are taken into account. For the purposes of this study its essential homogeneity will reside solely in its mythic core and then only ideal-typically. The premise of this book is that it is heuristically useful to base a definition of generic fascism on this mythic core, or what Sorel called the 'body of images', which crystallizes the rationale for fascism's unilateral 'war against modern society'. Our ideal type of fascism's 'lowest common denominator' is summed up in the second part of our initial definition: *a palingenetic form of populist ultra-nationalism*, a phrase which clearly calls for considerable amplification.

'Palingenetic myth' and 'populist ultra-nationalism'

Palingenetic Myth

The first of these components is perhaps one of the most common ingredients of human experience, despite the highly uncommon, not to say obscure, name we have given it here, namely the myth of renewal, of rebirth. Etymologically, the term 'palingenesis', deriving from *palin* (again, anew) and *genesis* (creation, birth), refers to the sense of a new start or of regeneration after a phase of crisis or decline which can be associated just as much with mystical (for example the Second Coming) as secular realities (for example the New Germany). Even in the spheres of theology and biology the term is unusual, not to say obsolete in modern English (see the *Oxford English Dictionary*), though it would be a mark of the heuristic value of this book to fascist studies if it eventually underwent its own palingenesis as a term of current social scientific usage. It was used extensively in this way by the French theorist Ballanche (1833) in his *Palingénésie sociale* and is occasionally applied by Italian academics in the context of fascism just as I propose to do here (for example Gentile, 1975, p.5; Lazzari, 1984, p.55). I intend to employ it as a generic term for the vision of a radically *new* beginning which follows a period of destruction or perceived dissolution.

The most obvious well-head of palingenetic myth in the wider sense is religion. The resurrection of Jesus Christ places one such myth at the very centre of a whole faith (a point I make with due deference to readers for whom this is a 'lived' reality: like ideology, myth is identifiable as such only by someone who is cognitively and spiritually 'outside' it). Notions of metaphorical (to believers, metaphysical) death and rebirth pervade the symbolism of baptism, communion, and Easter celebrations, while generations of Christian mystics have elaborated intricate verbal, pictorial and ritual mythologies to invoke the reality of spiritual rebirth on a higher plane of being after dying to the world of the flesh. Palingenetic myth is also central to the 'political religions' which Christianity has inspired in the past, notably the millenarianism exhaustively studied by Cohn (1970) and in which Sorel saw a major example of myth's power to act as an agent of historical change.

Again we must stress that an important premise to the way generic fascism is being approached in this book is that secular palingenetic myth is not derived from religious myth but is simply the expression of an archetype of the human mythopoeic faculty in secular form. In any case it is absurd to assume that the symbolism of death and renewal is peculiar to Christianity or even the 'West'. It is a central motif of religious, mythical and magical thought encountered literally the world over. Different aspects of its prevalence in cosmological thinking, mystical imagery and ritualistic practice have been extensively documented by Eliade (for example 1964, 1971), Jung (for example 1958), Frazer (1957), Schnapper (1965) and Campbell (1968, 1990). It became a well established topos in secularizing societies as well, especially from the mid-nineteenth century onwards, once renegades from the official Western cult of progress became convinced that the decadence gripping society was not inexorable but could be reversed (see Swart, 1964; Fromm, 1963, ch.6; E. Weber, 1982). One example is Dostoevsky's vision of Russia becoming a Third Rome, (see Voegelin, 1952, p.113), a notion also explored with quite different connotations by Mazzini.

The theme of regeneration can set the tone for economic projects (for example the 'New Deal'), or architectural schemes (for example the megalomaniac architectural projects of Ceauşescu, or the high-rise solutions to slum housing favoured by the town-planners of the sixties). In modern art, too, the myth of rebirth is a familiar theme. It surfaces, for example, in D.H. Lawrence's obsession with regeneration (which led to his adoption of the phoenix as a personal symbol) and in the preoccupation of many modern writers with achieving a new sense of (non-linear) time (for example Kermode, 1967). It need hardly be added that palingenetic myth was central to the Renaissance vision of the West's cultural history, as the term itself testifies. The longing for regeneration can also express itself in quests for the transformation of consciousness, whether of the sort aspired to by the Flower Power generation (for example Reich, 1971), or in modern psychotherapy (for example in Jungian, EST or rebirthing therapy). It may express itself in something as commonplace as the urge to 'turn over a new leaf' or the sense of magic personal regeneration which accompanies falling in love after a period in an emotional wilderness.

However, it is the power which palingenetic myth can display in the arena of political ideology which concerns us in the present context. Significantly one of the most universal and multivalent symbols of palingenesis, the phoenix, was frequently used in medieval, and even in classical times, to refer to entire eras of secular history when a period of decay had burgeoned into one of 'dynastic, social and political' renewal (Reinitzer, 1981, p.82). In modern society, too, moments in history when an old order seems doomed to total annihilation still create the ideal climate for palingenetic myth (even if it is not specifically expressed through the imagery of the phoenix) to be projected on to the contemporary situation and crystallize the hopes that a 'new era' is dawning. Thus it was that members of the French National Assembly felt that their 'liberal' revolution represented the 'regeneration of the world' (see Skocpol, 1985, p.88), and that liberal intellectuals nurtured visions of a new world order in the darkest days of the Second World War (for example Buchman, 1941; Wells, 1942; Dawson, 1943; Croce, 1944). The EEC was born partly out of highly pragmatic geo-political considerations, but also from utopian dreams of a regenerated Europe united by common economic and social goals (for example Schuman, 1963), while *perestroika* owed much of its initial success at home and favourable reception abroad to the way it conjured up mythic visions of Russia's metamorphosis into a liberal and capitalist democracy. (The Russian Revolution itself had originally been a profoundly palingenetic event – see Stites, 1992.)

'Dark' green politics, too, are a rich source of palingenetic myth, scenarios of planetary catastrophe being countered with rhapsodic evocations of a new global order if structural changes are introduced in time (see Capra, 1982). Obviously the most spectacular manifestations of palingenetic politics in recent history were provided during the autumn of 1989, when state communist regimes in several East-bloc countries were dramatically overthrown. Within the space of a year contemporary history had generated yet another secular palingenetic myth in the nebulous shape of George Bush's dream of a 'New World Order' (which strikes an ominous note into those who see it as a euphemism for *Pax Americana*). Ironically, this heady vision, which outstrips in scope even that of another American president, Woodrow Wilson, at the end of the Great War, grew out of the (First-)world crisis brought about when Saddam Hussein lived out territorial ambitions reinforced by a political ideology saturated with palingenetic myth (a point to which we will return in Chapter 6). Incidentally, none of these examples have anything to do with political religions, even if late in the day Hussein started cynically blending elements of (Islamic) 'religious' politics into his self-legitimation.

Against this background, the expression 'palingenetic myth' comes to denote the vision of a revolutionary new order which supplies the affective power of an ideology, even if, as in the case of liberalism and communism, its ultimate goal is a society which is dynamic but neither violent nor war-like. When this is a political ideology it will centre on a new society inaugurated through human agency and not a millenarian vision of a new world in a metaphysical and supra-historical sense. At the heart of pal-ingenetic political myth lies the belief that contemporaries are living through or about to live through a 'sea-change', a 'water-shed' or 'turning-point' in the historical process. The perceived corruption, anarchy, oppressiveness, iniquities or decadence of the present, rather than being seen as immutable and thus to be endured indefinitely with stoic courage or bleak pessimism, are perceived as having reached their peak and inter-preted as the sure sign that one era is nearing its end and a new order is about to emerge.

A characteristic sub-myth of such hopes of transformation is the idea that a 'new man' is destined to appear, a politicized version of the archetypal 'hero myth'. For example, the 'new communist man' was a well-known figure in the Marxist–Leninist evocation of the new era (and was satirized in Wajda's *Man of Steel*) and is still encountered in recent works informed by socialist hopes of renewal (for example Rossi-Landi, 1990, p.89; Attwood, 1990). Here again it is possible to find strictly religious analogies, as in the cosmological speculations of medieval Christian poets about the New Man (for example Silvestris, 1978; Alan of Lille, 1973) or *homines noves* (see Voegelin, 1952, p.112), cultural parallels (cf. the late 1980s magazine cult of the 'new man'), as well as 'purely' aesthetic equivalents, as in the longing for the 'New Man' in German Expressionism (see Riedel, 1970; Gordon, 1987). Voegelin is thus misleading when he insists on seeing the frequency of the concept in modern ideologies as a symptom of 'eschatological extravaganza' (Sandoz, 1981, p.242).

Though etymologically 'palingenetic political myth' could be taken to refer to a 'backward-looking' nostalgia for a restoration of the past (that is rebirth of the *same*), its value as a term in the analysis of ideologies would be diminished if it were to be extended to ultra-conservative or reactionary movements which involved no sense of revolutionary progress or 'new birth'. It is well known that a similar ambiguity is inherent in the word 'revolution', which within a cyclic scheme of history meant returning to an idealized vision of an earlier stage of society. But in an era dominated by linear conceptions of time and progress, 'revolution' now generally denotes the emergence of a substantially *new* order of society, no matter how much it is inspired by historical precedents or the myth of a past golden age. In palingenetic political myth (which is secular in orientation even when 'religious politics' are involved) the new order will be created within a secular and linear historical time. The arrow of time thus points not backwards but forwards, even when the archer looks over his shoulder for guidance on where to aim. It is with the particular connotations of political myth and in this radically non-restorationist sense of a *'new birth' occurring after a period of perceived decadence* that I propose to use the term 'palingenetic' in this study. Even with these qualifications, however, we are clearly dealing with a phenomenon which in medical terms might be termed 'non-specific' in that it can be a symptom of all but the most nostalgic ideologies in their utopian, revolutionary phase. It is only in combination with the next political term that it serves to designate something peculiar to fascism.

Populist Ultra-nationalism

One of the pervasive ideological forces in the shaping of modern history is nationalism, and if anything its virulence shows every sign of increasing rather than diminishing. It may well be that the history of the next few decades will be substantially shaped by the conflicts between centrifugal liberal nationalisms with a pacifistic and universalistic orientation on the one hand and centripetal illiberal nationalisms of a violent and separatist impetus on the other. The prospects of achieving any substantive 'green revolution' in time to save the ecosystem clearly depends partly on the triumph, or at least predominance, of the former.

However, as a taxonomic term in the social sciences 'nationalism' is, like 'ideology', a victim of its own success. It has been identified as an ingredient in a wide range of conflicting political systems and ideologies and has generated a plethora of sub-categories, such as 'tribal', 'pan-ethnic', 'dynastic', 'religious', 'liberal', 'communist', 'Third World', 'imperialist', 'Enlightenment', 'Romantic', 'integral' nationalisms (see Minogue, 1967; Smith, 1979; Alter, 1989). This rampant 'diversification' stems from the fact that the root concept 'nation' admits a wide range of definitions according to whether the criteria invoked are religious, geographical, historical, constitutional, cultural, linguistic, ethnic or genetic. Moreover, even when the same criteria are used, the connotations of the term necessarily vary according to the particular historical and political conditions which relate to the grouping in question. For example the core entity undergoes significant semantic shifts as we consider in turn 'British', 'Welsh', 'Arabic', 'African', 'Islamic', 'Aboriginal' nationalisms.

To refine the term so that it becomes useful for the investigation of fascism I propose to use the more specialized sub-category 'populist ultranationalism'. I follow Eley, (1990, p.281) in using 'populist' not to refer to a specific historical experience (for example late nineteenth-century American or Russian Populism) but as a generic term for political forces which, even if led by small elite cadres or self-appointed 'vanguards', in practice or in principle (and not merely for show) depend on 'people power' as the basis of their legitimacy. I am using 'ultra-nationalism', which already has some currency in the political sciences, to refer to forms of nationalism which 'go beyond', and hence reject, anything compatible with liberal institutions or with the tradition of Enlightenment humanism which underpins them. It approximates to what has also been referred to as 'integral' (Alter, 1989) or 'radical' (Eley, 1980) nationalism.

Combined into a single expression, 'populist ultra-nationalism' precludes the nationalism of dynastic rulers and imperial powers before the rise of mass politics and democratic forces (for example that of the Habsburgs or the Pharaohs), as well as the populist (liberal) nationalism which overthrows a colonial power to institute representative democracy (for example that of Mazzini in the Italian *risorgimento* and of many Czechoslovakians in late 1989). In other words, populist ultra-nationalism rejects the principles both of absolutism and of pluralist representative government. In Weberian terms (see M. Weber, 1948) it thus repudiates both 'traditional' and 'legal/rational' forms of politics in favour of prevalently 'charismatic' ones in which the cohesion and dynamics of movements depends almost exclusively on the capacity of their leaders to inspire loyalty and action (see Roth, 1963, for the notion that populist revolutionary movements in which myth in the Sorelian sense plays a central role are essentially charismatic). It tends to be associated with a concept of the nation as a 'higher' racial, historical, spiritual or organic reality which embraces all the members of the ethical community who belong to it. Such a community is regarded by its protagonists as a natural order which can be contaminated by miscegenation and immigration, by the anarchic, unpatriotic mentality encouraged by liberal individualism, internationalist socialism, and by any number of 'alien' forces allegedly unleashed by 'modern' society, for example the rise of the 'masses', the decay of moral values, the 'levelling' of society, cosmopolitanism, feminism, and consumerism. For the sake of succinctness 'ultra-nationalism' will henceforth be used exclusively with the qualifying connotations of 'populist' outlined here.

Defined in these terms, numerous forms of ultra-nationalism can be seen to have emerged since the breakdown of absolutist *ancien régimes* and 'the rise of the masses': in the many movements of racism and xenophobia which operate within liberal democracies while completely rejecting the pluralism and universal human rights on which these are based (for example the Ku Klux Klan, anti-immigration leagues in several EC countries); in those separatist nationalisms which eschew the liberal goal of instituting substantive democratic institutions after secession (for example those which have arisen in Azerbaijan now that the bonds holding together the Soviet Union are weakening); in the many nationalistic authoritarian regimes which have attempted to maximize genuine popular consensus rather than reign simply through manipulation and terror (for example the regimes of Vargas, Perón, Schuschnigg, Qadhafi) – which are to be distinguished from the pseudo-populism of many other modern dictatorships which cultivate the illusion of popular consensus as the justification for their despotism (for example Marcos, Pinochet, Pol Pot, Ceauçescu, Saddam Hussein). Genuinely populist ultra-nationalism plays a determining role, too, in generic fascism.

The 'Fascist Minimum': Palingenetic Ultra-nationalism

When the terms palingenetic ultra-nationalism are combined they delimit each other in such a way that, like 'nation-state', or 'social democracy', they become a relatively precise political concept. Just as the combination of two lenses in a telescope can bring a distinct object suddenly into focus, the binomial expression which they create defines a genus of political energy far more circumscribed than the vast areas of phenomena embraced by them separately, namely one whose mobilizing vision is that of *the national community rising phoenix-like after a period of encroaching decadence which all but destroyed it.*

To treat a mythic core based on this vision as the 'fascist minimum' is an example of what Max Weber called 'idealizing abstraction' at work, for both components have been identified independently in previous scholarship without being consciously combined within a synthetic ideal type. Nationalism (by which scholars clearly mean a profoundly illiberal form which corresponds to what we have called ultra-nationalism) is practically the only common denominator of all previous accounts of fascism's definitional characteristics, whether proposed by Marxists (for example Frolov, 1985, p.194) or non-Marxists (for example E. Weber, 1964, pp.17–25; Hayes, 1973, pp.51–62; Linz, 1979, pp.28–9; Mosse, 1980, p.189; O'Sullivan, 1983, pp.161–7; Sternhell, 1986, p.148; Payne, 1980, p.7).

Independent corroboration for the centrality of its 'palingenetic' component is inevitably far more patchy, but Payne alludes to it when under the heading 'ideology and goals' he includes the creation of a '*new* nationalist authoritarian state', a '*new* . . . integrated economic structure', a '*new* form of modern, self-determined, secular culture' (Payne, 1980, p.7; my emphasis). Implicit recognition of it can likewise be detected when Smith (1979, p.54) acknowledges that fascism offered 'a new solution to the old nationalist problems of the decay and decline of community' and associates this with the theme of the 'new fascist man'. In similar vein Mosse's 'general theory of fascism' (1979, ch.1) states that the 'new fascist man provided the stereotype for all fascist movements' (ibid., p.26), and a number of other scholars see the concept of the new man as a central fascist myth (for example, ibid., pp.82, 128, 265–7; Cannistraro, 1972, p.130; De Felice, 1982, p.214). Mosse also takes seriously fascist claims to represent a revolutionary 'Third Force' in European history in which 'utopianism and traditionalism' merged (op. cit., p.8). Sternhell, goes even further. He sees as the central thrust of fascist ideology the awakening of 'a desire for reaction and regeneration that were simultaneously spiritual and physical, moral, social and political' in an all-embracing 'revolt against decadence' (Sternhell, 1979, pp.356–7). In fact the whole thrust of the major essay on fascist ideology in which he makes this observation is the recognition of the centrality of what we have called 'palingenetic myth' to the ethos of fascism (ibid., pp.325–406).

Once the generic fascist minimum is conceived ideal-typically as a mythic core of palingenetic ultra-nationalism, it throws into relief two fundamental traits which have a considerable bearing on the immediate and long-term success of any particular permutation of it which emerges.

The Structural Weakness Implied by Fascism's Palingenetic Mythic Core

We have already argued that all ideologies assume a palingenetic dimension when they operate as a revolutionary force to overthrow an existing order. However, fascism radically diverges from liberalism, socialism, conservatism and most religious ideologies by making the 'revolutionary' process central to its core myth to the exclusion of a fully thought-through 'orthodox' stage when the dynamics of society settle down to becoming 'steady-state', namely when its internal and external enemies have been eliminated and new institutions created. In other words, the mythical horizons of the fascist mentality do not extend beyond what the social theorist Saint-Simon called the 'critical' stage in society's development to envisage clearly any sort of 'organic' stage which would have to ensue sooner or later. In terms of personal psychology this is perhaps analogous to someone with a pathological addiction to the heady emotions of 'falling in love' without any temperamental capacity to imagine or endure a steady relationship, let alone a marriage, which might eventually grow out of the passion when it cools.

The centrality of the palingenetic component to fascism's permanent mythic core explains much of its initial appeal. In the 'right' conditions (which it will be the task of the last two chapters to identify) the fascist vision of a vigorous new nation growing out of the destruction of the old system can exert on receptive minds the almost alchemical power to transmute black despair into manic optimism and thus enable a party which promotes this vision to win a substantial mass following. It promises to replace gerontocracy, mediocrity and national weakness with youth, heroism and national greatness, to banish anarchy and decadence and bring order and health, to inaugurate an exciting new world in place of the senescent, played-out one that existed before, to put government in the hands of outstanding personalities instead of non-entities. If the times are ripe, the vague or contradictory implications of the policies proposed to realize such nebulous goals do not diminish their attraction because it is precisely their *mythic* power that matters, not their feasibility or human implications.

Yet the predominance of the utopian component in fascist ideology also has two important practical consequences which severely *limit* its effectiveness as a political force. First, the core myth of palingenetic ultra-nationalism is susceptible to so many nuances of interpretation in terms of specific 'surface' ideas and policies that, more so even than socialism before Marx, it tends to generate a wide range of competing currents and factions even within the same political culture unless one of them is able through particularly effective leadership and tactics to weld them into a relatively cohesive 'movement'. Even then it is only in ideal circumstances that this movement may hope to achieve a substantial rank-and-file following which enables it to make an impact on the political developments of the day. Second, it means that fascism is in its element as an oppositional ideology only as long as the climate of national crisis prevails – generally a combination of social, economic, political, and psychological factors – which is necessary for some degree of mass or populist appeal to be generated. Since fascism's mythic power is automatically sapped by the renewed ascendancy of the private over the public sphere of life which ensues once political stability and relative social harmony are restored, it can only maintain its momentum and cohesion by continually precipitating events which seemed to fulfil the promise of permanent revolution, of continuing palingenesis.

In the case of Fascism and Nazism, the only two fascist movements (that is identified as such by the ideal type which we have constructed) which autonomously achieved the transition from oppositional force to regime, this posed no problem as long as the elaborate process of dismantling the institutions of the old 'decadent' order and introducing the structural foundations of the new one lasted. But thereafter it was only because both movements pursued imperialist expansion against enemies abroad and precipitated a series of military campaigns culminating in a new world war that the manic climate of 'permanent revolution' could be partially sustained. In the long term such a situation is clearly untenable. On the domestic front the heady visions of building a radically new society will run up against practical constraints which doom to failure even the most systematic attempts to use terror combined with benign programmes of social engineering so as to fascistize the whole of society. Meanwhile if it pursues a foreign policy of unlimited territorial expansion (and not all fascisms nurture the dream of empire), it will sooner or later face insuperable difficulties in continually making war on new enemies or even in finding sufficient resources to sustain military conquest and occupation indefinitely (cf. Kennedy, 1988). In a grotesque travesty of Faustian restlessness, fascism cannot permit itself to linger on a bed of contentment: its arch-enemy is the 'normality' of human society in equilibrium, its Achilles heel as a form of practical politics the utopianism which the fear of this enemy breeds. Eugen Weber clearly sensed this when he wrote:

> Without precise objectives the fascist must move forward all the time; but just because precise objectives are lacking he can never stop, and every goal attained is but a stage on the continuous treadmill of the future he claims to construct, of the national destiny he claims to fulfil. Fascist dynamism comes at the price of this, and therein lies its profound revolutionary nature, but also it seems the seeds of its eventual fall. (E. Weber, 1964, p.78)

It is thus entirely predictable if within a few years of seizing state power, Fascism was accused of becoming yet another gerontocracy by a new generation of zealots who took its claims to be a 'permanent revolution' seriously (see below p.70). Moreover, the problems of long-term viability which flow from fascism's commitment to palingenetic myth are compounded by its ultra-nationalist component.

The Structural Weakness Implied by Fascism's Populist Ultra-nationalism

Though the ultra-nationalist myth of fascism centres on the creation of a national community, this does not imply that it is democratic in any substantive sense. The driving force behind its formation is initially not a spontaneous protest mass movement on a par with the 'people power' which overthrew state communism in several East bloc countries in the autumn of 1989. It derives instead from a self-appointed elite which arrogates to itself alone the ability to interpret the 'true' needs of a people and the mission to install and direct the many new organizational structures necessary to guarantee its coordination and growth as a revolutionary force. The fascist cannot leave revolution to the people because he sees the instincts of the mass of the population as contaminated by decadent forces, leaving it a mere 'society' riven by class divisions and debilitated by levelling ideologies. Though it may seek through agitation and propaganda to develop into an 'irresistible' mass movement, fascism must always in the last analysis be imposed by an elite in the name of a national community *yet to be realized*, and whose realization, even once the movement is installed in power, will initially (and in practice indefinitely) involve re-education, propaganda and social control on a massive scale. The situation is analogous to the one which Lenin, despairing of the capacity of ordinary Russians to recognize their heroic role of 'historical subject', attempted to resolve with the formation of a 'vanguard' of dedicated political terrorists. The revolution would be pioneered by an elite, the diffusion of socialism would follow later.

However, unlike Leninist socialism, fascism is not just elitist in its tactics for seizing power (as most ideologies tend to be in their activist, revolutionary phase) but in its basic conception of society. Admittedly, the concept of the organic national community connotes classlessness, unfettered social mobility and an abolition of the inequities of *laissez-faire* capitalism in a way which allowed some of its ideologues to claim to represent 'true' democracy, egalitarianism and socialism. Yet power in the new community would remain descending rather than ascending even after the rebirth (in any case an ongoing process) had been inaugurated in a new order, for it would be concentrated in the hands of those who had risen 'naturally' through the ranks of the various hierarchical organizations in which all the political, economic and cultural energies of the nation were to be channelled and orchestrated. In a mystic version of direct democracy, the representation of the people's general will in a fascist society would mean entrusting authority to an elite or (especially in its inter-war versions) a leader whose mission it is to safeguard the supra-individual interests and destiny of the people to whom it (or he) claims to be linked by a metaphysical bond of a common nationhood. A paradox thus lies at the heart of fascist ultra-nationalism. It is populist in intent and rhetoric, yet elitist in practice. (Again it is to be stressed that fascism's elitist populism is to be distinguished from the *pseudo*-populism of many modern dictatorial regimes which impose mass-mobilizing programmes of social engineering *from above*, a distinction which will be elaborated further in Chapter 5.)

The peculiarly undemocratic mode of populism represented in fascism expresses itself in the influence exerted on its ideology by elitist theories of society (for example Nietzsche, Pareto, Sorel), in its pervasive racism (because in practice fascism, apart from rejecting multi-ethnicity or cosmopolitanness as intrinsically unhealthy, usually implies the ethnic or cultural superiority of the reborn nation over certain peoples and cultures judged inferior) and in the recurrent myth of the new 'fascist man' (*homo fascistus*) who is instinctively prepared to sacrifice himself to the higher needs of the nation. Fascists typically imagine themselves in the front line of an historical and cultural battle to turn back the tide of mediocrity and loss of vitality and so reinstate the exceptional, the outstanding, the heroic as the driving force of history. The elitism is also epitomized in its two characteristic organizational manifestations of the inter-war period: the paramilitary elite (for example the SS, the Romanian Legionaries) and the leader figure (for example Hitler, Codreanu). Though the leader cult, like corporatism, militarism and imperialism, is not a core component of generic fascism according to our ideal type (all of which are conspicuous by their absence in some contemporary forms of neo-fascism as we shall see in Chapter 6), it epitomizes the structural weakness that flows from fascism's pursuit of political transformation through an elitist form of populism.

We have already pointed out that by axiomatically rejecting (in Weberian terms) both 'traditional' and 'legal' concepts of authority and making political power depend instead on an 'inspired' elite at the head of an 'irresistible' mass movement, fascism is an essentially charismatic type of political force. It is entirely consistent with this if Nazi studies reveal the intrinsically unstable nature of the political institutions and policy-making machinery of the Third Reich despite its own myth of itself as perfectly 'co-ordinated': indeed one expert has attributed this instability specifically to the charismatic nature of the power it wielded (Kershaw, 1989, 1991). An identical argument could be made to account for the chronic inconsistency which characterized the government of Fascist Italy. The most obvious symptom of the reliance of both on charismatic power is, of course, the leader cult, which in both regimes became increasingly important to paper over the widening cracks between propaganda and reality. Even if according to our ideal type the leader cult is not a definitional component of fascism, it is a pragmatic necessity if any organization is to become what its palingenetic ultra-nationalism dictates it must be, namely a movement. However, the very success of an individual in becoming the charismatic leader of a fascist movement, and even mounting an assault on state power, is also its Achille's heel. In the long run the law of entropy which applies to the innovatory or expansionist momentum of a regime will also affect the leader himself. It will do so inexorably and in a way which the most efficient propaganda machine in the world cannot conceal indefinitely: he will grow infirm and eventually die.

The strength of a liberal democracy is that it creates for itself constitutional mechanisms which allow for ministers, the head of state and the government itself to change without recourse to violence. Even the most autocratic forms of 'democratic centralism', which, as all twentieth-century communist states have shown, need the artificial charisma of an official leader cult to generate a degree of social cohesion and credibility, resemble the Catholic Church in having evolved procedures to allow a new leader to emerge when the old one dies. Fascism is different. With a major programme of social engineering the charisma of a fascist movement can, in Max Weber's phrase, be 'routinized' to some extent even after it seizes power. But the growing senility and eventual death of a fascist leader could only mean the dissolution of the regime which he incarnated: the 'movement' would grind to a halt. In the event, the declining physical powers of Mussolini and Hitler only gave a foretaste of this devastating process of self-destruction to which fascism is exposed by its own mythic core. Their regimes were destroyed by force from without, so that the new world they had sought to create ended in a bang rather than whimper. Yet even before this the myths of their infallibility had worn very thin, their mortality had become apparent to all but the most fanatical proselytes (see Mack Smith, 1981; Kershaw, 1989).

The Intrinsic Inviability of Fascism Both as Regime and as a Movement

The need to prolong indefinitely the palingenetic phase of revolutionary transformation combines with the necessity of routinizing and prolonging indefinitely its charismatic appeal in a way which utterly destroys fascism's viability as the blueprint for a new type of society. Even in travestied form the new order is doomed not to survive more than a few years, let alone a millennium. To plug at least temporarily the widening gap between the utopian promises and reality, any fascist regime is forced to resort to social engineering on a massive scale. Since the breakdown of religious consensus in the West (which was itself never total), ideological energy has been directed into several main streams and countless smaller tributaries and rivulets, rather like an enormous delta without an estuary. Since only a minority of the population can be temperamentally susceptible to converting spontaneously to fascism or becoming the new breed of *homo fascistus*, and since even at the height of its popularity, no modern regime can enjoy total support, the thorough-going ideological coordination of the national community could never come about 'naturally'. A grotesque parody of it has to be enacted through the extensive use of propaganda and terror.

In practice, fascism's inability to take account of the essential pluralism of modern society or the complexity of human psychology means that attempts by any regime erected in its name to realize the utopia of the reborn nation must necessarily lead to the dystopia of physical and mental coercion satirized in *1984*. However, in contrast to the situation described in Orwell's book, the totalitarian control of national life attempted by fascism (that is in the name of the 'totalitarian state' under Mussolini or the *Volksgemeinschaft* under Hitler) is bound to remain a chimera, as is the total transformation or control of any modern society, independently of the vision underlying it (which is not to say that differences in the contents of this underlying vision are not significant, a point blurred by some Cold War theorists of totalitarianism such as Friedrich and Brzezinski, 1967). Fascism is therefore doomed by its nature (that is by the one which we have ideal-typically identified here) to be an impotent and ephemeral political force as the basis of a regime, no matter how destructive it is and irresistible it may seem in the upward sweep of its short parabola through human history.

We have concentrated on the implications of fascism's mythic core for its viability as a regime because of the enormous impact which Fascism and Nazism had on the lives of millions of Europeans in this century. It is, however, important to point out that the essentially utopian, elitist and charismatic implications of this core which determine the structural weaknesses of any fascist new order also prevent fascism ever becoming a powerful political force in the first place, let alone achieving power, except in an exceptionally rare conjuncture of factors, a point to be considerably expanded in Chapters 7 and 8. Apart from the freak exceptions to the rule represented by Fascism and Nazism, fascism has generally only been able to play a highly marginalized role in shaping the socio-political order of modern societies, whether liberal or authoritarian.

A Discursive Characterization of the Nature of Fascism

The various points made in the course of our amplification of the succinct definition with which we opened this chapter can now be built into a more discursive one. The schematic references which it makes to the ultimate inviability of Fascism and Nazism, the inevitably abortive nature of the most fascist movements, the radical heterogeneity of fascist myth and tactics, and the dependency for the success of fascism on specific historical conditions will all be fleshed out with empirical detail and sustained argument as the book progresses.

Fascism: a genus of political ideology whose mythic core in its various permutations is a palingenetic form of populist ultra-nationalism. The fascist mentality is characterized by the sense of living through an imminent turning-point in contemporary history, when the dominance of the allegedly bankrupt or degenerate forces of conservatism, individualistic liberalism and materialist socialism is finally to give way to a new era in which vitalistic nationalism will triumph. To combat these rival political ideologies and the decadence they allegedly host (for example the parasitism of traditional elites, materialism, class conflict, military weakness, loss of racial vitality, moral anarchy, cosmopolitanism), fascist activists see the recourse to organized violence as both necessary and healthy. Though they may well make some concessions to parliamentary democracy in order to gain power, the pluralism of opinion and party politics upon which it rests is anathema to their concept of national unity, which implies in practice the maximum totalitarian control over all areas of social, economic, political and cultural life.

The destruction which is necessitated both in theory and in practice by the fascist revolution is seen by its activists not as an end in itself but as the corollary of the regenerative process by which society is to be purged of decadence. As this process gains momentum the masses are to be gradually forged into a new national community, one drawing where possible on traditions which have supposedly remained uncontaminated by degenerative forces, but whose cohesion is assured by new institutions, organizations and practices based on a new political hierarchy and a new heroic ethos which uniquely equip its members to thrive in the modern age. As a result of the wide variations in the historical situations and cultural traditions in which fascists formulate their world-view, there are considerable variations in how they have conceived the revitalized nation and the scale of violence and destruction it has implied. For some it is associated with biological conceptions of racial purity, while for others it is simply a matter of cultural homogeneity. Some pursue aggressive policies of imperialist expansion, whereas for others the regeneration of the nation does not involve subjugating other nations or actively persecuting ethnic minorities and may, so they hope, even be inaugurated through the conquest of cultural hegemony instead of through the legal or violent seizure of state power.

However fascism conceives the reborn nation, the nebulous but radical moral and social revolution which it calls for and its rejection of all existing political ideologies severely limits the mythic appeal which it can exert either in a relatively stable pluralist democracy or in an authoritarian regime. Those fascist movements which have broken out of their highly marginalized position in political culture have been able to do so because they have been sufficiently well organized and ably led to take advantage of a genuine crisis in existing liberal institutions which has undermined traditional adherence to other parties and values. The vast majority of the many fascisms which have arisen in the twentieth century have never grown into mass movements powerful enough to mount a credible assault on state power.

The two regimes which did install themselves as regimes on the basis of palingenetic ultra-nationalist myth, Fascism and Nazism, held power long enough to demonstrate the wide differences in territorial ambitions and genocidal potential that flow from different permutations of the same mythic core, but also the intrinsic unrealizability of the fascist revolutionary project. A regime whose legitimacy depends on sustaining the myth of rebirth, and for which any social energies unco-ordinated by the state are symptoms of decadence, cannot perpetuate indefinitely the illusion of permanent revolution and renewal and is condemned in practice to degenerate into an oppressive authoritarian regime. In the event Mussolini and Hitler died as a result of military defeat, and thus did not have to face the insuperable problem of succession which the leader-cult would have bequeathed to the regimes they had created. Despite the failure and inhumanity associated with Fascism and Nazism, mimetic and new varieties of palingenetic ultra-nationalism continue to be cultivated in highly marginalized but vigorous sub-cultures in Europe and the United States, and still play an active role in South African politics. As an active factor in the transformation of history, however, fascism is a spent force.

The Basic Features of Fascism in the Light of the New Ideal Type

In Chapter 1 I raised a number of questions which the lack of consensus in fascist studies has left wide open such as whether there was a Japanese fascism and if the age of fascism extends beyond 1945. The answers which suggest themselves to such problems when the new ideal type is applied will hopefully emerge naturally in the course of what follows without further comment being necessary. However, in the same chapter we also established a number of specifications (above p.13) which any new ideal type should satisfy if it is to be an improvement on existing models. Before I apply the model I have constructed as the basis for an empirical account of actual fascist movements, it might be helpful to take stock of how far it has already met these criteria even at this purely theoretical stage of exposition.

Once the specific implications of palingenetic myth and populist ultra-nationalism have been internalized by the reader (which should become easier once it starts being applied to concrete phenomena), fascism becomes definable in a single binomial expression, thereby representing 'an advance in succinctness on existing models'. Moreover, by stressing that the mythic core which this expression encapsulates is capable of any number of permutations at a 'surface level' (which, it is worth stressing once more, is not to suggest that the differences are superficial in terms of historical events and their human consequences), this definition allows for the radical contrasts which commentators have rightly insisted exist between Nazism and Fascism and all other fascisms. As will hopefully be clear from Chapters 7 and 8, the new definition is also compatible to a great extent both with the existing empirical knowledge and with the theory concerning the dynamics of particular movements.

The new ideal type is also specific enough to clarify how the term 'fascism' relates to a number of other terms frequently encountered in fascist studies. I have already had cause to delineate the connotations which concepts such as 'ideology' and 'myth' acquire in the context of fascism and to point out the gulf which divides it both from 'political religions' and from 'millenarianism'. In doing so I underlined how the 'totalitarian' aspirations of fascism stem from a vision of the new national community which makes them quite distinct from those of regimes which legitimate themselves by invoking a different political myth (for example Stalinism). This point, and the fact that such aspirations are doomed to be frustrated in practice because of the essentially utopian, unrealizable nature of the core vision, also qualifies the heuristic value of the term 'totalitarianism'. The ground covered so far also enables specifying fascism's relationship to a number of other political phenomena which have not been specifically referred to in my argument so far.

Is Fascism Nihilistic or Idealistic?

No matter how gratuitously destructive its goals and methods appear to upholders of other value systems and how many of its recruits are motivated by cynical or base motives, the commitment of a significant percentage of fascist activists is intensely idealistic, rooted as it is in a profound urge to transcend the existing state of society and find a radical cure to the alleged evils which afflict it. One of the cultural preconditions for fascism may be a diffuse sense of cultural pessimism or 'despair' (cf. Stern, 1961), but only in the sense that it encourages fascists to believe their movement is a panacea to the ills of the age, tackling the underlying causes of the decay of healthy values through the creation of a radically new type of national order led by a heroic elite. Fascism thus embodies a manic charge of cultural *optimism*, ready to swing back to pessimism if the new order does not materialize. Unfortunately for the human embodiments of the decadence to be extirpated, fascists believe the destruction unleashed by their movement to be the essential precondition for reconstruction, giving rise, as we shall see later, to the paradoxical term 'creative nihilism' as a description of fascist violence.

Is Fascism Anti-modern or Modernizing?

Some forms of fascist myths are radically anti-urban, anti-secular and/or draw on cultural idioms of nostalgia for a pre-industrial idyll of heroism, moral virtue or racial purity. However, even in these cases it is only the allegedly degenerative elements of the modern age which are being rejected. Fascism's essentially palingenetic, and hence anti-conservative, thrust towards a *new* type of society means that it builds rhetorically on the cultural achievements attributed to former, more 'glorious' or healthy eras in national history only to invoke the regenerative ethos which is a prerequisite for national rebirth, and not to suggest socio-political models to be duplicated in a literal-minded restoration of the past. It thus represents an alternative modernism rather than a rejection of it. Thus when a fascist text bears the title 'Revolt against the Modern World', as in the case of Evola (1934), it is the *decadent* features of modernity that are being attacked in order to outline the prospect of a totally different type of society. When used in fascist scholarship (for example by Turner, 1975), 'anti-modern' invariably betrays a set of value judgements about what constitutes the ideal path of modernization for societies to follow and thus assumes a teleological myth of its own which makes it highly dubious as a useful ideal type for analysing alternative ideologies. Phrases such as 'reactionary modernism' (Herf, 1984) or 'modernist anti-modernism' (Soucy, 1980) point to the degree of confusion which can still arise when scholars try to make sense of the presence in some strands of fascism of such an obviously anti-traditionalist element as the celebration of technology, when they have not recognized the centrality to it of the myth of renewal. (This stress on fascism's revolutionary rather than reactionary dimension is also central to the very different ideal types used by Sternhell, 1979 and Payne, 1980.)

Is Fascism Revolutionary or Reactionary?

All revolutions 'react' to a perceived crisis in society and seek to install an ideal order in the place of the corrupt or repressive one which preceded it.

But when Marxists claim that fascism is reactionary, they are arguing in one way or another that it is a 'counter-revolution' to preserve the vested interests of the ruling classes, monarchy, Church, landowners and the bourgeoisie against their destruction by 'genuine' revolutionary forces (for example Mayer, 1971). This once again betrays an inability on the part of some scholars to accept that some of its idealists were (and still are) genuinely looking for an alternative to liberalism, communism, conservatism and capitalism as the formula for resolving the problems of the modern age. Fascism in practice colluded with traditional ruling elites in order to gain and retain power and left capitalist structures substantially intact. However, at the level of ideological intent both Fascism and Nazism aimed to co-ordinate all the energies of the nation, including conservative and capitalist ones, in a radically new type of society, characterized by new political, economic and cultural structures and a new ethos and went some way towards doing this. The sweeping measures which they undertook to achieve this degree indicates that their fascism was a revolutionary force in its own right (cf. Kershaw, 1985, ch.7; E. Weber, 1979; Mosse, 1979, pp.5, 36, 118, 132).

Is Fascism Essentially Racist?

The basic drive of a fascist regime is to create a strong state as the protector of a national community immune from the 'anarchic' forces of dissent so that its distinctive culture can flower once more. The attempts to generate a sense of the uniqueness and common destiny of this community means that fascism is essentially racist, just as all forms of chauvinism, imperialism and colonialism are whether military, economic or cultural.

An important rider to this is that fascism does not necessarily invoke the myth of a pure race or go beyond vague cultural and historical notions of nationhood to conceive it in biological and genetic terms. As such, varieties of it can well remain within the bounds of the common or garden racism which was so pervasive in European societies, 'liberal' or otherwise, at the turn of the twentieth century (see Mosse, 1978), and it is not *intrinsic* to fascism that particular groups (for example Jews, Slavs, Asians) should be picked out for persecution, let alone for systematic genocide. The virulence and object of fascist racism will depend on contingent factors, especially the prior existence of a tradition of xenophobic obsessions and racial persecution which the movement can incorporate as an integral part of its palingenetic vision and as an instrument of mass-mobilization.

Is Fascism Essentially Imperialist?

As a form of ultra-nationalism fascism will campaign against any visible signs of alleged national weakness such as foreign domination, occupation of 'unredeemed' home lands, demographic decline or humiliation in the sphere of international politics. However, the stress on the imminent rebirth of the national community does not necessarily express itself in the alleged need for increasing its 'vital space' through foreign conquests and can have various implications for relations with other countries: that is it can be (i) treated as an exclusively domestic matter (*neutralist*); (ii) equated with the nation's historical destiny to achieve ascendancy over other nations and expand the territory under its rule (*imperialist*); (iii) associated with a sense of common cause with other nations attempting to regenerate themselves (*universalist*). Thus fascism is essentially racist, but not intrinsically anti-Semitic or genocidal, and it is nationalistic but not necessarily imperialistic or anti-internationalistic. In fact a major theme of contemporary fascism is a 'Europe of nations' (see p.171).

What is Fascism's Relationship to Conservatism and 'the right'?

From everything that has been said, it follows that fascism is in principle as radically anti-conservative (cf. Payne, 1980, pp.14–15) as it is anti-liberal or anti-Bolshevik (though its 'anti-socialism' is less clear cut: cf. Sternhell, 1979, pp.371–9). Two points are liable to confuse this issue in practice. First, when fascists appeal to healthy, uncontaminated elements of the national tradition (for example the Roman Empire, the Aryan past, chivalric culture) this can create the impression that they long to return *literally* to a legendary golden age, whereas such elements are being used with an essentially mythic force as the inspiration of the new order because of the 'eternal' truths they contain for the nascent national community. Second, for tactical and pragmatic reasons fascism is liable to form alliance with, and make propagandistic concessions to, traditional conservative forces in order to achieve and maintain power. Hence the relationship between the two in practice is much more complex and intertwined than it is in theory (see Blinkhorn, 1990).

As far as the relationship with 'the right' is concerned, this is a particularly slippery and problematic ideal type (see Eatwell, 1989). Conservatism, whether deeply antagonistic to liberal society (see McClelland, 1970) or largely accommodatable within it (see Aughey, 1989), is generally classified as 'right', as are military movements and regimes which lack the elaborate ideological apparatus involved in palingenetic myth (see Pinkney, 1990). Thus an appropriate sub-genus of right is called for when locating fascism within it. This has not always been recognized. For example Rogger and Weber (1966), Rees (1984) and Ó Maoláin (1987) ignore the distinction, while Jonathan Cape's Roots of the Right series includes McClelland (1970) talking about the ultra-conservative de Maistre as well as Lyttleton (1973) discussing various tributaries of Fascism. Certainly the ultra-nationalism, anti-egalitarianism, hostility to internationalist socialism, collusion with traditional right-wing or conservative forces and constant appeal to primordial 'spiritual' values all point to the conclusion that fascism belongs to the extended family of rightist ideologies.

However, the term 'New Right' in the Anglo-Saxon context to refer to forms of anti-socialist neo-liberalism (that is 'Thatcherism') impairs its precision as a term (for a confusion of the two see Seidel, 1986) which underlines the importance of distinguishing the liberal 'right' from the illiberal 'ultra-right'. The taxonomic tangle that comes about once attempts to suggest a more appropriate one is well exemplified by Eatwell (1989), where Billig equates fascism with the 'extreme right', while the 'reactionary right', 'conservative revolutionary' right and the 'radical right' are used to cover phenomena which fit our ideal type and are treated in this book as forms of fascism.

Not only does the location of fascism within the right pose taxonomic problems, there are good grounds for cutting this particular Gordian knot altogether by placing it in a category of its own 'beyond left and right'. After all, like radical Catholicism in the inter-war period and present-day ecologism and feminism, it claims to fight for a new vision, a Third Way pioneering a radical break with all traditional ideologies and parties, a point which we have seen is central to Sternhell's conception of fascism (Sternhell, 1979 and 1987). Nevertheless, deeply ingrained habits of liberal and socialist thought make it counter-intuitive for most political scientists to deny that fascism belongs to the right rather than the left. It seems reasonable to regard it for practical purposes as a sub-category of the ultra-right but with special qualities of its own, that is we are dealing once again with a particular and thus unique manifestation of a generic ideal type. Perhaps the reader might come to feel comfortable with some such category as 'palingenetic ultra-right' by the end of this work, though once again the concept 'ultra-right' would have to be given specifically populist (and not merely pseudo-populist) connotations for the phrase to be coterminous with 'fascism'.

What is Proto-fascism?

While on the subject of fascism's relationship to the right, some unnecessary confusion should be avoided if we explain the connotation of one term which will recur several times in our analysis of fascist movements but whose meaning in specialist studies varies considerably: *proto-fascism*. As with all taxonomies in the human sciences, there are bound to be border-line cases where phenomena do not fall neatly into one category or another. The profusion of phenomena associated with the 'right' is an outstanding example of this, and while the ideal type we have constructed draws clear distinctions between fascism and the liberal conservative right, the illiberal conservative right, and the fundamentalist (religious) right, there are a number of movements which have a palingenetic ultra-nationalist core but do not fit unambiguously into the category 'fascist'.

The most problematic taxonomically are those which, while using the rhetoric of the reborn nation and rejecting liberalism in theory, are too elitist or utopian to set about creating a cadre-led mass movement which is dedicated to using a combination of legality with violence to seize state power. They thus hold back from any serious attempt to break with both parliamentary democracy and traditional (restorationist) conservatism and so create a genuinely new order which will eventually mould all the people (considered ethnically sound) into a national community under the leadership of a new elite or political class. Such movements in practice are insufficiently radical in their populism to destroy traditional ruling elites, and in their ultra-nationalism to destroy the existing political system, and hence never place themselves in a position to translate their visionary words into revolutionary deeds. By contrast, 'genuine' fascism *is* sufficiently radical in its aspirations, extremist in its tactics and action-oriented in its mentality at least to attempt to create a cadre-led mass revolutionary force capable of seizing power. Nevertheless, the shared core of palingenetic ultra-nationalism points to a kinship which can be recognized by terming the former 'proto-fascist'. This term does not imply that the movement in question necessarily precedes the appearance of a genuine form of fascism, even if this is often the case.

A special problem is posed by ideologues who explore visions of a new society whose mythic core is demonstrably that of palingenetic ultra-nationalism but who never attempt to become activists so as to implement their ideas, even though some sort of cadre-led mass movement would eventually be necessary to overthrow the existing order so that they could be realized within (what would prove to be) an authoritarian regime. These 'literary fascists' (for example Papini, Drieu la Rochelle, Evola, Alain de Benoist) could be considered proto-fascists in terms of their obvious elitism and indirect impact on events, but when (as in the case of all four figures) their works are used indirectly to legitimate fascist activism it is clear that they are still an integral part of the fascist phenomenon. Much *völkisch* and 'conservative revolutionary' thinking in pre-Nazi Germany (for example Moeller van den Bruck, Ernst Jünger, both of whose ideas have been revived by Italian neo-fascism) hovers on the cusp between the two.

From the Abstract to the Concrete

Having located the thesis of this book within the current debate on generic fascism and constructed the ideal type with which we propose to investigate it, we are now in a position to flesh out the skeletal schema of the book's contents given at the end of Chapter 1. The next four chapters consider concrete manifestations of fascism 'at work' as an ideological and political force in modern history. Clearly they can do no more than scratch the surface of the historical and scholarly complexities of the events involved. They should be regarded as synthetic rather than analytic in intent, written with a view to evaluating the role played by fascism in twentieth-century politics and to throw into relief its salient traits as an ideological force in the light of the conceptual framework we have specially constructed in order to investigate it.

We will start with Fascism, not only because it bequeathed the generic term which has come to plague generations of scholars ever since, but it also made the transition from movement to regime and in doing so exemplifies many of the features which characterize fascism when translated into the bases of political policies and institutions, including its radical failure to realize its own utopian scheme of the reborn nation. The next chapter will focus on Germany, and Nazism in particular, giving an account of it in terms of its attempt to realize a syncretic vision of national regeneration which, though radically distinct in specific contents and in destructive potential from the one which animated Fascism, shared the same structural core we have made central to our ideal type and thus justifies treating it for heuristic purposes as a permutation of generic fascism.

Chapter 5 then casts the net wider by surveying other permutations of generic fascist ideology which emerged in Europe before 1945 but failed to seize power, thus underlining just how impotent fascism is as a revolutionary force except in the most exceptional of circumstances, and just how anomalous were the ephemeral 'triumphs' of Fascism and Nazism. Chapter 6 will look at non-European and post-war fascisms, basically to indicate just what a prolific and heterogeneous source of revolutionary movements fascism has been, but also to draw attention to the emergence of new forms of fascist myth quite distinct from inter-war models. We will then be in a position to indulge in some cautious speculation about the psychological and socio-economic preconditions for fascism's emergence and successes in Chapters 7 and 8.

References

Alan of Lille. 1973. *Anticlaudius* (trans. James Sheridan), Universal, Toronto.

Alter, P., 1989. *Nationalism*, Edward Arnold, London.

Aughey, A., 1989. The modern right: the conservative tradition in America and Britain, in R. Eatwell (ed.), *The Nature of the Right*, Pinter Publishers, London.

Attwood, L., 1990. *The New Soviet Man and Woman. Sex-role Socialization in the USSR*, Macmillan, London.

Ballanche, P.S., 1833. *Palingénésie sociale: prolégomènes*, Vol.4 of *Oeuvres complètes*, Bureau de l'encyclopédie des connaissances utiles, Paris.

Billig, M., 1978. *Fascists: A Social-psychological View of the National Front*, Harcourt, Brace, Jovanovich, London, New York.

Billig, M., 1989. The extreme right: continuities in anti-Semitic conspiracy theory in post-war Europe, in R. Eatwell (ed.), *The Nature of the Right*, Pinter Publishers, London.

Blinkhorn, M., 1990. *Fascists and Conservatives*, Unwin Hyman, London.

Buchanan, T. and Conway, M. (eds), 1996. *Political Catholicism in Europe, 1918–1960*, Oxford University Press, Oxford.

Buchman, F., 1941. *Remaking the World*, William Heinemann, London.

Capra, F., 1982. *The Turning Point*, Wildwood House, London.

Campbell, J., 1968. *The Hero with a Thousand Faces*, Princeton University Press, Princeton.

Campbell, J., 1990. *The Hero's Journey*, Harper, New York.

Cannistraro, P.V., 1972. Mussolini's cultural revolution: fascist or nationalist?, *Journal of Contemporary History*, Vol.7, Nos.3–4.

Cohn, N., 1970. *The Pursuit of the Millennium*, Palladin, London.

Conway, M., 1990. Building the Christian city: Catholics and politics in inter-war francophone Belgium, *Past & Present*, No. 128.

Croce, B., 1944. *Per la nuova vita dell'Italia. Scritti e discorsi 1943–44*, Ricciardi, Naples.

Dawson, C., 1943. *The Renewal of Civilization*, National Peace Council, London.

De Felice, R., 1982. Fascism, in P.V. Cannistraro (ed.), *A Historical Dictionary of Italian Fascism*, Greenwood Press, Westport, Connecticut, London.

Eatwell, R. (ed.), 1989. *The Nature of the Right*, Pinter Publishers, London.

Eley, G., 1980. *Reshaping the German Right. Radical Nationalism and Political Change after Bismarck*, Yale University Press, New Haven.

Eley, G., 1990. *From Unification to Nazism*, Allen & Unwin, Boston.

Eliade, M., 1964. *Shamanism: Archaic Techniques of Ecstasy*, Routledge & Kegan Paul, London.

Eliade, M., 1971. *The Myth of the Eternal Return or Cosmos and History*, Princeton University Press, Princeton.

Evola, J., 1934. *Rivolta contro il mondo moderno*, Hoepli, Rome.

Evola, J., 1972. *Il cammino del cinabro*, Scheiwiller, Milan.

Frazer, J.G., 1957. *The Golden Bough*, Macmillan, London.

Freeden, M., 1986. *Liberalism Divided*, Oxford University Press, Oxford.

Friedrich, C.J. and Brzezinski, Z.K., 1967. *Totalitarian Dictatorship and Autocracy*, Praeger, New York.

Frolov, I., 1985. *Dictionnaire Philosophique*, Editions du Progrès, Moscow.

Fromm, E., 1963. *The Sane Society*, Routledge & Kegan Paul, London.

Gentile, E., 1975. *Le origini dell'ideologia fascista*, Laterza, Bari.

Gentile, E., 1990. Fascism as political religion, *Journal of Contemporary History*, Vol.25, Nos 2–3.

Goodwin, B. and Taylor, K., 1982. *The Politics of Utopia*, Hutchinson, London.

Gordon, D.E., 1987. *Expressionism*, Yale University Press, New Haven.

Guerra, P. and Revelli, M., 1983. Bibliografia essenziale per la conoscenza della nuova destra italiana, in P, Bologna and E. Mana (eds), *Nuova Destra e cultura reazionaria negli anni ottanta*, Istituto storico della Resistenza, Cuneo.

Hayes, P. M., 1973. *Fascism*, George Allen & Unwin, London.

Herf, J., 1984. *Reactionary Modernism*, Cambridge University Press, London.

Jesi, F., 1979. *Cultura di destra*, Garzanti, Milan.

Jung, C.G., 1958. *The Undiscovered Self*, Routledge & Kegan Paul, London.

Kennedy, P., 1988. *The Rise and Fall of Great Powers. Economic Change and Military Conflict 1500–2000*, Unwin Hyman, London.

Kermode, J.F., 1967. The modern apocalypse, in *The Sense of an Ending*, Oxford University Press, Oxford.

Kershaw, I., 1985. *The Nazi Dictatorship*, Edward Arnold, London.

Kershaw, I., 1987. *The Hitler Myth*, Oxford University Press, Oxford.

Kershaw, I., 1989. Defining the Nazi State, *New Left Review*, No. 176.

Kershaw, I., 1991. *Hitler*, Longman, London.

Kumar, K., 1987. *Utopia & Anti-utopia in Modern Times*, Oxford University Press, Oxford.

Lasky, M.J., 1976. *Utopia and Revolution*, Macmillan, London.

Lazzari, G., 1984. Linguaggio, ideologia, politica culturale del fascismo, *Movimento Operaio e Socialista*, Vol.7, No.1.

Ledeen, M., 1972. *Universal Fascism*, Howard Fertig, New York.

Linz, J.J., 1979. Some notes towards the comparative study of fascism, in W. Laqueur, *Fascism: a Reader's Guide*, Penguin Books, Harmondsworth.

Lyttleton, A., 1973. *Italian Fascisms from Pareto to Gentile*, Jonathan Cape, London.

Mack Smith, D., 1981. *Mussolini*, Weidenfeld & Nicolson, London.

Mannheim, K., 1960. *Ideology and Utopia*, Routledge & Kegan Paul, London.

Mayer, A.J., 1971. *Dynamics of Counter-revolution in Europe 1870–1956*, Harper and Row, New York.

McClelland, J.S., 1970. *The French Right (from de Maistre to Maurras)*, Jonathan Cape, London.

Minogue, K.R., 1967. *Nationalism*, B.T. Batsford, London.

Moeller van den Bruck, A., 1923. *Das Dritte Reich*, Ringverlag, Berlin.

Mosse, G.L., 1978. *Towards the Final Solution*, Dent, London.

Mosse, G.L., 1979. *International Fascism. New Thoughts and Approaches*, Sage Publications, London.

Mosse, G.L., 1980. *Masses and Man*, Howard Fertig, New York.

Ó Maoláin, C., 1987. *The Radical Right: A World Directory*, Longman, London.

O'Sullivan, N.K., 1983. *Fascism*, J. M. Dent & Sons, London.

Nolte, E., 1988. Ein Höhepunkt der Heidegger-Kritik? Victor Farias' Buch *Heidegger et le nazisme*, *Historische Zeitschrift*, Vol.247.

Payne, S.G., 1980. The concept of fascism, in S.U. Larsen, B. Hagtvet, J.P. Mycklebust, 1980. *Who Were the Fascists?*, Universitetsforlaget, Bergen and Oslo.

Pinkney, R., 1990. *Right-wing Military Government*, Pinter Publishers, London.

Pois, R.A., 1986. *National Socialism and the Religion of Nature*, Croom Helm, London.

Popper, K., 1966. *The Open Society and its Enemies* (2 vols), Routledge & Kegan Paul, London.

Rees, P., 1984. *Fascism and Pre-fascism in Europe 1890–1945. A Bibliography of the Extreme Right*, 2 vols, Harvester Press, Sussex.

Reich, C., 1971. *The Greening of America*, The Penguin Press, Harmondsworth.

Reinitzer, H., 1981. Vom Vogel Phönix, in W. Harms and H. Reinitzer (eds), *Natura loquax*, Peter D. Lang, Frankfurt-on-Main.

Reszler, A., 1981. *Mythes politiques*, Presses Universitaires de France, Paris.

Rhodes, J. M., 1980. *The Hitler Movement*, Hoover International Press, Stanford.

Riedel, W., 1970. *Der neue Mensch*, Bouvier und Co. Verlag, Bonn.

Rogger, H. and Weber, E. (eds), 1966. *The European Right*, University of California Press, Berkeley.

Rossi-Landi, F., 1990. *Ideology*, Oxford University Press, Oxford.

Roth, J., 1963. Revolution and morale in modern French thought: Sorel, and the Sorelians, *French Historical Studies*, Vol.3, No.2.

Roth, J., 1980. *The Cult of Violence. Sorel and the Sorelians*, University of California Press, Berkeley.

Sandoz, E., 1981. *The Voegelinian Revolution*, Louisiana State University, Baton Rouge, London.

Schnapper, E.B., 1965. *The Inward Odyssey*, George Allen & Unwin, London.

Schuman, R., 1963. *Pour l'Europe*, Nagel, Paris.

Seidel, G., 1986. Culture, nation and race in the British and French New Right, in R. Levitas, *The Ideology of the New Right*, Polity Press, Cambridge.

Sewell, W.H., 1985. Ideologies and social revolutions: reflections on the French case, *Journal of Modern History*, Vol.57, No.1.

Silvestris, B., 1978. *Cosmographia*, ed. P. Dronke, Brill, Leiden.

Sironneau, J-P., 1982. *Sécularisation et religions politiques*, Mouton, The Hague.

Skocpol, T., 1985. Cultural idioms and political ideologies in the revolutionary restructuring of state power: a rejoinder to Sewell, *Journal of Modern History*, Vol.57, No.1.

Smith, A., 1979. *Nationalism in the Twentieth Century*, Martin Robertson, Oxford.

Sorel, G., 1961. *Reflections on Violence*, Collier-Macmillan, London (1st French edition 1908).

Soucy, R.J., 1979. The nature of fascism in France, in G.L. Mosse (ed.), *International Fascism. New Thoughts and Approaches*, Sage Publications, London.

Soucy, R.J., 1980, Drieu la Rochelle and the modernist anti-modernism in French fascism, *Modern Language Notes*, Vol.95, No.4.

Stern, F., 1961. *The Politics of Cultural Despair*, University of California Press, Berkeley and Los Angeles.

Sternhell, Z., 1979. Fascist ideology, in W. Laqueur, *Fascism: A Reader's Guide*, Penguin Books, Harmondsworth.

Sternhell, Z., 1987. Fascism, in David Miller (ed.), *The Blackwell Encyclopedia of Political Thought*, Basil Blackwell, Oxford.

Stites, R., 1992. *Revolutionary Dreams. Utopian Dreams and Experimental Life in the Russian Revolution*, Oxford University Press, Oxford.

Swart, K.W., 1964. *The Sense of Decadence in Nineteenth-century France*, International Archives of the History of Ideas, The Hague.

Tudor, H., 1972. *Political Myth*, Pall Mall, London.

Turner Jr, H.A., 1975. Fascism and Modernization, in H.A. Turner, Jr (ed.), *Reappraisals of Fascism*, Franklin Watts, New York.

Voegelin, E., 1938. *Die politischen Religionen*, Bermann-Fischer, Vienna.

Voegelin, E., 1952. *The New Science of Politics*, University of Chicago Press, Chicago and London.

Voegelin, E., 1968. *Science, Politics and Gnosticism*, Gateway Editions, South Bend, Indiana.

Weber, E., 1964. *Varieties of History*, D. Van Nostrand, New York.

Weber, E., 1979. Revolution? Counter-revolution? What revolution?, in W. Laqueur, *Fascism: a Reader's Guide*, Penguin Books, Harmondsworth.

Weber E., 1982. Decadence on a private income, *Journal of Contemporary History*, Vol.17, No.1.

Weber, M., 1948. *From Max Weber* (ed. and trans. by H.H. Gerth and C. Wright Mills), Routledge & Kegan Paul, London.

Wells, H.G., 1942. *Phoenix. A Summary of the Inescapable Condition of the World Reorganization*, Secker & Warburg, London.

3 Italian Fascism

Proto-fascism in Italy

If we were concerned simply with reconstructing the evolution of Fascism then it might be sensible to start with the inaugural meeting of Mussolini's *Fasci di combattimento* held in March 1919 and thus before the full extent of the structural damage which the war had inflicted on Italy's liberal institutions had become apparent. Our primary concern, however, is to establish how forces at work in the political culture of modern Italy exemplify the nature of *generic* fascism. Thus we must go back several years earlier to consider the pro-war lobby which formed in the autumn of 1914 when, despite its conspicuous failings, Italian liberalism still seemed unassailable. Some of these 'interventionists' were democrats and included Radicals, right-wing Liberals, reformist Socialists and several cabinet ministers, as well as the two most important members of the government, the prime minister, Salandra, and the foreign minister, Sonnino. They all hoped that by fighting on the winning side Italy would not only secure territorial gains and enhanced international prestige but create a new style of dynamic, authoritative parliamentary government, so finally putting an end to the rise of revolutionary socialism and the weakness they identified with the Giolittian system.

What interests us here, however, is the intensive extra-parliamentary campaign mounted between August 1914 and the 'radiant days of May' when Italy formally joined the *Entente Cordiale*. Though highly disparate in their surface ideology and in the degree to which they constituted a recognizable political grouping, the different elements which joined forces to become revolutionary interventionists had one thing in common: the belief that entry into the war would inaugurate a new post-liberal Italy. In other words, the shared mythic core which made their alliance possible was a palingenetic variety of ultra-nationalism, so that, according to our ideal type, the pressure group they formed can be considered the first significant manifestation of fascist politics in Italy.

The oldest component had no organizational form as such but was essentially a publicistic phenomenon. It nevertheless represented an important current in the political counter-culture of pre-war Italy. One of its foremost representatives was Papini, who as early as 1904 had co-written 'A

Nationalist Programme' attacking the decadence of liberalism and the divisiveness of socialism. Presented as a lecture in several Italian cities that year, the programme called for the diffusion of the allegedly aristocratic virtues of authority and heroism to revitalize the middle classes so as to create a 'world of revived energy' in which not only would the arts flourish once more, but patriotic armies and entrepreneurs would work together to create a flourishing colonial empire in Africa (see Lyttleton, 1973b, p.116–9). Palingenetic myth is not only the *Leitmotif* of Papini's publicistic activity in these early years, even dictating the titles of some of his articles, 'Italy is Reborn', 'Campaign for the Forced Reawakening of Italy' (see Papini, 1963), but three decades later it still provided the central theme of *Italia mia*, his most famous work of propaganda for the Fascist regime: 'Italy's nature is like that of the phoenix: cut in two it reconstitutes itself, and hardly has it arisen once more than it soars even stronger than before' (ibid., p.509). He made important contributions to a number of periodicals such as *Il Leonardo*, *Regno*, *La Voce*, *Lacerba* and *L'Anima* which helped establish the respectability of anti-socialist, anti-liberal and ultra-nationalist ideas in pre-war Italy.

The most influential of these was *La Voce*, edited by Prezzolini who had set up *Leonardo* with Papini in 1903 and co-written with him the Nationalist Programme. The articles and editorials of these two men, along with the contributions of the poet Soffici, preached an eclectic blend of aesthetic politics which drew on Nietzsche and other currents of anti-materialist philosophy (Crocean idealism, Bergsonian vitalism, as well as conservative nostalgia for a strong unitary state). The result was a sustained critique of the mediocrity of Italian society and the call for a revolution in Italy, not merely cultural but ethical and political which would place the country in the hands of a new spiritual elite. As early as 1904 Prezzolini had been arguing that the 'old Italy' of corruption and decadence had to give way to the 'new' one of energy and heroism (for example Prezzolini, 1904). This vision of Italy's rebirth became the central creed not only of the *Voce* circle in Florence (1908–16), but of numerous self-appointed *Vociani* who felt they belonged to a new generation destined to complete the *risorgimento* in a political order which was not merely post-Giolittian but post-liberal. In 1914 all three men threw their publicistic energies into the pro-war campaign. Prezzolini turned *La Voce* into an uncompromisingly interventionist magazine, while in the pages of *Lacerba* Papini and Soffici fused avant-garde art with heady visions of an Italy regenerated through the war experience (see Gentile, 1972; Adamson, 1989).

Another component of revolutionary interventionism was closely related in its origins to Papinian and Vocian 'cultural ultra-nationalism' but operated as a formally constituted political pressure group. In December 1910, amid the heightened nationalist passions aroused by Austria's expansion into Bosnia in 1908 and the imminent prospect of a colonial war with Libya, a Nationalist Congress was held in Florence, home of the *Voce* circle. At this congress Corradini, who had co-edited *Il Regno* with Papini in 1904, and his close collaborator Federzoni founded the *Associazione Nazionale Italiana*. The core ideology of the ANI's more radical members, spelt out emphatically in its periodical, *L'Idea Nazionale*, perpetuated the Vocian myth of the 'new Italy' but also contained two distinctive elements. The first, elaborated by Corradini on his return from Latin America in 1908, was a quasi-Marxist justification of Italian expansionism as the act of a 'proletarian' nation asserting its right no longer to submit to the hegemony of plutocratic 'capitalist' ones such as Britain and Germany. The second was provided by the legal theorist, Rocco, who had been recruited by the ANI in 1913. His drive to promote a new post-liberal order in Italy was rooted in a philosophy of history which focused on the decline of state authority allegedly brought about by the diffusion of liberal and socialist principles ('demosocialism') in the wake of the French Revolution. The remedy he proposed to the corruption and class conflict he saw about him was a peculiar blend of technocratic faith with both conservatism and modern imperialism. He proposed the replacement of the liberal system by a corporativist order in which a powerful industrial class would control sectors of the economy under the auspices of a strong state in which the authority of the monarchy, the military and the Church had been restored. In 1914 *L'Idea Nazionale* predictably turned itself into a major organ of interventionist argument (Roberts, 1979, ch.5; De Grand, 1971, 1978).

Both Vocian and ANI ultra-nationalism was of a distinctly elitist, right-wing complexion and represented a transformation of the conservative tradition, albeit in a revolutionary rather than a restorationist direction. In this respect they can be placed at the opposite end of the spectrum from a third component of anti-democratic interventionism, neo-syndicalism. This term refers to a number of revolutionary socialists who since the turn of the century had, in contrast to the 'maximalist' (that is revolutionary Marxist) mainstream, increasingly looked to a technologically advanced Italy as the precondition for the creation of a heroic proletariat and for the subsequent realization of socialism through a network of worker-led unions. Though an attempt was made to make this political vision the basis of a formal organization with the setting up of the *Unione Sindacale Italiana* in 1912, it remained essentially a diffuse current of revolutionary agitation represented by some trade-union activists and propagated in periodicals (for example *Avanguardia socialista* and *Il divenire sociale*) and books (for example Labriola, 1910).

The openly palingenetic and increasingly nationalist trend of neo-syndicalist thinking predisposed a number of its most prominent theorists, notably Lanzillo, De Ambris, Rossoni, Corridoni and Panunzio, to campaign alongside their natural enemies, the 'right-wing' extra-parliamentary interventionists in 1914. They believed that 'the war would bury for good the forms and ideologies of the past and prepare the way for something radically new . . . Whoever remained passive would be left behind as history accelerated and Italy entered a new era' (Roberts, 1979, p.112). The only vestige of socialism in their belief in the revolutionary virtues of national war was the underlying assumption that society would one day belong politically and economically to the 'producers' rather than to the parasitic ruling, landowning and industrial classes who had dominated Italy hitherto. To promote their cause they set up a network of pressure groups, the *Fasci di azione rivoluzionaria* (the adjective '*internazionalista*' which originally appeared in their name had been quietly dropped), while Corridoni proved his mettle as one of the most effective speakers at the mass rallies held in Milan to whip up public pressure against neutrality (see Roberts, 1979, ch.5).

A fourth political grouping which promoted interventionism in 1914 had an even less orthodox pedigree than the neo-syndicalists: the Political Futurists. In 1909 their leader, Marinetti, had achieved international fame with the publication in Paris of the Futurist Manifesto announcing a radical break with all tradition (*passatismo* or 'pastism') in the name of an art which would celebrate the dynamism of the modern machine age. In this respect 'Futurism' was a child of the same age which gave rise to fauvism, expressionism, abstractionism, surrealism and constructivism (see Hughes, 1980, pp.40–3). What set it apart from such aesthetic movements was that from the beginning the inauguration of a 'futurist' age was inextricably bound up with the call for national regeneration. The legacy of Italy's imperial, religious or cultural past was regarded by futurists as a dead weight preventing her from becoming a technologically advanced, militarily strong national community. Liberalism, which embodied the 'pastist' mentality had to go. The mythic core at the heart of such ideas was again unmistakably palingenetic: 'Political futurism was the irrational and activist commitment to the violent destruction of the old world and the creation of a new society whose form was as yet ill-defined, in which Marinetti intended to have the role of leader and ideologue' (Gentile, 1982, p.146).

The policies which flowed from this curious form of aesthetic politics were distinctly bellicose ('war is the sole hygiene of the world' was one of Marinetti's more memorable aphorisms). Futurism thus managed to combine chauvinism and imperialism with policies in keeping with its anti-establishment pose, namely republicanism, egalitarianism and anti-clericalism. As a result, Futurists such as Boccioni were to be found campaigning against the Church and for national expansion in the 1909 elections, and in 1914 were eager to support the interventionist cause: indeed, Marinetti became one of its most effective spokesmen. In addition, the urge to translate avant-garde aesthetics into political change drew support from the periodical *Lacerba*, produced by Papini and Soffici in their short-lived Futurist phase (Joll, 1965; Gentile, 1982, ch.4; Mosse, 1990).

Another permutation of aesthetic politics was to be found in the interventionist alliance, this time embodied not in a formally constituted political group, nor even a current of political culture, but in a single ideologue of visionary politics: D'Annunzio. His personal discovery of Nietzsche in 1893 had been the starting point for a decisive shift from exploring the perverse delights of the 'decadent' sensibility (that is in *Il piacere* of 1891) to a self-appointed 'superman'. Though initially he felt his role was to resist the rising tide of mediocrity unleashed by modern mass society (that is *Le vergine delle rocce* of 1895), the wide-spread food riots of 1898 left a deep impression on him. From then on he saw himself as a seer called upon to use his lyric and dramatic genius to inspire patriotic fervour in the masses and bring about 'the rebirth of Italy' (*La Gloria* of 1899; *Il fuoco* of 1900) as an heroic, imperialist, modern nation. But D'Annunzio was not content to be the poet laureate of nationalism. True to his new vision of himself as a synthesis of artist and leader, he was drawn irresistibly into the political arena. Having been elected deputy in 1897 on an extreme right-wing ticket, he eventually gravitated away from parliamentary politics altogether. Though by 1911 he had been drawn into the orbit of the newly formed ANI, he never formally joined it. He greeted the interventionist crisis as an ideal opportunity to convert the masses to the cause of nationalism, and his rallies soon established him as a born demagogue (see Ledeen, 1977, ch.1).

In October 1914 Mussolini found himself in a similar position to D'Annunzio, a flamboyant outsider figure with a reputation for exceptional journalistic gifts but no longer identified with any established political faction since his dramatic rupture with the neutralism of the revolutionary 'maximalist' socialists. In contrast to the poet's well-established nationalist credentials, however, Mussolini's earlier achievements as the editor of *Avanti!* and ardent neutralist made his espousal of interventionism a dramatic U-turn, confirming the view many commentators have subsequently formed of him as an unscrupulous opportunist with no ideological backbone (for example Kirkpatrick, 1964; Hibbert, 1975; Mack Smith, 1981). Painstaking research by several scholars (for example Settembrini, 1976; Gregor, 1979; De Felice, 1965; Gentile, 1982, ch.3) has shown, however, that more was involved in his sudden switch to a bellicose chauvinism than mere opportunism. After several years of intense preoccupation with a personal 'revision' of Marxism and revolutionary theory, the myth of cultural regeneration preached in a Nietzschean key by the likes of Papini and Prezzolini hit him with the force of a 'revelation' (Gentile, 1982, p.104). He had 'the sensation of being called to announce a new epoch', (ibid., p.106) and became convinced of being a 'man chosen by destiny to belong to the small ranks of the elect, one of the new breed of new men and free spirits like the *Vociani* themselves, harbingers of a new era and apostles of the greatness of the Third Italy' (ibid., p.106). By the time the European war broke out, Mussolini's Marxism had been all but washed away, and his internationalism and pacificism had worn very thin. He already felt some affinity with the national syndicalists (Roberts, 1979, pp.98–9) and while still editor of *Avanti!* he had founded his own journal, *Utopia*, which was more 'Vocian' than socialist. It was thus a small, not to say inevitable, step for him to throw in his lot with the neo-syndicalist *Fasci* (whose leftist brand of ultra-nationalism was closest to his own, though the vitalism and anti-establishment radicalism of the Futurists also appealed to him), taking with him a small band of faithful supporters already convinced of his charismatic powers.

When Mussolini brought out his new paper *Il Popolo d'Italia*, dedicated to the cause of war and revolution, it was as a bid to turn the interventionist movement into a dynamic constituency of revolutionary politics with himself at its head. In this he was only following the example of all the main groupings in the interventionist alliance, for the ANI Nationalists, the Political Futurists and the syndicalists were producing a flood of articles in their own periodicals attempting to impose their interpretation of the turning point in Italy's history as the orthodoxy of the day.

The First Italian Fascism: Some Inferences

Clearly it would be excessive to claim that revolutionary interventionism marked the appearance of fully fledged fascism in Italy. Apart from the *Fasci di azione rivoluzionaria*, which co-ordinated the agitation of neo-syndicalists and Mussolinians, the alliance between the different components of revolutionary interventionism remained a loose one and there was no concerted attempt to harmonize tactics or produce a joint blueprint for the post-liberal society which might ensue from the war. Therefore, while its core myth of palingenetic ultra-nationalism classifies revolutionary interventionism as a form of fascism at the level of ideology, its lack of organizational cohesion and tactical radicalness marks it out as no more than a harbinger of things to come, as *proto-fascist*, in fact. Nevertheless, with the benefit of hindsight several features of this embryonic fascism assume particular significance because of the way they already prefigure important aspects of the phenomenon in its more 'mature' manifestations.

First, it emphasizes the crucial role played by the existence of an objective crisis of political institutions in allowing discrete currents of ultra-nationalism to coalesce and move from the wings towards the centre of the political arena. The various factions of revolutionary interventionism would have been condemned to isolation and impotence but for the bitter divisions between politicians over the intervention issue and the deepening crisis of public confidence in official government policy. This breakdown of consensus politics was in turn the culmination of ten years of mounting social unrest, growing threats from the revolutionary left and rising nationalist fervour over irredentist claims, Austrian expansionism and the need for colonies. It was only the special political conjuncture which unexpectedly emerged in October 1914 that temporarily allowed ultra-nationalist elements, which till then had been both disparate and minute to transform themselves into a *movement* as such (though, except briefly in Milan, not a *mass* movement). Clearly, then, the fundamental entity in which fascism exists is not the movement, for this is something which only materializes when 'objective conditions' are propitious for alliances to form between individual ideologues (for example D'Annunzio, Mussolini), cultural currents (for example Vocianism, Political Futurism) and political groupings (for example neo-syndicalists, Nationalists).

The recognition that fascism does not essentially manifest itself in the form of a movement, let alone a regime, relates to the second inference to be drawn: neither leader-figures or paramilitary uniforms are to be considered among its core definitional properties. In its chrysalis stage fascism is but a publicistic and activistic (or 'agit-prop') phenomenon on the fringe of mainstream political culture and developments, condemned to lead a marginal existence in articles, pamphlets and books, often with negligible readerships and in the radicalism of ineffectual political factions. Even the progression to the columns of large-circulation newspapers and well-attended public meetings represents a quantum leap for the diffusion of fascism which is still far removed from nation-wide mass rallies, extensive paramilitary violence and the 'seizure' of state power. Implicit in this observation is the fact that the original fascist activists always represent a small (self-appointed) elite inspired by an esoteric vision of a new order which awakens no spontaneous response in the vast majority of the population they dream so ardently of integrating into a new national community. All the interventionists saw themselves as a vanguard political force creating new values which they felt to be necessary precisely because the vast majority of both the ruling classes and the masses lacked a unifying vision, an epic historical perspective with which to rise above inertia and decadence. The dream of fascists is somehow to inspire an irresistible surge of revolutionary 'people power' which they nevertheless co-ordinate and control from above. The interventionists acted as catalysts rather than spokesmen, and their populism was accordingly of the abstract, elitist kind common among ideologues who claim to be the sole interpreters of what the people 'really' need.

Third, interventionist fascism embodies the factiousness typical of an alliance provisionally forged by a common cause (the overthrow of the 'old Italy') and a common utopian goal (the inauguration of a 'new Italy'), both of which accommodated widely divergent diagnoses and remedies at the level of detailed analysis. In particular two poles are discernible: a 'right' wing embodied in the ANI, which sought to re-establish the authority of the state through the creation of a new ruling and entrepreneurial class capable of co-ordinating the energies of the people from above in conjunction with traditional elites, and a 'left' wing represented by the neo-syndicalists, who sought eventually to create new institutions in which the economic power of the country's productive forces could be translated into political power. D'Annunzio, Mussolini and Marinetti produced their own unique blends of elitism and populism, leftist and rightist ultra-nationalism.

Fourth, whatever combination of revolutionary nationalism with conservatism or socialism each component upheld, what characterized all of them was a stress on the primacy of action over carefully conceived political programmes. Though all the leading ideologues involved had elaborate rationales for their political activism, their priority was to strike while the iron was hot and exploit the crisis into which the Giolittian system was plunged in October 1914 by using intensive propaganda and *piazza* politics to enlist public support for a simplified, propagandist version of their esoteric vision of the future. The result was a synthesis of visionary utopianism with calculating pragmatism, typical of 'mature' fascism. Moreover, the demagogic use of crowd power, together with the celebration of war, sacrifice and heroism which characterized the interventionist campaign, all establish Italy's proto-fascism as a renunciation of both traditional and rational forms of politics in favour of 'charismatic' politics born of and tailored to the age of the masses.

Finally, what stands out about the campaign of the anti-democratic interventionists and underlines its charismatic nature is that its momentum was attributable directly to the irrational appeal which a vision of national renewal enjoyed at least among a significant minority of the politicized public in northern cities. The war fever of the 'radiant days of May' was not just the resolution of a domestic political crisis but the Italian manifestation of a powerful wave of palingenetic expectancy which was sweeping the whole of Europe at a time when intellectuals, political activists and a large number of 'ordinary people' looked to war as a source of renewal and redemption (see Stromberg, 1982). This in turn was fed by a diffuse cultural climate in which irrationalist and elitist theories of society were gaining ground among wide sections of the European intelligentsia in the so-called 'revolt against positivism' (see Hughes, 1958) to which Italian social theorists such as Michels, Mosca and Pareto made a significant contribution. According to our ideal type it is precisely fascism's ability to draw strength from such mythic forces that conditions its nature as a political force.

Post-war Italian Fascisms

Though the interventionists had succeeded in changing Italy's policy of neutrality in 1915, they had not succeeded in making the war a popular cause except among a vociferous minority. Paradoxically it was the disastrous defeat at Caporetto which was effective where heady rhetoric had failed. Once the army had been driven back to the Piave and was defending Italian soil against the Austrian invaders, both civilian and military enthusiasm for the war soared. A 'Parliamentary Group (*Fascio*) of National Defence' was formed by a cross-party lobby of pro-war deputies, while all over the country local patriotic committees (*Fasci*) formed, whipping up a McCarthy-like animosity against neutralists, especially Giolittians and Socialists, for their lack of patriotism.

The effect of this new climate of populist nationalism was that the vengeance wreaked on the Austrians at Vittorio Veneto and the final victory of the Entente powers heightened the generalized climate of heady expectancy that Italy would make substantial territorial gains from the eventual peace settlement. The frustration of these hopes ('the mutilated victory') spread waves of dissatisfaction, with a liberal ruling class tarred with the reputation for neutralism and now demonstrably out of touch with the acute social and economic crisis which followed the demobilization of the army. Nowhere were these frustrations more acute than within the ranks of those who had risked their lives for their country and now felt betrayed by it: the *ex-combattenti*, or war veterans. Ex-officers and demobilized members of the crack regiments formed after Caporetto, the *Arditi*, were especially susceptible to the idea that the spirit of the trenches (*trincerismo*) could somehow become the basis of a new political system now that the war was over. The syndicalist and interventionist Lanzillo articulated their feelings at the time thus:

> We are all convinced that a radical, profound transformation awaits us, unpredictable in its consequences. All of us feel that millions and millions of men do not die without such an enormous hecatomb giving rise to prodigious innovations. A new society, different in its institutions, its goals, its economic, moral and political structures will issue forth out of this decisive turning point in history. (Lanzillo, 1918, p.160)

In other words, a new political constituency had been formed by the war, *combattentismo*, based on a nebulous but powerful mood of palingenetic ultra-nationalism (for the generational dimension of this mood see Mosse, 1986; Wanrooij, 1987). The consequence of this was predictable: the diverse ideologues and groupings who had formulated revolutionary interventionism in 1914 strove to channel paramilitary radicalism into a movement tactically cohesive enough to overthrow the liberal system and replace it with a 'new state', a concept redolent with palingenetic overtones (see Gentile, 1982). The ANI set up their own paramilitary force, the *Sempre Pronti*, the Political Futurists set up their own *Fasci* and formulated political programmes designed to attract the increased electorate. Meanwhile, neo-syndicalists, now more fervently nationalistic than ever, intensified their publicistic activities and, since many had fought in the war, were natural recruits of the new paramilitary organizations, especially Captain Vecchi's *Arditi*.

It is against this background that Mussolini made his own bid to become the undisputed leader of the new revolutionary forces. His paper, *Il Popolo d'Italia* had already established itself as the main mouthpiece for the revolutionary interventionist spirit throughout the war, and he now judged the time ripe to set up his own political organization. The name he chose for it spoke volumes. *Fascio* had once been a generic term for a political grouping of right or left, but ever since 1914 it had been used by many of the pro-war organizations so that it came to be indissociable from the interventionist spirit. As a result the neologism *fascismo* had already gained currency to refer to this spirit, a usage reinforced when several of the new ex-servicemen's organizations also called themselves *Fasci* (the exclusive associations of the word with Mussolini's movement and with the Lictor's symbol of authority came later). Thus, the name *Fasci di combattimento* in itself celebrated the anti-democratic ethos of interventionism and the radicalism of *combattentismo*. At the same time it implied a cellular movement based on sustained revolutionary action and struggle (*combattimento*), rather than on empty rhetoric and political machinations which only perpetuated an ailing political system.

Thus in broad outline the ideology of Mussolini's *Fasci* was clear before a word had been spoken at their inaugural meeting in March 1919, attended mostly by ex-servicemen, but also by neo-syndicalists and Futurists. The programme to be announced mattered less than the event itself, which symbolically celebrated the interventionist and veteran myth that the war had acted as the midwife of a new Italy. To reinforce the link with *trincerismo* the chairman of that first meeting was Captain Vecchi, while the two speeches made that day echoed the mood of the 1914 *Fasci*: they pledged that the sacrifices of the Italian armies would be vindicated with territorial expansion and a new place for Italy in international politics and sketched out the restructuring of Italy in terms broadly consistent with the 'leftist' radicalism of Futurist and neo-syndicalist theories. The public impact of this 'Sansepolcro Fascism' was, however, minimal. Even when *Arditi*, Futurists and Fascists formed a bloc to fight the Milan elections later that year, they polled a mere 0.5 per cent of the vote.

It was to be not Mussolini but D'Annunzio who showed that it was possible for a revolutionary interventionist to create a fully fledged fascist movement out of Italy's post-war crisis. Backed by Nationalists, top army officers and a few industrialists he marched into the city of Fiume at the head of 2,000 self-styled 'legionaries' (mostly army deserters), to the obvious delight of Italians who formed the bulk of the local inhabitants. Once safely installed, representatives of all the main Italian currents of palingenetic ultra-nationalism, apart from Fascism, flocked to join him: ANI members, neo-syndicalists, Political Futurists and war-veterans (in fact in June 1921 when the Arditi Association officially broke with Mussolini it would go over to D'Annunzio). Confident of the backing of revolutionary nationalists and the general public in the 'Regency of Carnaro', the *Comandante* enthusiastically set about turning it into a microcosm of the New Italy. He maintained the highly charged emotional climate crucial to a regime based on charismatic politics and palingenetic myth with a series of ceremonial 'happenings' and high-flown rhetorical speeches laden with metaphors of transformation. Equally importantly, he worked on the new policies and structures needed for the metamorphosis of society. In collaboration with De Ambris, a prominent theoretician of national syndicalism, he drafted the Carnaro Charter to lay the basis of a new corporativist order. He also planned the formation of the Fiume League, an international alliance of 'Oppressed Peoples' to forge solidarity between the new Italians and other peoples who were due for their own *risorgimento* since their nationhood too had been suffocated by colonization. The palingenetic thrust of both projects is obvious and nowhere more so than in the Charter's declaration that the tenth corporation was to be left empty, 'dedicated to the unknown genius, to the appearance of the New Man (*nuovissimo uomo*), to the ideal transfiguration of human industry and time' (see De Felice, 1978; Ledeen, 1977; Mosse, 1980).

D'Annunzio's practical experiment in creating a fascist new order was brusquely terminated after fifteen months when the Giolittian government ousted the *dannunziani* by force on 25 December 1920 or the 'Christmas of Blood' as it became known in Dannunzian legend. This marked the effective end of Dannunzian fascism. The plans he nurtured to remobilize his legionaries in a *coup d'état* against the liberal government came to naught. In the meantime Mussolini's fascism, which seemed to have suffered a cot death in the elections of November 1919, had quite unexpectedly become not only a movement, but a mass movement. A month after the *Fasci di combattimento* were formed, a group of *Arditi*, led by Marinetti and Vecchi acting on Mussolini's behalf, burnt down the offices of *Avanti!* From these modest beginnings the paramilitary arm of Fascism was deliberately expanded by orders from Milan into a network of what would now be called terrorist cells, every *Fascio* being encouraged to set up its own 'action squad'. Then in the autumn of 1920 *squadrismo* suddenly 'took off' spontaneously, especially in the rural areas of northern and central Italy, where it acted as an anti-communist vigilante movement.

The *squadristi* were responding to a combination of factors: the Rapallo Treaty frustrated Italy's territorial claims in Dalmatia and spelt the end of the Fiume occupation, while the government appeared to the ultra-right and to alarmed property owners as spineless as ever in combating the ominous rise of bolshevism in what came to be called the *biennio rosso* (1919–21). The result of Mussolini's *fascismo* becoming identified with the most effective formation of ultra-nationalism and anti-bolshevism was spectacular. Whereas so far it had consisted of a handful of ineffectual urban groupings, it was now transformed into a nation-wide and largely agrarian movement (though the headquarters remained in cities and towns). Whereas in December 1919 it consisted of 31 *Fasci* with a total of 870 members, within two years it had 830 cells with nearly a quarter of a million members. Moreover, it was no longer Mussolini who was effectively in charge, but the provincial bosses, often ex-officers (called *ras* after Ethiopian chieftains) who enjoyed a free hand to tailor recruitment, propaganda and anti-bolshevik tactics to local conditions.

The 'punitive expeditions' which *squadristi* carried out so zealously served the interests of anti-socialist and conservative forces and pushed Fascism decisively to the right, despite the fact that many Dannunzian legionaries of 'leftist' syndicalist persuasion also joined the squads after the 'Christmas of Blood'. The intransigent opposition of *ras* forced Mussolini to abandon his plans for a 'pacification pact' with the Socialists in 1921, and the rhetoric of republicanism and anti-clericalism was dropped. This cleared the way for the decisive collusion of Victor Emmanuel III with Mussolini's political ambitions between October 1922 and July 1923, as well as for the Lateran Pacts of 1929 which assured the connivance of the Vatican with the new regime. It also enabled the Fascism to absorb in January 1923 the last significant independent strand of proto-fascism (and the one which was most elitist in its populism), the ANI. But although the possibility of Fascism forging an alliance with the authoritarian right dates from the rise of *squadrismo*, it would be erroneous to explain the dynamism and violence of the squads solely in terms of counter-revolutionary terrorism devoid of any elaborate ideological purposes. However mindless the violence of the lower-middle-class youths and students from professional backgrounds who became the most fanatical recruits, their leaders were overwhelmingly ex-servicemen, ensuring a direct continuity with the 'interventionist' myth of national renewal. The diaries of *squadristi* which have survived (for example Banchelli, 1922; Piazzesi, 1980; Farinacci, 1934) confirm the fact that many of them saw themselves as the 'trenchocracy' (*trincerocrazia*) called upon to lead the revolution of the new Italy against the old, precisely the scenario Mussolini had been predicting in *Il Popolo d'Italia* even before the war was over (for example 15 December 1917, 14 February 1918: see Gentile, 1975, ch.1).

It was *squadrismo* which not only transformed Fascism from an impotent grouping to a powerful paramilitary movement but eventually forced Mussolini's hand by making further compromise with liberalism imposs-ible. The first problem it posed for him was how to regain control of the movement which he had founded and how to pursue a more constitutional path to power which the failure of the Fiume adventure had convinced him was the only practical option. Flying in the face of vociferous *ras* opposition and of earlier claims that Fascism was an 'anti-party' he created the *Partito Nazionale Fascista* in 1921. The following year he staged a mock *putsch* by the *squadristi* in what came to be known as the March on Rome, a gamble which paid off when on 28 October Victor Emmanuel III not only revoked the decree of martial law under which Fascism could have been crushed but two days later appointed Mussolini prime minister of a coalition government. After years of indecisive Liberal government he was widely welcomed as the young, forceful head of state needed to put an end to the climate of anarchy and violence which his movement had done so much to create, an image that seemed confirmed when soon after his appointment he disbanded the squads and recruited their members into the newly formed Militia (MVSN). But hard-core Fascists were not prepared to take what they saw as the emasculation of 'their' revolution lying down. Former *squadristi* continued to carry out sporadic acts of violence against anti-Fascists, culminating in the murder of the reformist socialist Matteotti in June 1924.

The assassination of the only deputy to have had the courage to attack the Acerbo Law (which rigged the electoral system to give the Fascists an inflated majority in parliament) provoked a protracted crisis within Fascism, thus bringing to a head the conflict between legalitarians and extremists, party and *squadristi*, as well as revealing for the first time an extraordinary lack of decisiveness and consistency in Mussolini's leadership. However the failure of the legal opposition to Fascism to take advantage of the unique opportunity handed to them to force Mussolini's resignation enabled him to ride out the storm. It took the publication of proof of his implication in the Matteotti murder and a threatened coup by the Militia to force him finally into crossing his own Rubicon by making a speech before parliament on 3 January 1925 in which he assumed full responsibility for the actions of his followers since he had been in office. Anti-Fascist purges started within days and the transition to the Fascist dictatorship had begun (see Lyttleton, 1966; Gentile, 1984).

In its first three years Mussolini's highly heterogeneous form of fascism had completed the transition from a minute grouping on the fringe of politics (its 'natural' state), to a mass movement (possible only in circumstances of extreme state crisis), both of which were broadly consistent with its palingenetic myth. Its next incarnation as a constitutional party operating as an integral part of a coalition government (a development only made possible by contingent forces) was a radical contradiction of its palingenetic myth, as the 'intransigents' of all denominations pointed out vociferously. It had now been metamorphosized, almost against its leader's own will or better judgement, into an authoritarian regime exercizing power in the name of a populist revolution. This was the logical fulfilment of the revolutionary goals of Fascist political myth but also the stage in which the ultimately chimeric nature of the 'new Italy' would eventually become all too apparent, except, that is, to those among Mussolini's followers who were not merely intransigent but fanatical.

Fascism: the Esoteric Ideology of the Fascist Regime

When Mussolini formally announced the creation of a state based on fascism he had finally emerged as the only one of the countless agitators and political theorists of his generation to achieve the goal of being in the position to direct the restructuring society from top to bottom. Paradoxically, he had been able to succeed where others failed partly because his palingenetic vision was not associated with any clearly focused blueprint of the ideal society, so that he had been able to chop and change alliances and policies according to the situation, a flexibility denied to more single-minded activists. But even his highly malleable brand of fascism would have got him nowhere had not four national emergencies provided him with concrete situations to exploit: the interventionist crisis, the socio-political unrest following the war, the *biennio rosso* and the murder of Matteotti. Just as he had made himself the most authoritative spokesman of the interventionist spirit through his newspaper, he had finally succeeded in becoming the leader of *combattentismo*. In the process the neo-syndicalists, Political Futurists, Nationalists and many former Dannunzians came to look to Fascism as the only viable vehicle for the realization of their own, more clearly thought through (though no less utopian) revolutionary schemes, as, with more reluctance, more individualist ideologues such as D'Annunzio, Papini, Soffici, Prezzolini and Marinetti would do.

An immediate consequence of Mussolini's vagueness about what policies and structural changes Fascism stood for was that in January 1925 he was in no position to give concrete form to the Fascist revolution himself. It was now that the proto-fascist currents which had become tributaries of his movement came into their own, for there was no shortage of fervent political idealists only too anxious to turn their idiosyncratic vision into the orthodoxy of the new state. Thus it was that the leading representatives of neo-syndicalism, the ANI and *squadrismo* all found key positions in the Fascist regime, enabling them to leave their stamp on legislation and the new institutions. To see this one only has to consider the careers of such individuals as Panunzio, Lanzillo, Rossoni, Rocco, Davanzati, Federzoni, Balbo, Starace or Farinacci (see Cannistraro, 1982; De Grand, 1978).

But it was not just the survivors of proto-fascism who moved to the ideological front of the Fascist revolution. They were joined by revolutionary theorists, currents of thought and groupings which only surfaced after the March on Rome, providing vital new sources of dynamism and legitimation. Just one example among many is Giovanni Gentile, whose definition of Fascism in the 1932 *Enciclopedia Italiana* has led some scholars to treat him (quite misleadingly) as Fascism's principal ideologue. His own interpretation of the Fascist revolution was based on a highly individual philosophy known as 'actualism' which he had evolved by fusing neo-Hegelian conceptions of the 'Spirit' with a philosophy of history which focused on the decay of faith and heroism induced by the forces of secularization and individualism. The solution was to be a new type of post-liberal state in which individuals would be educated into internalizing the principles of authority and idealism, so collectively forming an 'ethical state'. It was precisely this type of state which he convinced himself that Mussolini was inaugurating with the March on Rome, and within weeks he was pouring his intellectual energy into formulating the theoretical bases of the new Italy and the educational reforms which would complete the *risorgimento*.

Like Gentile, all the most articulate hierarchs or ideologues who served the regime nurtured the illusion that they could be the mid-wives of a new Italy reborn in their image. What is striking is the wide variation in the visions of the New Italy formulated by its apologists, such as Bottai (see Gentile, 1982, ch.6), Malaparte (see De Grand, 1972), Evola (see Griffin, 1985), Grandi (for example Cannistraro, 1982), a feature observed by a number of historians of the regime (for example Tannenbaum, 1969; Lyttleton, 1973b; Roberts, 1979, ch.8). Attempts to establish the relative coherence of Fascist ideology at the level of specific theories (for example Gregor, 1969; Sternhell, 1987) excessively homogenize and intellectualize the 'ideology of Fascism', for it is the core of palingenetic ultra-nationalism which provides the common ground among the ideologues of Fascism and not how they rationalized it in detail. This can be seen when we consider the new currents of thought which emerged under the regime. One was associated with Mussolini's son Vittorio, and went by the name of *Novismo* ('Newism'), an iconoclastic campaign fought in periodicals and meetings in the early thirties. 'Novists' took seriously the claims of Fascism to be inaugurating a new stage in Western civilization, but so radical was their longing to be at the cutting edge of history that they attacked not only Gentilean 'actualism' but even Futurism as the stale orthodoxies of an older generation (see Ledeen, 1972, pp.38–9). They warned that the innovating thrust of Fascism should be compromised neither by the complacency or corruption of its hierarchs nor by the constraints imposed by its conservative fellow-travellers, especially the Church.

It should be pointed out in this context that the relationship between Fascism and Catholicism was in fact a complex one. There were examples of clergy who remained implaccably hostile to Fascism's overt secularizing and anti-Christian ethos, especially after it adopted racism, and many who gave the regime its full support because of its anti-bolshevism and promotion of family life (see Tannenbaum, 1972, ch.7). There was however a powerful movement of political Catholicism which sought to bring about a rebirth of Italian and even European society on its own religious terms, thus forging its own Third Way, this time between liberalism and fascism (see Pollard, 1986). The ambiguity of Fascism's relationship to orthodox religion is highlighted by the fact that in 1930 concerns similar to those of the Novists led one of Mussolini's nephews, Vito, to help set up the *Scuola di mistica fascista* to act as a sort of ideological think-tank for elaborating Fascist ideology. The 'mysticism' in question was not of any religious or occultist variety but a code word for the vitalism and heroism which had supposedly inspired the Fascist revolution. Nevertheless in February 1937 Cardinal Schuster delivered a major speech at the School justifying Fascism's occupation of Ethiopia as the synthesis of Italy's Roman and Catholic heritage which was Mussolini's greatest achievement – after all, as he assured readers of *Il*

Popolo d'Italia on 27 February 1937, 'Christ is Roman' (Marchesini, 1976, p.208).

The 'Novist' and 'mystic' strands of Fascism were just two elements of a diffuse movement of 'revisionist' Fascism which arose spontaneously in the thirties, dubbed by Ledeen (1972) 'Universal Fascism'. It expressed the utopian hopes of those within the post-war generation who took the regime's palingenetic claims at their word and consisted both of the writings by number of ideologues (for example Ricci, Carella, Gravelli, Ferri) as well as the conferences run by organizations such as the Lausanne-based International Centre of Fascist Studies. It was this 'universalist' form of Fascism (cf. above p.49) which exerted the greatest influence on one of its most enthusiastic evangelists abroad, the one-time British major and secretary-general of CINEF, James Strachey Barnes (see Barnes, 1928). One of its most influential periodicals was *La Sapienza*, founded in 1933 by Spinetti who went on to write three books expounding his vision of the new Italians as the precursors of a new era of civilization. The last one was published when all but the most fanatical could see that the party was over, a vivid illustration of the way in which palingenetic myth could create tunnel vision not just in die-hard Fascists of the 'first hour' such as Farinacci, but even idealists of the second generation, if their elective affinity with it was sufficiently strong.

The relationship of Fascist artists to the regime directly mirrors that of its ideologues: Mussolini's indifference to the detail of what should constitute the new Italy combined with his pragmatic urge to harness all genuine enthusiasm for it, so that the most contradictory aesthetics were channelled willy-nilly into sources of legitimation (see Tannenbaum, 1972, chs 9 and 10). In the case of several individuals we have already encountered, these two spheres of activity substantially overlap. Papini, Prezzolini, Soffici, Marinetti, D'Annunzio and Malaparte all served the new Italy both as ideologues and artists. Papini edited his own periodical *Frontispizio* to promote a Fascistized version of cultural nationalism, while Marinetti continued to write extensively, and the movement he founded became one of Fascism's most prolific approved artistic styles (so-called 'second Futurism'). Both were naturally showered with honours by the state. In complete contrast both Malaparte and Soffici, the latter especially through his periodical *Il Selvaggio*, became associated with *strapaese*, a theory that the *squadrista* phase of the Fascist revolution expressed its true nature as a social and moral crusade against the pernicious forces of modern urban values and a celebration of rural ones, so that this should be reflected in its official ethos as well as its art.

New aesthetic creeds also emerged to lay claim to being the best expression of the regime's revolutionary *élan*. One was promoted by Bontempelli's periodical *Novecento* (20th Century) which called for a synthesis of the past and future, avoiding the excesses of Dannunzian neoromanticism, *strapaese's* anachronism and Futurist iconoclasm. Meanwhile, in the pages of the avantgarde review *Kn*, Belli argued that the abstract art he was producing epitomized the radicalness of the regime's innovations in every sphere of society better than the figurative art championed by

Bontempelli or Marinetti. Significantly, the personal palingenetic myth crucial to the elective affinity of all such figures with the regime emerges clearly from studies of their lives carried out by art historians with no interest in the mysteries of 'generic fascism'. Thus an analysis of Bontempelli's artistic vision identifies at its heart 'the myth of *renovatio* destined to resuscitate Western culture': he wanted 'with a prophetic gaze' to locate his own 'aesthetic palingenesis' [sic!] within the framework of a naive 'cyclic' or 'biological' philosophy of history' so as to generate a 'New Era' (*Annitrenta*, 1982, pp.202–4: compare p.153 on Belli).

In architecture, too, similar conflicts grew up. Thus practitioners (for example Piacenti) and theorists (for example Ojetti) of an august monumental neo-classical style appropriate to the Third Rome vied to impose their aesthetics as the official idiom of Fascism with advocates of a rationalist style modelled on the 'modern movement', also referred to as *Novecento*. A fervent champion of the latter was Sarfatti-Grassini, one of the *duce's* more durable mistresses, while the deep attachment of its most famous architect, Pagano, to his own vision of modern buildings as the concrete expression of the new Italy eventually led him to break with Fascism with tragic personal consequences (he died in Mauthausen concentration camp). As ever, Mussolini presided over such conflicts with sovereign indifference to seeing them resolved.

The Exoteric Ideology of Fascism

In talking about architecture we have already crossed over the thin threshold dividing the esoteric sphere of Fascist ideology, where its fundamental ideas were generated by committed ideologues and activists, from the exoteric sphere, where it was experienced by the mass of Italians who had no deep elective affinity with the myth of a total and permanent revolution. For them Fascism manifested itself outwardly in the regime's political policies, social programmes and institutional changes which personally affected their lives, but above all in the ceaseless flow of rhetorical claims and gestures legitimizing the regime as the creator of the new Italy which dominated all areas of communications and so established the dominant 'cultural filter' through which the events of contemporary history were perceived.

The policies and changes were designed to affect every sphere of life, thus justifying the boast that the regime was a 'totalitarian' one. Politically this meant the systematic replacement of the liberal system by a new authoritarian order in which executive power was concentrated in the Fascist Grand Council, the numerous state ministries and the *duce* himself. By 1929 Italy had been changed constitutionally and 'legally' from a liberal to a single-party state, a development unprecedented in history. In the sphere of economics a series of new legislation was introduced to create the juridic and institutional basis of the corporativist state, presented as a 'Third Way' between the anarchy of the liberal market economy and the strictures of the

Bolshevist planned one. The dynamic industrial and agricultural growth which the new economic order was supposed to generate was the premise for the other main plank of Fascist economic policy, autarky. This led to tariff barriers, a drive to boost agricultural output (the 'Battle for Grain'), an extensive programme of land reclamation (*bonifica integrale*) and the creation of state-owned monopolies set up to exploit new mineral resources, develop natural fibres, maximize the efficiency of the petro-chemical industries and lessen dependency on oil and coal imports through hydroelectric schemes (see Tannenbaum, 1972, ch.4). It should be pointed out that though Fascist propaganda presented such initiatives as symbols of the revolutionary new ethos which was transforming the nation, many of them bore a distinct resemblance to schemes for the economic modernization of Italy proposed even before the war by the agrarian-industrial bloc and drew on the *dirigiste* precedents set by the war economy between 1915 and 1918 (see Kelikan, 1986).

For most Italians the impact of these political and economic transformations were less visible than the innovations made in the sphere of social life, where comprehensive organizations were set up to regiment the lives of Italians from childhood to early adulthood (see Tannenbaum, 1972, chs. 5,6,8). Intensive efforts were also made to integrate adults into the new state through a major initiative to organize their leisure time, co-ordinated by the *Opera Nazionale Dopolavoro*, through which millions of 'ordinary Italians' were given the opportunity to participate in such 'modern' spare-time activities as sport, excursions, cycling, picnics, cinema outings, trips to the seaside and listening to the radio. *Dopolavoro* also encouraged the retention of popular festivals and rituals in agricultural areas and so reinforced the *strapaese* emphasis on the purity of rural life. It was against this background that football and cycling first became mass spectator sports and that Cinecittà was built as Italy's answer to Hollywood. The cumulative effect was that popular culture generally became indistinguishable from Fascism. A parallel process of assimilation and appropriation took place in high culture as well where distinguished institutions such as the Royal Academy of Italy, and prestigious projects such as the *Enciclopedia Italiana* secured at least luke-warm collusion from many of the country's most gifted artists, academics and scientists, thus causing their achievements to be equated with the success of Fascism.

The regime's monopoly of the press and newsreels meant that the myriad events both great and small set in train by the creation of the single-party state, corporativism, nation-wide youth and leisure organizations, and by the increased access of the urban masses to 'modern' life, could all be exploited as vindications of Fascism's claim to be the creator of the New Italy. Indeed anything suggestive of dynamism and innovation, such as the land-reclamation and hydroelectric power schemes, the new motorways, FIAT cars, Olivetti typewriters, Balbo's transatlantic formation flights ('cruises'), the achievements of Italian athletes at the Berlin Olympics naturally tended to be associated in the public mind with the success of the Fascist revolution in creating a modern, strong, youthful, advanced nation (cf. Cannistraro, 1972).

The general ethos of renewed national health was promoted by two major areas where innovative government policy and intensive propaganda fused: the demographic campaign and imperialism. Mussolini seems to have genuinely convinced himself that modern urban civilization was the main factor for falling birth rates and that this in turn was a symptom of national decadence, very much in line with the theories of the *strapaesani* and the propaganda surrounding the land-reclamation schemes and the Battle for Grain. Accordingly, a number of initiatives were launched to stem the decay of rural life, encourage large families and assign women to their traditional roles as wives, mothers and the source of domestic, emotional and moral sustenance of their offspring and spouses (see De Grand, 1976). The concern to overcome decadence was central to Fascist foreign policy as well. In his encyclopedia definition of Fascism written in 1932, Mussolini had affirmed that 'peoples who rise or rise again are imperialist'. The ruthless suppression of resistance by Haile Selassie's poorly equipped forces three years later meant that he was able to announce to ecstatic crowds that Fascist Italy had at last emulated the Romans in having an African Empire. Mussolini's ambitions for an imperialist Italy did not end there. There were long-term plans to oust the British and French from their Mediterranean colonies, and Italy's occupation of Albania (April, 1939), her participation with Nazi Germany in the partition of Croatia, as well as the ill-fated attempts to invade Greece, point to a bid to create not just an African, but a European empire.

Because of the intensive propaganda which accompanied all the policies and structural changes undertaken by Mussolini's government, they contributed, irrespective of their practical results, to the complex mesh of legitimating myths on which the regime depended for its viability. What is significant about these myths for the light they throw on the nature of generic fascism is that, despite their surface contradictions, they all share a common core of palingenetic ultra-nationalism. For example, the original *squadrista* myth of the reckless, self-sacrificing front-line soldier as the ideal type of the new Italy was perpetuated in the martial ethos of the youth organizations, the lionization of the Militia volunteers who were sent to support Franco's troops as the flower of the nation and the countless military parades which punctuated civilian life. It was also used to justify the conquest of Ethiopia and the mobilization of millions of troops to fight in France, North Africa, the Balkans, Russia and finally in Italy itself between 1939 and 1943.

The *squadrista* myth was conflated with that of *Romanità*, which invited Italians to see themselves as having directly inherited the virtues of the Italic race. This was not meant in an arch-conservative sense: the Italians were to become a new race imbued with the spirit of 'eternal Rome', not to regress literally to the civilization of their forebears. Taken together with the demographic campaign and imperialism, *Romanità* points to the presence of a deep-seated ethnocentrism and chauvinism at the heart of the Fascist world-view which is undoubtedly a form of racism, albeit a far less virulent form than those incited by the Aryan myths propagated by Nazism. Even ignoring the small minority of avowed anti-Semites Fascism had attracted since the beginning (for example Farinacci), this indigenous 'cultural' Fascist racism was intrinsic to Fascism, long predating the aberrations of 1938 and after, though it only became apparent as official policy shifted from 'neutralist' and 'universalist' to 'imperialist' modes of ultranationalism (see De Felice, 1961; Michaelis, 1978; Gregor, 1969, ch.6; Robertson, 1988). As a result, the conquest of Ethiopia was justified as the recreation of the Roman Empire and the Albanian and Greek companies were to turn the Mediterranean into a 'Roman Lake', a notion which underlay one of the rare propaganda feature films made by the regime, *Scipione l'Africano*. 'Romanness' was also invoked as justification of the classical style favoured by the Piacenti camp of architects and led to a renaissance in archaeological classical studies which the regime promoted. It affected the regime's 'image' in other ways: the proliferation of the lictor's *fasces* as the symbol of Fascism, the stress on athleticism and sport as part of a classical heritage, the introduction of the 'Roman salute' and eventually a 'Roman step' (that is the Nazi goose step) (see Cofrancesco, 1980).

Other prevalent myths with unmistakably palingenetic connotations were that Fascist Italy was the fulfilment of the Mazzinian *risorgimento* tradition which had been diverted from its true course by the aberrations of the decadent Giolittian one (see Woolf, 1965); that war is an intrinsically regenerating force in the life of the nation (cf. Gentile 1975, chs 1 and 2); that the regime was a revolution of 'Youth' (cf. Ledeen, 1971; Wanrooij, 1987); that the national character would undergo a transformation under Fascism to become that of the 'new man' or 'Fascist man' (*uomo fascista*), purged of the deformations of personality engendered by 'demo-liberalism' (see Cannistraro, 1972, pp.129–34); that Italy was pioneering a new type of state, in which all citizens would eventually find fulfilment of their human potential as part of a heroic, supra-individual reality (see Cannistraro, 1972; and especially Gentile, 1982, ch.7); that Fascism was the true incarnation of the twentieth century, marking the dawn of a new civilization (see Lyttleton, 1973b, pp.50–7; Tannenbaum, 1969, p.1,200; Sarti, 1970). The same notion of an historical turning-point after an age of decay underlay the designation of 1922 as year 0 of a new calendar (see Cannistraro, 1972, p.132) – here Fascism was aping the French Revolution in the introduction of its own 'immortal principles'.

Even the language used in the regime's propaganda bears out this analysis: a Marxist scholar has concluded that among the most characteristic *tropes* of Fascist discourse are words suggesting rebirth: Fascism promised to 'revalue, renovate, heal, renew, reconquer, remould, restore a nation that is resurrected, regenerates itself', in short to bring about 'the palingenesis [*palingenesi*] of the Fatherland' (Lazzari, 1984, pp.53, 55). It has also been shown that the dominant themes of Mussolini's own speeches include the notion of the 'new man' and 'new aristocracy' as well as the theme of Italy living 'in the transition from one civilization to another' and winning 'supremacy in the decline of the West' (Simonini, 1978, pp.99–101, 113–5).

All these myths of national renewal were subsumed in the leader-cult or *ducismo*. Mussolini was the *dux*, a modern Caesar, the restorer of the Augustan age, the heir of Mazzini and Garibaldi combined, the inaugurator of a new age. One of the earliest hagiographies of Mussolini to be written after the March on Rome was Beltramelli's celebration of the triumph of Fascism entitled *L'uomo nuovo* (1926), the 'new man' being, of course, the *duce* himself who incarnated the triumph of youth over the liberal gerontocracy (cf. Cannistraro 1972, p.136). The carefully orchestrated personality cult which presented him as a *uomo universale* unparalleled even in Renaissance times was, till 1938, one of the most successful populist myths to serve the legitimation for the regime. In short, whatever aspect of the Fascist regime we consider, the underlying myth is that of national renewal, of a dramatic turning-point from the decadence of the 'old' Italy, to the glories of the 'new'.

Independent corroboration of this analysis is provided by Zunino's study of Fascist ideology based on the vast profusion of books and periodicals which appeared in the first five years of the regime. He breaks down his subject into a number of sub-topics: the way individual liberty, democracy, society, and the nation were conceived under the new regime, its demographic policy, foreign affairs, the economy, the corporations, education and the *duce*. Despite the highly nuanced picture that emerges of the various positions adopted, Zunino identifies as the basic premise underlying all of them the assumption that the era preceding Fascism had been one of 'progressive decadence, of decline, of decomposition' owing to the anarchic individualism promoted by the liberal system and by the threat to the nationalist principle posed by socialism. This conviction did not lead to cultural pessimism, or a 'paralysing anguish' but to the conviction that, as *Critica Fascista* put it in 1927 (1 March, p.82), Fascism marked the transition to 'the era of a new civilization whose essence no one could know'. Mussolini's regime thus represented for Fascists the 'beginning of a new cycle' in history, 'the dawn of a new epoch' (Zunino, 1985, pp.133–5). With a mixture of idealism and pragmatism, Fascist ideologues believed they were inaugurating an unprecedented 'new order', a heroic response to an objective historical crisis of global properties.

Further corroboration of the centrality of palingenetic myth to Fascism is that it forms one of the few elements of continuity between Mussolini's regime and the Italian Social Republic (RSI), the rallying point and refuge for all convinced Fascists after the armistice, among them such luminaries of inter-war Fascism as Gentile, Marinetti, Ricci, Preziosi, Starace, Farinacci, Graziani and Pavolini. The ideology of the new regime represented both a reversion to some of the 'leftist' principles of Sansepolcro Fascism which Mussolini had abandoned after 1921 (that is anti-clericalism, antimonarchism, anti-capitalism and proletarian syndicalism) but at the same time a radicalization of the *squadrista* strain of Fascism modelled on the SS (hence the formation of the *Brigate Nere* for anti-partisan operations, the use of terror, the active persecution of Jews). By contrast, one component of the RSI's myth of renewal reflected a significant shift in Mussolini's worldview away from the parochial perspectives of early Fascism, though it keyed in with some of the global scenarios of cultural regeneration nurtured by 'universal' Fascists such as Spinetti. It also can be seen as a distant cousin both of D'Annunzio's plans for a League of Oppressed Nations and of the

ANI's conception of 'proletarian' and 'plutocratic' nations which they had taken up from Corradini even before the First World War. According to this scenario Italy was one of a handful of youthful nations (which included Germany, Japan and even Russia) which were locked in battle with decadent ones such as France, Britain and America. The Fascist regime, it was alleged, had failed in its mission of rejuvenation because it had made too many concessions to *fiancheggiatori* or fellow travellers (that is the monarchy, the industrialists, the bourgeois spirit, the old ruling class) but in its new uncompromising form was now fighting alongside its natural ally, Nazism, for the survival of European civilization (see De Felice, 1982, p.216. Cf. below p.171).

As the Republic shrank before the Allied advances, the tone of its propaganda became increasingly apocalyptic and the brutality of the Brigades became increasingly violent. By the time Mussolini fled from Milan on 25 April 1945 to meet his fate at the hands of partisans two days later, republican Fascism had already ceased to exist as a regime or a co-ordinated movement (it had never been a mass movement). In the end of Fascism was its beginning. It was now little more than the desperate longing for a new order carried in the heads of a few die-hard revolutionary nationalists, with the difference that instead of seeing a new day dawning they felt the world crumbling around them. It is bitterly ironic that the powerful partisan movement which sprang up after the Armistice to drive Fascism and its Nazi allies out of the peninsular was a sustained expression of spontaneous populism, heroism and revolutionary idealism which Mussolini's new Italy could never inspire.

The Gulf between Fascist Image and Reality

In practical terms Fascism had failed long before 1939, let alone 1943 or 1945. The results of the two major planks of Fascist economic planning, corporativism and autarky, were dismal travesties of the claims made for them in propaganda (see Tannenbaum, 1972, ch.8). The first created a stagnant manufacturing sector with built-in inefficiency and waste of resources, and instead of integrating workers in the production and decision-making process only abolished their bargaining rights and artificially depressed their wages. The second held back Italy's technological revolution, which flourished in only a handful of sectors, and did practically nothing to regenerate the agricultural sector, especially in the south where the peasants' lot had changed little since Bourbon times even when war broke out (cf. Levi, 1959). The demographic campaign did not succeed in boosting the birth rate significantly, nor did the ruralization drive do anything to alleviate the acute deprivations experienced by the majority of peasants. The devastating defeats of Italian armies in the first two years of the war gave the lie to the image of Italy's fighting forces as the most superbly trained and equipped in the world. The colonization of 'Italian East Africa' was so badly planned and poorly resourced that no effective settlement by Italian peasants took place: the whole invasion had been no more than a propaganda coup which carefully omitted any allusion to the unexpected difficulties the Italian forces had experienced in subduing the Ethiopians or the distinctly 'racist' mass atrocities committed on poorly armed soldiers and defenceless civilians in the process (Steer, 1936; Robertson, 1988). In all over 200,000 died (Sbacchi, 1989, p.33).

The most signal failure of Fascism was in its 'totalitarian' bid to destroy class divisions and integrate all Italians within a dynamic new order. Corporativism exacerbated class divisions rather than healed them, autarky and ruralization did nothing to bring the peasants into the state any more than Liberalism had done, and Gentile's school reforms reinforced the prestige traditionally enjoyed by classical studies, making social barriers based on educational background harder to overcome than ever. The regime in practice did nothing to undermine the privileges and prestige enjoyed by the monarchy, the nobility, the traditional landowning aristocracy, the army, industrialists or the Church, nor did it even attempt to bridge the acute divides between popular and high culture or wipe out the snobbery associated with class distinctions, education and wealth. Furthermore, it actively reversed the progress some sectors of educated urban women had started to achieve in emancipating themselves from traditional roles before 1922 (De Grand, 1976).

The main targets of the regime's mass organizations and propaganda were the urban working class, the lower middle classes and youth. The rapid decline in mass support for the regime between the conquest of Ethiopia and the outbreak of war, and the powerful anti-Fascist consensus which grew up in all liberated areas after the armistice except for a small hard-core of fanatics, suggests that what the deliberate manufacture of consensus by the regime achieved was not the Fascistization of the urban masses but, in Mosse's phrase, their 'nationalization'. If under Fascism the nation-state became a reality for the majority of Italians for the first time since unification it was thanks to the national and civic pride which it fostered rather than through any esoteric visions of a supra-individual new order. Similarly, the youth organizations, despite their impressive numerical strength, succeeded in regimenting the lives of the young, but not in inculcating a deep sense of loyalty to the regime or in breeding a new Fascist elite. Indeed, the point was not lost on those members of the new generation who did grow up with a genuine commitment to Fascism that, despite the regime's bombastic claims about its youthfulness and dynamism, it had rapidly developed bureaucratic and ministerial hierarchies dominated by men of the war generation, who by the thirties were well on the way to becoming the very sort of gerontocracy that Fascism was theoretically bent on destroying. The result was mounting frustration at its loss of momentum and lack of broader vision (see Ledeen, 1972).

In their Carnaro Charter, D'Annunzio and De Ambris had left the tenth corporation empty to be filled by the *uomo nuovissimo*. After nearly two decades in power Fascism had not succeeded in filling it: no breed of heroic Italians had emerged ready to give themselves mind and body to the new Italy. Moreover, the main effect of *ducismo* had been to paper over the widening cracks in Fascism's cohesion and credibility as a political system

(Melograni, 1976). Once Italy's foreign and domestic policies were perceived even by ordinary people to be dictated by Nazism and to be heading inexorably towards a second world war, the myth of Mussolini as a leader who was 'always right' quickly went sour. After several disastrous military campaigns culminated in the Allied invasion, only those most blindly committed to the regime could fail to see that, after the briefest of flights, Italy's phoenix was consigning itself once again to the ashes. With the connivance of several 'hierarchs', the army and the monarchy, Mussolini was formally removed from power by his own Fascist Grand Council in July 1943. His charisma, his mass following and all but his most fanatical right-hand men had deserted him.

Structural Reasons for Fascism's Failure

Whatever aspect of Fascism in practice we consider the picture is the same: unresolved conflicts in the interpretation of fundamental policy issues and a glaring gap between official theory and practice, propagandistic pronouncements and reality. Though it would possible to look for the reasons for these contradictions and discrepancies in detailed reconstructions of what happened in each sphere of Fascist policy, an enormous amount of scholarly effort has already been dedicated to such an undertaking over the last six decades. In the present context it is thus more fruitful to consider four areas of structural weakness which the regime created for itself from the moment it became committed to fascism as the basis of its institutions, its populist support and its policy-making.

The first concerns fascism's innate tendency towards ideological disunity and factiousness. We have seen that leftist and rightist versions of populism and corporativism, universalist and imperialist permutations of nationalism, different complexions of racism, radically opposed evaluations of the role technology and rural values should play in the new order all jostled for position to become the ideological well-head of the regime. That Fascism consisted of a plurality of ultimately irreconcilable fascisms was no doubt due in part to the vagueness of Mussolini's own palingenetic myth. He had no definitive blueprint of the New Italy, and it was precisely this which enabled him to become the leader of Italian fascism in its formative phase as a mass movement. Nevertheless, the contradictions between different currents of fascism which hampered the formulation of single-minded and effective policies were intrinsic to fascism itself as a utopian myth of national renewal and hence liable to generate a number of rival versions of itself precisely when a crisis of the established political culture favoured its rise as an alternative ideology. Their advocates can only be welded into an effective *bloc* if circumstances combined with outstanding leadership make their common cause weigh more heavily than their differences.

The second factor concerns fascism's dependency for success on collusion with conservative forces. Even though diverse Italian fascisms had by 1922 aggregated themselves into a powerful extra-parliamentary opposition movement, Mussolini would never have been able to conquer state power without the passive compliance or active support of a whole range of conservative forces: the monarchy, many large landowners and industrialists, much of the army and the Church, the more fervently reactionary, anti-socialist sections of the middle classes and initially even some right-wing Liberals, such as Croce, who longed for an end to weak government. Their support of Fascism was motivated not by ideological commitment but by self-interest: in their different ways they hoped Mussolini would use the political clout conferred on him by the violence of his followers to restore socio-political stability and so strengthen rather than weaken their position. Once they saw their own interests being threatened by the regime's actions, the basis for their collusion crumbled, leaving a small minority of fanatics to continue what they alone perceived as a last-ditch stand against decadence.

Fascism, then, was not merely an alliance between heterogeneous fascist forces, but between them and disparate conservative ones in a way which made it intrinsically polycentric and unstable. However, here too it would be naïve to trace this simply to Mussolini's indecisiveness or chameleonic approach to politics. By definition, conservatives will only be fellow-travellers of fascism as long as it seems to be fulfilling a restorationist programme (putting an end to anarchy, destroying union power, defending religious or family values etc.). Yet fascism will always need to forge an alliance with conservatism to conquer the state because it can never spontaneously be a powerful enough mass movement to do so through the sheer strength of 'people power'. This is because, even in the most ideal conditions for its propagation, palingenetic ultra-nationalist myth can only appeal spontaneously to a small minority who sees itself as a natural elite called upon by destiny to save the nation from disintegration not by restoring the past but by creating a new order. It will not have a spontaneous constituency among those temperamentally repelled rather than attracted by the prospect of cathartic destruction (for example most women, wide sections of the middle and upper classes), the more apolitical or 'passive' sections of the population (for example the old, illiterate peasants, children) or those deeply committed to other political or religious values (for example fervent humanists, liberals, socialists, Marxists, Christians).

This leads to a third structural weakness of fascism borne out by Mussolini's regime: no matter how refined or well orchestrated the techniques of social control, there will always be severe limitations to the degree to which the mass of the population can ever be genuinely fascistized. The esoteric visions of a heroic national community cultivated by Farinacci, Gentile or Bottai remained alien to the vast mass of Italians because they were essentially a myth projected on to contemporary history by a self-appointed and profoundly unrepresentative elite. The atypical social background and psychological make-up of most ideologues made it inevitable that their myth of the ideal society took no account of the affective realities which give meaning to most people's lives or of the practical political and economic implications of creating a 'new order'. What assured a degree of mass consensus behind Fascism was not the utopian visions of its theorists but its promise to most people of a stable system in which to plan their lives as well as access to a life-style associated with modern urban civilization (e.g. cinema, sport and mobility), both of these prospects infused with a fervent patriotism. The popular chauvinism which underpinned Fascism and the *duce* cult was combined not with a profound commitment to revolutionary politics as its ideologues intended but with a sense of stability and conformism. The Ethiopian campaign was a temporary propaganda success because it fed a sense of national pride while disrupting relatively few lives at home. The spectres of destruction summoned up by the outbreak of the Second World War meant that for millions the thin threads of affective attachment to the regime simply snapped.

The extensive intrusion of the state into most areas of life, the wide-spread use of overt and covert propaganda, the creation of special tribunals and a secret police (the OVRA) to stamp out dissent could not create a Fascist Italy in any meaningful sense of the term. Only a grim (and, as Fellini's film *Amarcord* points out, sometimes farcical) travesty resulted in which the public were fed with lies, their values manipulated and their consensus deliberately fabricated but without creating any deep understanding of or unconditional loyalty to the regime. Just as *autarchico* became a colloquialism not for abundant but for frugal, so *totalitario* came in practice to mean, not the dynamic co-ordination and integration of all citizens into the life of the new Italy but the stifling of individuality, freedom and truth. Even this coercive aspect of the state could never be 'total' because of the intrinsic limitations to the capacity of any regime to control *all* aspects of its citizens' lives.

A fourth factor in Fascism's failure is the loss of revolutionary dynamism at the heart of government which any fascism will tend to experience sooner or later on becoming the basis of a regime. The inefficiency, inertia and corruption which crept into Fascist ministries, organizations and institutions were certainly exacerbated by Mussolini's personal style of leadership. His reluctance to devolve power, his lack of loyalty towards his most zealous followers, his readiness to chop and change policies, his preference for mediocrities and sycophants over men of natural ability, and, most of all, his increasing tendency to believe his own rhetoric about the state of the nation ensured that the new state was never going to be a meritocracy (see Mack Smith, 1981). Yet, no matter how efficient Mussolini might have been as a manager of the Fascist enterprise, a loss of momentum was inevitable sooner or later. To construct and run a new regime necessitates the emergence of a new caste of civil servants, bureaucrats, officials and managers whose careerist or reactionary mentality is far removed from the revolutionary impulses and violent instincts which enabled the movement to seize power in the first place. This entropy of radicalism may not be detrimental to the credibility of a political system if the fundamental ideology in whose name it was established celebrates continuity and stability, as do conservatism, socialism and liberalism in their different ways. But Fascism celebrated permanent revolution as the *raison d'être* of the new order. The bulk of party members and civil servants who exercized power in Italy after 1925 were opportunists. As such they were indifferent to

Fascism's esoteric visions of its regenerating mission and made a mockery of the cult of youth and of *squadrista* virtues proclaimed by the state.

Fascism's Achilles heel as a regime thus proved to be precisely what had been the source of its strength in its formative years when in the eyes of millions the country seemed to be at the mercy of socialists and threatened by immediate collapse: its ability to embody the nebulous promises of a new order. As we argued in the last chapter (pp.42–3), a regime based on the myth of permanent revolution and the reborn nation depends on its 'charismatic' power and is thus automatically caught between the Charybdis of entropy through normalization and the Scylla of self-destruction through war. Mussolini's experiment in creating an unprecedented type of socio-political system started to flounder on the reef of normalization in the early thirties till the Ethiopian campaign temporarily restored some of its credibility. It then embarked on the road to self-destruction by becoming embroiled in Hitler's expansionism and pursuing new imperialist policies in the Adriatic and the Balkans till it was checked by the Allies on all fronts, by which time it had long since collapsed from within as a mass movement.

When someone falls off a high cliff fatal injuries are inevitably sustained no matter how contingent those which actually result. Obviously the *way* Fascism failed was contingent, and is a matter for historians to establish in detail, but the ultimate inevitablility of that failure is something which can be deduced from political theory *a priori* (at least when the ideal type we have proposed is applied to it). In the event, hardly was the institutional and legislative apparatus of the New Italy in place than it started functioning as an oppressive counter-revolutionary regime, retarding any authentic integration of the Italians into the state, hampering the emancipation of the peasantry and of women, consolidating conservative institutions and attitudes, stifling initiative, curtailing individualism, abolishing political debate outside certain parameters, reversing the gains of workers, imposing an uneasy blend of petty bourgeois values with a mindless ethos of chauvinism, militarism and personality cult, slowing down the industrialization of the economy and creating an everyday reality for millions which was conformist and banal. After 1935 Italy was launched into a quick succession of military campaigns (Ethiopia, Spain, the Balkans, North Africa) which exposed the myth of Italy's military power and caused incalculable human suffering for the Italian armed forces and their victims. This led in turn to Italy's invasion by the Allies, her occupation by the Nazis and the creation of the Salò Republic, in the course of which many thousands of former soldiers were deported to Nazi labour camps, while millions of Italian citizens were exposed to hunger, fear and random violence. A worse fate awaited those who joined the massive ground-swell of anti-fascist 'partisans' if they fell into enemy hands.

However pathetic then squalid the Fascist regime turned out to be, its failures were not due to a lack of ideology. If anything the original movement had accommodated *too many* rival versions of what it stood for ideologically, all of which shared a core which could only produce a grotesque travesty of a reborn nation once translated into practical policies. It was not nihilistic but utopian, not anti-modern but modernizing in a palingenetic and thus a contradictory and unrealizable sense. It was not the nemesis of a fatally flawed liberal system because a high degree of contingency was involved at every stage of its rise to power. Nor was it a mere 'parenthesis' in Italy's history as Croce suggested in a much quoted remark, for, on the contrary, it grew out of a deep-seated structural crisis in the country's liberal institutions and was rooted in its pre-war ultra-right political culture. However, Fascism's bid to inaugurate a new era in Italian, let alone world civilization, was doomed. As a permutation of generic fascism it was bound to be no more than a parenthesis in the unfolding of modern history, Mussolini or no Mussolini.

References

For those unfamiliar with the course of Italian Fascism, useful overviews are offered by Cassels (1969) and the relevant chapters in Seton Watson (1967), Mack Smith (1981), Clark (1984). More detailed reconstructions are offered by Lyttleton (1973a) and Tannenbaum (1972).

Adamson, W.L., 1989. Fascism and culture: avant-gardes and secular religion in the Italian Case, *Journal of Contemporary History*, Vol.24.
Annitrenta, 1982., Nuove Edizioni Gabriele Mazzotta, Milan.
Banchelli, F., 1922. *Memorie di un fascista*, Edizioni della VAM, Florence.
Barnes, J.S., 1928. *The Universal Aspects of Fascism*, Williams and Norgate, London.
Cannistraro, P.V., 1972. Mussolini's cultural revolution: fascist or nationalist?, *Journal of Contemporary History*, Vol.7, Nos.3–4.
Cannistraro, P.V. (ed.), 1982. *A Historical Dictionary of Fascism*, Greenwood Press, Westport, Connecticut.
Cassels, A., 1969. *Fascist Italy*, Routledge & Kegan Paul, London.
Clark, M., 1984. *Modern Italy 1871–1982*, Longman, London and New York.
Cofrancesco, D., 1980. Appunti per un'analisi del mito romano nell'ideologia fascista, *Storia Contemporanea*, Vol.11, No.3.
De Felice, R., 1961. *Storia degli ebrei italiani sotto il fascismo*, Einaudi, Turin.
De Felice, R., 1965. *Mussolini. Il rivoluzionario*, Einaudi, Turin.
De Felice, R., 1978. *D'Annunzio politico 1918–1938*, Laterza, Bari.
De Felice, R., 1982. Fascism, in P.V. Cannistraro (ed.), *A Historical Dictionary of Fascism*, Greenwood Press, Westport, Connecticut.
De Grand, A., 1976. Women under fascism, *The Historical Journal*, Vol.19, No.4.
De Grand, A.J., 1971. The Italian Nationalist Association in the period of Italian neutrality. August 1914–May 1915, *Journal of Modern History*, Vol.33, No.3.
De Grand, A.J., 1972. Curzio Malaparte: The Illusion of the Fascist revolution, *Journal of Contemporary History*, Vol.7, Nos.1–2.
De Grand, A.J., 1978. *The Italian Nationalist Association and the Rise of Fascism in Italy*, University of Nebraska Press, London.
Farinacci, R., 1934. *Squadrismo*, Edizioni Ardita, Rome.
Farinacci, R., 1937. *Storia della rivoluzione fascista*, Cremona Nuova, Cremona.
Gentile, E., 1972. *La Voce e l'età giolittiana*, Einaudi, Milan.
Gentile, E., 1975. *Le origini dell'ideologia fascista*, Laterza, Bari.
Gentile, E., 1982. *Il mito dello stato nuovo*, Laterza, Bari.
Gentile, E., 1984. The problem of the party in Italian Fascism, *Journal of Contemporary History*, Vol.19, No.2.

Gregor, A.J., 1969. *The Ideology of Fascism: The Rationale of Totalitarianism*, Free Press, New York.

Gregor, A.J., 1979. *The Young Mussolini and the Intellectual Origins of Fascism*, University of California Press, Berkeley.

Griffin, R.D., 1985. Revolts against the modern world: the blend of literary and historical fantasy in the Italian New Right, *Literature and History*, Vol.11, No.1.

Hibbert, C., 1975. *Benito Mussolini*, Penguin, London.

Hughes, H.S., 1958. *Consciousness and Society*, MacGibbon & Kee Ltd., London.

Hughes, R., 1980. *The Shock of the New*, BBC Books, London.

Joll, J., 1965. F.T. Marinetti: futurism and fascism, in *Three Intellectuals in Politics*, Pantheon Books, New York.

Kelikan, A.A., 1986. *Town and Country under Fascism*, Oxford University Press, Oxford.

Kirkpatrick, I., 1964. *Mussolini: Study of a Demagogue*, Odhams, London.

Labriola, A., 1910. *Storia di dieci anni: 1899–1909*, Casa Editrice *Il viandante*, Milan.

Lanzillo, A., 1918. *La disfatta del socialismo: Critica della guerra e del socialismo*, Libreria della Voce, Florence.

Lazzari, G., 1984. Linguaggio, ideologia, politica culturale del fascismo, *Movimento Operaio e Socialista*, Vol.7, No.1.

Ledeen, M.A., 1971. Fascism and the generation gap, *European Studies Review Quarterly*, Vol.1, No.3.

Ledeen, M.A., 1972. *Universal Fascism*, Howard Fertig, New York.

Ledeen, M.A., 1977. *The First Duce: D'Annunzio at Fiume*, John Hopkins University Press, Baltimore.

Levi, C., 1959. *Christ Stopped at Eboli*, translated by Frances Frenaye, Landsborough Publications, London.

Lyttleton, A., 1966. Fascism in Italy: the second wave, *Journal of Contemporary History*, Vol.1, No.1.

Lyttleton, A., 1973a. *The Seizure of Power: Fascism in Italy 1919–1929*, Charles Scribner's Sons, New York.

Lyttleton, A. (ed.), 1973b. *Italian Fascisms from Pareto to Gentile*, Jonathan Cape, London.

Mack Smith, D., 1968. *The Making of Italy. 1796–1870*, Macmillan, London.

Mack Smith, D., 1981. *Mussolini*, Weidenfeld & Nicolson, London.

Marchesini, D., 1976. *La scuola dei gerarchi*, Feltrinelli, Milan.

Melograni, P., 1976. The cult of the Duce in Mussolini's Italy, *Journal of Contemporary History*, Vol.11, No.4.

Michaelis, M., 1978. *Mussolini and the Jews*, Clarendon Press, Oxford.

Mosse, G.L., 1980. The poet and the exercise of political power: Gabriele D'Annunzio in G.L. Mosse (ed.) *Masses and Man*, Howard Fertig, New York.

Mosse, G.L., 1986. Two world wars and the myth of the war experience, *Journal of Contemporary History*, Vol.21, No.4.

Mosse, G.L., 1990. The political culture of Italian futurism: a general perspective, *Journal of Contemporary History*, Vol.25, Nos 2–3.

Ó Maoláin, C., 1987. *The Radical Right: A World Directory*, Longman, London.

Papini, G., 1963. *Politica e civiltà*, Vol. 8 of *Tutte le operei*, Arnaldo Mondadori, Milan.

Piazzesi, M., 1980. *Diario di uno squadrista toscano 1919–22* (ed. M. Toscana), Bonnaci, Rome.

Pollard, J., 1986. *The Vatican and Italian Fascism, 1929–32*, Cambridge University Press, Cambridge.

Prezzolini, G., 1904. Le due Italie, *Il Regno*, 22 May.

Roberts, D.D., 1979. *The Syndicalist Tradition in Italian Fascism*, Manchester University Press, Manchester.

Robertson, E.M., 1988. Race as a factor in Mussolini's policy in Africa and Europe, *Journal of Contemporary History*, Vol.23, No.1.

Sarti, R., 1970. Fascist modernization in Italy: traditional or revolutionary?, *American Historical Review*, Vol.75, No.4.

Sbacchi, A., 1989. *Ethiopia under Mussolini*, Zed Books, London and New York.

Seton Watson, C.I.W., 1967. *Italy from Liberalism to Fascism*, Methuen, London.

Settembrini, D., 1976. Mussolini and the legacy of revolutionary socialism, *Journal of Contemporary History*, Vol.11, No.4.

Simonini, A., 1978. *Il linguaggio di Mussolini*, Bompiani, Milan.

Steer, G.L., 1936. *Caesar in Abyssinia*, Hodder & Stoughton, London.

Sternhell, Z., 1987. Fascism, in D. Miller (ed.), *The Blackwell Encyclopedia of Political Thought*, Basil Blackwell, Oxford.

Stromberg, R.N., 1982. *Redemption by War*, The Regents Press of Kansas, Lawrence.

Tannenbaum, E.R., 1969. The goals of Italian Fascism, *The American Historical Review*, Vol.74, No.4.

Tannenbaum, E.R., 1972. *The Fascist Experience: Italian Society and Culture 1922–1945*, Basic Books, New York.

Valeri, N., 1963. *D'Annunzio davanti al fascismo*, Le Monnier, Florence.

Wanrooij, B., 1987. The rise and fall of Italian Fascism as generational revolt, *Journal of Contemporary History*, Vol.22, No.3.

Woolf, S.J., 1965. Risorgimento e fascismo: il senso della continuità nella storiografia italiana, *Belfagor*, Vol.20.

Zunino, P.G., 1985. *L'ideologia del fascismo*, Il Mulino, Bologna.

4 German Fascism

Proto-fascism in Germany

If Italy's proto-fascism could be pictured as a few rivulets or trickles of ultra-nationalist sentiment whose confluence was only made possible by the interventionist crisis, then Germany's evokes a meandering network of tributaries which had still to find a common channel by the time the First World War broke out. The catalyst for both countries' *risorgimento* or 'national awakening' had been the Napoleonic Wars, but whereas the visions of a regenerated post-liberal Italy being promoted by the ANI before the interventionist crisis were atypical of Italian society as a whole, German equivalents of this 'integral' (Alter, 1989) or 'radical' (Eley, 1980) nationalism had been proliferating throughout the century and making deep inroads into the country's intellectual and political culture. Fostered by the complex factors which had caused Germany to exist as a *Kulturnation* long before 'belatedly' becoming a *Staatsnation*, its numerous ideologues sought to persuade Germans to see themselves as something far more significant than mere citizens of the juridic nation-state or partners in the contractual 'civil society' on which liberal theorists set their sights. Their true destiny was to reconstitute themselves as members of the organic, national/racial community (*Volksgemeinschaft*) which had supposedly existed before the waning of the cultural forces sustaining it.

By the late nineteenth century many educated Germans both inside and outside the Second Reich were familiar with the idea that they were heirs to a past and a destiny as a homogeneous culture which set them apart from the superficial 'civilization' of established Western nations (in particular France, Britain and America). The diffusion of such assumptions fostered the glorification of patriotic history, national heroes and powerful leaders, providing a fertile soil for various brands of statism, militarism, imperialism and xenophobia. The word '*Volk*', and especially its adjectival form *völkisch*, thus became endowed with untranslatable connotations of racial solidarity and collective mission. In its radical forms, moreover, *völkisch* thought implied that the nation was endowed with a mysterious essence which could be sapped by such 'decadent' forces as socialism, materialism, cosmopolitanism and internationalism, all of which came to be epitomized for some in the Jews (see Mosse, 1966, Part 1; Bracher, 1970, ch.1; Smith, 1979, ch.2).

It would be wrong-headed to assume that *völkisch* nationalism was somehow the product of a pathological cultural tradition peculiar to Germany which found its natural culmination in Nazism, as was sometimes argued in the past (for example Vermeil, 1938; Shirer, 1964). Local variants of integral and racist nationalism were making their presence felt in most European countries by the end of the century (see Rogger and Weber, 1966) and were themselves but one manifestation of a broader wave of irrationalism commonly referred to as 'the revolt against positivism' (see Hughes, 1958). The permutations of vitalism, often drawing on bastardized Nietzscheanism, and theories of natural inequality based on perversions of Darwinism and anthropology which swept *fin de siècle* Europe, may have been particularly rife in Germany and created an ideal glasshouse in which indigenous species of ultra-right elitism could thrive (see Struve, 1973). Yet, it was only a special, and in no ways 'inevitable', conjuncture of forces that enabled a number of them to be channelled into a cohesive revolutionary movement under Hitler.

Several other facts warn against seeing *völkisch* nationalism as a direct precursor of Nazism. Firstly it lacked the ideological, structural or tactical cohesion of a political grouping such as the Italian Futurists, let alone the post-war *Fascisti*, and was a 'movement' more in the sense that reformist socialism or political anti-Semitism was: a diffuse current with many nuclei of associated organizations and publications. There could thus be no direct continuity between it and a relatively well-co-ordinated political organization such as Hitler's National Socialists. Second, even as a diffuse political sub-culture, it could never become a dominant force in the Second Reich. By the 1890s, liberalism, albeit of a variety adulterated by extreme patriotism and elitism, was well established as a rival to radical nationalism within the German *Mittelstand* ('middle class' but with specific connotations), while outside them conservatism and social democracy had formed powerful political constituencies of their own in the upper and working classes respectively (Eley, 1980). In addition, the prevalence of conservative and nationalist interests over liberal and socialist ones in the government of a Reich successfully pursuing expansionist industrial and imperialist policies, meant that *völkisch* nationalism could be extensively accommodated as a fractious lobby of radical right-wing opinion, so that its various currents were both marginalized and defused as revolutionary forces. Finally, the ideologues of *völkisch* nationalism, like many of the socialists dubbed 'utopian' by Marxists, generally showed little interest in developing the strategies for mobilizing mass opinion, seizing power or creating a new type of state, all of which were necessary if their visions were ever to leave the drawing board or the drawing room. The rejuvenated *Volk* which lay at the centre of their speculation remained for most a nebulous abstraction.

What gives *völkisch* thought its historical importance was therefore not its cohesion as a political force but the fact that the common denominator of its many permutations was the myth of the German nation reborn in a post-liberal new order. It thus created an abundant reservoir of proto-fascist political myth which Nazism would be able to transform into full-blown fascism once the war had changed the political situation out of all recognition. The striking feature of the sub-culture it formed before 1918 was just how prolific and variegated it was, each of its permutations exhibiting an unique pattern of handwoven palingenetic myth even if belonging unmistakably to the same type of ideological cloth. For example, Richard Wagner's vision of a regenerated German people blended Nietzschean art theory with Romanticism, German paganism, anti-Semitism and the Aryan myth, and both he and his Circle tried to turn Bayreuth into the spiritual birthplace and powerhouse of the future Germanic *Volksgemeinschaft*. A similar eclecticism, but this time in art-historical and theosophical key, provided the rationale for the gospel of the reborn nation preached in Langbehn's bestselling *Rembrandt als Erzieher* (1890; see Stern, 1961). The circle of artists who formed round Stefan George (the *Georgekreis*) presented yet another permutation of the same theme, though in this case the value they attached to Germany's long tradition of initiatic societies gave their ideas a distinctive colouring. They saw themselves as the nucleus of an exclusively male order of seer–poets uniquely imbued with the primeval energies which had forged the nation's heroic pagan past and thus called upon to use their creative gifts to inaugurate a new age in her history.

Given its esoteric leanings, it is no coincidence if one of the *Georgekreis*, Schuler, played a significant role in another sphere of *völkisch* thought by feeding Austro-German circles of occultist racism with pseudo-anthro pological speculation about Aryan history. One of his more enduring achievements was to have helped establish the Swastika as an Aryan sun-symbol denoting the imminent rebirth of the *Volk* (see Pulzer, 1988). The most famous figures associated with this murky current of ultra-nationalism, however, were the Austrians Guido von List and Lanz von Liebenfels, both of whom elaborated 'alternative' world-views based on a phantasmagorical mish-mash of theosophical, racial, historical and anthropological speculation. The title of Liebenfels's major work, *Theo-Zoology or the Lore of the Sodom-Apelings and the Electron of the Gods*, speaks volumes for the bizarreness of the thesis it expounds but betrays little of its central theme: the imminent regeneration of the German people through otherworldly powers once they have thrown off the literally sub-human influence of feminists, socialists, homosexuals and Jews (see Goodrick-Clarke, 1985).

Aesthetic and occultist theories of the reborn nation form only two idioms of *völkisch* discourse. They included schemes by Dinter (see Hartung, 1990), Diedrichs, and Lagarde (see Stern, 1961) for grafting radical nationalism on to a highly edited (per)version of Christianity so as to produce a rejuvenating 'Germanic religion'; wide-ranging attempts to stimulate a pagan Renaissance (for example Dahn, Burte, Blunck; see Mosse, 1966, ch.4), as well as a growing torrent of cultural, anthropological or biological speculation about the Germans' unique mission as the purest heirs of an Aryan ancestry (see Poliakov, 1974). The chief vulgarizers of this school of thought were a number of self-appointed racial experts such as Houston Chamberlain, Woltmann and Schemann (see Pulzer, 1988) who found elaborate ways to rationalize, not only the innate superiority of the Germans, but, as a corollary, the portrayal of the Jews as an 'anti-race'. Other important contributions to integral nationalism in Wilhelmine Germany were made by academics in the fields of economics (for example Sombart), geo-politics (for example Haushofer) and educational reform (for example Lietz). Even the distinguished historian and former liberal Treitschke produced a history of modern Germany which corroborated many themes of integral nationalism, including its anti-Semitism.

It should be stressed that there was little consensus among such ideologues in detail. Their world-views ran the full gamut from mysticism and occultism to secularism and scientism, from thorough-going ruralism to dreams of Germany's cities and industrial economy regenerated on racial lines, as when Fritsch, a prolific source of anti-Semitic propaganda, also contributed to a European current of utopian town planning theory with a work on the Garden City. Nor was there any consensus on the 'Jewish question'. According to how it was framed, solutions to it ranged from progressive assimilation of Jews to the systematic eradication of their commercial or cultural influence, though this was rarely couched in biological, let alone genocidal terms. The only denominator common to all was the myth of national rebirth, or as a foremost expert on the subject put it, the belief 'in an inner spiritual revival which would bring about the true flowering of the German *Volk*' (Mosse, 1966, p.7). This flowering was no mere restoration of an idealized pagan or medieval Golden Age but the completion of German unification. In this respect, what Mosse says of Diedrichs applies to the whole movement: his neo-romantic rejection of modern society 'did not mean a return to the past, a peasant utopia', for he assumed that 'the adoption of an irrational, emotional and mystical world-view by each individual German would automatically produce . . . a *new* community of thought' (Mosse, 1966, p.55; my emphasis).

The *völkisch* sub-culture was not an exclusively publicistic phenomenon. Its assumptions underlay the schemes for utopian communities hatched by racial theorists such as Fritsch and Häckel, pervaded student associations such as the nation-wide *Verein Deutscher Studenten-Kyffhäuser Bund* (1881) and also infiltrated the hugely successful *Wandervogel* youth movement founded in 1901 (Laqueur, 1962). Incubators of *völkisch* ideas in a more overtly ultra-nationalist spirit were provided by some of the social and political 'leagues' whose proliferation after 1870 (they soon numbered tens of thousands with a combined membership of millions) was so symptomatic of the social and political tensions left unresolved by the official channels for the aggregation of public opinion created by the Bismarckian state. The Agrarian League, The National Union of Commercial Employees, The School Association, The Colonial Society, The Language Association, The Society for the Eastern Marches and The Navy League all contained radical factions which promoted a myth of the nation based on ethnicity rather than on statehood (see Eley, 1980).

Yet, instead of coalescing into a coherent force of opposition to the Reich, the political sub-culture formed by *völkisch* and other ultra-right formations remained profoundly fragmented and centrifugal. The 'Cartel of the

Productive Estates' formed to promote the common interests of the Agrarian League, the Central Association of German Industrialists and the Imperial German Middle Class League in 1913 was the closest the extra-parliamentary radical right came to forming an effective bloc, but it was an organization to whom the very idea of mobilizing mass support, resorting to physical violence against political and cultural enemies or declaring open war on the *mésalliance* of monarchism and parliamentarism bequeathed by Bismarck were anathema. The same picture emerges in the case of the contemporary formations of political anti-Semitism. Its different factions were divided over the Christian, pagan, monarchist, socialist, elitist and populist orientation of their policies and lacked both the tactics and leadership to form the nucleus of concerted extra-parliamentary opposition of the right, let alone a revolutionary mass movement. By 1912 even one of its most tireless campaigners, Fritsch, had given up any hope that it would break through into the political mainstream (Pulzer, 1988, p.283).

The overall picture that emerges is that 'proto-fascism' in pre-war Germany, far from being an irresistible force, was only the most radical element within a highly fractious political sub-culture of the right which, instead of threatening the stability of the state, merely strengthened the hegemony of the conservatives within the Second Reich. A case study which illustrates this situation is provided by the *Alldeutscher Verband*, or Pan-German League, which had a membership of over 20,000 in 1905 as well as a sister organization in Austria–Hungary. Detailed research has shown that it was only after the end of the Boer War in 1902 led to a decline in its membership that the AV's central symbol of nationalism moved from Bismarck and the emperor to the German people (Chickering, 1984, ch.11). This change in direction was signalled when the league's leadership was taken over by Class, whose major work of political analysis, *If I Were the Kaiser* (1912) reveals his profound debt to *völkisch* political theory. Class argued that if the process of dissolution wrought by socialists, Jews, liberals and foreigners continued unchecked, Germany would suffer the same fate as the Roman Empire. Salvation lay in the creation of a true *Volksgemeinschaft* under an inspired leader, but to bring this about Class looked, not to a new elite or mass mobilization, but a 'parliament in which education and virtue have the influence they deserve'. Hence, though Class envisaged a *coup d'état* as being necessary for his 'reforms' to be carried out, it was to the right-wing alliance of the Cartel that he looked to carry it out, no less a paper tiger than the patriotic leagues (see Chickering, 1984, pp.286–7).

The Pan-Germans came no closer to becoming the vanguard of revolutionary nationalism when in 1917 they formed part of the *Vaterlandspartei* (Fatherland Party) made up of Conservatives, integral nationalists and some National Liberals to counter the left-wing faction in the Reichstag which pressed for a negotiated peace. However ardent the rhetoric of the radicals within this 'national opposition' about the need to 'awaken' the whole German people from its slumber and resist the seditious attempts of the left to sabotage the war effort, they acted in practice as a lobby of radical right middle-class opinion operating from within the existing system rather than as a violent 'extra-systemic' movement of demagogic populism (see Eley, 1990). But while its presence did not destabilize the political institutions of Wilhelmine Germany, it had ensured the currency in pre-war Germany of a discourse of politics which vested legitimate power not in particular institutions but in the regenerated *Volk*. After 1914 this creed was to become widely diffused in the premature celebrations of the 'imminent' German victory as the triumph of a healthy *Kultur* over a senescent and alien *Zivilisation* (Stromberg, 1982). Events in 1918 were to give *völkisch* nationalism more radical connotations than ever.

The Aftermath of 1918: the Proliferation of Proto-fascisms

If in July 1918 the war still looked winnable to the German High Command, within a year a series of major upheavals had transformed, not just the institutional but the country's ideological structures out of all recognition. Just as General Ludendorff began to sue for peace, the outbreak of a naval mutiny and of revolutionary unrest in Berlin and Munich, ominously reminiscent of events in Russia a year before, led to the *de facto* abdication of Kaiser William II and with it the end of the Second Reich. Power was left in the hands of the social democrat Ebert, heading an alliance of majority and independent socialists. Two days later the provisional government signed the armistice demanding unconditional surrender, thus giving rise to a nationalist myth that not defeat on the battle field but the peace-mongering of traitors had cost Germany the war. However, the threat to its authority was perceived as coming not from the right but from the left. Revolutionary socialists attempted to fulfil the prophecy of the newly formed Communist Party (KPD) that the Bolshevik Revolution would spread throughout Europe. The result was a wave of Spartacist demonstrations starting in Berlin in January 1919 and culminating in the soviet-style Republic (*Räterepublik*) set up in Munich in April. To restore parliamentary rule the Socialist-led coalition government saw it necessary to rely on the support not only of conservative forces, the civil service, the judiciary and the Army but of even more hostile opponents of the Weimar State, the paramilitary squads organized as Free Corps to defend, not the Republic, but the *nation*.

It was precisely these powerful anti-socialist forces whose disaffection from the new state was bound to be exacerbated even further by the government's next major act: the signing of the Versailles Treaty. Under its terms Germany effectively gave up any aspirations to great power status in international politics. Not only did it implicitly acknowledge guilt for starting the war but agreed to massive restrictions to her military capacity, the loss of overseas colonies, the return of Alsace–Lorraine to France and the payment of reparations on a scale calculated to cripple for decades an already exhausted economy. If Italy's peace had been 'mutilated', Germany's was placed in intensive care. As a result, by the time the Republic's highly advanced democratic constitution was adopted on 31 July 1919, the new state had in the eyes of a considerable section of the public already sacrificed the precondition for any democracy to function, its credibility as an authoritative voice of the national interest.

The new Weimar Republic was therefore faced from its very inception not only with profound economic and social problems but with an even more profound crisis in its legitimacy. By the Marxist–Leninist left it was rejected as a bourgeois state created amid the death agonies of the capitalist system. By the extreme right it was identified with left-wing revolution, treacherous surrender (the *Dolchstoss* or 'stab in the back') and national humiliation, and rejected as a form of constitution foreign to German history. A sign of the times was that the Conservatives joined forces with other former members of the *Vaterlandspartei* from the Pan-German League and the Agrarian League, as well as with remnants of two pre-war anti-Semitic parties, the Christian-Socials and the *Deutschvölkische Partei*. The result was the *Deutschnationale Volkspartei* (DNVP), which signalled both the disappearance of 'East Elbian' conservatism, a mainstay of the Second Reich, as an autonomous force in German politics and, simultaneously, the formation of a bloc of integral nationalists at the centre of German politics, just as Class had dreamed might happen before 1914 (see Mosse, 1966, ch.13).

But the DNVP was not the only mouthpiece of *völkisch* politics in the new Republic. The same preconditions which created it also prompted a vigorous growth in its varied extra-political manifestations. There were new experiments in creating rural utopias (Mosse, 1966, ch.6), the youth movement took on a new vitality (Laqueur, 1962) and the pre-war patriotic groups such as student associations and the right-wing German National League of Commercial Employees (DHV) welcomed a new influx of members. In each case *völkisch* racism and a hatred of Weimar was embraced as an article of faith. The same axioms were taken up by the numerous *völkisch* groups which now began to form such as Fritsch's German Community of Renewal. Underpinning all these developments was a welter of *völkisch* publications such as Lehmann's *Deutschlands Erneuerung* (Germany's Renewal), Wulle's *Deutsches Tagblatt* and Eckhart's *Auf gut Deutsch*, promoting their own vision of the regenerated nation on pagan, Christian or eugenic lines. As a publicistic phenomenon, however, this form of ultra-nationalism was still so diverse that its major taxonomist (and one father-figure of the French New Right), Mohler (1972), has to devise no less than twenty-one sub-categories to accommodate the hundred or so writers who fuelled the *Los-von-Weimar* (Out of Weimar!) groundswell.

Though regenerated by the war, *völkisch* ideologues no longer enjoyed a monopoly of integral nationalism. They were now just one component in a cluster of ultra-right theories which are referred to variously as the 'New Right' (Schulz, 1975), the 'New Nationalism' (Sontheimer, 1968) or the 'Conservative Revolution' (Mohler, 1972). The new currents of ultra-nationalism looked nearer afield than the primordial Germans for inspiration. One group of writers saw the solution to Germany's ills, not in the restoration of the monarchy, but in the founding of a new type of dynamic authoritarian Reich to replace the republic and harness national energies. Their most influential publicist, Moeller van den Bruck (see Stern, 1961, part 3), helped give currency to the phrase 'The Third Reich' by making it the title of a book published in 1923 to offer a definitive diagnosis of the state of the nation. In it he depicted Germany's current problems as symptoms of a malaise affecting the whole of Europe, turned by materialism, Marxism and liberalism into a 'decaying world', 'too beneath contempt to be saved' (Moeller, 1923, p.245). The only remedy was for Germany to heal itself through an heroic 'reconnection forwards' (ibid., p.163) in which eternal values would be enshrined in a *new* order. Edgar Jung and Spengler (whose *Decline of the West* is erroneously associated outside Germany with morbid pessimism rather than heady nationalist optimism) offered their own versions of 'Conservative Revolution', the first invoking a German 'Christianity', the other a Caesarist (that is Prussian) 'socialism' as the key to national rebirth. Far from being inspired by 'cultural despair', all three placed their faith in a new national order in which the blend of discipline, virtue, heroism and socialism peculiar to the race would give a new lease of life to a civilization plunged into materialism, internationalism and decadence.

An even more radical departure from pre-war ultra-nationalism was 'National Bolshevism'. The writers and agitators who were associated with this paradoxical label, such as Niekisch, saw the key not only to 'the political, but the religious, spiritual and moral renewal of the German people' in a *rapprochement* with revolutionary Russia, which they saw as a national culture which had just dramatically rejuvenated itself rather than as the source of an internationalist subversive movement (Schüddekopf, 1960, p.397). Another source of assault on the Weimar Republic found its inspiration not in the primordial *Volk*, eternal truths or the rebirth of Russia, but in the war. In terms which strongly echo the 'trenchocratic creed' of the *squadristi* in contemporary Italy, the key theme of the disparate ideologues who became known as National Revolutionaries was that the *Zusammenbruch* ('collapse') of 1918 had been but one stage in the German Revolution which started in 1914 and which was leading to the creation of a new type of nation. The war had exposed the bankruptcy of the Second Reich just as much as the Weimar Republic laid bare the impotence of liberal parliamentarism. The experience at the front, the *Fronterlebnis*, however, had given birth to a new generation 'capable of breaking through to new values and to the belief in a new ordering of things' (Sontheimer, 1968, p.99; cf. Hüppauf, 1990).

A major literary genre in which this myth was expressed consisted of visionary evocations of the ecstasies of combat in the key of what was sometimes called 'soldierly nationalism' (see Prumm, 1974). Its foremost exponents were Schauwecker, Ernst von Salomon but above all Ernst Jünger. By the 1930s the front soldier, Jünger's prototype of the New Man, had been subsumed within his new ideal type, 'the Worker' in whom the modern forces of total mobilization first displayed in the First World War were creating a new technocratic aristocracy. This vision is expressed in the palingenetic imagery so characteristic of Jünger (see Herf, 1984). 'We are witnessing the spectacle of the collapse [*Untergang*] of a civilization which can only be compared to geological catastrophes . . . But the epoch of the masses and of machines represents the titanic workshop of an empire which is arising' (quoted in Mohler, 1972, p.82.) One need hardly add that the empire envisaged by Jünger was destined to be quintessentially *German* in the best Prussian tradition.

No matter how utopian or 'metapolitical' such interpretations of contemporary history may seem today, they offered elaborate rationalizations for rejecting the Weimar system lock, stock and barrel which captured the mood of wide sectors of the inter-war intelligentsia. Circles sprang up to disseminate their ideas such as the *Juniklub* round Moeller, the *Widerstandsbewegung* (Resistance Movement) round Niekisch and the *Tatkreis* round Zehrer, another national revolutionary with 'Bolshevik' leanings (see Struve, 1973), while Jung had a direct influence on von Papen, who was to show such open contempt for democratic principles after he became chancellor in 1932. The sentiments and arguments of national revolutionary chauvinism also had an impact on the radical demands formulated by the leaders of the wave of peasant unrest in 1928 known as the *Landvolkbewegung* (see Mohler, 1972) and were taken up by the veteran and vigilante paramilitary leagues (*Kampfbünde*) which mushroomed in the early years of the Republic to perpetuate both the spirit of the trenches and the militant anti-communism of the Free Corps which had helped crush the left-wing unrest of 1919. Over seventy such leagues sprang up all over Germany within months of the armistice, the largest and most durable being the *Stahlhelm*. The countless newspapers and leaflets produced by formations such as *Wiking*, *Werwolf* and the *Jungdeutscher Orden* preached hostility to the Weimar Republic in unmistakably palingenetic terms. A leader in *Der Stahlhelm*, for example, reassures the reader that the league 'fights for the German Volk and therefore for the renewal of the Germanic race; it fights to strengthen German self-consciousness so that foreign racial influences will be eliminated from the nation' (quoted in Mosse, 1966, p.255).

It is this sense that Germany's decadence and decline was about to give way to an age of rebirth and rejuvenation which provides the common denominator of the heterogeneous currents of the 'new nationalism'. This is recognized by Sontheimer, who identifies its hallmark as 'a great turning point in history which is putting an end to the age of the liberal nation state and will lead to a new era with new values, new human beings and a new type of politics with new institutions' (Sontheimer, 1968, p.199). Mohler, too, dwells on the palingenetic component of the 'Conservative Revolution', seeing its central thrust as 'an attitude which calls into question everything which has already been achieved and constantly longs for a rebirth to take place out of annihilation', an attitude which he approvingly dubs 'German nihilism' (Mohler, 1972, p.38). He claims that the effect of the First World War was to impress on integral nationalists the 'conception of a turning point: one age was being replaced by another' (ibid. p.35), thus intensifying the 'hope of a rebirth [*Neugeburt*, or literally 'new birth', the exact German equivalent of 'palingenesis'] on the other side of destruction' (ibid., p.95).

Yet despite the visionary tone of its rhetoric, all the forms of the 'new nationalism' we have considered were either an exclusively publicistic phenomenon or were taken up by pressure groups campaigning on behalf of special sectors of society such as students, commercial employers, veterans or peasants. An inveterate utopianism and an in-built elitism made them stop short of waging a war on Weimar even if they repeatedly declared it. This explains the ultimate impotence of even the most important organization set up to aggregate ultra-nationalist resentment of Weimar nation-wide, the German *Völkisch* Defensive and Offensive League (DVSuTB), which could boast 160,000 members before it was outlawed in the summer of 1922 (see Lohalm, 1970). Though it was rhetorically committed to the vision of a regenerated *Volksgemeinschaft*, Eley stresses that the DVSuTB's conception of a populist revolutionary movement was 'an *authoritarian* as opposed to a *participant* one', so that 'rather than agitating the [masses] directly, they preferred a combined strategy of working for influence in high places and mobilizing the masses at one remove' (Eley, 1990, p.63). This observation holds for nearly all formations of the inter-war integral right. The one exception was not only going to prove the rule but to change all the rules.

The Rise of German Fascism

In February 1920, a meeting was held in Munich's Hofbräuhaus beer hall of an obscure organization pursuing vague racist, nationalist and anti-capitalist goals, the 'German Workers' Party' (DAP). The packed audience learnt from the main speaker, a recent recruit to the party called Adolf Hitler, that it had added 'National Socialist' to its official title and that the NSDAP would henceforth be committed to a twenty-five-point programme. Though its relaunch had been well-staged, there was little to distinguish the party's goals from those of any number of chauvinist and *völkisch* groups then active in Germany, a point not lost on some elements within the DVSuTB at the time. The need for all Germans to be united in a militarily strong *Volksgemeinschaft* to end the humiliation inflicted on them by hostile foreign powers and 'the November traitors' (socialists and Jews) broadly summarized the common ground of all integral nationalists since the *Zusammenbruch* of 1918, and even the attacks on usury and capitalism in the name of a 'German socialism' was an idea mooted by some pre-war radical nationalists. Knowledge that several of the leading members of the DAP, Harrer, Feder and Eckhart, had been associated with an esoteric racist society, the *Thulegesellschaft* (Thule Society), would only have confirmed expectations that, despite the extravagant claims and promises made that evening, the NSDAP was doomed to be as ineffectual as any of the other formations of the far, not to say 'lunatic', right which were mushrooming throughout Germany. What made this party different was that its rising star, Hitler, had no illusions about the chasm which separated wishful thinking from reality. As he wrote in an internal memorandum two years later, 'an idea is of no value, as long as the wish does not turn into action, but eternally remains a wish' (quoted Broszat, in 1960, p.43): his driving ambition was to use the NSDAP to transform *völkisch* utopianism into a 'political power'.

It is this determination that marked Hitler out temperamentally as a fascist rather than a proto-fascist and ensured that the movement and regime he created would be in his own image.

By August 1921 Hitler had become party chairman and began to exercize total control over its policies and tactics. These concentrated not on winning elections, but on following a 'putschist' path to power by making the NSDAP a cadre party with a strong internal organization, propaganda machine and paramilitary wing. In practice this meant strengthening the party's hierarchical command structure, absorbing where possible other radical right groups, such as the German Socialists, tightening his control over the Austrian National Socialists, turning the former *Thulegesellschaft* newspaper, the *Völkischer Beobachter*, into an effective party newspaper and recruiting anti-Marxist veterans and would-be soldiers so as to build up the strength of the party's paramilitary arm, the *Sturmabteilung* (SA). Significantly, though much impressed by the success of Mussolini's March on Rome the year before, he did not yet see himself as *Führer*, but rather as the 'drummer' of the 'national revolution' which the socio-political tensions unleashed by the Ruhr crisis and hyperinflation of 1923 seemed to make imminent (Tyrell, 1975). This putschist strategy proved a major miscalculation on Hitler's part, leading to the spectacular flop of the attempted military coup of 9 November, his imprisonment in the Landsberg fortress prison and the outlawing of his party in southern Germany (it had been banned elsewhere the year before), whereupon its membership splintered into a number of minute parties and factions. The degree of the party's disarray which resulted can be measured by the readiness of the Rosenberg/ Gregor Strasser wing of the newly formed Greater German Peoples' Community (GDVP) to enter a tactical alliance with elements of a rival formation, the German *Völkisch* Freedom Party (DVFP) led by Wulle and von Graefe to form the *Völkisch*-Social-Block (VSB) to fight the May 1924 Reichstag elections. But with or without Hitler's extraordinary organizational and demagogic powers, the ultra-right was becoming increasingly marginalized. Ebert's democratic application of the presidential emergency powers to preserve liberal institutions rather than undermine them, coupled with the refusal of the army under Seeckt to back the national opposition had allowed the Republic to ride out the immediate crisis and inaugurated a period of relative economic and political stability in which ultra-nationalism had no chance of breaking through as a mass movement. In the elections the Block polled a mere 6.6 per cent, which was still twice as much as was won by yet another party which grew out of the alliance, the *Völkisch* Social Freedom Party, seven months later. However, this was to prove to be no more than a lull before the hurricane.

The publication of the first volume of *Mein Kampf* in 1925 was not only a testimony to the privileges Hitler enjoyed while in the Landsberg jail but to his need to reassess his overall strategy. He now set about becoming the undisputed leader of a type of opposition force unprecedented in history. It was to be made up of three integrated components: a disciplined but openly terroristic private army indispensible for the 'seizure of power' and the maintenance of order once it had been achieved; a 'shadow state' ready to take over the various functions of government immediately the Republic had fallen; and a mass political and social movement, not only providing the electoral strength essential for the constitutional assault on government but the basis for a substantial public consensus for the new order once it had been formally created (Bracher, 1970, p.169–83). By building up the NSDAP as a paramilitary and 'para-state' vanguard party with a nation-wide base in as many social strata as possible, Hitler dreamt of placing himself in a unique position to carry out the *Machtergreifung* (seizure of power) by a combination of electoral success, the surgical deployment of violence and political manoeuvring.

On his release from prison Hitler characteristically set about putting his plan into practice with enormous energy and single-mindedness. He skilfully resolved the internal wrangles and leadership struggles which had riven his movement since its outlawing by reestablishing his own absolute authority over former party hierarchs (Orlow, 1967) and duly refounded the NSDAP in February 1925. Temperamentally lacking the capacity for methodical planning, he relied heavily on Gregor Strasser to carry through the next stage, the transformation of the party into a nation-wide mass movement. What slowly emerged was a highly centralized hierarchical and cellular structure, on which Hitler personally imposed strict internal discipline to prevent rival factions emerging which might challenge his position. By the late 1920s the 'new' NSDAP had started to become an embryonic 'state within a state', with specialized departments developing Nationalist Socialist policies on major social and political issues and a number of 'para-state' organizations formed through the affiliation to the party of various organizations representing particular sectors in society (for example students, school pupils, teachers, law officials, doctors, women), most of which had already been softened up for Nazism by the influence of *völkisch* thought. Meanwhile the SA was built up as a highly trained armed wing strictly subordinated to Hitler and independent of other paramilitary groups. At the same time Hitler carried out to the letter the excursi in *Mein Kampf* concerning the techniques of mass manipulation which, apart from being the most original sections of the book, reveal in true fascist manner just how elitist was his concept of populist politics. In 1928 a school was set up in Bavaria to train NSDAP members in public speaking and in 1930 the propaganda machine was given a powerful new engine by the appointment of Joseph Goebbels as head of propaganda. Even before this the party had established its unmistakable 'style', designed to maintain a high public profile irrespective of its real electoral strength. Well co-ordinated poster and leaflet campaigns, the invention of political rituals, and the holding of mass rallies were carefully designed not merely to impress Nazi slogans on the general public but to generate the cumulative sense that a vast movement was afoot heralding a new era in Germany's history.

To give his movement a nation-wide base Hitler entrusted Gregor Strasser with increasing party membership in the north while he concentrated on the south. The energetic recruitment campaigns orchestrated by both men soon bore fruit in a quadrupling of the 1925 membership figure to 100,000 within three years. Yet this did nothing to halt its decline as a party-political force, a fate it shared with all extremist parties in the new conditions of stability. In the May elections of 1928 it managed to poll only 2.6 per cent of the vote. It was the renewed structural crisis unleashed on German society by the world depression, which caused unemployment to rise to an average figure of 5,600,000 in 1932, that was the necessary condition for Nazism to be transformed into a genuine mass movement. It not only triggered off a major crisis in the agricultural sector but, occurring in a country where liberalism as a socio-cultural force had failed to put down healthy roots, immediately generated powerful centripetal political forces just at a time when incumbents of the presidency were predisposed by their ultra-conservative sentiments to suspend the democratic process in order to solve the problems assailing it. As the economic and constitutional crisis bit deeper, the spectres of total anarchy or a Bolshevik take-over loomed ever larger for increasing numbers of Germans disaffected with the 'system' and inclined by over a decade of propaganda against it to have ultra-nationalist convictions. The *Los-von-Weimar* movement had prepared the ground well, and the NSDAP's growth was spectacular, peaking in July 1932 with 37.3 per cent of the vote. In the event, however, it was not to be electoral success, a paramilitary '*Machtergreifung*' or sheer 'people power' which won the day for Nazism. A series of crucial personal decisions taken between 1930 and 1933 by Brüning, Hugenberg, von Papen, von Schleicher and Hindenburg effectively replaced parliamentary government by presidential dictatorship and thus lowered the drawbridge to invite Hitler's group to enter 'legally' into the citadel of state power. These men were apparently deceived by the same illusion that Hitler could be 'tamed' which lured many arch-conservatives into a tactical alliance with Nazism in order to ward off the perceived twin threat of Marxist revolution or total anarchy (see Noakes, 1990). It is one of the more tragic pieces of irony in history that he was let in just when there were signs that the tide of grass roots support for Nazism was starting to ebb. However, Hitler would never have been in the position to demand the chancellorship had his party not become firmly identified both with a message of radical change and the only vehicle by which it stood a chance of being implemented.

The message, spelt out turgidly in *Mein Kampf* (which had nevertheless sold some 300,000 copies *before* its author became the German Chancellor), and implicit in the thousands of articles and speeches by Nazi faithful great and small thereafter, was a cluster of interlocking themes current in radical right circles ever since the war: the *Zusammenbruch* of 1918 as the work not only of treacherous socialists, but especially of the Jews, who had set in train a process of national decadence which long predated 1918; the need for racial regeneration at a biological, spiritual and political level which would enable Germany to rescind the terms of the Versailles Treaty, eliminate the Jewish-Bolshevik assault on the nation, rearm, create a Greater Germany by uniting all ethnic Germans into a single homeland, and proceed to conquer 'vital space' in the East. The mission of the NSDAP would be to make this possible by replacing the Weimar Republic with the Third Reich, which unlike the previous two, would be based not just on the leadership principle but on the primacy of the *Volk*, in other words the *Volksgemeinschaft*. Like a Rorschach test of integral nation-alist convictions, this programme invited all those of ultra-right leanings to project their own visions and aspirations on to the 'Hitler-movement'. While some prominent spokesmen for different currents of ultra-nationalism stayed aloof, (for example Jünger, Jung, Fritsch, Spengler), many more succumbed even before 1933. For them the practical impli-cations or coherence of specific policies faded into insignificance behind the overriding sense that Germany was rising from the ashes, that a national rebirth was taking place. As Sontheimer puts it:

> Because the longing for this new reality and its concrete realization burnt so intensely in their hearts, in their struggle with their own conscience most of them gave in to the temptation to side with the National Socialist mass movement from the moment they saw that it offered the only way of eventu-ally reaching a new Germany. (1968, p.288)

Thus countless publicists and organizations infected with *völkisch* racism could savour the virulent anti-Semitism and the racial philosophy of history which underpinned it. Conservative Revolutionaries could be heartened by the prospect of a Third Reich in which authority and hierarchy would prevail once more in a new order. National Revolutionaries could endorse the interpretation of the war as the beginning of a national resurgence pioneered by that new breed of men, the 'front-soldiers'. National Bolsheviks could seize on the attacks on the capitalist ethos as an alien, that is Jewish, force and the need for a German socialism. After 1928 the programme was deliberately modified to appeal to the new constituency formed by the militant farmers of the *Landvolkbewegung*. Within two years the party had recruited Walter Darré, the most important ideologue of anti-urbanism and enforced re-ruralization, to flesh out Nazi policies for making the *Nährstand* (the food-producers estate) the mainstay of the new Germany and the peasantry the nucleus of a new aristocracy of 'blood and soil'. With its *passe-partout* programme for an imminent German rebirth, Nazism thus established itself as an ecumenical movement of the diffuse and fragmented *Los-von-Weimar* movement.

What enabled the NSDAP to eclipse all other ultra-right formations after 1925, however, was not just the ideological appeal of its policies to ultra-right activists and intellectuals who, after all, represented a small percentage of the population. Far more important in the long run was its impact on the increasing number of 'ordinary' Germans who became convinced that Nazism really was *different*, that it could break the mould of the Weimar 'system', that the NSDAP was the nucleus of a national revolution which was already under way, no matter how many seats it held in the despised Reichstag. For those who came under its spell, the Hitler movement alchem-ically transformed a generalized despair at the present order of society, a sense of being a foreigner in one's own country, into hope for the future, a sense of belonging. This, rather than anti-Semitism or middle-class reaction as such accounts for the steady build-up of the party and the SA before 1928, despite the pathetic showing at the ballot box. The ethos of paramilitary discipline and hierarchy, the omnipresence of the SA, the demagogic techniques used by the speakers, the carefully timed emotional crescendo leading up to the climax of Hitler's appearance on the podium, the theatrical effects produced by lighting effects and banners deliberately transformed the superbly organized mass meetings, rallies and congresses into initiatic rites for those who longed for Germany's rebirth.

It was when the depression started biting deep into German society that the NSDAP finally began to harvest the rich crop of mythic energies which countless publicists and activists of integral nationalism had been sowing since the late nineteenth century. A guru of the Conservative Revolutionaries, Edgar Jung was prompted to observe ruefully that 'the spiritual preconditions for the German revolution were created *outside* National Socialism' and that thinkers like himself had carried out the 'meticulous preparatory work' which provided each Nazi candidate with his votes (quoted in Sontheimer, 1968, p.288). Though convinced Catholics, socialists and Communists generally, and Jews universally, were inoculated against the fascination of the brave new world Nazism was promising, those who did succumb were not just former DNVP voters or frightened bourgeois, but came from a wide spectrum of social milieux and walks of life. This explains the profound heterogeneity of the party's social base after its 1929 'take-off' (Mühlberger, 1987; 1991). That about one-third of the NSDAP's 850,000 members were classified in the *Partei-Statistik* of 1935 as workers does not reflect the desire of a middle-class movement (*Mittelstandsbewegung*) to have the public image of a mass movement (*Massenbewegung*), as generations of Marxist scholars have tried to make out, but the fact that it exerted a genuine trans-class and trans-generational appeal.

Against the background of the sustained crisis of confidence in liberal democracy unleashed by economic collapse, the new converts were lured by the cumulative effect of Nazism's demagogic, paramilitary and terroristic style of campaigning. For millions who after 1929 despaired of the 'old' system and rejected the communist alternative, it generated a powerful subjective impression that the Germans were being transformed before their eyes from a degenerate and anarchic mass to a majestically co-ordinated new nation. This was the subliminal message of the numerous ceremonies and special days invented by the party, one of which even turned the failed putsch of 9 November 1923 into a Nazi holy day (see Vondung, 1971, 1979). In the carefully contrived climate of hysteria whipped up by party meetings and congresses, the slogan 'Germany awake', the omnipresent Swastika with its connotations of mystic regeneration and the appearance of Hitler as the embodiment of a new order could symbolize the hopes and certainties which the Weimar state could no longer provide.

It was not only the public who fell for the palingenetic message of Nazism, however. An examination of the NSDAP leadership before 1933 illustrates vividly that the power of Nazism to weld disparate currents of proto-fascism into fascism was just as crucial in attracting its top 'hierarchs' as its lesser luminaries. They represent *völkisch* theories on law (for example Frank), Germanic Christianity (Dinter, until he was ousted in 1927 for peddling a rival brand of Nazism), radical agrarianism (Darré), imperialist geopolitics (Hess), National Bolshevism (Feder, the Strasser brothers), the 'national revolutionary' fervour of war veterans (Röhm, von Salomon, Goering and, until 1925, Ludendorff) and various dialects of racial history and anti-Semitism: cultural (Rosenberg), conspiratorial (Streicher), genetic (Günther) and occultist (Himmler). Several can be shown to have developed personal permutations of ultra-nationalism of their own before the rise of Hitler (see, for example, Bramwell, 1985, on Darré and the 'ruralist' pole of *völkisch* thinking; Lutzhöft, 1971, on Günther and the *völkisch* current called 'nordic thought'; Stachura, 1983, on Gregor Strasser and the anti-capitalist strand of Nazism), a private palingenetic vision which they then had no qualms about translating into the discourse of Nazi ideology once they allowed their energies to be harnessed to its cause.

A case study in this pattern is provided by Goebbels. However opportunistically he carried out his crucial services to the movement and regime as head of propaganda, the study of a novel he wrote before joining the NSDAP, *Michael. A German Destiny* (first published in 1929) points to a profound continuity between the desperate hopes for national rebirth which he was nurturing before Hitler came on the scene and the speeches he made later as Reich Minister of Public Enlightenment and Propaganda. Goebbels' *alter ego* Michael is a listless student in Munich who feels assailed by the ubiquitous symptoms of social pathology he sees around him. The targets of his diatribes include intellect, the press, internationalism, money, cosmopolitanism, relativism, Marxism, Bohemianism, parliament and pacifism, all embodied in the Jew: 'we are all sick! Only a battle against this putrefaction can save us at all' (Goebbels, 1931, p.76). Yet this is no 'cultural pessimism', but the prelude to 'German nihilism'. Michael comes to see himself as embodying the vitality of a new class of (German) workers produced by the last creative act of a dying bourgeoisie. Their task is to revolt against the present corrupt order for 'if things are to be made anew then it is first necessary to destroy' (ibid., p.98). It is not by chance that in 1933, newly installed as Reich Minister for Public Enlightenment and Propaganda, Goebbels presented the burning of 'un-German literature' as an act which consigned the depraved spirit (*Ungeist*) of the past to the flames and razed to the ground 'the spiritual foundations of the November Republic'. Far from being wanton destruction, though, this was but the prelude to the regeneration of Germany, for 'out of the rubble the phoenix of a new spirit will rise up' (Wulf, 1963, p.46; palingenetic motifs also recur throughout the 1934 collection of Goebbels' speeches *Signs of the New Age*).

There is every indication that Hitler's psychological 'elective affinity' with the movement he had done so much to create fits this pattern. The ruthlessness with which he dismantled the liberal foundations of the Weimar Republic, orchestrated an escalating campaign of anti-Semitism or liquidated a number of rivals in the Night of the Long Knives is only one side of the picture. The other is his passionate commitment to a programme of national unification, reconstruction and expansion which, after the failed putsch of 1923, he became convinced that only he could implement. This in turn is the expression of an underlying palingenetic myth of history in which he seems genuinely to have believed. One of his many biographers,

Fest, senses this when he writes that what underpinned Hitler's obsession with the need for vital space and racial purity was: 'once again, the concept of a great turning point in the history of the world. A new age was beginning; history was once more setting the mighty wheel in motion and apportioning lots anew' (Fest, 1974, p.215).

Such a concept accounts for the way the dialectic of decadence and rebirth gives *Mein Kampf* any cohesion and structure it has and is the central axis of innumerable speeches. It would also throw light on several speeches which Rauschning attributes to Hitler and quotes as illustrations of the fundamental 'nihilism' of the Nazi revolution. Though unreliable as a stenographic record of what Hitler said, a passage such as the following certainly rings true, and points to a palingenetic obsession of which Rauschning himself is seemingly oblivious:

> We had come to a turning-point in world history – that was his constant theme . . . He saw himself as chosen for superhuman tasks, as the prophet of the rebirth of man in a new form. Humanity, he proclaimed, was in the throes of a vast metamorphosis . . . The coming age was revealing itself in the first great human figures of a new type . . . 'Those who see in National Socialism nothing more than a political movement know scarcely anything of it. It is even more than a religion: it is the will to create mankind anew'. (Rauschning, 1939, pp.240–2)

In other words, Hitler's boundless lust for power was inextricably bound up with his genuine commitment to the ultimate goal of founding a Greater German Reich in Europe based on the subjugation, enslavement or extermination of its subjects according to racial principles, a particularly virulent *völkisch* variant of the *Lebensraum* strand of German imperialism which had developed under the Second Reich (see Smith, 1986). The creation of this new empire would begin 'the new racial millennium over the entire globe under the ruthless domination of the Germanic Aryan elite' (Hauner, 1978, p.25; cf. Bracher, 1970, pp.504–5). He thus seems seriously to have seen himself as heralding a new phase of human civilization based on the racial–nationalist rebirth of the German people.

The Third Reich as a Fascist Regime

Armed with a radical palingenetic myth which could be translated much more readily into immediate decisions and medium-term strategies than Mussolini's, Hitler showed little of the hesitancy or aimlessness that characterized so much of the *duce*'s style of leadership. As a result, whereas Fascism remained a loose alliance of fascist, proto-fascist and conservative factions, displaying considerable ideological ambiguity and contradictions throughout its career, Nazism behaved in an altogether more single-minded and uncompromising manner.

Once Hitler had been appointed chancellor on 30 January 1933 he immediately set about destroying liberalism and eroding pluralism through the same insidious blend of sham legality, pressure and violence that he had used so masterfully to turn Weimar's post-1930 constitutional crisis to his advantage. In the political sphere the process euphemistically known as *Gleichschaltung* (co-ordination) was carried out in such a way that many potential sources of opposition 'voluntarily' dissolved themselves or even allowed themselves to be absorbed by Nazi organizations. Technically operating within the legitimacy afforded by a series of emergency decrees and the Enabling Act of 23 March 1933 (which meant that the republican constitution was never formally rescinded), all civil liberties and constitutional rights were indefinitely suspended and a series of coups and capitulations put paid to the regional autonomy of the *Länder*. The Communist and Social Democratic Parties were soon banned (March and June 1933 respectively) and within months the other political parties retired from the arena one by one. On Hindenburg's death in August 1934 the presidency was allowed to lapse so that the presidential dictatorship became a nakedly autocratic one, rationalized by convoluted juridic theories of the leader principle and by the occasional use of plebiscites. From then on, even if much of the Weimar Civil Service structure was technically left intact, in practice all crucial areas of state policy became the responsibility of Nazi 'para-state' quangos, organizations and offices, individual Nazi leaders or Hitler himself. Thus for a time the Foreign Office coexisted with the party bureau for formulating foreign policy run by Ribbentrop, while the police and judicial system, too, continued to operate, but soon found itself doing so strictly subordinated to Himmler's SS and the 'People's Courts', which together operated a system of terror institutionalized in a growing network of Gestapo (Secret State Police) headquarters and concentration camps.

The same pattern of destruction, neutralization or absorption took place in the sphere of 'extra-parliamentary' power. The socialist Free Union Movement, which had once boasted millions of members and been the mainstay of the most consistently powerful party till 1933, the SPD, was smashed and its membership forcibly absorbed into the German Labour Front (DAF) along with (less recalcitrant) members of Christian and 'yellow' (that is employers') unions. Larger entrepreneurs were left to make their own peace with the new regime on which their survival now totally depended. With a few exceptions, collaboration by the owners and managers of the industrial cartels such as IG Farben and Krupp, who had so much to gain from the transformation of Germany into a gargantuan war-machine, was enthusiastic, and was to remain so to the very end (see Hayes, 1987). The fate of the *Wehrmacht* followed a similar pattern of being infiltrated rather than summarily placed under NSDAP control. Its internal structures were not interfered with, but after 2 August 1934 each soldier took a personal oath of allegiance to Hitler and the autonomy of its high command was increasingly encroached upon by the SS. Meanwhile, for the hundreds of thousands of Germans belonging to rival currents of integral nationalism the choice was between giving up their activities or being recruited by an organization tolerated or created by the regime. Hence the Pan-Germans were disbanded in 1933 and the *Stahlhelm* absorbed by the SA, which in turn was effectively neutralized as an independent force in the Night of the Long Knives of June 1934. Similarly, all youth movements were wound up and absorbed into the *Hitlerjugend*, though the Catholic one survived till 1936 under the protection of the 1933 concordat with the state.

The concordat was just one component in the complex strategy the Nazi leadership had to adopt in order to neutralize the opposition potentially offered by both the Protestants and Catholic Churches after 1933. They succeeded in resisting attempts to found a 'National Church' on thinly veiled racist principles and in preserving the tradition of Christian worship sufficiently intact for it to become a major force in the post-war politics of both Germanies. Nevertheless, illiberal nationalism and anti-Bolshevism had been sufficiently rife among both Protestant and Catholic clergy to ensure extensive collusion or passivity in the crucial early years of the regime. Thus, while many individual priests and pastors made stands against the barbarity of the regime at great personal cost, it was only on the issue of euthanasia that the Catholic Church displayed its potential for effectively applying pressure for inhuman policies to be silently dropped from official policy.

In contrast, another potential source of dissent, the schools and universities, were Nazified with extraordinary rapidity, a process vastly facilitated by the deep inroads *völkisch* thought had already made into academic spheres before 1933. Curricula, text books, student assignments and lectures were soon applying Aryan principles to every discipline, from musicology to physics, while chairs were created in racial theory and eugenics. The training of the future SS and party cadres could not be entrusted to existing institutions, however, and special schools were created to prepare them for their duties in the front line of the German revolution (yet another symptom of the elitism of Nazi populism). The press, areas of which had been a powerful source of anti-Nazi propaganda throughout the Weimar years, called for more Draconian measures and was brought into line by buy-outs, censorship, thinly veiled coercion and the enforced Nazification of personnel. The exclusively propagandistic function it now performed was supplemented by official Nazi journals and publications, but these were just one fruit of the monopoly which the party exercized over every sphere of mass communications. This monopoly was enforced so rigorously and exploited so effectively that the parallel efforts of the Fascists seem sloppy by comparison. The creation of a Reich Cultural Chamber drove most potentially anti-Nazi artists into exile or 'inner emigration', while ensuring the enthusiastic collusion, or at least tactical collaboration, of countless writers, painters, broadcasters and film-makers.

In the Third Reich the 'co-ordination' of society through totalitarian measures was not an end in itself, as it had seemed to be for the first decade of the Fascist regime (namely till 1935 when the Ethiopian campaign started in earnest), but the prelude to an unbroken sequence of dynamic events set in train by the new state which fully merit the concept of 'permanent revolution' with all its ultimately self-defeating and unsustainable connotations. There is considerable controversy among historians about the degree to which either the escalating programme of imperial expansion or the Final Solution were the inexorable culmination of a personal blueprint for absolute power which Hitler conceived soon after the failed putsch of 1923 (the 'intention-alist' school), or resulted 'structurally' on a largely ad hoc basis from the type of militaristic and ultra-nationalist authoritarian state which the Third Reich quickly became, despite, and even because of, its internal organizatio-nal chaos. There are many nuanced positions within this debate and no shortage of empirical data or cogent theorizing to support most of them (see Kershaw, 1985, ch.6). Nevertheless, however complex the dynamics of Nazi policy-making and accidental some of its consequences, there can be no doubt that from the moment it had 'taken out', 'attritted' or 'degraded' (to use American military 'Gulfese') potential sources of opposition, the Third Reich embarked on the construction of a state terror apparatus and a military machine which had to lead to an ever-widening circle of persecution and aggression as long as Hitler was in power. Fuelled by genuine popular enthusiasm for the signs of spectacular recovery from a devastating social and economic crisis, as well as for a series of triumphs in foreign affairs which ended a prolonged period of national humiliation, the Nazi state developed a self-perpetuating revolutionary momentum. This could only have stopped of its own accord had it been prepared to abandon its claim to be a New Order and thus to degenerate into a stagnant neo-conservative regime like those of Salazar and Franco, with no genuine commitment to creating a national community. Such a tame capitulation was alien to Hitler and the leadership around him, as well as to his paramilitary troops and party faithful who supported them. It is thus pedantic, if not perverse, to argue the toss about whether Hitler personally gave a written order to sanction a particular military campaign or launch the Final Solution. The invasions, persecutions, occupations and mass executions, like the extensive use of torture, slave labour, and not least the attempted genocide of gypsies and the Jewish race, no matter how contingent the precise circumstances in which they were carried out, were all consistent with the general thrust of this vision.

The horrific human consequences of Hitler's bid to create a new Reich, unparalleled in European history, have tempted some observers to see in Nazism the expression of nihilism just as Rauschning maintained (see above p.6). Perhaps what makes Nazi brutality even more disturbing for a human-ist than wanton and therefore pathological violence is the fact that it was conceived, if not executed, in the spirit of Mohler's chilling phrase '*German nihilism*', destruction as the prelude to building anew. Seen in this perspect-ive even Auschwitz is indeed to be seen as 'the poisonous fruit of Utopia' (Geoghegan, 1987, p.4). Certainly, the regime recruited many criminals and psychopaths who revelled in sadism for its own sake, and the Third Reich gave rise to literally millions of inhuman acts which it would be grotesque to rationalize away within some neat explanatory model. For example, it would be obscene to read palingenetic symbolism into the abundant crops of strawberries grown for SS guards alongside the Treblinka extermination camp which used as fertilizer the ashes from incinerated human corpses. Nevertheless, at the level of Nazi ideology and policy-making there are good grounds for seeing even the extermination of the Jews and other social categories whom the Nazis regarded as 'sub-human' as the destructive aspect of what was conceived by convinced Nazis as a purging of society, the 'positive' corollory of which war elaborate attempts to 're-Aryanize' or 're-nordify' the Germans spiritually and physically to create a healthy ethos and athleticism embodied in the 'new Man'. The short-lived *Lebensborn* experiment in spawning a master race by applying the principles of livestock breeding was just one of the more grotesque episodes in the attempt to realize the 'idealistic' phase of what the eugenics 'expert' Günther called *Aufnordung*, the project of restoring to the Germans the pristine qualities of their Nordic heritage and heredity.

The dialectic of destruction and creation ran through every sphere of Nazi policy. For example, the burning of books deemed 'alien to the people' and the banning of degenerate art went hand in hand with a profusion of literature and painting which, no matter how devoid of genuine creativity by non-Nazi standards, cannot be dismissed simply as propaganda (see Hinz, 1979). They were just as much an attempt to embody a new healthy ethos as the extensive plans to build monumental civic buildings to mark the end of anarchic individualism and (Jewish) speculation which, so Hitler claimed in *Mein Kampf*, had relegated the public sphere to the private (Taylor, 1974). The onslaught on the whole ethos of individual freedom and privacy had its corollary in the mass regimentation of leisure in the name of the healthy communal life so central to the activities of such organizations as the Hitler Youth, the League of German Girls, and *Kraft durch Freude* (Strength through Joy), the Nazi equivalent of the highly successful *dopolavoro* organization in Fascist Italy (see Grunberger, 1974).

What emerges is the perverse paradox that, however barbaric the connotations of the Swastika for the untold millions of victims of Nazi violence, for those mesmerized by its mythic power it symbolized not death but rebirth, not herd-like somnambulism but national reawakening. This is most clearly documented in the mass of written testimonies to the hopes aroused by the Nazi destruction of Weimar liberalism. Palingenetic myth pervades the books of party leaders, and is even reflected in their titles such as *Blood and Honour. A Fight for German Rebirth* (Rosenberg, 1934) or *The Rebirth of Europe as the History of our Times* (Rosenberg, 1939) or *On the Rebirth of the Peasantry* (Darré, 1934). It is equally central to the fantasies of a regenerated Aryan race elaborated by the accredited 'scientific' expert on racial hygiene, Günther (e.g. 1933), to the ecstatic eulogies of the new regime by the expressionist Benn (for example 1933), to the vindications of its legality put forward by the juridic theorist Schmitt (for example 1934), to the ontological defence of its revolutionary mission offered by the philosopher Heidegger (for example 1933; see Brown, 1990) or to the prophecy of the Nazi technological revolution by an engineer such as Schröter (1934; see Herf, 1984).

The importance of the myth of national rebirth was that it could operate in a far less articulate and articulated form as a vague set of 'gut' feelings. For millions of citizens who were lured into active collusion with Nazism the basis for their elective affinity with it boiled down to little more than the vague feeling that a corrupt 'system' had finally been destroyed and the prospect the new order offered everyone who was 'racially sound' of finding 'a niche where he could feel secure and respected: in short a true "national community" from which all sources of friction and unease had been removed' (Peukert, 1987, p.41). The image which encapsulated the mythic force of Nazism was thus the community held together by a common racial heritage (*Volksgemeinschaft*) and destiny (*Schicksalsgemeinschaft*). It was the fostering of this mythical entity which formed the hidden agenda of the 'Winter Help' campaigns to give to the poor (Aryans), of the annual Bückeberg Day of Honour held to celebrate the peasantry (attended by a million farmers in 1935), of the drives to modernize factory conditions organized by the offshoot of the German Labour Front, the 'Beauty of Work' Office (Rabinbach, 1976), and of the many 'instant' traditions, ceremonies and rituals such as the *Thingspiel* or the oath of allegiance to the *Blutfahne* (blood banner) on the anniversary of the failed putsch of 9 November 1990. Every public event, even the unveiling of the first Volkswagen or the opening of a motorway (see Shand, 1984), was stage managed in order to create a collective sense of 'cultic fraternity' (Benz, 1990), of 'magic consciousness' (Vondung, 1971; 1979), the premise for the transformation of world history in the new age which had dawned.

The most persistent focus for these utopian longings was obviously Hitler himself, who became the subject of a cult which was not purely the fruit of the elaborate ritual, propaganda campaigns and academic theories designed to sustain the myth of his genius and infallibility (Kershaw, 1987). Its palingenetic core emerges clearly in the countless sycophantic homages paid to him in print after 1933, as when an editor of a collection of Nazi poetry declares, 'A new man has come from the depths of the people. He has nailed new theses to the door and brought with him new tablets. He has created a new people' (Loewy, 1966, p.270). The writer of a book celebrating the seizure of power chose to preface it with the following lines (quoted in Kershaw, 1987, p 53):

> Now has the Godhead a saviour sent,
> Distress its end has passed.
> To gladness and joy the land gives vent:
> Springtime is here at last.

The Fascist Nature of Nazism

Nazism highlights just as emphatically as Fascism the total dependency of any fascist movement on a grave socio-political crisis to develop a mass base and shows again that only a unique concatenation of events and accidents enables it to seize power. But the Third Reich demonstrated even more devastatingly than the Third Rome the enormous revolutionary potential of fascism as an ideology once these conditions *are* met. Not only were the legal, political and social structures of the Weimar Republic systematically destroyed or perverted wherever they impinged upon the Nazi value system but entirely new structures were created specifically to implement a totalitarian domestic policy and an expansionist foreign policy of boundless ambition and aggression: the SS and the extermination camps are just the most notorious examples.

The scale of systematic, mass-produced inhumanity which resulted can be attributed in no small measure to the fanaticism of its leadership, especially that of Hitler himself, and to the radicalness of the palingenetic vision they pursued. Their vision of a racially pure German empire implied far greater destruction even than Mussolini's ultimate dream of an Italian Mediterranean, and the extraordinary extent to which elements of the programme for its realization had been carried out by the time they had been forced to surrender underscores the gulf which separates 'true' fascism from even the most dynamic conservatism (see Noakes, 1990). The primary locus of the Nazi revolution may have been 'subjective consciousness' (see Kershaw, 1985, p.141; cf. Vondung, 1979), and its deeply paradoxical long-term effect may have been to facilitate the 'modernization' of Germany in a liberal-democratic sense (cf. Dahrendorf, 1969). It should not be forgotten, however, that in its own day and on its own terms it had shattering *objective* consequences at every level of society, quite independently of the gruesome practical consequences it had for the flesh and blood of untold millions of its victims.

However, an evaluation of Nazism's 'achievements' also casts a particularly baleful light into the chasm which must always yawn between what fascism promises as a movement and the reality it delivers. With the possible exception of Nazi anti-Semitism, which only achieved a systematic genocidal dimension once the *Blitzkrieg* against Russia had failed, whereupon it gathered a momentum which could only be stopped by total military defeat (see Mayer, 1990), there is no sphere in which Hitler's new order showed signs of ever fulfilling its objectives. In practice the thorough-going *Gleichschaltung* necessary to create the 'total State' dreamed of by Nazi ideologues (for example Forsthoff, 1933) was never realized and was unrealizable. The Third Reich remained irreducibly 'polycratic', political power being unevenly distributed between Hitler, rising and falling Nazi leaders, the party, the state, old Weimar and new Nazi offices, central, regional and local authorities, the police, the SS and the army.

The resulting decision- and policy-making, legislative, executive and bureaucratic system was so Byzantine that some commentators have gone so far as to talk of the 'institutional anarchy' of the Third Reich (see Kershaw, 1985, ch.4) or its 'bedlam of rival hierarchies' (Williamson, 1982, p.20). Even if this may be an exaggeration, the regime's political apparatus was characterized by extensive overlapping and duplication of authority as well as by corruption and inefficiency (Bracher, 1970, pp.289–97; Kershaw, 1985, ch.4), structural flaws which Draconian censorship and incessant propaganda covered up and therefore exacerbated. Hitler's power was constrained by the very system he had created to the point where some experts of 'structuralist' persuasion argue that he was in effect a 'weak dictator' within it (see Kershaw, 1985, ch.4). The reality of the Nazi state thus fell far short of the perfect efficiency, co-ordination and totalitarianism to which it aspired and which has become part of an 'image' accepted in the past even by many of its enemies and critics. The fate of literature and poetry under the Third Reich can be seen as a microcosm of the regime as a whole: the facts in no way bear out the stereotype of a coherent policy being adopted towards aesthetic issues or of all writers being coerced into serving as docile propagandists for Nazi values (Travers, 1990).

A symptom of the intractable problems of translating the myth of the Third Reich into reality was the impossibility of resolving conflicting Nazi theories of a new economic order into a coherent set of policies and structural innovations. The principle of centralized economic planning and industrial output found expression in Ley's Labour Front, Göring's Four-Year-Plan office, the Hermann Göring steel works, the Todt organization, the Ministry for Arms and Munitions, the Reich Economic Chamber and the Central Agencies of the Reich. But this 'corporatist' strategy coexisted with a policy of minimal intervention into large sectors of big business and heavy industry. The result was a complex patchwork of planned and unplanned, co-ordinated and autonomous, private and *dirigiste* spheres. Nazi industry, eventually supplemented by the ruthless use of forced and slave labour, may have proved immensely more efficient as the basis of a modern war machine than its Italian counterpart, which remained largely a figment of intensive party theorizing, yet its reality did not live up to the myth of perfect technocratic co-ordination that still flutters around the slogan *Vorsprung durch Technik*. Moreover, the enormous increase in industrial output and technological progress which did take place as the war approached meant abandoning once and for all the utopian schemes for the revitalization of the agrarian sector and the settlement of the Eastern empire with farmers of 'pure stock' nurtured by Darré as National Peasant Leader and Minister of Food and Agriculture in the early days of the regime, even if the rhetoric of 'blood and soil' lingered on. As for the 'socialist' measures outlined in the 'unalterable' NSDAP programme, the only sense in which they were implemented was that Jewish property was systematically confiscated by the state or fell into private hands. In practice Nazism succeeded merely in creating a 'behemoth-like' war economy in which industry was geared to the needs of the armed and occupying forces, domestic shortages could be supplemented by wholesale looting of the conquered territories, and unlimited supplies of 'human material' became available for use as forced or slave labour. The exceptional conditions created by a world war masked the acute structural shortcomings of autarkic policies and camouflaged the minimal progress being made towards a sustainable economic order which would survive the war (cf. Bracher, 1970, pp.411–22; Kershaw, 1985, ch.3).

Foreign policy, both military and racial, was more consistent than economic policy, largely because Hitler's fanatical commitment to major territorial expansion in the East and a war to the death against the Jews was widely shared at all levels of the hierarchical executive structures which he had created. Yet here again only intense propaganda could paper over the cracks and failures of Nazi imperialism. Hierarchs such as Darré, Rosenberg and Himmler pursued rival visions of the post-war settlement of the conquered territories, and by 1943 teams of economists and contemporary historians were preparing plans for the new Europe many of which were at variance with the one envisaged by Hitler to the point of anticipating a sort of ultra-nationalist EEC (see Herzstein, 1982). Meanwhile, Hitler's short-term strategies and individual decisions were increasingly dictated by intuitive and opportunistic reactions to a complex and rapidly shifting international situation, a situation shaped not only by the international repercussions of his own revolution but by independent developments in other countries such as the Spanish Civil War and the imperial expansion of Italy and Japan (see Kershaw, 1985, ch.4). Up to the invasion of France in the summer of 1940 each stage of escalating German aggression which he masterminded and sometimes imposed on his chiefs of staff was nevertheless crowned with success. Thereafter, both *Blitzkrieg* campaigns and conventional campaigns on land, sea and air met with a chain of protracted but cumulatively disastrous setbacks. Britain and Russia were not conquered, and after America's entry into the war and Italy's capitulation Germany was faced with precisely the war of encirclement its army commanders had feared.

Unresolved tensions in Nazi foreign policy were grotesquely highlighted when the policy of an anti-Semitic programme to exterminate the Jews was pursued to the bitter end, despite the fact that it consumed material and human resources which could have been better deployed from a military point of view to ease the logistical problems created by the war effort to hold the encroaching Allies at bay. But even if Britain and Russia had been defeated and Japan had not forced America's entry into the war, the result would have been a multi-national European Empire so huge that the 'Kennedy law' of the decline of great powers (Kennedy, 1988) would sooner or later have come into effect, even before the death of Hitler himself signalled the brain-death of the Nazi revolution. Meanwhile, the survival of the Jewish race would have been assured by the number of Jews safely established in New York alone, surely a city beyond the clutches of imperial Germany and Japan even if they had worked in close collaboration. A new and fully Aryanized and 'Jew-free' world order was as much a mirage as The Thousand Year Reich.

In another sphere the failure of Nazism to translate utopian myth into the semblance of reality was in some respects even more dramatic. The 'Third Empire' was not an end in itself but, like Mussolini's African Empire, the outward manifestation of the regenerated *Volksgemeinschaft*. Certainly, the rebuilding of Germany's economy and military strength, the creation of a Greater Germany and the success of the first *Blitzkrieg* campaigns won Nazism a solid base of popularity among millions whose understandable longings for an end to economic chaos and political instability were bound up with visceral anti-Semitic and anti-communist sentiments. Even so, a fanatical commitment to the regime did not spread beyond a small percentage of the population, and the pluralism and polycracy which had come to be such a conspicuous feature of German society by the inter-war period remained stubbornly resistant to the intense measures of social engineering designed to fabricate a mass consensus for the New Order through propaganda or fear. Not only did pockets of resistance continue to be organized within the new Germany by socialists, Christians, conservatives and youth, 'national community' remained a chimera (Bracher, 1985, ch.7; 1989; cf. Baldwin, 1990, p.22). The most persistent nucleus of us for the regime resided in loyalty to Hitler as an inspired states-arlord and the saviour of Germany, a loyalty which outweighed and d any commitment to the party and its hierarchy. But even the myth of *his* infallibility went into rapid decline as the war perceptibly turned against Germany and the civilian population started to become victims rather than victors (Kershaw, 1987).

While the precise trajectory of Nazism's rise and fall is a matter for historians to establish, the fact that it *would* fall sooner or later was predictable *a priori* from its core myth of national rebirth. By identifying itself in a time of acute socio-political crisis with the vision of the Germans as a regenerated racial community forged out of chaos by a charismatic leader, it succeeded in mobilizing mass (though far from universal) support in the short term but doomed itself ultimately either to wither away as a corrupt, decaying, leaderless empire or to a catastrophic defeat at the hands of the enemies it inevitably created. Mercifully for those who survived the Holocaust, both Jewish and non-Jewish, it was brought to its knees from without before collapsing from within, so that its programmes of persecution and genocide were cut short.

The Uniqueness of Nazism

Like any permutation of fascism, Nazism was necessarily unique, because every nation follows its own *Sonderweg*, its own special path of development, and in so doing generates a unique cultural tradition on which ultra-nationalists can draw. Suggestions that the exceptional ideological radicalness of Nazism sets it apart generically from Fascism (Weber, 1964), or that its biological racism makes it a rule unto itself (Sternhell, 1979), tend merely to confuse the issue (cf. Kershaw, 1985, pp.35–41). Clearly, if our exclusive concern is to reconstruct the history of Nazism in its particularity (idiographically), then the 'fascist minimum' it shares with other movements is irrelevant. But once attempts made by the human sciences to make the dynamics and fate of Nazism more intelligible involve locating it within wider kinship systems of historical phenomena, then its generic traits as a form of fascism become of central importance.

From a humanistic point of view, the most disturbing point which emerges from investigating the fascist nature of the Third Reich in the light of the new ideal type is that it was no cynical or gratuitous experiment in the perfection of a totalitarian state apparatus but a broad-fronted crusade against decadence. Its visionary goal was to regenerate *every* aspect of society, even if it inevitably only succeeded in partially destroying the old order and producing horrendous travesties of a new one. A synergy of palingenesis and destruction (with the latter prevailing over the former) is a feature of many modern ideologies in practice – one only has to think of Jacobinism, Stalinism or the regimes of Pol Pot, Ceauşescu and Saddam Hussein – but rarely has the need to destroy been made so central to the *theory* by which a political system legitimates itself as it was in Nazi thought, whether the ideologue in question is Hitler, Rosenberg, Darré or some obscure party official writing in *Nationalsozialistische Monatshefte*. The driving force behind Nazism's radical destructiveness (see Kershaw, 1991) was therefore not rear-guard action by capitalism or the middle classes (see Kershaw's survey of Marxist approaches, 1985, pp.23–30), nihilism (Rauschning, 1938), or cultural despair (Stern, 1961), but a manically optimistic form of ultra-nationalism which embraced particularly virulent varieties of imperialism and biological racism as well as a broad spectrum of other components ranging from ruralism and occultism to technocratic and scientistic fantasies.

Once the new ideal type of fascism is applied to Nazism it becomes equally evident that the affective driving force of Nazism owed little to 'a religion of nature' (Pois, 1986) or 'millenarianism' (Rhodes, 1980), no matter how much the psychological mechanisms on which it depended for support have affinities with either. The use of terms such as 'initiatic', 'convert', 'sect' and 'ritual' in accounts of Nazism (and mine is no exception), though steeped in religious connotations, merely emphasize that we are dealing with a *charismatic*, and hence intrinsically unsustainable, mode of politics where complex psychological processes determine the fanatical commitment of militant followers and the logic of their violent acts (see Kershaw, 1991). They do so in a way impossible to model even approximately from the safe distance of academia unless rationalistic assumptions about the dynamics of ideology are abandoned, but this is no reason to treat Nazism as something other than a modern political phenomenon, a child of *our* age. Its palingenetic core ensured that it was not reactionary, but revolutionary, not anti-modern, but a bid to create a new type of modernity, even if the sense of historical destiny which legitimated this vast undertaking often drew on mythical images of its historical and racial past. Moreover, the fact that Nazism took many of these images directly from currents of pre-war *völkisch* nationalism refutes simplistic 'revisionist' notions that it was essentially anti-Marxist and symbiotically related in its goals and tactics to Stalinism, as alleged by Nolte (1988).

Our model also highlights the fact that but for a fatal conjuncture of events the utopian dreams of Nazis would have been relegated to the highly marginalized existence to which practically all other fascist utopias have been condemned (a point to be developed below). Instead, they became the ideological basis, not just of a movement, but of a regime which for twelve years systematically set about turning its nebulous goals into policies and concrete historical realities. Precisely because it was a modern political myth rather than a traditional religious one, Nazism could be systematized, rationalized and executed with all the bureaucratic, technological and productive efficiency of an industrial society, creating not just killing fields, but killing factories. The Third Reich finally collapsed, not because of any widespread loss of nerve within the ranks of the Nazi leadership, but because its armed forces were overwhelmed by the sheer size and resources of the war-machine assembled by the Americans, the British and the Russians. Even the utter destruction of Berlin could not shake the loyalty to the cause of at least one of the Nazi faithful. The political testament which Adolf Hitler dictated within hours of his suicide on 30 April 1945 records his hope that:

> Out of the sacrifice of our soldiers and out of my own solidarity with them to the point of death, the seed will inevitably grow once again in German history which will lead to the glorious rebirth of the National Socialist Movement, and thereby the realization of the true national community. (Benz, 1990, p.288)

Once again palingenetic myth had shown its power to make death seem a *rite de passage* to a new life, and once again the manic hopes that were generated by this alchemy had proved illusory. It remains to be seen how far the breaching of the Berlin Wall on 9 November 1989 heralded the emergence of a German national community in the liberal democratic sense. What is certain is that such a community in the ultra-nationalist sense which Hitler meant can never be realized. Many seeds of a new Nazism continue to germinate, but they will always shrivel up long before they flower into a new mass movement of racial hatred and imperial aggression. The reasons why these predictions can be made so confidently lie in the nature of fascism itself, or, more precisely, the dependence for its success on particular conditions, conditions which, at least in Europe, disappeared for good with the defeat of Nazism. But before we examine these conditions in Chapters 7 and 8, we should take stock of the many seedlings of fascism that have sprouted in other countries only to remain stunted or to wither away entirely, thereby throwing into relief just how exceptional the Fascist and Nazi conquest of state power really were.

References

For excellent overviews of the complex events which make up the rise and fall of Nazism see especially Bracher (1970), Hildebrand (1984). For an invaluable overview of the considerable debate surrounding Nazism see Kershaw (1985).

Alter, P., 1989. *Nationalism*, Edward Arnold, London.

Baldwin, P., 1990. Social interpretations of Nazism: renewing a tradition, *Journal of Contemporary History*, Vol.25, No.1.

Benn, G., 1933. *Der neue Staat und die Intellektuellen*, Deutsche Verlagsanstalt, Stuttgart.

Benz, W., 1990. The ritual and stage management of National Socialism, in J. Milfull (ed.), *The Attractions of Fascism*, Berg, New York.

Bracher, K.D., 1970. *The German Dictatorship*, Penguin, Harmondsworth.

Bramwell, A., 1985. *Blood and Soil: Walther Darré and Hitler's Green Party*, The Kensal Press, Bourne End, Buckinghamshire.

Broszat, M., 1960. *German National Socialism, 1919–45*, Clio, Santa Barbara, California.

Brown, K., 1990. Language, modernity and fascism, in J. Milfull (ed.), *The Attractions of Fascism*, Berg, New York.

Chickering, R., 1984. *We Men who Feel Most German*, George Allen and Unwin, Boston.

Dahrendorf, R., 1969. *Society and Democracy in Germany*, Doubleday, Anchor Books, New York.

Darré, W., 1934. *Zur Wiedergeburt der Bauerntums*, Lehmann, Munich.

Eley, G., 1980. *Reshaping the German Right*, Yale University Press, New Haven and London.

Eley, G., 1990. Conservative and radical nationalists in Germany: the production of fascist potentials, in M. Blinkhorn (ed.), *Fascists and Conservatives*, Unwin Hyman, London.

Fest, J., 1974. *Hitler*, Weidenfeld & Nicolson, London.

Forsthoff, E., 1933. *Der totale Staat*, Hanseatische Verlagsanstalt, Hamburg.

Geoghegan, V., 1987. *Utopianism and Marxism*, Methuen, London.

Goebbels, J., 1931. *Michael. Ein deutsches Schicksal*, Eher, Munich.

Goebbels, J., 1934. *Signale der neuen Zeit*, Eher, Munich.

Goodricke-Clarke, N., 1985. *The Occult Roots of Nazism*, The Aquarian Press, Wellingborough.

Grunberger, R., 1974. *A Social History of the Third Reich*, Penguin, Harmondsworth.

Günther, H.F.K., 1933. *Kleine Rassenkunde des deutschen Volkes*, Lehmann, Munich.

Hartung, G., 1990. Artur Dinter: a successful fascist author in pre-fascist Germany, in J. Milfull (ed.), *The Attractions of Fascism*, Berg, New York.

Hauner, M., 1978. Did Hitler want a world dominion?, *Journal of Contemporary History*, Vol.13, No.1.

Hayes, P., 1987. *Industry and Ideology. IG Farben in the Nazi Era*, Cambridge University Press, London.

Heidegger, M., 1933. *Die Selbstbehauptung der deutschen Universität*, Korn, Breslau.

Herf, J., 1984. *Reactionary Modernism*, Cambridge University Press, London.

Herzstein, R.E., 1982. *When Nazi Dreams Come True*, Abacus, London.

Hildebrand, K., 1984. *The Third Reich*, Allen & Unwin, London.

Hinz, B., 1979. *Art in the Third Reich*, Blackwell, Oxford.

Hüppauf, B., 1990. The birth of fascist man from the spirit of the front: from Langemarck to Verdun, in J. Milfull (ed.), *The Attractions of Fascism*, Berg, New York.

Hughes, H.S., 1958. *Consciousness and Society*, MacGibbon & Kee Ltd., London.

Kennedy, P., 1988. *The Rise and Fall of Great Powers: Economic Change and Military Conflict, 1500–2000*, Unwin Hyman, London.

Kershaw, I., 1985. *The Nazi Dictatorship*, Edward Arnold, London.

Kershaw, I., 1987. *The Hitler Myth*, OUP, Oxford.

Kershaw, I., 1991. *Hitler*, Longman, London.

Laqueur, W., 1962. *Young Germany: A History of the German Youth Movement*, Transaction Books, New Brunswick.

Loewy, E., 1966. *Literatur unterm Hakenkreuz*, Europäische Verlagsanstalt, Frankfurt-on-Main.

Lohalm, U., 1970. *Völkischer Radikalismus. Die Geschichte des Deutschvölkischen Schutz- und Trutzbundes 1919–1923*, Leibniz-Verlag, Hamburg.

Lutzhöft, H-J., 1971. *Der Nordischer Gedanke in Deutschland 1920–1940*, Ernst Klett, Stuttgart.

Mayer, A.J., 1990. *Why Did the Heavens not Darken?*, Verso, London.

Moeller van den Bruck, A., 1923. *Das Dritte Reich*, Hanseatische Verlagsanstalt, Hamburg.

Mohler, A., 1972. *Die Konservative Revolution in Deutschland*, Wissenschaftlich Buchgesellschaft, Darmstadt.

Mosse, G.L., 1966. *The Crisis of German Ideology*, Weidenfeld and Nicolson, London.

Mühlberger, D., 1987. Germany, in D. Mühlberger (ed.), *The Social Basis of European Fascist Movements*, Croom Helm, London.

Mühlberger, D., 1991. *Hitler's Followers. Studies in the Sociology of the Nazi Movement*, Routledge, London.

Noakes, J., 1990. German Conservatives and the Third Reich: an ambiguous relationship, in M. Blinkhorn (ed.), *Fascists and Conservatives*, Unwin Hyman, London.

Nolte, E., 1988. *Der europäische Bürgerkrieg. Nationalsozialismus und Bolschewismus*. Propyläen, Berlin.

Orlow, D., 1967. The conversion of myths into political power: the case of the Nazi Party 1925–26, *The American Historical Review*, Vol.72, No.3.

Peukert, D.J.K., 1987. *Inside Nazi Germany. Conformity, opposition and racism in everyday life*, Penguin, Harmondsworth.

Poliakov, L., 1974. *The Aryan Myth*, Chatto & Windus, London.

Pois, R.A., 1986. *National Socialism and the Religion of Nature*, Croom Helm, London.

Prumm, K., 1974. *Die Literatur des Soldatischen Nationalismus der 20er Jahre*, 2 Vols, Scriptor, Krönberg.

Pulzer, P., 1988. *The Rise of Political Anti-Semitism in Germany and Austria*, Peter Halban, London.

Rabinbach, A., 1976. The aesthetics of production in the Third Reich, *Journal of Contemporary History*, Vol.11, No.4.

Rauschning, H., 1938. *Die Revolution des Nihilismus*, Europa Verlag, New York.

Rauschning, H., 1939. *Hitler Speaks*, Thornton Butterworth, London.

Rhodes, J.M., 1980. *The Hitler Movement*, Hoover International Press, Stanford.

Rogger, H. and Weber, E. (eds), 1966. *The European Right*, University of California Press, Berkeley.

Rosenberg, A., 1934. *Krisis und Neubau Europas*, Junker und Dünnhaupt, Berlin.

Rosenberg, A., 1938. *Blut und Ehre. Ein Kampf für Deutsche Wiedergeburt. Reden und Autsätze von 1919–33*, Eher, Munich.

Schmitt, C., 1934. *Bewegung, Staat, Volk*, Hanseatische Verlagsanstalt, Hamburg.

Schröter, M., 1934. *Die Philosophie der Technik*, Oldenbourg, Munich.

Schüddekopf, O-E., 1960. *Linke Leute von Rechts*, Kohlhammer, Stuttgart.

Schulz, G., 1975. *Der Aufstieg des Nationalsozialismus*, Propyläen Verlag, Berlin.

Shand, J.D., 1984. The *Reichsautobahn*: symbol for the new Reich, *Journal of Contemporary History*, Vol.19, No.2.

Shirer, W.L., 1964. *The Rise and Fall of the Third Reich*, Pan Books, Harmondsworth.

Smith, A.D., 1979. *Nationalism in the Twentieth Century*, Martin Robertson, Oxford.

Smith, W.D., 1986. *The Ideological Origins of Nazi Imperialism*, Oxford University Press, Oxford.

Sontheimer, K., 1968. *Antidemokratisches Denken in der Weimarer Republik*, Nymphenburger Verlagshandlung, Munich.

Stachura, P.D., 1983. *Gregor Strasser and the Rise of Nazism*, George Allen & Unwin, London.

Stern, F., 1961. *The Politics of Cultural Despair*, University of California Press, Berkeley.

Sternhell, Z., 1979. Fascist ideology, in W. Laqueur (ed.), *Fascism: A Reader's Guide*, The Penguin Press, Harmondsworth.

Stromberg, R.N., 1982. *Redemption by War*, The Regents Press of Kansas, Lawrence.

Struve, W., 1973. *Elites against Democracy*, Princeton University Press, Princeton.

Taylor, R., 1974. *The Word in Stone*, University of California Press, Berkeley.

Travers, M., 1990. Politics and canonicity: constructing 'Literature in the Third Reich', in J. Milfull (ed.), *The Attractions of Fascism*, Berg, New York.

Tyrell, A., 1975. *Vom Trommler zum Führer: der Wandel von Hitlers Selbstverständnis zwischen 1919 und 1924 und die Entwicklungsgeschichte der NSDAP*, Fink, Munich.

Vermeil, E., 1938. *Doctrinaires de la révolution allemande*, Sorlot, Paris.

Vondung, K., 1971. *Magie und Manipulation: ideologischer Kult und politische Religion des Nationalsozialismus*, Vandenhoeck and Ruprecht, Göttingen.

Vondung, K., 1979. Spiritual revolution and magic: speculation and political action in National Socialism, *Modern Age*, Vol.23, part 4.

Williamson, D.G., 1982. *The Third Reich*, Longman, Harlow.

Weber, E., 1964. *Varieties of Fascism*, D. Van Nostrand, New York.

Wulf, J., 1963. *Literatur und Dichtung im Dritten Reich*, Gütersloh, Hamburg.

5 Abortive Fascist Movements in Inter-war Europe

The nature of fascism as the ideological basis of a regime can only be explored by examining the history of Fascism and Nazism. However, to concentrate exclusively on these is to lose sight of two outstanding features of its nature as the rationale of a *movement*, namely (i) the systematic failure of fascism to seize power, whether in non-liberal or liberal states, except in inter-war Italy and Germany; (ii) the protean quality of palingenetic ultra-nationalism as a mythic core which has enabled fascism to surface in an unbroken stream of new ideological permutations and organizational forms right up to the present day. This second feature will be thrown into relief particularly in the next chapter when we consider non-European and post-war fascisms. Towards the end this chapter will also stress the structural homogeneity of the wide variety of fascist movements which surfaced in inter-war Europe, but its primary focus will be on their inability to emulate the achievement of either Fascism or Nazism in seizing power autonomously either from an authoritarian or a liberal regime. Once the full range of *abortive* manifestations of fascism referred to in the two chapters are taken into account, it is tempting to conclude that its essential characteristic is an inverse relationship, and an ironic tension, between the radicalness of revolutionary ambitions and claims inspired by its utopian myth and its impotence to achieve actual power or results.

Fascism's Paths to Failure in Inter-war Europe

There are a number of ways in which a particular fascist movement can fail in its declared aim to take over the state and embark on the total transformation of society. Whatever the dreams of a new order which inspire it, the fate of any fascism in reality is generally one of the following:

(i) to be spontaneously dissolved by its members out of despair at the lack of headway;

(ii) to be merged with a more dynamic, but in the long-term no more successful, formation;

(iii) to be marginalized and condemned to exist with no significant public support;

(iv) to be thwarted or outmanoeuvred by the state in its assault on power even when it has developed into a revolutionary movement with a significant mass following;
(v) to be officially banned or suppressed whether by an authoritarian or a liberal regime.

In inter-war Europe, a phrase being used here with a degree of historical licence to embrace the period 1918–45, two further destinies could befall a fascist movement which put paid to its revolutionary effectiveness less dramatically but just as conclusively, namely to be:

(vi) co-opted and neutralized by a para-fascist regime (that is a radical right regime with fascist trappings);
(vii)incorporated by Nazism into a puppet regime of the Third Reich and hence reduced to a purely collaborationist role.

Clearly each of these seven potential destinies was lived out historically as a series of unique events whose complexity and texture will be lost in a panoramic survey of the sort undertaken here. As ever, it is the underlying patterns which are of central concern in an investigation of generic fascism, not the singularity of the phenomena which comprise it. However, before considering concrete examples of how fascism failed, we must first delimit the scope of the phenomena under investigation by distinguishing between fascism 'proper' and those movements and regimes which have sometimes come to be conflated with it owing to the use of ideal types more accommodating or less discriminating than the one we have constructed.

The Non-fascist Radical Right

Our ideal type distinguished between fascism and all movements which, though undoubtedly both anti-liberal and anti-communist, sought to fulfil goals which were insufficiently palingenetic or ultra-nationalist in their inspiration to lead even in principle to the creation of a new national community through the radical overhaul of existing political, economic, ideological and social structures. In other words fascism as we define it embodies a vision of the regenerated nation which is not just anti-parliamentarian and anti-communist, but also anti-conservative, aiming to mobilize not only the traditional ruling elites but the whole people. It does not focus on a single issue, such as the need to take action against the threat allegedly posed by Jews or communists, or to create a separatist homeland, but looks towards a total transformation of the status quo.

These criteria exclude not only chauvinistic pressure groups like the Navy League and Round Table groups of Edwardian England but also a number of political formations which arose before the First World War to promote illiberal forms of nationalism without embracing openly revolutionary goals (which is not to deny that they made a significant contribution to the social climate which incubated both proto-fascism and fascism). Some were manifestations of a 'new right' with populist leanings such as Déroulède's *Ligues des Patriotes*, Drumont's *Jeunesse Antisémite* and *Ligue de la Patrie Française*; some were dynamic forms of conservatism (neo-

conservatism) such as the 'regenerationist' movements in Spain, the Union
of the Russian People or the Austrian Pan-Germans led by Schönerer.
Others were formations which combined a more distinctly populist brand of
nationalism with non-Marxist socialism in a way pioneered by Barrès, such
as Lueger's Christian Social Party, the National Federation of the Yellows in
France, the Czech National Socialist Party and the Bohemian German
Workers' Party.

A qualified exception might be made, however, for elements within
Maurras's *Action Française* (AF). Maurras himself was a federalist rather
than a centralist, while the corner-stone of his 'integral nationalism' was a
neo-conservative blend of royalism and Catholicism which precluded any
idea of seizing power through mass mobilization. Nor can the *Camelots du
roi*, the AF's paramilitary wing, be seen as direct forerunners of Roehm's SA
or Mussolini's *squadristi*. Nevertheless, after 1911 some of the AF's ideologues, notably Valois, were blending Maurrasian elitism with the genuinely
palingenetic myths of anarcho-syndicalists and Sorelians sufficiently to
qualify as proto-fascist (Mazgaj, 1979). Significantly, though, when
Maurras's ideas were taken up elsewhere, it was in a neo-conservative spirit
rather than a fascist one. For example, the *Action Française* was one of the
main influences on *Integralismo Lusitano*, a movement which emerged in
Portugal on the eve of the First World War with the aim of creating a
bulwark of 'integral' Catholic values to ward off the threat of anti-clerical
liberalism and socialism, but not to launch a populist revolution. Our
taxonomy thus differs from Nolte's (1965), who treated the *Action Française*
as one of the 'three faces of fascism'.

Another illustration of the essentially non-fascist impact of the *Action
Française* outside France is the influence it had under the Spanish Republic
on the Alfonsine neo-monarchists, whose journal was called *Acción
Española*. This was only one of a number of radical right groups which
sprang up in inter-war Spain whose political platform was ultimately reactionary (anti-liberal, anti-communist but in a reactionary Catholic or monarchist spirit) even if they resorted to 'modern' forms of political discourse and
agitation. Some had already come into prominence under the dictatorship
(1923–30) of General Miguel (for example the *Unión Patriótica* or the Carlist
Communión Tradicionalista), others sprang up in the early thirties to fight
Spain's Republican left in the name of a regenerated Catholic and national
tradition such as the Spanish Confederation of Autonomous Rightist
Groups (CEDA) or the more radical *Renovación Española*, and the National
Bloc. The outstanding ideologue of this neo-conservative right was Calvo
Sotelo, who sought to revitalize traditional elites and structures not to create
new ones. It is hardly surprising to find outside the Marxist camp a wide
consensus that none of these are truly fascist (for example Payne, 1980,
p.153; Blinkhorn, 1990, pp.134–5).

The criteria which we are using also disqualify from consideration a
number of anti-conservative right-wing movements of the inter-war period
which, although often associated with fascism, never committed themselves
unequivocally to the overthrow of liberalism and acted in practice as right-
wing pressure groups. Examples are such chauvinist groups as the Belgian

Front Party, the Swedish National League and the Norwegian Patriotic League, as well as the many veteran, youth and paramilitary leagues which surfaced after the armistice (for example in Belgium the *Action Nationale*, and in France the *Union Nationale des Combattants*, the *Jeunesses Patriotes*, the *Solidarité Française*). Using the same criteria neither the paramilitary *Croix de Feu*, nor the party which grew out of it, the *Parti Social Français*, are genuinely fascist, a point corroborated by Austin (1990) but not by Plumyène and Lasierra (1963) or Soucy (1986), who use different ideal types. Other groupings which our taxonomy locates on the margins of fascism rather than within it are such terrorist organizations as France's secret anti-communist *Cagoule*, and Poland's Catholic and anti-Semitic *Falanga*. In a quite different national context, The Army Comrades Association in Ireland, better known as the Blue Shirts, may have been patriotic and radically anti-communist, but their militarist trappings and flirtation with corporatist theory were far removed from the sphere of truly demagogic or putschist politics, even if their leader, O'Duffy, openly admired Mussolini and Salazar. When he did attempt to found an out-and-out fascist force, the National Corporate Party, it came to nothing (see Cronin, 1997).

A somewhat more complex case in this context is presented by the Estonian *Vabadussõjalaste Liit*, or Central League of the the Veterans of the War of Independence, formed in 1929 as a reaction to the crisis which hit the country's fledgling liberal institutions when the depression struck. Influenced in externals by such contemporary role models as the Nazi SA and the Finnish Lapua movement, Vaps (as it is known for short) soon radicalized itself into an extra-parliamentary paramilitary organization claiming to defend the interests of the Estonian people. However, Vaps had no comprehensive plans for a new post-liberal order and corresponds closer to what we have called proto-fascism than the full-blown version. At first, rather than attempt to seize power by force, it used its massive popular support to bring about a legal show-down with the government over its plan for a new constitution which would have strengthened the executive powers of the head of state. In the referendum held in October 1933 it won 73 per cent of the votes, but the prime minister, Tõnisson, used emergency powers to ban its campaign meetings (July 1933). His successor Päts then dissolved the organization (March 1934) as part of a bloodless palace revolution on Bonapartist lines. This did not prevent its members attempting to carry out an armed coup in December 1935, though the police were able to preempt it. It was only after four years of rule by decree that Päts was able to restore democratic institutions, albeit with some elements of fascistization (see Parming, 1975).

Another group of inter-war movements often associated with fascism in secondary literature but which do not satisfy the criteria established here are those based on a narrow ethnic racism or separatist nationalism. Examples are Gömbös's Party of Racial Defence in Hungary, the National Democrat Party in Poland, the Czech National Socialist Party, the National Christian Party and League of National Christian Defence in Romania: none of which seriously set out to create for themselves a mass base or erect a radically new order on ultra-nationalist lines. This applies equally well to

the many unitary and separatist nationalist parties, organizations and movements which sprang up in inter-war Yugoslavia, even if several of them,
notably the Macedonian radical nationalist IMRO, the Serbian separatist
movement SRONAO and its Croatian counterpart HRANAO, all used
tactics and an organizational style reminiscent of Fascist and Nazi hit-
squads. Another candidate fascist force, Ljotić's radical unitary (anti-federal)
movement *Zbor* formed in 1935, resembled the Polish *Falanga* in adopting a
number of fascist features (leader-cult, corporativist theory, anti-Semitism,
anti-communism) and in blending Christianity with ultra-nationalism, but
the mythic core of its ideology was not sufficiently focused on a regenerated
Yugoslavian national community thriving within a new type of post-liberal
order to make it more than proto-fascist (see Sugar, 1971).

A similar taxonomic verdict must also be passed on the fascist credentials
of the extremely violent Croatian separatist movement UHRO, normally
referred to as Ustasha (uprising). When its *poglavnik* (leader), Pavelić, was
installed as head of an independent Croatian state by the Nazis in April
1941, he immediately promulgated laws for the creation of a corporatist state
based on workers and the peasantry and for the protection of 'Aryan blood
and honour of the Croatian people'. These edicts were a blank cheque for
the ruthless persecution of non-Croatian minorities, leading to the murder
of up to a million Serbs, 35,000 Jews and thousands of gypsies at the hands
of the ruthless Ustasha militia. Moreover, the movement's ideology had its
roots in an indigenous equivalent of *völkisch* thought which drew inspiration from the national energies which had created the Great Croatia ruled
over by Tomislav in the Middle Ages and fuelled the heroic rebellion of
Croatian peasants in the sixteenth century. However, while the rabid anti-
Semitic and anti-Serbian feelings it stood for ensured that the Ustasha state
became a compliant tool of Nazi racial policies, Pavelić's national socialism
amounted to little more than the mass-expropriation of Serbs and Jews. The
central role played in Ustasha by the Catholic clergy, the absence of any
serious vision of the mobilization of the Croatian people or of the social
reconstruction which would follow once the destructive xenophobic phase
of palingenesis had been completed all tend to suggest that we are dealing
with a form of proto-fascism rather than fascism (Hory and Broszat, 1964;
Meneghello-Dinsic, 1969).

The Ustasha state raises the taxonomic problem posed to students of
fascism by the many authoritarian regimes which mushroomed in inter-war
Europe (see Huntington and Moore, 1970). Not only did all of them, with
the obvious exception of Stalin's Russia, appeal to ultra-nationalist sentiments in their self-legitimation, but many showed the unmistakable influence of either Fascism or Nazism in their characteristic style and
institutions. They thus demand special attention in an account of generic
fascism.

Para-fascism

When Fascist Italy and Nazi Germany are compared with the other authoritarian regimes which established themselves in Europe after 1918, a crucial

difference soon emerges: namely, that none of them grew directly out of a seizure of state power by an 'extra-systemic' revolutionary movement of populist nationalism bent on creating a new national order. All of them in one way or another came to power as attempts by sections of the ruling elites or their military representatives to restore stability and strong government in a way which did not threaten the basis of the existing class structure or of traditional values. Their dynamics were thus essentially reactionary and conservative. This difference is obvious in the case of attempts by the premier of Yugoslavia's infant parliamentary system, Stojadinović, to align himself first with Fascist Italy and then with the Axis between 1935 and 1939. Though he created a green-shirted youth organization and encouraged crowds to chant the Serbo–Croat equivalent of '*Duce! Duce!*', he never sought the real demagogic or paramilitary power necessary to seize power and his fascistization of national politics was no more than cosmetic (see Sugar, 1971, p.136). The same applies to the more genuinely authoritarian regimes presided over by Piłsudski of Poland (1926–35) or King Boris of Bulgaria (between 1935 and 1943), neither of whom attempted to rationalize their suspension of political liberalism in revolutionary terms or present their dictatorial powers as the incarnation of the general will.

The situation is more complex, however, in the case of a number of counter-revolutionary regimes (that is not just anti-communist but anti-fascist) which masqueraded as revolutionary (that is pro-fascist) ones. Now that the last *ancien régime* had been swept away, the ideology of legitimist or restorationist conservatism was bankrupt, and since the age of mass politics had spread to all parts of Europe, most authoritarian leaders felt the need for a façade of popular legitimation. So impressive was the apparent success first of Fascism and then Nazism in welding revolutionary nationalism into a 'third way' between communism and liberalism, that their externals were bound to be imitated by both conservative and military regimes as a cosmetic ploy to retain hegemony, to manipulate rather than to awaken genuine populist energies. The result has been described in such terms as 'fascistized', '*fascisant*', 'pseudo-fascist', 'proto-fascist' or 'semi-fascist'. I propose to use instead the term 'para-fascist', in which the prefix 'para-' connotes an 'alteration, perversion, simulation' (*Oxford English Dictionary*) of 'real' fascism as we have defined it. It was in this autocratic and anti-fascist spirit, for example, that the colonels who succeeded Piłsudski set up an official state party, the Camp of National Unity (OZN), and Miguel de Rivera, Spain's military dictator between 1923 and 1930 made gestures towards introducing a leader-cult and corporatism on Fascist lines, leading one expert to use the paradoxical expression 'fascism from above' (Shillony, 1983). The same ploy of apeing Fascism to secure popular support was used by Smetona, Lithuania's dictator between 1926 and 1939, who also set up an official political front, the *Tautinakai*, (Lithuanian National Union) represented at the International Fascist Congress held at Montreux in 1934, and a youth movement, Young Lithuania.

A para-fascist regime, however ritualistic its style of politics, well orchestrated its leader cult, palingenetic its rhetoric, ruthless its terror apparatus, fearsome its official paramilitary league, dynamic its youth organization or monolithic its state party, will react to genuine fascism as a threat, and though it may be forced to seek a fascist movement's co-operation to secure populist support or ward off common enemies (notably revolutionary socialism), such a regime will take the first opportunity to neutralize it. This pattern is exhibited with exemplary clarity in the case of Latvia, whose infant democracy seemed to have overcome a number of teething troubles when the Depression plunged it into crisis in 1929. Of the several groups which sprang up to pursue ultra-nationalist goals (for example the National Revolutionary Workers and the Latvian National Socialist Party), by far the most important was the *Ugunkrust* (Firecross), subsequently renamed *Perkonkrust*. The Thundercross pledged itself to rid the country of the influence of its many minorities (Poles, Russians, Germans, Jews, Lithuanians) and create a regenerated Latvian national community. Using its newspaper *Latvis* to preach its own form of *völkisch* myth, it attracted some 6,000 members (mainly from students) and a wide popular following. But its plans to seize state power were dramatically thwarted when the leader of the Peasants' League, Ulmanis, staged a palace revolution and set about creating an authoritarian regime extensively modelled in its rhetoric, institutions and leader-cult on Fascist Italy. Despite concerted attempts by this para-fascist regime to smash the Thundercross in 1935 and 1937, this genuine fascism was still tenacious enough to re-emerge in the summer of 1941 to aid and abet the Nazi occupation of the Baltic states (see Hehn, 1957).

Under King George II, Greece experienced 'fascism from above' on an even more grandiose scale when former Chief of Staff Metaxas (1936–41) embarked on an intensive campaign to persuade Greeks that they formed a 'blood community' and that a long period of decadence was giving way to the 'Third Hellenic Civilization' under the aegis of the 'new state'. His 'Regime of the 4th of August' created the National Youth Organization (EON), which by 1940 boasted 600,000 members, introduced a measure of state corporatism and deployed a Special Security Service of considerable brutality. Nevertheless, there was no sense in which the regime was based on a spontaneous mass movement or envisaged any sort of social revolution, so that its declared aim of creating 'the new Greek' remained the empty rhetoric of para-fascist dictatorship (Andricopoulos, 1980; Dambassina-Kamara, 1983).

A more thorough-going experiment in fascistization was undertaken in contemporary Portugal. The interim military dictatorship headed by Carmona which replaced the republic in 1926 was even less concerned with legitimating itself through mass-mobilizing organizations and myths than was Primo de Rivera's in Spain. However, the ascent of the former professor of economics, Salazar, from finance minister to virtual dictator was accompanied by growing concern with creating a modernizing and regenerationist ethos. This culminated in 1933 in the restructuring of the economy on state corporatist lines and the official baptism of Portugal with the palingenetic title *Estado Novo*. Before long this 'New State' had equipped itself with a paramilitary organization (the *Legião Portuguesa*), a national youth organization (the *Mocidade Portuguesa*) and a secret police (the PIDE) backed up by special tribunals. It was also careful to adopt the other prerequisite externals of Italian Fascism (state propaganda, censorship, constant political rituals, a leadership cult) in a declared attempt at 'total integration' (Martins, 1968). The essentially para-fascist nature of Salazar's 'New State' is underlined by the fate suffered by Preto's National Syndicalists which in 1935 staged a coup against the regime in the name of a genuinely new type of populist and corporatist order. The crushing of the rebellion was entirely consistent with the fact that Salazar's principal ideological inspiration was neither Fascism nor Nazism but a blend of social Catholicism wih elements of Maurrassian integral nationalism. Not surprisingly, Salazar showed himself as willing to defascistize his regime as he had been to fascistize it (which he had been particularly keen to do after Preto's attempted coup) once he saw the war starting to turn inexorably against the Axis powers (see Gallagher, 1990).

If the *Novo Estado* crushed indigenous fascism, inter-war Spain illustrates another way the fundamental conflict between para-fascism and the real thing could work itself out. The *Juntas de Ofensiva Nacional-Sindicalista* started out in 1931 as a party bent on realizing a vision of the new Spain strongly influenced by the corporatist strand in Fascism. Three years later its impact on the nation's politics was still so insignificant that it took one of the options open to failed fascist movements by merging with the equally insignificant *Falange Española* to form the *Falange Española de las JONS*. The new party's article of faith was that the energies of the masses could be harnessed and the country regenerated only through a revolution which went beyond left and right by synthesizing traditional Catholic moral values with a syndicalist state under the leadership of José Antonio Primo de Rivera, son of the former dictator and leader of the FE. But despite some aggressive campaigning and the backing of the radical monarchist *Renovación Española*, the Falange obtained a mere 0.7 per cent of votes in the 1936 elections, ignored by the left and the right. It was the outbreak of the Civil War in July 1936 which began to turn the Falange into a significant paramilitary and political force. In the process it even recruited the bulk of the Popular Action Youth (JAP), which, while starting out as a militant Christian youth organization, had come to stand for a genuinely populist form of palingenetic ultra-nationalism. Their vision of the nation's regeneration through a fusion of the modern age with the quintessential quality of Spanish nationhood, *Hispanidad*, became sufficiently populist and revolutionary for them to despair of orthodox formations of political Catholicism as the architects of post-liberal Spain (see Preston, 1978).

Yet hardly had the Falange's membership and paramilitary recruitment begun to soar when, in April 1937, General Franco, now recognized as 'Chief of the Spanish State' by the anti-Republican forces, created a state party, the *Falange Española Tradicionalista y de las JONS*, which, as this mouthful implies, imposed a shot-gun marriage between Falangists and the traditional (that is non-fascist) radical right. With the formation of this deliberately hybrid force, Spanish fascism was formally co-opted from above to provide a façade of revolutionary dynamism for a military dictatorship whose policies remained fundamentally reactionary and authoritarian. Thus, despite the extensive fascistization of 'Franquism' in this and other aspects of the regime (leader-cult, totalitarian mechanisms of social control, the limited adoption of corporatist economics), it never went beyond para-fascism. Its success in neutralizing fascism's revolutionary impetus by absorption has nevertheless deceived numerous historians into mistaking Franco's regime for the real thing, and even Hitler and Mussolini deluded themselves into reading into it a kinship with their movements which did not exist in any positive sense (Payne, 1961; Blinkhorn, 1990). Between them, the regimes of Salazar and Franco exhibit two possibilities open to a para-fascist regime when faced with the challenge of a genuine fascist movement: either to suppress it by force or to exploit its populism for its own purposes while depriving it of real power. The fate of fascism under three other para-fascist regimes introduces some important modifications to this pattern.

The Fate of Fascism under Para-fascism in Austria, Romania and Hungary

The first real threat to Austria's fledgling democracy posed by the right came, not from the populist ultra-right movements which had flourished before 1914, such as Schönerer's *völkisch* Pan-Germans and Lueger's pro-Catholic Christian–Socials, but from the paramilitary *Heimwehren*. Often referred to collectively as the *Heimwehr*, these were regional units of National Guards who, like the *squadristi* and the *Freikorps*, were recruited overwhelmingly from war veterans only too eager to fight the nation's alleged enemies, whether external (for example Yugoslavs making incursions over the border in the south) or internal (i.e. Communists and Social Democrats).

In the first decade of their existence the *Heimwehr* lacked the organizational or ideological cohesion to constitute a fascist force, its only core principles being virulent patriotism and anti-Marxism. What reversed its gradual decline into a negligible paramilitary movement was the uprising of Viennese workers in 1927 supported by the Social Democrats' paramilitary arm, the *Schutzbund*. The energetic role played by the voluntary National Guard in helping the government restore 'law and order' not only established them as a key factor in state politics, but ushered in a phase of internal upheaval from which it would emerge a more united and radical movement, a development which won it the material support of both Mussolini and the Hungarian prime minister, Bethlen, as a possible bridge between their two countries. The openly proto-fascist orientation of its politics was formalized when in May 1930 its leaders took the Korneuburg Oath committing the movement, albeit in nebulous terms, to replacing parliamentary democracy by a Catholic, German and corporatist state.

In 1931 the Styrian *Heimwehr* units under Pfrimer made a bid to translate revolutionary rhetoric into deeds with a putsch, but the pathetic outcome underlines the continued imperviousness of Austrian liberalism to fascism despite the growing political and economic crisis. That the bulk of the *Heimwehr* stopped short of full-blown fascism was clear, not just from the way that Pfrimer's units had to go it alone, but from its reaction to Dollfuss's decision of September 1933 to solve the protracted crisis of the liberal state by replacing it from above with a 'Christian corporative' one. Instead of rejecting out of hand the new regime as a counterfeit of the new order he had pledged to create, the national leader Starhemberg agreed to become vice-chancellor and to head the Patriotic Front, a pseudo-populist umbrella organization for a wide range of conservative, Christian and nationalist groups. Much of the movement's rank and file tamely followed suit. The scene was thus set for the final stage in the neutralization of the *Heimwehr*, when, in April 1936, Dollfuss's successor, Schuschnigg, removed Starhemberg from both his offices, disbanded his movement and absorbed its members into the *Front-Miliz*, the new paramilitary arm of the Patriotic Front. Para-fascism had successfully absorbed proto-fascism (cf. Rath and Schum, 1980 and the contrasting taxonomy used by Lewis, 1990).

If the *Heimwehr* proved to be a prevalently proto-fascist force in national politics which posed no serious threat to a neo-conservative regime, it co-existed with another movement which never left its fascist credentials in doubt, Austrian National Socialism. It had grown out of the German Workers' movement, originally formed as an anti-Czech but, before long both an anti-Marxist and anti-Semitic (but reformist) strand of trade unionism in the late 1880s. In 1918 its party, the DAP (1904), was rebaptized the DNSAP, only to be split by the new frontiers into a Bohemian and Austrian section. The subsequent history of the Austrian Nazis was fraught by fractiousness and leadership battles over leftist and rightist interpretations of national socialism, the degree of Austrian autonomy within a Greater Germany and how far the movement should become an extension of its younger but more powerful German *confrère*. With no charismatic leader to unite the party (which even split into two in the mid-1920s), it was inevitable that Hitler would gradually gain ascendancy over the movement, which by 1926 had significantly changed its name to NSDAP to bring it into line with the German movement. Even so, many Austrian Nazis struggled to retain some autonomy from Munich, and one faction, led by Seyss-Inquart, cultivated a Catholicizing version of Nazism, turning it into a form of religious politics which had no counterpart in Germany (Kitchen, 1980).

Until 1930, the Nazis were successfully marginalized by the parliamentary system. After that, Hitler's growing success in Germany, the impact of the Depression and especially the prolonged state crisis of 1932–34 helped the NSDAP to become a genuine populist force, though never a mass movement on the scale of its German blood brother. While the majority of *Heimwehr* colluded with Dollfuss, the Nazis stayed true to the radicalness of their palingenetic vision. Though outlawed in July 1934, they staged a putsch to act as a catalyst for the long-awaited chance to enforce the *Anschluss*, but despite German backing it fared little better than the Munich putsch eleven years earlier, its chief result being Dollfuss's barbaric assassination. Para-fascism had stood firm against fascism. Yet the Austrian NSDAP continued relentlessly to build up its organization and membership throughout the country and provided a natural haven for the increasing number of *Heimwehr* members disenchanted at the emasculation of their movement. They thus found themselves in a position to play a crucial role in the sequence of events so carefully stage-managed by Hitler which in 1938 led to Schuschnigg's overthrow and the *Anschluss*. The Nazi rank-and-file and many *Heimwehr* radicals were automatically incorporated by the Nazi state, some of them achieving high office within it, but the individuality and autonomy of Austrian fascism was sacrificed for good. It had finally overthrown para-fascism, not autonomously, but as a fifth column of a Nazi regime bent on reducing Austria to a province of the Greater Germany. But for this external factor it would have doubtless remained as ineffectual as all other fascist movements in overthrowing a para-fascist regime (Pauley, 1981).

Between 1938 and 1942 Romania exhibited an even more complex set of permutations in the relationship between fascism and state power, both liberal and authoritarian. The Legion of the Archangel Michael had started out as an ultra-nationalist terrorist organization dedicated to its own esoteric vision of a regenerated Romania, before building up a mass following through an electoral party, the Iron Guard (formed 1930). This was suppressed by the liberal (though extraordinarily right-wing) system in 1933, but reconstituted in 1934 as All for the Fatherland. Notwithstanding the fanaticism of its activists and the loyalty of its supporters, the new party's electoral success peaked in 1937 with 15.5 per cent and it never threatened to gain power constitutionally. Its fortunes changed after King Carol's *coup d'état* but initially for the worse. Seeing it rightly as a threat to his authority, the king set about ruthlessly destroying it through mass arrests and executions which only stopped in January 1940 when, in a remarkable U-turn, he started to woo its support to help ingratiate himself with the Nazis and complete his own superficial programme of fascistization. This involved setting up the Front of National Revival as an official state party, founding a youth movement (*Strajeri* or Watch) and announcing his own nebulous version of the corporatist economic planning favoured by most illiberal regimes in the inter-war period. Unlike the *Heimwehr*, but like the Austrian Nazis, the Legionaries spurned such appeals to rally to the travesty of a genuine fascist state, and once Germany forced Romania to surrender Bessarabia to the (then still allied) Soviet Union as well as giving up territory to Bulgaria and Hungary, they took advantage of a tide of popular anti-monarchism to stage a putsch. This forced King Carol to turn to the support of the military general and political activist, Antonescu, who for his part insisted on the monarch's abdicating in favour of his son, Mihai.

With the reins of power now in his hands the general formed a tactical alliance with Horia Sima, the leader of the Iron Guard since the execution of Codreanu on Carol's orders in the repressions of 1938–9. In September 1940 the country legally became the National Legionary State, with the Iron Guard as the only official party. However, while Antonescu's concern was with maintaining law and order, the Legion, many of whose second generation of recruits were now little more than cynical opportunists, carried out a bloody campaign of pogroms and vendettas, and were rumoured to be plotting against the General himself. Their fate was decided by Hitler, who, recognizing they would be far from compliant with Nazi political and economic hegemony in Eastern Europe, refused to back them. Instead, Antonescu was given the go-ahead to liquidate them, which he set about doing with relish. Several hundred of the Iron Guard were murdered, thousands imprisoned and thousands more were forced to go underground. Many fled, ironically enough, to Germany where they were interned. Having been marginalized, then suppressed and then marginalized again by liberalism, a fascist movement had in quick succession been crushed, wooed, co-opted, and liquidated by two types of para-fascist regime, one of them with the full backing of the Third Reich (Weber, 1965; Nagy-Talavera, 1970).

Hungary provides yet more instances of the incapacity of both fascist and proto-fascist movements to make headway against a para-fascist regime, but also shows that even if fascism did break through with Nazi assistance it automatically sacrificed its autonomy. In November 1919 the Bolshevik regime of Béla Kun was overthrown in an army-led counter-revolution which culminated in violent pogroms against communists and Jews. But even as Admiral Horthy set about building a stable neo-conservative government on semi-pluralist lines to consolidate his victory, a more radical ultra-right political culture was emerging in Hungary. A number of patriotic societies sprang up cultivating a myth of the nation's decline and imminent rebirth such as the Awakening Hungarians or the esoteric Etelköz Association (EKSZ). Nationalists from such organizations were involved in negotiations with Hitler in 1923 to co-ordinate a putsch in Hungary against the Horthy regime with the one he was planning in Munich, were associated with the creation of a Party of Racial Defence, and were instrumental in engineering the appointment of their most dynamic spokesman, Gömbös, as head of government from 1932 until his death in 1936.

Though Gömbös's bid to align Hungary with the Axis powers endowed Horthy's neo-conservative system with a markedly fascistized complexion, little structural change occurred under his premiership. Extra-systemic fascism was similarly marginalized. Meskó's Hungarian Hitlerite Movement formed in 1932, sporting green-shirts and the arrow cross symbol, or Count Festetics' Hungarian National Socialist Party, offered little more than crude Hungarianized versions of the Nazi Aryan myth, with no scheme for seizing power and thus remained proto-fascist. In contrast Böszörményi's Scythe Cross, formed in 1931, for a time mobilized a peasant following with vague slogans of land reform and social justice laced with attacks on liberals, Bolsheviks, the Habsburgs, cosmopolitanism and, of course, the Jews, all presented as standing in the way of the regeneration of the Hungarian race. As usual such palingenetic wishful thinking fell at the first hurdle when put to the test. Despite attracting 20,000 members and forming a paramilitary arm, the Scythe Cross's bid to stage a peasant revolt against 'decadent' Budapest in 1936 was a fiasco.

By the outbreak of war scores of minute parties had sprung up hawking different blends of Scythe Cross and Arrow Cross fascism, but the only significant attempt at a fascist take-over of state power was mounted by Szálasi. His Party of National Will was formed in 1935 and renamed the

Arrow Cross Party–Hungarist Movement in 1937. Backed by Nazi funds it quickly grew strong enough to make Horthy fear a coup against his regency. Szálasi was therefore arrested in 1938, but this did not prevent the party winning over 30 per cent of the vote in the next elections. On his release in 1940 he built up party organization and propaganda so successfully that membership rose to half a million. Frustrated in his attempts to achieve power under Horthy, who had ensured that the Nazification of Hungary was a largely cosmetic one, he started negotiations with the Germans. His moment finally came when the Germans, alerted to the regent's plans to surrender to the Russians, occupied Hungary in October 1944.

With Horthy deposed and imprisoned, Szálasi was legally appointed by parliament as prime minister and 'national leader'. Blinded by an illusory sense of the underlying compatibility of Nazism with Hungarism, he soon turned the Arrow Cross government into one of the Nazis' most compliant puppet states. Right up to the liberation of Budapest in February 1945, it afforded Eichmann every assistance in the rounding up of thousands of Jews for slave labour and extermination as well as co-operating in the transport to Germany of any materials that could prolong the Nazi war effort. Szálasi's attempts to implement his own fascist vision were confined to bombastic proclamations of the new post-war order he planned for Central and Eastern Europe. It took Nazi intervention to force Hungary to make the transition from a para-fascist regime, in which a variety of native fascisms was consistently marginalized, to a collaborationist regime in which Hungarism officially became the basis of state power while in reality remaining a solely rhetorical force for change (Déak, 1965; Nagy-Talavera, 1970; Szollosi-Janze, 1989).

Indigenous Fascisms under Liberalism

Only five liberal democracies in inter-war Europe held out against authoritarianism and were spared Nazi occupation. Hence their states were denied the option of absorbing, co-opting or physically liquidating indigenous fascism, yet in all but one the threat which it posed was so small that even to have banned it would have been an overreaction. In Eire, Duffy's minute fascist movement was not even worth outlawing. Electoral support for the Icelandic Nationalist Party (1934), which sported a Swastika and spouted eugenic theories, peaked at 0.7 per cent in 1924 and had dwindled to 0.2 per cent in 1937 (Gudmundson, 1980). At first sight Sweden seems to have been a more propitious environment for fascism, with no less than five fascist movements wooing mass support through party political and publicistic campaigns proposing visions of a new Sweden based on various mixtures of corporatism, blood and soil ruralism, anti-Semitism, anti-capitalism and Fascism or Nazism. Yet even when two of them, called at the time the National Socialist Workers' Party and the Swedish National Socialist Party, joined forces in 1936, they only obtained 0.7 per cent of the vote and a de-Nazified and more Swedish version of the NSAP polled a mere 0.14 per cent in 1944 (Hagtvet, 1980). The extra-parliamentary 'New Sweden' movement formed in 1930 also had a negligible impact.

The situation was little different in Switzerland. By 1937 each language area had its own fascist party, the philo-Nazi National Front (German), the *Unione Nationale* (French) and the philo-Fascist *Lega Nazionale Ticinese* (LNT) (Italian: see Cerutti, 1986), the Romansch cantons being contested by the latter two. None of them posed a serious threat to Swiss democracy. For example, the National Front, which, while adopting elements of Nazi ideology strove for a post-liberal Switzerland to become part of an international fascist order, did comparatively well in local elections in Schaffhausen (27 per cent in 1933) but elsewhere never obtained more than 6.2 per cent. The party dissolved itself in 1940 but resurfaced in a number of para-political organizations only to be banned in 1943 (Glaus, 1980). The fact that Switzerland hosted several of fascism's more ambitious 'internationalist' initiatives, such as the International Centre for Fascist Studies (CINEF) and the 1934 congress of the Action Committee for the Universality of Rome (CAUR), did little to ruffle the Swiss state's official commitment to democracy and pluralism, even if the country's foreign and economic policy was significantly influenced by the presence of philo-Nazis in high places during the war.

In Britain fascism, at first sight, may seem to have been more of a threat to democracy. It produced not only a cluster of mimetic Fascist and Nazi parties with negligible followings, but an indigenous movement which for a time enjoyed considerable notoriety, the British Union of Fascists (BUF). This was due partly to the prominence which its leader, Mosley, had achieved as a politician before leaving the Labour Party, but mainly to the (largely anti-fascist) violence with which the BUF was regularly associated after the Olympia meeting of June 1934 and which culminated in the Battle of Cable Street, when 1,900 marchers were opposed by 100,000 anti-fascists. Yet the high public profile of the BUF belied its signal failure to achieve a nation-wide mass following. When the electoral popularity of its programme for a 'Greater Britain' was tested in sixty-six metropolitan boroughs and provincial towns in November 1937, BUF candidates did badly everywhere except in the party's stronghold, the East End, and even here they were as easily beaten by Labour and Conservatives as they had been in the London County Council elections the previous spring. In the meantime, membership, having quickly reached 50,000 members in the early days, slumped to 5,000 after the first episodes of public disorder, and by the time it was outlawed in 1940 recruitment stood at about 25,000, less than a thirtieth of NSDAP membership when Hitler became chancellor. This partial recovery had only been achieved by deliberately cultivating a paramilitary and anti-Semitic ethos (which were scarcely present in the early propaganda) to appeal to hard-line racists and Nazi sympathizers. The decision to ban the BUF was prompted more by fears that it represented a potential source of enemy espionage than that it posed any serious risk to British democracy (Thurlow, 1987; Stevenson, 1990).

The one country in this group where an indigenous fascist movement severely tested the strength of democratic institutions was Finland, significantly a new nation-state born in 1917 in the wake of the Russian Revolution (though enjoying considerable antonomy even before) and

immediately rent by a ferocious civil war between nationalists and communists. Drawing on powerful currents of ultra-nationalist speculation, the
Lapua Movement had started out in 1929 as a radical right pressure group
campaigning for the banning of communism and social democracy (the
communists were in fact outlawed between 1930 and 1934). It became
overtly fascist in 1930 when it launched a terrorist campaign against its
enemies and attempted a coup against the state, but the state managed to
survive the crisis and ban Lapua's activities. Two years later the government
allowed the formation The People's Patriotic Movement (IKL) which soon
radicalized itself on fascist lines under its leader Vihtori Kosola, developing
its own militia and youth movement and announcing a revolutionary programme for the creation of a new order. Yet, though it remained an active
extra-parliamentary force in Finnish politics till 1944, successfully resisting
an attempt to ban it in 1938, it failed either to pursue a successful putschist
strategy or create for itself an 'irresistible' electoral following, managing to
poll a mere 8.3 per cent in its best year, 1936. The outbreak of the Second
World War made the prospect of a Finnish new order recede even further
and caused the mythic appeal it generated to fade (Rintala, 1965; Karvonen,
1988).

Fascism in Democracies Occupied by the Nazis

In tracing the fate of fascism under para-fascist regimes we saw how illusory
it would be to think that indigenous fascisms prospered under the auspices
of the Third Reich. As a genuine form of fascism, Nazism could not absorb
other fascisms as a para-fascist one might want to. Nor could it allow them
any autonomous state power, for apart from a small corps of 'universalist'
fascists in the Nazi think-tank for the post-war Europe (see Herzstein,
1982), the war-lords of the Third Reich had no intention of allowing the
nations they had conquered to be run by indigenous versions of palingenetic
ultra-nationalism: if they could not be turned like the Arrow Cross into the
basis of a collaborationist regime, they would be simply marginalized.

Henlein's Sudeten German Party was, like the Austrian Nazis with
whom they were so closely aligned, a special case. Formed in 1933, this
movement had roots in an indigenous tradition of anti-Czech 'national
socialism' reaching back to the 1890s but modelled itself slavishly on the
'Hitler Movement', including its anti-Semitic Aryan myth. After the
Munich Agreement of September 1938, the majority wishes of Sudeten
Germans were granted and they were assimilated into the Third Reich along
with their fascism. On the surface Slovakian fascism seems to constitute
another exception. Hlinka's Slovak People's Catholic Party started out life
after the war as a separatist nationalist movement and achieved up to 40 per
cent of Slovak votes in the 1920s. However in the course of the 1930s, it lost
its mass base as it became increasingly infiltrated by extremists who aimed
to create an independent Slovakia modelled on the Third Reich. Once the
Slovak Republic was proclaimed in 1938, their dreams seemed to be

realized. Hlinka's successor, Tiso, became head of state and leader of the party, the Hlinka Guard and the Hlinka Youth. Before long corporatist doctrines were adopted, and the apparatus of totalitarianism and anti-Semitic racial policy energetically applied. Yet Tiso's single-party state along with its official ideology of 'Slovak National Socialism', a crude mish-mash of Nazism and Catholicism, remained alien to Slovak traditions and values, thus precluding mass support. It had changed from a marginalized fascist party to a collaborationist and basically para-fascist regime.

Czech fascism was an even more compromised force. On the country's dismemberment, what was left of Czech territory was governed by a coalition of philo-Nazi fascists and conservatives headed by the former leader of the Agrarians, Beran. On the creation of the Protectorate in March 1939 this transitional government was baptized the 'National Confederation', but despite its name, the new government remained totally subservient to the Nazis and deeply unrepresentative of the Czechs. Indeed, one of its first acts was to ban the country's only autonomous fascist formation, Gajda's National Fascist Community which, as its name implied, had spurned the example of Nazism. Thus there is no suggestion that authentic Czech or Slovak fascism broke through under Hitler's 'protection' and every reason to believe that without it the Czechoslovakian liberal system would have continued to marginalize both of them. Support for Gajda's party, formed on the Fascist rather than the Nazi model in 1926, peaked at a mere 8 per cent of the votes in 1935 (Havránek, 1971; Zacek, 1971).

In Northern Europe too indigenous fascist movements, whether Nazified or not, failed to achieve autonomous power under the Third Reich. Quisling founded his *Nasjonal Samling* (National Unity Party) in 1933, yet, even after three years of campaigning, its programme for a national rebirth based on corporatism, autarky, Christianity and traditional Norwegian virtues still only convinced a mere 1.8 per cent of the electorate. When the German forces overran the country in April 1940, Quisling took advantage of the chaos to set up an NS government, but after only a week Norway was placed under the control of Reichskommissar Terboven. The hour of the NS seemed to have come when soon after it was made the only legal party its membership quickly rose to 35,000. Yet Quisling's appointment as head of state in February 1942 did not mean that Norwegian fascism had prevailed. As far as Berlin was concerned, the NS was simply a vehicle for Norway's Nazification. Quisling's aim of building up his party as the foundation for national sovereignty within the German New Europe was thwarted at every turn, both by the fervent opposition of his fellow-countrymen and by Hitler in Berlin, who was determined that the country should remain a vassal state (Hayes, 1971; Hoidal, 1989). Denmark's fascism got even less of a look-in, largely because the system of constitutional monarchy was anomalously allowed to go on working 'normally' after the invasion. As a result, Frits Clausen, head of the mimetic Nazi DNSAP (Danish Nationalist Socialist Workers' Party), was no closer to power after German occupation than before it, for his party polled 2.1 per cent in the elections of 1943, a mere 0.3 per cent more than its pre-war best (Poulsen and Djursaa, 1980, Djursaa, 1981).

Pre-war Netherlands hosted two rival largely mimetic currents of fascism, a highly fragmented philo-Italian and pro-Catholic one which made several attempts to form a joint front (for example the 1932 General Dutch Fascist Union, the 1935 Black Front) and the more secular National Socialist Movement (NSB) founded in 1931 and enthusiastically led by Mussert. It was only after 1935, by which time it had 47,000 members, that the NSB leadership started identifying itself closely with Nazism and introduced anti-Semitic racism into its programme (which might partially account for the steady decline in membership thereafter). The electoral support of the Dutch Fascists was minimal (0.2 per cent in 1937), while that of Mussert's party peaked at 7.9 per cent in 1935, slipping back to 4.2 per cent two years later. Once the Nazis occupied the Netherlands both movements tried to take advantage of the suspension of democracy, but despite the NSB's surge in membership to 75,000 and the extreme philo-Nazism of the faction that formed under van Tonningen, Berlin refused to devolve any authority to indigenous collaborators and the country was ruled by the former Austrian Nazi, Seyss-Inquart. Except for its propaganda value Dutch fascism was left to dwindle into total irrelevance (Hansen, 1981).

Inter-war Belgium saw the emergence of a number of paramilitary organizations which in the 1930s came to adopt overtly Fascist or Nazi elements but without ever making a serious attempt to seize power at the head of a mass movement. The most important of these proto-fascisms were De Clerq's Flemish National Federation (VNV) and Van Severen's *Verdinaso* (League of Netherland-National Solidarists), both of which defended the cause of Flemish separatism, and Hoornaert's *Légion Nationale*, which wanted Belgium to become a corporatist and monarchist authoritarian state on Maurrassian lines (Stengers, 1965; Schepens, 1980). The most spectacular manifestations of anti-liberal populism in Belgium, however, were associated with *Rex*. Degrelle's initiative to found this movement in 1936 grew out of his work as a propagandist for militant Catholicism in the pages of the journal *Christus Rex*. But while the original Rexist programme outlined (in nebulous terms deeply indebted to Maurrassian ideas) a crusade against the decadence of liberalism, capitalism and Bolshevism, a corporatist restructuring of the economy, as well as measures to regenerate rural and family values, it proposed radical *reform* of parliament (that is reduction of its authority), not its overthrow. After remarkable successes in the 1936 elections which brought him 11.5 per cent in Belgium as a whole and considerably more in the Walloon provinces, Degrelle's campaigning became more overtly fascist in tone and style, but he still did not commit himself to destroying constitutional democracy, seemingly pinning his hopes instead on being swept to power thanks to irresistible public support at the ballot box.

At this stage, then, *Rex* cannot even be treated 'technically' as a proto-fascist movement, but rather as a highly idiosyncratic democratic one under charismatic leadership. It was his crushing personal defeat in a by-election against the future prime minister, van Zeeland, in April 1937, in which he obtained only 19 per cent of the vote, which caused him to resort to an extensive Nazification of the movement, including the adoption of anti-

Semitic and anti-parliamentary rhetoric in the party newspaper, *Le Pays Réel*, and the staging of mass rallies with a paramilitary ethos. This signalled *Rex*'s transformation into a proto-fascist force but simultaneously its collapse as a populist one because in the 1939 elections it polled a mere 4.4 per cent (Étienne, 1968; Stengers, 1965; Schepens, 1980). Though Degrelle's highly personal challenge to liberalism had failed, the Nazi occupation of Belgium occasioned *Rex*'s gradual metamorphosis into a collaborationist movement and simultaneously into a fully fascist one. But the complex machinations on the part of Degrelle and a hard core of his followers determined to take advantage of the Nazi era for the revitalization of their nation came to naught. Historically speaking they had, like all other Nazi collaborators, backed the wrong horse, and in any case the new European order envisaged by the Nazi hierarchy was to be based on subjugation not on partnership. While philo-Nazi Flemish separatists pursued the chimera of a Greater Holland and some of their Walloon counterparts that of a reborn Burgundy, their only practical impact was to become the compliant stooges of Nazi military rule at home or prolong the agony of the Russian campaign as part of the German army. Degrelle has survived outstanding services to fascism in both roles to become a doyen of post-war neo-Nazism (Conway, 1986).

Fascisms in France

As Zeev Sternhell has rightly pointed out, France 'offers particularly favourable conditions' for the study of fascism (1983, p.15). We have seen earlier that, even using our own very different ideal type, France provides a major case study in the often subtle distinctions which separate fascism from new forms of radical right that emerged after 1870 such as the anti-Semitic leagues, prototypes of national socialism associated with Boulanger and Barrès, the mainstream *Action Française* or the veteran anti-socialist leagues such as the *Croix de Feu* which were such a feature of inter-war France. But France is no less important to fascist studies because it illustrates several of the ways in which inter-war fascism could fail in its revolutionary mission, whether it operated under a liberal, a para-fascist or a Nazi regime.

Valois formed *Le Faisceau* in November 1925, and both its name and its division into paramilitary, youth, civic and producers' sections clearly reflect the degree to which he took as his role model, Mussolini, who had granted him an audience in 1923. Ideologically speaking, however, it was based on the fusion of Maurrassian integral nationalism with anarcho-syndicalism, which a breakaway leftist faction of the *Action Française* had been exploring just before the war in the Cercle Proudhon, despite the heretical nature of such radicalization to Maurras himself. So seriously did Valois take his concept of the syndical state that, by 1928, when some Italian national syndicalists still deluded themselves that Fascism would be the vehicle of their revolution, he was condemning the way Mussolini had abandoned socialism for reaction. Among the more original features of his scheme for France's regeneration was that it should form a Latin fascist bloc with Spain and Italy and the way he expressly invited Jews to contribute their creativity to the 'New Age' (the suitably palingenetic name of the party newspaper). However, *Le Faisceau* never attracted more than 60,000 members and, by 1927, Valois began to come to the conclusion that fascism could make no headway in France. A year later, after a vain attempt to reorganize the movement, he dissolved it (Soucy, 1986, chs 4–5).

Though Bucard's *Francisme* was formed months after Hitler's seizure of power in Germany, its role model was Fascism, and especially Mussolini, rather than Nazism. Bucard not only repudiated anti-Semitism, but represented France at the international fascist congress held in 1934 on the instigation of Italy's idealistic 'Universal Fascists'. Though it attacked Bolshevism and parliamentarism, plutocracy and democracy, left and right, its positive programme was thin. In 1934 it sprouted an anti-Semitic faction with its own organ, *La Libre Parole*, but this schism was academic, because *Francisme* never won more than 10,000 proselytes. It remained safely marginalized by liberalism (Plumyène and Lasierra, 1963, pp.57–63).

By contrast *Parti Populaire Français* (PPF) seemed for a time to be a force to be reckoned with. It was formed in 1936 by Doriot as a response to the formation of a coalition government by the Popular Front. With financial backing from conservative businessmen and landowners, the PPF soon had 130,000 followers, a high percentage from the working class. Doriot, who had been a prominent communist activist before 1935, attracted many activists from other right-wing formations. The PPF's ideology was a radical critique of Bolshevism, class warfare, liberalism and capitalism and by the spring of 1938 had adopted elements of 'cultural' anti-Semitism. It merged ultra-nationalism (symbolized in Joan of Arc), with a celebration of productivism and technology, and its newspaper, *L'Emancipation nationale*, which at one point was regularly selling 200,000 copies a day, attracted articles by France's most articulate fascist ideologues. In 1937 the government relieved Doriot of his office as mayor of St. Denis and subsequently banned his meetings, but PPF membership continued to grow, reaching 300,000 in 1938. Lacking the pragmatic tactical flair of Hitler or Mussolini, Doriot refused to pursue a legal route to power by contesting elections or to build up the paramilitary force needed for a putsch. Nor did he show any interest in forging alliances with other right-wing forces such as the *Parti Social Français*, which by mid-1937 had over 600,000 members. Thus his scheme for the social, economic and moral regeneration of the nation remained the utopian myth of an impotent extra-parliamentary movement (Wolf, 1969). Despite its many structural weaknesses, France's liberal system had successfully resisted the fascist challenge.

The country's defeat in 1940 was followed by the creation of perhaps the most complete of all para-fascist regimes, namely Vichy. With the collusion of the Nazis it was set up under Marshal Pétain in the French 'Free Zone' and continued to exercize power as a fully collaborationist government after the Zone was occupied in 1942. What was involved here was no slavish imitation of Mussolini's Italy or Hitler's Germany, but a dynamic form of home-grown neo-conservatism that produced 'from within' doctrines, policies and structures which had many points of external affinity with the restructuring of society undertaken in both countries. The 'national revolution' which Pétain's government set out to implement was rationalized by a wholesale condemnation of the decadence of republicanism in general and of the Third Republic in particular, which, so they claimed, had allowed all the forces which the ultra-right saw as degenerate (materialism, socialism etc.) to sap the moral fibre of the nation to a point where defeat at the hands of the Nazis in 1940 was inevitable. In the four years of its government, though its room for autonomous policy-making was severely restricted by the escalating demands made by Berlin on its economic and political cooperation, Vichy voluntarily took major steps towards creating a new order based on a moral revolution, the revitalization of agriculture, the modernization of industry and a renewed sense of national identity and solidarity.

Predictably the attempt to fulfil this ambitious programme as a Nazi fief involved Vichy not just in turning the media and the educational system into a vast propaganda machine but in creating a number of para-fascist institutions of social control or engineering such as a youth organization (the *Compagnons de France*), a grassroots organization for the mass mobilization of men (*Légion des Anciens Combattants*), an elite paramilitary body (the *milice*), a sophisticated secret service (the *Service du Contrôle Technique*). It also promulgated eugenic measures and actively pursued a campaign of anti-Semitism which, while not based on biological principles, in practice guaranteed extensive and active collusion with Nazi racial and genocidal policies.

Yet, no matter how closely aligned it was with the Third Reich, Vichy was far from fascist in its inspiration. Not only had it been brought to power by military defeat and not by a populist revolution, but its upper échelons represented a wide spectrum of rightist forces whose only common denominator was a hostility to the liberal weakness and socialist strength of the Third Republic. It brought together elements from the armed forces and the paramilitary leagues, the civil service and the police, the Church hierarchy and proponents of political Catholicism, royalists, Bonapartists and admirers of Salazar's Portugal, anti-liberal technocrats and re-ruralizing visionaries, federalists and centralists. Where this Babel of illiberal nationalisms converged was in the stress on such nebulous notions as stability, law and order, patriotism, Catholicism, respect for family, all embodied in Pétain himself, who, as an aging hero of the First World War, was more reminiscent of Hindenburg than of Hitler (Paxton, 1972).

The fate of genuine fascism under this fully fledged para-fascist regime was predictable. Despite their prolific publicistic output and collaborationist zeal, its ideologues were marginalized by Vichy in terms of real influence and continued to be so even after the Free Zone was occupied by the Nazis in November 1942 and the regime's break with France's venerable liberal–humanist tradition became more radical in every respect. They were reduced to the role of giving Vichy a cosmetic sheen of ideological radicalism which assisted collusion with the Nazis but had a minimal impact on policy-making as such. As for their role in the Nazi occupied zone, they provided a valuable source of collaboration and propaganda, but their dreams of forming the nucleus of an autonomous French government in a post-war European federation of fascist states were as illusory as that of all other philo-Nazis in the occupied nations of the Third Reich. Either vicariously (via Vichy) or directly, the several dialects of French fascism were thus co-opted, absorbed and neutralized as an authentic force for change.

Two examples stand out. Doriot went through a series of major ideological contortions to convince himself that Nazism embodied the higher synthesis of proletarian socialism and nationalism he had sought to realize in the PPF and became converted to the belief that a fascist France would be ideally placed to become a full member of the Nazi's new European order. This act of cognitive dissonance, so common among fascists desperate to accommodate the Nazi conquest of Europe, led him to fight on the Eastern front as part of the *Légion des Volontaires Français*, but it did no more to win him influence with the Nazis than the willingness to fight at the head of a Walloon brigade of the SS had done for Degrelle. Doriot's main rival for 'left-fascist' influence on the new France, Déat, fared somewhat better. He too projected on to the Nazis the syncretic political myth which he had elaborated before the war and which went by the name 'neo-socialism'. Turning a blind eye to Hitler's liquidation of the Strasserite 'socialist' faction in 1934 and to the virulent anti-Semitism and aggressive imperialism which had increasingly dominated the policies of the Third Reich ever since, he persuaded himself that the Nazi occupation was the chance for France to undergo a 'second French revolution' on neo-socialist principles which would make it the worthy equal of Germany in the new European order. His self-deception led him to found the *Le Rassemblement National Populaire* in 1941 to be the nucleus of a second French Revolution. The RNP soon boasted a membership of half a million, but could no more avoid being a servile collaborationist force than the war-time movements of Quisling, Szálasi and Degrelle. When late in the day he accepted high office within the Vichy government, it showed just how far from his former ideals a 'communist' can be lured if the affective core of his idealism is not socialist compassion but abstract visions of a reborn humanity (Plumyène and Lasierra, 1963, pp.150–8; Baker, 1976).

The Diversity and Homogeneity of Inter-war Fascism

By concentrating on the common destiny of inter-war fascisms outside Italy and Germany to fail in their revolutionary enterprise, there is a danger of losing sight of the the extraordinary heterogeneity in the types of movement they represent. Some are political parties, some paramilitary cadre parties, some are both, some have a mass following, some do not. The style of leadership, the role of religion, the type of racism, the socialist content, the social base and, of course, the specific contents of their ultra-nationalist myth all vary in ways which are entirely consistent with the kaleidoscopic picture which emerges when all the strands, aspects and phases making up the history of Fascism and Nazism are taken into account.

So what did such a motley collection of movements have in common? It is precisely this vital question, of course, which any ideal type of generic fascism has been tailored to answer. The answer which ours gives is by now entirely predictable. If a movement has been included in this chapter as a manifestation of fascism, it is because the specialist studies and primary sources relating to it point to the presence of an ideological core of palingenetic ultra-nationalism. There is space here only to give a hint of the varied and complex philosophies of history which enabled the most fervent ideologues of fascism to conceive the possibility of an imminent transfiguration of their nations and rationalize their activism.

The leading ideologues of mimetic Fascist or Nazi movements simply reworked the theme of national rebirth associated with their role models to make them applicable to their national situation, though even in this case more authentic personal ideological energies could be involved. Quisling, for example, originally dreamt up a scheme for Norway's regeneration which made no reference to Aryan eugenics but pinned hopes on a national form of socialism which took account of the country's Nordic heritage and Lutheran tradition, as well as the vital contribution to be made by its sailors and farmers. It was this vision which prompted him to found the Nordic Folk Awakening in 1931, and which re-emerged in the political theory of 'universalism' he intended to bequeath as the distillation of his wisdom at the end of the war. As late as 1937 he was still inviting the Anglo-Saxons, through the pages of the *British Union Quarterly* to 'unite in a Nordic World Movement to create peace and cooperation between all Nordic peoples throughout the world', thus fulfilling their 'mission . . . to do away with an obsolete world and create a new world' (Weber, 1964, p.156), a notion inconceivable to all but the most Europeanist ideologues of the Third Reich (cf. Herzstein, 1982). However, his 1941 essay 'National Decay and National Resurrection', published for a German readership by the NSDAP, shows how prompt he was to edit out of his political message any element, especially Christianity, which might jar a Nazi ear. Having evoked the racial qualities exhibited by the Vikings, he laments Norway's subsequent reduction first to a vassal state of the Danes, then to a pawn of the British in the Napoleonic Wars, before finally being contaminated by the spirit of 'Anglo-Jewish world capitalism', (though it should be noted that Quisling's anti-Semitism never extended in theory beyond the insistence that Jews should have their own homeland in some such place as Madagascar). The war having awakened Norway from her slumber, the age of inner 'collapse' (*Zusammenbruch*) was over. Once the nation was transformed through a revolution based on a Nordic form of socialism, it could fulfil its destiny, namely to work side by side with its blood brothers, the Germans, and so enter a new era of greatness as a 'free people within the new Europe' (Quisling, 1942, pp.118–41).

In the case of other movements, mimetic trappings could cloak a synthesis of ideas which were even more original than Quisling's. For example, the political theatre staged by the BUF fused elements of both Fascism and

Nazism, but the core notions of Mosley's world-view owed little to either. It was informed by a mix of Lamarckian genetic theory, Spenglerian speculations about the Faustian genius of the West and its contemporary decay, Nietzschean and Bergsonian vitalism and the Shavian vision of the emergence of a new type of man. A chauvinist belief in Britain's imperial and civilizing mission (the British equivalent of *völkisch* thought) came to be supplemented by an increasingly emphatic ingredient of cultural anti-Semitism as the decade wore on, even if from Mosley's point of view this may have been largely for tactical reasons. His vision of Britain's economic renewal, one of his major preoccupations, drew on socialist and Keynesian theories of the planned economy and Douglas's theory of 'social credit'. Mosley concocted out of this pot-pourri of ideas a panacea for Britain's acute socio-economic problems, which he attributed to the bankruptcy of the parliamentary and capitalist system as well as a pervasive moral decline. The country would retain the monarchy but could only continue to fulfil its civilizing mission by revitalizing its colonial and trading empire under a single party state with himself as its charismatic leader. The palingenetic myth at the heart of this vision became a constant theme of BUF propaganda, as when the *Blackshirt* of November 1933 confidently announced that 'slowly but surely the New Order emerges, Phoenix-like, from the smouldering ashes of the old'. But this was no aggressively imperialistic fascist vision (after all, Britain already had a vast empire), nor was it a narrow neutralist one. When in the run-up to the war Mosley adopted a policy of appeasement towards Hitler and Mussolini, it was a symptom of his belief that the fascistization of Britain was an integral part of the West's (international) regeneration. This belief had been a major factor behind his decision to found a new type of party. As he wrote at the time of the BUF's formation in 1933: 'A humanity released from poverty and from many of the horrors and afflictions of disease to the enjoyment of a world reborn . . . will . . . need a fascist movement transformed to the purpose of a new and nobler order of mankind' (Mosley, 1968, p.326). Such 'universalist' sentiments, so alien to the mentality of Hitler or Goebbels, form a recurrent theme of Mosley's most elaborate formulations of his political vision (1934, 1939) and inform his definition of fascism as 'the embodied and organized determination of young manhood to rescue great nations from decadence, and march together towards a higher and nobler order of civilization' (Mosley, 1936, p.7).

Szálasi's Hungarism is set against a quite different ideological landscape. The small ultra-nationalist groups that sprang up in the twenties had developed their own equivalent of *völkisch* Aryanism centred on the myth that the Hungarians were a 'pure' Turanian race descended from a judicious blend of Persians, Hittites, Egyptians and Sumerians, Jesus himself being a Turanian! Now that the Habsburg yoke had been removed, Hungary could regain its historic greatness but only if the threat posed to it by Bolshevism and Judaism and the debilitating force of parliamentarism could be eradicated by a new political elite. Turanianism established itself as a common denominator of all fascist groups from then on. Szálasi blended it with Christian notions of moral regeneration based on a 'social national' (that is corporatist) reconstruction of the economy which would put an end to class struggle and exploitation and a geo-political vision of a radically restructured new European order reflecting the natural hegemony of certain nations.

Freely using millenaristic imagery, his writings explained how the Hungarians were destined (possibly in an alliance with a Legionary Romania, an extraordinary idea given the profound ethnic tensions between Hungarians and Romanians) to establish the 'Carpathian–Danube Greater Homeland' on a par with the European empires of the two other 'leading races': the Germans and the Italians. Under the tutelage of these three chosen peoples Europe would be healed of the ravages of secular liberalism and materialistic socialism, and a new age of peace would emerge. Like Quisling, Szálasi saw the Jews as 'only' constituting a cultural threat to the new-born nation. They were to be physically removed from Europe, not to extermination camps but to an unspecified homeland of their own (though a 'benign' form of anti-Semitism, one which deterred Szálasi even less than Quisling from co-operating with the SS in the Final Solution). A speech he made ten days after the Russians took Budapest demonstrates how deeply he was imbued with a palingenetic myth that could turn total defeat into victory: 'Without Good Friday there is no resurrection . . . We shall drink the bitter cup to the last drop so that the new world can arise which gives human life a new meaning' (Szollosi-Janze, 1989, p.225).

The Romanian Iron Guard, which Szálasi at one time had obligingly conceded a privileged position within his scheme for a regenerated Danube Basin, had other ideas about their national destiny. They were based on a blend of Orthodox Christianity, xenophobia and anti-Semitism rooted in peasant culture, with a Romantic nationalism cultivated in university circles. The Legionary elite fused the commitment to Romania's rebirth that grew out of these ideas with an initiatic leader worship and death cult which is unparalleled in other fascist movements, except, perhaps, among the most fanatical paramilitary supporters of Hitler and José Antonio. As a result a visionary, not to say pathological, intensity pervaded the otherwise familiar diatribes against materialism, democracy, Bolshevism and especially against Jews, and found expression in the ritualistic acts of violence carried out by the Legionaries themselves, lending the movement a quasi-mystic tone rarely found in other fascisms. Yet, no matter how different the ideas of the Iron Guard are from those of the various strands of Fascism, Mosley's BUF or Doriot's PPF, they share with them the same core of palingenetic ultra-nationalism. Indeed, the Legionaries themselves sensed an inner kinship with Fascism, Nazism and (mistakenly) Franco's stand against Communism in the Spanish Civil War, and a number of Legionaries volunteered to fight the Republicans. The Legionary leader Moţa wrote shortly before being killed in Spain, 'We are fighting, we are dying here in defence of our ancestral law, for the happiness of the Romanian people, for its rebirth which is being made possible by our Captain's [Codreanu] reconstruction of it' (Motza, 1984, p.42). For Legionaries like Moţa and Codreanu the ultimate goal of history was 'the Resurrection of nations in the name of Jesus Christ' (Nagy-Talavera, 1970, p.266). The symbol of national resurrection would be *omul nou*, the new man. Legionaries were told 'the new man or the renewed nation presupposes a great spiritual renewal, a great spiritual revolution of the whole people . . . Before being a political, theoretical, financial, economic movement, the Legionary Movement is a spiritual school, in which if a man shall enter, a hero must come out at the other end' (quoted in Weber, 1964, pp.167–9. Predictably, almost every passage Weber has chosen to illustrate the ideologies of different fascisms contains palingenetic language of this type).

A major influence on Romanian fascism had been the supercharged racist nationalism expressed in the works of Romantic poets such as Eminescu at the turn of the century and which was given a new dimension by university professors, notably the political economist Cuza and the historian Iorga. An even more central role in the evolution of Finnish fascism was played by the Academic Karelia Society (AKS), founded in 1922 by soldiers freshly returned from fighting Russians in East Karelia. One of its animating myths was that as each civilization became 'soft', the centre of human progress had moved continually outwards from the hospitable soil and climate of Babylonia and Egypt towards ones where the struggle to survive became increasingly arduous. Having been passed from the Mediterranean to Northern Europe, the torch of human progress now fell to the Russians, the Scandinavians or the Finns. As a unique mixture of Nordic, East Baltic and Cro-Magnon man the Finns were the most dynamic, the other two being too racially pure (!) to win hegemony. The historical mission of the Finns was thus to fight Bolshevism (hence the war which they had fought between 1917 and 1922), eradicate Swedish contamination of their culture and recreate a Greater Finland (*Suur-Suomi*) stretching to the Urals. For good measure this Darwinian geo-political fantasy was laced with allusions drawn from Lutheran revivalism to a divine law which sanctioned the Finns' territorial ambitions.

The AKS lacked any strategy for implementing this vision of the nation's rebirth and thus remained a proto-fascist force. It was the students and veterans recruited by Lapua who attempted to translate it into reality in the form of anti-communist terror campaigns and an attempted coup. When Lapua was banned in 1932, Karelian ultra-nationalism resurfaced immediately in the IKL. Its militant stand against socialists, the bourgeoisie, Freemasons and Jews was no traditional conservatism, but flowed from the belief that world history had reached a critical phase in which liberal individualism was dying and being replaced by Bolshevist materialism. The only healthy solution to the dilemma was for Finland to recreate itself as a *kansankokonaisuus*, the 'national community', within an organic corporatist state. Predictably, this diagnosis of contemporary history expressed itself in palingenetic imagery, as in this arboreal simile used by one of the major figures of Finnish fascism:

> [The war] was a storm over the old Europe that violently shook its nations which were sinking into the softness of excessive culture. That which was weak or rotten disintegrated or perished. But a healthy tree even when bruised, rises again out of the turmoil of the storm. With a broken top and with branches stripped bare it sinks its roots twice as deep and again pushes forth

new buds. Soon it stands more erect than before, spreading a new, stronger crown of leafy branches. (Rintala, 1965, p.413)

Inter-war Fascism: an Abortive Revolt Against Alleged National Decadence

Whatever fascist movement we consider, the myth of death and rebirth, of decadence and renewal forms the core of its ultra-nationalism. Thus Preto announced to his National Syndicalists the death of the 'absurd era' of liberal–democratic constitutions. In the new state a regenerated Catholicism and family life would provide the moral linchpins of society, while a 'hierarchic and organic' state syndicalism would heal class divisions and channel the creative and productive energies of the whole people. The consequence would be Portugal's *risorgimento*, based on heroic will, economic strength and national solidarity (Medina, 1978, pp.216–18). As a result it would revitalize its military and colonial tradition and enter a new period of imperial greatness. Preto emphasized this was no conservative nostalgia for past glories: 'Nationalism can no longer signify "Tradition" – but a breaking of the mould – a break with the old ideological restraints so that the spirit may fly and rise ever higher' (ibid., pp.231–9). In similar vein José Antonio explained to his followers that:

> Revolution . . . is the task for a determined minority whose first steps will not be understood by the masses, since understanding is the most valuable thing the masses lose as the victims of an era of decadence. But revolution will eventually replace the barren confusion of our collective life with the joy and radiance of a new order. (Thomas, 1972, p.204)

Degrelle's 'progress' from the advocate of Belgium's moral rearmament through a revitalized and integral Catholicism to a philo-Nazi, but still Belgian, fascism is unique. Yet looking back with pride to when he fought alongside the German SS on the Russian front, he has no doubts as to what united all fascists in a common bond. The elusive 'fascist minimum' turns out to be precisely what we have termed 'palingenetic ultra-nationalism':

> 'Fascism' had sprung up everywhere, in Europe, spontaneously, under very different forms, from this vital need, a total and general one, of renewal: *renewal of the State* to break free from the games of dice played by political anarchy; renovation of society liberated from the asphyxiating conservatism of bourgeois with gloves and stiff collars . . . ; *social renewal*, or more precisely, social revolution, liquidating paternalism, . . . putting capital in its place as a material instrument, the people, a living substance, becoming once more the essential base, the primordial element of the life of the Fatherland; finally a *moral revolution* . . . which would teach the nation, the youth once more to rise up and give its all. (Degrelle, 1969, pp.31–2)

As we have already pointed out, Zeev Sternhell applies a different ideal type from the one we have put forward, namely one which sees fascism as the synthesis of (revolutionary) nationalism and (non-materialist) socialism. Yet on the basis of studying many thousands of pages of original materials relating to the ideology of French fascists he comes to the conclusion that the:

> . . . thirst for renewal, which is shared by a whole generation, constitutes a sort of common denominator for fascists and for *fascisants*, but also for all those who simply cannot resist the appeal of fascism, its ethos, its dynamism, its youthfulness . . . For men like Mounier who like depicting France as an 'exhausted invalid', as a country debilitated by the forces of 'decomposition', struck down by sickness of the will, for men who wonder 'is France finished?' the message of a Maulnier or a Brasillach cannot fail to strike a chord. (Sternhell, 1983, p. 239)

It was such concerns for the health of the nation which underlie the different projects for the restructuring of the nation proposed by the movements we have considered: the 'new man', the new national community, the new international order, the new civilization destined to emerge as a result of this revolution are seen as finally putting an end to the process of decay which has produced so many external symptoms of structural crisis in society and robbed modern life of meaning and dignity. In this context the writings of Drieu la Rochelle, especially the novel *Gilles* and his literary testament, *Récit secret*, are highly illuminating for the insights they afford into the nature of fascism. They bear eloquent witness to his personal conversion from deep cultural pessimism to a manic faith that a fascist revolution was transfiguring Europe, thus throwing vital light on to his motives for becoming one of the PPF's most effective propagandists (see Soucy, 1979). Drieu was obsessed with the cultural decay of the age he was living through, but even before the PPF was founded nationalism was at the heart of his personal revolt against decadence. In a significant passage he seems to be transposing the concept of *stirb und werde* (die and become) from the sphere of nature where Goethe located it to the realism of national politics: 'France is dying. But only external forms die; for life to die is already an act of living again . . . Life in France is undergoing one of its metamorphoses . . . Let France die so that she may live anew'. (quoted in Plumyène and Lasierra, 1963, p.166)

Whatever the base motives which caused millions of Europeans to become fellow-travellers or collaborators of Fascism and Nazism once those movements had seized power, the ideological mainspring of fascism was originally provided by idealists driven by an almost puritanical urge to purge society of degeneracy. It was as one of their most articulate spokesmen that Drieu could identify fascism with 'health, dignity, fullness, heroism' (Sternhell, 1983, p.270) or write: 'I am fascist because I have taken stock of the advance of decadence in Europe. I have seen in fascism the only way to contain and reverse this decadence' (quoted in Paxton, 1972, p.146).

At an affective level inter-war fascism was, for its true activists and 'believers' at least, rooted in a subjective experience of profound cultural malaise and historical crisis to which it seemed to offer a cure. For the vast majority who remained outside the magic circle of this logic, there was no shortage of objective indices pointing to social, economic problems and a crisis of civilization. Indeed, from a liberal humanist perspective the mush-rooming of ultra-right, racist and fascist movements and the installation of fascist and para-fascist regimes were themselves the most important signs that pathological processes were at work. Because only a minority could spontaneously feel drawn to be members of an ideological community based on fascism's drastic diagnosis of the problems of contemporary society and their remedy, the high public profile enjoyed by movements upholding it belied their essential impotence. Even when fascism suceeded in becoming a genuine mass movement (for example in Hungary, Finland, Romania), it proved just as incapable of seizing power from (neo-)conservative as from liberal regimes.

We have already considered at some length the only two exceptions to this rule, Fascism and Nazism. These demonstrated another sort of impotence, namely their incapacity to create more than a grotesque travesty of the regenerated national community promised in their rhetoric. Here too the revolt against decadence remained abortive, the new nation stillborn.

By now several important aspects of fascism's psychological dynamics and structural causes should already be coming into focus. But before we draw any conclusions about either we must consider the handful of non-European fascisms which were contemporaries of those in inter-war Europe, as well as the countless ones which have since emerged all over the world, so as to establish how far they confirm or modify the patterns which we have detected.

References

Clearly scholarly works in English relevant to the varieties of fascism and para-fascism touched on in this chapter run into many hundreds. Those cited in the chapter are generally the most accessible general treatments of the subject and most contain invaluable bibliographies for more specialized study. Particularly important texts which cover fascism and proto-fascism in several European countries are Rogger and Weber (1965); Laqueur (1979), Payne (1980), Larsen *et al.* (1980) and Blinkhorn (1990).

Andricopoulos, Y., 1980. The power base of Greek authoritarianism, in Larsen *et al.* (op. cit.).

Austin, J., 1990. The conservative right and the far right in France: the search for power, 1934–44, in M. Blinkhorn (ed.), *Fascists and Conservatives*, Unwin Hyman, London.

Baker, D.N., 1976. Two paths to socialism: Marcel Déat and Marceau Pivert, *Journal of Contemporary History*, Vol.11, No.1.

Blinkhorn, M., 1990. Conservatism, traditionalism and fascism in Spain, 1898–1937, in M. Blinkhorn (ed.), *Fascists and Conservatives*, Unwin Hyman, London.

Buchanan, T. and Conway, M. (eds), 1996. *Political Catholicism in Europe, 1918–1960*, Oxford University Press, Oxford.

Cerutti, M., 1986. *La Svizzera italiana nel ventennio fascista*, Franco Angeli, Milan.

Conway, M., 1986. Le Rexisme de 1940 à 1944: Degrelle et les autres, *Centre de Recherches et d'Etudes Historiques de la Seconde Guerre Mondiale*, Vol. 10.

Cronin, M., 1997. *The Blueshirts and Irish Politics*, Cork University Press, Cork.

Dambassina-Kamara, K., 1983. *Le regime du 4 août en Grèce*, Université de Paris VII, Paris.

Déak, I., 1965. Hungary, in H. Rogger and E. Weber (eds), *The European Right*, University of California Press, Berkeley and Los Angeles.

Degrelle, L., 1969. *Hitler pour 1000 ans*, Éditions de la Table Ronde, Paris.

Djursaa, M., 1981. Denmark, in S.J. Woolf (ed.), *Fascism in Europe*, Methuen, London.

Étienne, J.M., 1968. *Le Mouvement rexiste jusqu'en 1940*, Colin, Paris.

Gallagher, T., 1990. Conservatism, dictatorship and fascism in Portugal, 1914–45, in M. Blinkhorn (ed.), *Fascists and Conservatives*, Unwin Hyman, London.

Glaus, B., 1980. The National Front in Switzerland, in Larsen *et al.* (op.cit.).)

Gudmundson, A., 1980. Nazism in Iceland, in Larsen *et al.* (op. cit.).

Hagtvet, B., 1980. On the fringe: Swedish fascism 1920–45, in Larsen *et. al.* (op. cit.).

Hansen, E., 1981. Fascism and Nazism in the Netherlands 1929–39, *European Studies Review*, Vol.11.

Harrison, J., 1979. The regenerationist movement in Spain after the disaster of 1898, *European Studies Review*, Vol.9.

Havránek, J., 1971. Fascism in Czechoslovakia, in P.F. Sugar (ed.), *Native Fascism in the Successor States 1918–1945*, ABC, Santa Barbara, California.

Hayes, P., 1971. *Quisling*, David & Charles, Newton Abbot.

Hehn, J. von, 1957. *Lettland zwischen Demokratie und Diktatur*, Isar, Munich.

Herzstein, R.E., 1982. *When Nazi Dreams Come True*, Abacus, London.

Hoidal, O., 1989. *Quisling. A Study in Treason*, Oxford University Press, Oxford.

Hory, L. and Broszat, M., 1964. *Der kroatische Ustascha-staat, 1941–1945*, Deutsche Verlags-Anstalt, Stuttgart.

Huntington, S.P. and Moore, C.H., 1970. *Authoritarian Politics in Modern Society*, Basic Books, New York.

Karvonen, Lauri, 1988. From white to blue-and-black. Finnish fascism in the interwar period, *Commentationes Scientarum Socialium*, No.36.

Kitchen, M., 1980. *The Coming of Austrian Fascism*, Croom Helm, London.

Larsen, S.U., Hagtvet B. and Myklebust, J.P. (eds), 1980. *Who Were the Fascists: Social Roots of European Fascism*, Universitetsforlaget, Bergen.

Lewis, J., 1990. Conservatives and fascists in Austria, 1918–34, in M. Blinkhorn (ed.), *Fascists and Conservatives*, Unwin Hyman, London.

Martins, H., 1968. Portugal, in S.J. Woolf (ed.), *European Fascism*, Weidenfeld & Nicolson, London.

Mazgaj, P., 1979. *The Action Française and Revolutionary Syndicalism*, University of North Carolina Press, Chapel Hill.

Medina, J., 1978. *Salazar e os fascistas*, Livraria Bertrand, Lisbon.

Meneghello-Dinsic, K., 1969. L'état 'Oustacha' de Croatie (1941–45), *Revue d'Histoire de la Deuxième Guerre Mondiale*, No.74.

Mosley, O., 1934. *The Greater Britain*, BUF, London.

Mosley, O., 1936. *Blackshirt Policy*, BUF Publications, London.

Mosley, O., 1939. *Tomorrow We Live*, Greater Britain Publications, London.

Mosley, O., 1968. *My Life*, Nelson, London.

Motza, Ion., 1984. *Testamento di Ion Motza*, Edizioni All'Insegna del Vetro, Genoa.

Nagy-Talavera, M., 1970. *The Green Shirts and Others: A History of Fascism in Hungary and Romania*, Hoover Institution Press, Stanford, California.

Nilson, S.S., 1980. Who voted for Quisling?, in Larsen *et al.* (op. cit.).

Nolte, E., 1965. *Three Faces of Fascism: Action Française, Italian Fascism, National Socialism*, Weidenfeld and Nicolson, London.

Parming, T., 1975. *The Collapse of Liberal Democracy and the Rise of Authoritarianism in Estonia*, Sage, London, Beverly Hills.

Pauley, B.F., 1981. *Hitler and the Forgotten Nazis. A History of Austrian National Socialism*, Macmillan–University of North Carolina Press, London.

Paxton, R.O., 1972. *Vichy France: Old Guard and New Order*, Knopf, New York.

Payne, S.G., 1961. *Falange*, Stanford University Press, Stanford.

Payne, S.G., 1980. *Fascism. Comparison and Definition*, University of Wisconsin Press, London.

Plumyène, J. and Lasierra, R., 1963. *Les Fascismes français*, Macmillan, London.

Poulsen, H., and Djursaa, M., 1980. Social bases of Nazism in Denmark: The DNSAP, in Larsen *et al.* (op. cit.).

Preston, P., 1978. *The Coming of the Spanish Civil War*, Macmillan, London.

Quisling, V., 1942. *Quisling ruft Norwegen*, Eher, Munich.

Rath, J., and Schum, C.W., 1980. The Dollfuss–Schuschnigg regime: fascist or authoritarian?, in Larsen *et al.* (op cit.).

Rintala, M., 1965. Finland, in H. Rogger and E. Weber (eds), *The European Right*, University of California Press, Berkeley and Los Angeles.

Rogger, H., 1965. Russia, in H. Rogger and E. Weber (eds), *The European Right*, University of California Press, Berkeley and Los Angeles.

Schepens, L., 1980. Fascists and Nationalists in Belgium, 1919–40, in Larsen *et al.* (op. cit.).

Shillony, B., 1983. *Fascism from Above*, Clarendon Press, Oxford.

Soucy, R.J., 1979. *Fascist Intellectual: Drieu la Rochelle*, University of California Press, Berkeley.

Soucy, R.J., 1986. *French Fascism: The First Wave 1924–33*, Yale University Press, New Haven and London.

Stengers, J., 1965. Belgium, in H. Rogger and E. Weber (eds), *The European Right*, University of California Press, Berkeley and Los Angeles.

Sternhell, Z., 1972. *Maurice Barrès et le Nationalisme français*, Colin, Paris.

Sternhell, Z., 1978. *La Droite révolutionnaire, 1885–1914*, Editions du Seuil, Paris.

Sternhell, Z., 1979. Fascist Ideology, in W. Laqueur (ed.), *Fascism: A Reader's Guide*, Penguin, Harmondsworth.

Sternhell, Z., 1983. *Ni droite ni gauche. L'idéologie fasciste en France*, Edition du Seuil, Paris. (For English edition see above p.25).

Sternhell, Z., 1986. Fascism, in D. Miller (ed.), *The Blackwell Encyclopedia of Political Thought*, Basil Blackwell, Oxford.

Stevenson, J., 1990. Conservatism and the failure of fascism in inter-war Britain, in M. Blinkhorn (ed.), *Fascists and Conservatives*, Unwin Hyman, London.

Sugar, P.E. (ed.), 1971. *Native Fascisms in the Successor States*, ABC, Santa Barbara.

Szollosi-Janze, M., 1989. *Die Pfeilkreuzlerbewegung in Ungarn*, R. Oldenbourg, Munich.

Thomas, H. (ed.), 1972. *The Selected Writings of José Antonio Primo de Rivera*, Jonathan Cape, London.

Thurlow, R., 1987. *Fascism in Britain*, Blackwell, Oxford.

Weber, E., 1964. *Varieties of Fascism*, D. Van Nostrand, New York.

Weber, E., 1965. Romania, in H. Rogger and E. Weber (eds), *The European Right*, University of California Press, Berkeley and Los Angeles.

Whiteside, A.G., 1962. *Austrian National Socialism before 1918*, Nijhoff, The Hague.

Whiteside, A.G., 1975. *The Socialism of Fools. Georg von Schönerer and Austrian Pan-Germanism*, University of California Press, Berkeley and Los Angeles.

Wolf, D., 1969. *Doriot: du communisme à la collaboration*, Fayard, Paris.

Zacek, J.F., 1971. Czechoslovakian Fascisms, in P.F. Sugar (op. cit.).

6 Non-European and Post-war Fascisms

If the proliferation of abortive fascist movements in inter-war Europe necessitated a synoptic survey reminiscent of aerial reconnaissance, the sheer profusion of phenomena which in principle fall within the scope of this chapter is, to appropriate a Fascist expression, more 'oceanic' still, especially where post-war developments are concerned. For them to be included on the map at all means operating at an even higher altitude than before, so that only major topographical and geological features will stand out. Readers new to this area are thus urged to acquaint themselves in greater depth with any one of the fascisms touched on fleetingly here so as to break out of the series of abstractions and generalizations they encounter. Only in this way can they hope to acquire a feel for the unique texture and complexity which the subject exhibits at every turn when studied idiographically and which provide the sociological imagination with the raw material to work on so as to become 'real' (a point equally valid for the previous chapter). In the meantime, they are asked to take in good faith and in a heuristic spirit the schematic accounts of the non-European and post-war Europe ultra-right offered here, as well as the general inferences I have drawn about the light they throw on an important aspect of 'the nature of fascism', namely its almost Darwinian capacity for adaptation to its environment. Since these may well be novel to those who still tend to equate fascism essentially with the regimes of Mussolini and Hitler, and assume it was interred together with them in 1945, it is as well if they are summarized at the outset.

First, a consideration of events in inter-war Latin America and Japan underpins a central thesis of the last chapter: in poorly liberalized nations even sophisticated forms of indigenous fascism stand no chance of seizing and retaining power when pitted against dynamic conservative or neo-conservative opposition and are likely to have their populist appeal (that is political space) severely restricted by rival non-fascist forms of renovationist ultra-right. This picture of fascism's impotence as a revolutionary force is not essentially modified when South African fascism is considered, even though a unique ethnic and political situation has continued since the Second World War to give it a particular virulence, despite a high degree of ambient 'modernization' that shapes the lives of the ruling caste. The rest of the chapter is devoted mainly to an account of post-war fascism in Europe and the United States which adds two new elements. First, fascism clearly no longer requires objective conditions of developmental or socio-political crisis, let alone the threat of Marxist revolution, as a precondition for its existence for it appears to have established itself, at least among a numerically insignificant but highly unsilent minority, as a permanent idiom of Western culture. Second, European fascism has undergone several significant ideological and tactical transformations which underline its protean ability to adopt new formulations and guises, one of the most significant being a process of ideological and organizational internationalization, (an ecumenicalism which paradoxically continues to go hand in hand with the marked tendency to fractionalize which is a feature of most ideological forces when they are reduced to acting as a highly marginalized extrasystemic pressure group).

These general points, despite the lack of space to substantiate them in detail in these pages, are worth placing firmly on the agenda of the fascist debate, if only to rebut several common misapprehensions about fascism which some of the most commonly available works on the subject do little to dispel. First and foremost, fascism is not intrinsically a European phenomenon, nor did 'the fascist era' conveniently end in 1945. In fact, Payne's statement that fascism was 'an historical phenomenon primarily limited to Europe during the era of the two world wars' (1980, p.176) holds true only if considerable weight is placed on the word 'primarily'. In addition, when a number of indigenous fascist ideologues generally neglected in surveys of the subject, whether non-European (for example Salgado in Brazil, Nakano in Japan) or post-war (for example de Benoist in France and Evola in Italy), are considered in a depth precluded here, they prove to have taken their ideology from cultural and historical sources of political mythopoeia quite remote from those drawn on by Fascism or Nazism which, as we have seen in Chapters 3 and 4, were themselves heterogeneous in their ideological roots as well as being worlds apart at a surface level. This merely serves to underline the fact that palingenetic ultra-nationalism as we have ideal-typically defined it can draw on any number of raw ingredients, local or imported, religious or secular. Nakano and Evola in particular also demonstrate how fallacious it would be to assume that fascism necessarily draws ideological sustenance from exclusively European wells of cultural heritage, such as Christian millenarism (for example Joachim of Flora), elitist sociology (for example Mosca and Pareto) or the late nineteenth-century 'revolt against positivism'.

On the basis of premises quite at variance with Brecht's Marxist assumptions, this chapter thus concurs with his declaration in the closing words of *Arturo Ui* that 'the bitch which gave birth to [Nazism] is still on heat', even if it does not endorse the play's implication that the deformed runts which it continues to sire will ever again pose a major threat to the Western liberal humanist and parliamentary tradition. In case that should complacently imply the end, if not of ideology or of history, then at least of fascism, the chapter concludes with a fleeting allusion to two largely non-Westernized countries where regimes have in the recent past been installed by cadre movements whose rationale for systemic and systematic barbarity bears an uncanny structural resemblance to that of fascism, even if they spurn the principle of mass mobilization 'from below'. In other words, those studying or monitoring fascism should be on the look-out for scavenging new breeds of *zoón politikón* who feed on similar ideological food. But before venturing so far into *terra incognita*, we will start on a more familiar province for comparative fascist studies by considering Latin America.

Fascism in Latin America

The radical divergence between the taxonomic implications of Marxist paradigms of fascism and the ideal-typical definition offered in this book is nowhere illustrated more clearly than in the case of Latin America. What the radical left has throughout the twentieth century regarded as a hothouse of fascism in its most nakedly counter-revolutionary, dictatorial forms turns out, when seen in terms of our taxonomy, to have hosted hardly any political formations of substance which approximate to it. Certainly a tangle of factors have conspired to give many parts of Latin America a political culture in which (somewhat like Eastern Europe in the inter-war period) a 'healthy' parliamentary system, let alone a socialist one, has found it difficult to secure a footing. The result has been that on those rare occasions when democratic institutions have appeared to be establishing themselves in the hands of liberal or socialist elites, the threat of a left-wing coup, or (more usually) a right-wing military putsch which installs a regime ruled by a junta (*coronelismo*) or a personal dictator (*caudillismo*), has rarely been far away. Yet, paradoxically, the same conditions have also made it a hostile environment for an unadulterated fascism to thrive. Not only have populist energies been more easily excited by Catholicism, Marxism or charismatic dictatorship than by visions of an organic national community under a radically new order, but the few seedlings of palingenetic ultra-nationalism that did manage to germinate have sooner or later been trampled underfoot or absorbed by the non-revolutionary authoritarian right just like those which surfaced under Franco, Salazar or Pétain.

Hence to look for fascist regimes in Latin America is an exercise in snark-hunting. The only two plausible candidates are the *Estado Novo* which Vargas established in Brazil from 1937 till 1945 and the Perón government in Argentina (1945–55). Closer inspection shows, however, that the 'New State' succeeded only in being, like the Portuguese regime it plagiarized, both para- and anti-fascist. Certainly that of Juan Perón came closer because it not only blended elements of socialism with nationalism in an attempt to find a 'Third Way' between capitalism and communism but was legitimated by a populist movement which endowed the leadership, especially Evita Perón, with charismatic powers. But neither the ultra-nationalism nor the palingenetic myth of Peronism were sufficiently radical to lead to the full-scale programme of socio-economic transformation necessary to create an organic national community or to qualify as 'fascist' as we have defined it. Once the search for unambiguous specimens of fascism focuses not on regimes but on the yet more kaleidoscopic sphere of inter-war political movements (see Alexander, 1973; Hennessy, 1979), there are few direct hits, even if there is no shortage of 'near misses' which at least serves to demonstrate the exclusive function of our ideal type when used as a taxonomic category for nearly all the putative fascisms turn out on closer inspection to be lacking at least one definitional characteristic.

Thus, the Argentinean *Afirmación de una Nueva Argentina* (ADUNA), an alliance of eight ultra-right groupings formed in 1933 under the spell of the visionary poet Lugones, created neither the para-military or mass movement necessary to live up to the palingenetic promises of its name and hence remained a proto-fascist engine without gear-box or wheels till it broke up in 1938. Apparently closer to the mark, Mexico's *Acción Revolucionaria Mexicana*, or Gold Shirts (*Dorados*) consciously aped contemporary European para-military groups such as the SA in style and ethos but lacked the palingenetic vision needed to rank as anything more than a counter-revolutionary and anti-Semitic terrorist group. This cannot be said of another Mexican movement, the *Union Nacional Sinarquista* formed in 1937. Its crusade against the alleged *an*archism of the times, which it identified with the familiar fascist bug-bears (socialism, liberalism, secularism, the materialist decadence of the United States), was conceived as the first stage in a heroic national rebirth. Moreover, unlike ADUNA, the *Sinarquistas* rapidly became a genuine mass movement with as many as half a million members. However the centrality of the Christian faith to its vision of the new order classifies it as a radical form of political Catholicism rather than fascism, while the absence of a para-military dimension condemned it in any case to fade into an ineffectual right-wing pressure group, eventually superseded by the conservative *Acción Nacional*. Though anti-clerical, Peru's *Apra* also fails to measure up to the criteria we have established, even though its original blend of Marxism, Fabian socialism and *indigenista* nationalism was combined with the vision of a new national community of all Peruvians in a way which suggests a deep affinity with 'leftist' fascism (for example the Italian national syndicalists). Yet, despite developing a degree of popular support and spawning a paramilitary wing, the *bufalos*, the movement failed to win over the army and gradually evolved into the social democratic party which finally took power constitutionally in 1985 – a fate inconceivable for a genuine fascist movement. In the 1930s the Paraguayan *Febreristas* had the revolutionary intransigence which the *Sinarquistas* and *Apristas* lacked, and their programme had palingenetic overtones in its stress on the need to rebuild the country, introduce land reforms and move towards a semi-corporatist economy. Yet in the year between their successful coup in 1936 and being ousted by the army, the new state showed no sign of a commitment to radical populism or nationalism and in the post-war era this movement too evolved into a form of democractic socialism.

Of five political movements whose names specifically imply fascist aspirations, only one is of any significance in the present context. The Argentinean Fascist Party founded in 1938 soon disappeared without trace, and the equally mimetic and ineffectual *Falange Española Tradicionalista* set up by Spanish ex-patriates in Mexico was, as the name implies, Franquist and hence non-fascist. As for two other Falangist parties of the day, the Chilean one formed in 1938 turns out to have been a grouping of political Catholicism which formed the nucleus of what was to become the country's Christian democratic party. The *Falange Socialista Boliviana*, on the other hand, started out three years earlier as a more radical bid to transplant José Antonio's vision of a national syndicalist Spain to the New World, but it too gradually de-fascistized itself into a democratic right-wing opposition party after the war, despite the demagogic fantasies nurtured by its leader de la Vega at the outset. In contrast the Chilean *Movimiento Nacional Socialista*, formed by the Hispano–German González von Mareés in 1932, was more resolute in its revolutionary ambitions and finally provides the political entomologist with an authentic specimen of Latin American fascism. With considerable backing from *emigré* Germans and the urban middle classes, it set out to fulfil its self-appointed mission of regenerating Chile through the combination of single-party rule, corporatism and the solidarity of the whole population, and quickly built up a membership of 20,000, as well as a para-military force modelled on the SA. Though it started out as the crudely mimetic Nazi movement which its name implied, González, with the help of the party's leading intellectual Carlos Keller, soon turned the *Nacis* organizationally and ideologically into an indigenous form of fascism which by 1938 was strong enough to attempt a military coup. Yet once again fascism proved not only its fundamental antagonism to the conservative ultra-right, but its impotence to overthrow it, and the putsch was ruthlessly crushed by government troops. The party was renamed *Vanguardia Popular Socialista*, but disbanded in 1941 after the government had temporarily interned González on suspicion of insanity.

By far the most significant case of fascism in Latin America thrown into relief by the ideal type we are using was the *Ação Integralista Brasileira* (AIB). Its founder and leader, Plinio Salgado, had undergone an ecstatic conversion experience on his visit to Mussolini's Italy in 1930, returning convinced that 'the concept of fascism' would be 'the light of the new age' (Levine, 1970, p.81). Two years later he launched the AIB, which, in contrast to all the other initiatives we have considered, was not only based on an original form of palingenetic ultra-nationalism but 'took off' to become a revolutionary mass movement which posed a serious threat to the government. Accurate statistics are impossible to obtain, but by the end of 1934 it had as many as 180,000 members, and a year later was holding rallies of an estimated 42,000 party faithful. Three years later it controlled numerous provincial newspapers and had a network of over 4,000 cells covering every part of the country and co-ordinating a total of anything up to 200,000 activists (the party claimed 400,000). These are staggering figures given the poor politicization of Brazilian society as a whole and the attempts by Vargas, virtual dictator since 1930, to suppress the movement's activities.

With so many followers behind him, Salgado was able to develop an elaborate organizational structure for his movement which, while deliberately emulating Fascism, was far from being slavishly mimetic. It was effectively run by a 'Chamber of the Forty' (cf. the Fascist Grand Council), representing major personalities from the spheres of economics, education, culture, the professions, government, industry and the armed forces (the AIB was particularly influential among Navy officers), and which presided over a hierarchical institutional network covering district, municipal, state, regional and national levels. Attempting to emulate the NSDAP of the late 1920s in becoming a para-state organization, the AIB set up party organs to cover numerous aspects of national and social life, including first aid, scouting, sport, aviation – of particular importance were the party trade union movement (*Frente Unica Sindical*), a women's federation of 'Green Blouses', a comprehensive youth movement and a National Secretariat for Propaganda. Inevitably, it also instituted a party militia led by Barraso, an anti-Semite who openly admired Streicher's services to the NSDAP and was second only to Salgado in importance as party ideologue and propagandist.

'Integralist' doctrine (not to be confused with 'integrism', a post-war form of political Catholicism) is even less open to the charge of plagiarism. The central stress on 'Brasilian-ness' (*Brasilidade*, the elusive product of a unique amalgam of indigenous, negro and Portuguese cultures) may at first sight seem a reworking of the Fascist cult of 'Roman-ness'. But it differed from Fascism in folding into its ultra-nationalism from the outset both the commonplaces of cultural-economic anti-Semitism increasingly wide-spread in Brazilian society of the time and a defence of Christian values which went beyond Fascist concessions to political Catholicism and was more akin to the political piety of José Antonio's Falange. The AIB also designed its own version of the ritual politics which had impressed Salgado so much in Mussolini's Italy: the militia wore green shirts with black and blue armbands inscribed with the Greek letter 'Σ' (the mathematical sign of summation), members greeted each other with the Roman salute accompanied by the salutation 'anauê' (derived from the Tupi indian language) and the party held elaborately orchestrated ceremonies such as the Night of the Silent Drums to mark the party's founding. On such occasions the Integralist hymn *Avante* would be sung and the venue bedecked with national and party flags, lavish green and blue bunting and banners bearing such slogans as 'Our Hour Will Come'. Following in Mussolini's footsteps, Salgado baptized 1932 'Year One' of the new era (see Levine, 1970, ch.8).

What marks out the AIB as an authentic form of non-European fascism is the fact that both its agitation and propaganda were underpinned by an elaborate philosophy of history which had been homespun by Salgado himself and which bears the unmistakable stamp of palingenetic ultra-nationalist myth. In the true fascist spirit, a holistic vision of the state of human affairs banished in one fell swoop all the uncertainties and anxieties of the modern age, interpreting them as ephemeral symptoms of the painful transition from an age of decadence to a new age. There had already been three major phases in human evolution, and it was the destiny of an Integralist Brazil to act as the mid-wife of the 'fourth humanity' (see Trindade, 1974). Yet, though the ideological originality and momentum as both a mass and a cadre movement of revolutionary populism places the AIB in the same league as the Romanian Iron Guard as a major manifestation of native fascism, its failure to win over the army made it as impotent to topple Vargas's *Estado Novo* as the Legionaries were to oust King Carol or

Antonescu, and it was finally suppressed in December 1937. Two revolts by *Integralistas* the following year were easily put down, and any threat they posed to the state evaporated entirely when Salgado retired to Portugal soon after (see Hilton, 1972). The fate of the AIB seems to confirm the impression that if fascist movements are generally abortive in their bid to overthrow liberal systems, they are even more powerless when pitted against an established authoritarian regime of whatever complexion. Such a régime has few of the constraints of a liberal regime in taking Draconian measures to deal with a putschist threat or with an upsurge of populism (unless, that is, it develops the irresistible momentum attained by 'people power' in some East bloc countries in 1989 which fascism never did even in Weimar Germany).

Since 1945 Latin America has been awash with various denominations of ultra-right fighting crusades against the evils allegedly embodied by communists, liberals, Jews, and the United States, but few approximate to the Identikit of fascism which our ideal type provides. To take just two examples: the vicious anti-Semitic Tacuara movement in Argentina (see Eisenberg, 1967, ch.15) adopted Nazi trappings but lacked a palingenetic ideology, while Brazil's National Renewal Alliance (ARENA) no more attempted mass mobilization than ADUNA had. Chile's *Frente Nacional Patria y Libertad* formed in 1970 as the spearhead of terroristic opposition to Allende is a closer match. Drawing on a *nacista* legacy and an indigenous form of populist corporativism called 'gremialism' (*gremio*, a committee) whose roots stretched back into the nineteenth century, the FNPL quickly became an influential ultra-nationalist, anti-communist faction with definite palingenetic themes in its programme. Yet, like so many ultra-right formations in Latin America, it was too embroiled with traditional conservative and militarist forces to count as full-blown fascism.

The only vestiges of genuine fascism are of a nostalgic, mimetic or imported variety. The Brazilian Workers' and Peasants' Union was partly an attempt to revive Salgado's AIB, but by the 1970s it had faded from the scene, as had a bid to found a 'National Front' as the nucleus of a Brazilian neo-Nazi movement. The success of these initiatives was eclipsed by those of the clandestine Organization of Former SS Members (Odessa) and of the philo-Nazi elements within expatriate German communities to turn some Latin American countries into a second *Heimat* to thousands of unrepentant Nazis and war-criminals, Mengele being only the most infamous. The same countries continue to accommodate 'groupuscules' affiliated with some of the 'internationalist' fascist organizations which will be encountered later: Argentina, Bolivia, Ecuador, and Uruguay have links with the Spain-based neo-Nazi CEDADE, El Salvador and Peru with the neo-Nazi WUNS operating from the United States, and Mexico with Evolian neo-fascism originating in Italy (see Ó Maoláin, 1987). This does little to qualify the overriding impression that, as far as Latin America is concerned, the only notable specimens of fascism in the inter-war period were the Chilean *Nacis* and Salgado's AIB, and that it has been a spent force there ever since, even if in most countries the non-fascist ultra-right, both as movement and regime, has continued to be very much alive and frequently kicking.

Japanese Fascism

As early as 1934 Soviet Marxists were describing contemporary Japan as fascist when it was still far from the apogee of its imperialism or totalitarianism, and a number of post-war Japanese historians have been happy to take over this foreign model without even attempting to improve it. But if the homogeneity of Japan's cultural history compared with that of Latin America in principle makes it easier to answer questions about whether or not it hosted an indigenous form of fascism, then the dubious applicability of Western historical analogies and social scientific concepts to such a radically different society compounds even further the problematic nature of the term as a generic concept (cf. Sims, 1982; Payne, 1984; Kasza, 1984). Certainly, a concomitant of the industrialization and 'massification' of Japan in the early twentieth century was the embryonic emergence of a pluralist party-political system, an increasingly politicized general public, and an intelligentsia polarized into ultra-left and ultra-right. But the comforting sense of familiarity that a historian of inter-war Europe might have is quickly dissipated when the period is looked at in terms of the structural forces shaping it.

A major feature of Japan's particular *Sonderweg* (for, as I have already pointed out, every nation's modernization is a 'special path') was that its rapid metamorphosis from what had been a declining feudal society into an aggressively expansionist industrial–military giant was completed under the aegis of an *ancien régime* which had managed to carry out a gradualist but highly dynamic 'conservative revolution' from within. It was not in the wake of a 'bourgeois revolution' or a Marxist–Leninist coup but under an 'enlightened' emperor that Japan was for the first time opened up to technological and economic forces of modernization (the so-called Meiji Restoration, 1868–1912). This meant that what from a Euro-centric point of view are 'normal' socio-cultural concomitants of such forces – namely liberalism, secularism, rationalism and individualism – were largely filtered out by a pervasive conservatism. As a result the populist form of 'integral nationalism' called 'Japanism' which emerged in the late nineteenth century has telling analogies with *völkisch* nationalism in contemporary Germany except in one vital respect: it was not a sub- or counter culture but officially encouraged 'from above'. Its key concepts, such as *kokutai* (national essence or entity) and *kokumin* (people, *Volk*), were steeped in a mystical sense of the indivisible unity between the emperor and his subjects. These in turn were reinforced by such deeply rooted and pervasive structures of Japanese cultural life as Confucianism, Buddhism, the samurai ethos of *bushido*, emperor worship, 'familism', militarism and, above all, Shintoism. As a result populist ultra-nationalism in Japan did not arise to challenge an existing 'legal–rational' system (as the Second Reich was in part) but had the effect of altogether precluding such an 'alien' system from being installed in the first place. It thereby created the basis of a fusion of rapid modernization and aggressive imperialism with a blend of charismatic and traditional politics (see Barrington Moore, 1969; Gluck, 1985).

In short, the initial conditions for the emergence of a Japanese fascism of any moment were simply lacking. Despite the many points of superficial analogy between the Third Reich and post-1932 Japan when taken as case-studies in totalitarianism, none of its war leaders, even Tōjō, assumed the function of a Mussolini, let alone a Hitler, while the Imperial Rule Assistance Association, set up in 1940 when parties were dissolved, was, unlike the NSDAP, little more than a bureaucratic fiction. Even the military's ascendancy over all political, economic and social life did not mean the formal end of parliamentary processes. Indeed, when elections were held in 1942 more candidates stood than ever before (see Barrington Moore, 1969). A reference to 'the coming to power of the Japanese fascist movement' in the 1930s (Ó Maoláin, 1987, p.176) is thus as misleading as it is mysterious.

The result for comparative fascist studies is that, while inter-war Japan is seething with various complexions of rightist politics, the yardstick of an ultra-nationalism both radically populist and anti-conservative must be applied judiciously if genuine parallels to the European experience are to be identified, and sausages are not to be judged by their skins. For example, the New Order Movement turns out to have been a political current promoted by the Showa Research Association, an imperial and imperialistic government think-tank (see Fletcher, 1982), while what some Japanese historians have dubbed as *gun-fuashisumu* (Sims, 1982) refers to the fundamentalist militarism which did so much to revolutionize the country's conservatism and 'totalitarianize' its state apparatus from above, that is in an *anti-fascist* direction. It is only when attention is turned to schemes for transforming Japan through a popular revolution or a military coup that indirect parallels with the European fascist and proto-fascist experience do become discernible. A spate of such schemes were hatched in the inter-war period from within a sub-culture whose obsessions ranged from Japan's political and moral regeneration to her global mission to stem the tide of Westernization and found a new Asian or Pacific order. It is no coincidence that at the time Japan was undergoing a sustained socio-economic and politico-cultural crisis (see Brown, 1955, chs. 9–10; Morley, 1971).

One of the most important manifestations of this sub-culture was the burgeoning of a publicistic radical right, a phenomenon meticulously documented by police censors, (a fact which highlights the need to distinguish between the official regime and putative fascist movements in Japan). The records show that by February 1936 there were some fifty-one rightist journals which had a total circulation of over 89,000 and which offered various blueprints for a new order, ranging from radical programmes of re-ruralization ('idealist Japanism'), to blends of tradition and industrial capitalism ('renovationist Japanism'), to a combination of tradition with state socialism ('state socialism'). However, the centrality of the emperor cult to all of them bears out Kasza's verdict (1984) that we are dealing with something less than fascist in its radicalism.

The same judgement applies to the two abortive military coups known as the 'Incidents' of 15 May 1932 and 26 February 1936 respectively. In complete contrast to most putsches (see Pinkney, 1990), the Young Officers who carried them out were inspired by an elaborate political vision of the country's imminent metamorphosis. While the ethical creed which informed this vision drew on Nichiren Buddhism, *bushido*, and a form of Confucianism (Ōyōmei) which stresses the purity of the resolute deed (cf. above p.68 Gentile's 'actualism'), its underlying philosophy of history was based on a revolutionary interpretation of the Meiji Restoration and of Japan's historical mission to liberate Asia from Western imperialism and decadence. These two components had first been synthesized in the 'Plan for the Reorganization of Japan' published by Kita Ikki in 1919 and treated by the officers practically as a sacred text of the new order (see Wilson, 1969; Shillony, 1973). Yet though the language in which they couched the rationale for their revolt both in their manifestos and at their trial is steeped in palingenetic imagery, the fundamental place attributed to the divine emperor Hirohito as the corner-stone of the new Japan makes parallels with fascism quite specious, something they themselves knew only too well: 'We are neither rightists nor leftists. We oppose communism, but we also reject fascism. What we stand for is restoration-revolution (*ishin no kakumei*), which would establish direct Imperial rule' (Shillony, 1973, p.80).

There was, however, one ultra-right movement which was radical enough in its rejection of traditional Japanese institutions to meet the criteria set by our ideal type of fascism, namely *Tohokai* or The Society of the East. As with Salgado's Integralism, the movement was undoubtedly, as far as external trappings were concerned, a 'direct imitation of Hitler and Mussolini' (Payne, 1984, p.273) – for example, its supporters wore black shirts sporting arm-bands with the Japanese character meaning 'the East' – but it was far from being mimetic fascism at the level of ideology. Its programme was a highly original political myth elaborated by its founder, Nakano Seigō, who shared many key sources and theories with the Young Officers, in particular his adulation for the samurai Saigō who led the abortive Satsuma Rebellion in 1871. Like them, he saw this desperate bid to bring about the direct rule of the emperor over his people as embodying the 'true' potential of the Meiji Restoration which should now be fulfilled in the Showa period under Hirohito. But Nakano's vision of the imminent revolution differed in one vital respect from that of the Young Officers or Kita Ikki. For him, the emperor was no divinely enlightened autocrat but the symbol of the god-like potential in each individual which lay at the basis of popular sovereignty. Obsessed by the signs of national weakness and moral decadence he saw around him, he found profound parallels between Showa Japan and the crisis which had brought down the *ancien régime* in France, parallels which at one point made him gravitate towards the liberal camp.

However, in 1931 the signs of mounting anarchy caused Nakano to despair in reformism and look instead to a ground-swell of revolutionary populism which would transcend class divisions and the distinction between right and left. This would lay the basis for the 'moral community' which he believed had started to form in the early Meiji period, and which – led by a new national hero capable, like Saigō had been, of channelling the energies of the people – would regenerate the country culturally and spiritually. Concurrently it would be revitalized socio-economically by a form of what he called 'social nationalism' (influenced by, of all things, the British Fabians). Far from slavishly imitating European fascism, he saw in

Mussolini (whom he met in 1938) and Hitler proof that Italy and Germany had found 'their' Saigō, able to achieve the union of thought and action prescribed by Ōyōmei intuitionism and give their nations *tenka hitori o motte okoru*, roughly translated as 'the power to rise up alone in the world'. But despite concerted attempts to widen its social base, the electoral performance of the Society of the East even at the height of its success (eleven seats in 1937) and the attendance at the deeply 'un-Japanese' mass rallies were far too feeble as displays of populist fervour to stop the movement being snuffed out along with other parties in 1940. Undeterred, Nakano continued his crusade for a new Japan single-handed, a tenaciousness rewarded by his being placed under house arrest in 1942, whereupon he committed *seppuku*, or ritual disembowelling, the only way out for a true samurai (see Najita, 1971; Shillony, 1981).

The fate of Nakano epitomizes the fact that, even in a period of major socio-political upheaval which has created a vigorous ultra-right, it is impossible for even the most dedicated fascist ideologue to win a significant following for the vision of a radically new type of reborn national community if it is conceived in terms which go against the grain of the dominant culture. In any case, even if he had created a mass movement it could never have mounted an effective assault on a neo-conservative ruling imperial, aristocratic and military caste which was so well 'dug in'. However, the removal of that caste by military defeat in 1945 did not mean the end of the 'extra-systemic' right (see Morris, 1960). By the mid-eighties there were still fifty revolutionary nationalist groups in Japan with a total constituency of 120,000 activists and fellow-travellers (Ó Maoláin, 1987, pp.176–7). Significantly, neither of its two most influential 'Japanist' writers, Hayashi and Mishima, followed Nakano's example in their personal struggle to combat the damage to Japanese society they saw being wrought by such 'alien' forces as liberalism and consumerism. The cult-status which Mishima won for himself with his abortive attempt to re-enact successfully the Young Officers' rebellion in a carefully staged 'Incident' on 25 November 1970 (which ended with his committing *seppuku*), and the existence of a Showa Restoration League indicate that contemporary Japan is still eminently capable of generating (ineffectual) currents of its own, quite unexportable, 'conservative revolution' but not fascism as such.

Fascism in Africa

If these surveys of inter-war Latin America and Japan are considered 'nomothetically' in relation to the whistle-stop visits to Portugal, Spain and Eastern European countries made in the last chapter, a rudimentary pattern suggests itself. In every case where the breakdown of traditional society and a superficial liberalization of institutions came into conjunction with sustained socio-political instability, it favoured the ascendancy of the ultra-right over liberalism and socialism. However, movements claiming to tackle the root causes of national weakness and 'anarchy' tended to lack either the radical populism or the palingenetic myth needed to approximate to (our ideal type of) fascism, while authoritarian regimes promising the nation law and order, dynamism or imperial greatness were invariably anti-fascist, even when they encouraged populist consensus as the mainstay of their legitimacy. (The significance of the fact that Fascism and Nazism succeeded in countries where the process of liberalization was by contrast both *advanced* and *structurally imperfect* will be considered in the last chapter.) If we push this line of reasoning a little further it should be clear that countries where secularization and 'nationalization' are minimal cannot create the initial conditions for an ultra-right to emerge, let alone fascism.

In other words, those parts of the world, including former colonies and dominions, where traditional religious culture has substantially resisted Westernization, or which have been forcibly incorporated into state communist systems or their sphere of influence – that is the Middle East, the Indian sub-continent, Central and Far Eastern Asia, Indonesia – could not engender fascism because there was no basis for the historical consciousness, the populist ultra-nationalism or the phoenix myth which fascism presupposes. It is significant that the one proto-fascist movement in the iddle East that did emerge was the Lebanese Phalange, founded in 1936 by Arab nationalists who were not Muslim but Maronite Christians and who thus found it more natural to imitate the paramilitary fascism of contemporary Europe (though even this grouping has officially shed its fascist legacy since the war). This is not to say that fascism is an essentially European phenomenon, as the examples of Salgado and Nakano make clear, but that conjunctures of socio-political forces which were pervasive in inter-war Europe, such as a populist nationalism and a secular nation-state, have to be present before it can establish itself.

A corollary of this observation is that Africa too, both before and after colonization, has entirely lacked the initial conditions for fascism. Not only has traditional culture continued to exert a considerable hold over the lives of a vast, 'un-massified' majority, but in every case the 'nation' was the administrative fiction of the 'mother country' (that is colonizing power) and usually bore the scantiest relation to the pre-existing tribal cultures and their territorial relations. As a result no national phoenix myth could be invoked by the many liberation movements which arose after 1945, or by the personal and military dictatorships of both ultra-left and ultra-right leanings which preserved the artificial entity of the nation they had inherited at the expense of its equally artificial representative democracy. The major exception to this generalization is, of course, South Africa, where alone among the scores of the world's nation-states which were formerly European possessions, political and economic hegemony is still in the grip of a (long since indigenous) white minority which has perpetuated the conditions of nineteenth-century colonialism by imposing them autocratically *from within*.

The bitter fruit of this totally anomalous, and ultimately untenable, situation is what has been termed a 'racially exclusive bourgeois democracy' (Davies *et al.*, 1988, p.131), or what through a different ideological lens could also be seen as a unique form of ultra-right regime which has apportioned its citizens civil rights and freedoms on a sliding scale of alleged racial superiority from white to black. The grotesque adaptation of a Western-style democratic system to the task of running a regime forced by the perverse logic of its franchise to operate as a police state against the majority of its citzens has created a powerful (black and white) reformist and a (predominantly black) revolutionary opposition. It has also brought into being a highly active (and exclusively white) ultra-right pledged to prevent any 'softening' of official policy. The growing structural tensions resulting from the government's decision to adopt a Canute-like stance against the post-war tide of decolonization has meant that, in glaring contrast to all the other countries we have considered, the seed-bed which South Africa provides for fascism has become more, not less, fertile since 1945.

When in February 1991 de Klerk officially made known his decision to dismantle the legal and constitutional basis of *apartheid*, it only deepened further the gulf which divides both reformists and reactionaries from those who believe that only a radically new type of regime can prevent its destruction at the hands of liberals, communists, blacks and Jews. One source of such convictions is a strain of Nazism which dates back to the 1930s, and whose presence is made more intelligible by South Africa's annexation of German South West Africa after the First World War and an influx of German immigrants from depression-stricken Europe thereafter. This was one reason why South Africa proved remarkably permeable to the Nazis' attempts to transplant their institutions so as to work towards the eventual incorporation of the country into the Third Reich. By 1936 the proliferation of branches of the NSDAP, the Hitler Youth, the Labour Front and Winter Help was sufficiently alarming for Nazi organizations to be banned by the ruling Union Party, but this only intensified the anti-Semitic agit-prop of the Greyshirt movement which had been formed in 1933 to emulate the SA.

But South Africa had no need to import German fascism, for it had long had a source of indigenous ultra-nationalism in the *Broederbond*, or Brother's Association. It was originally formed in 1918 to conserve a distinctive Afrikaner identity within the shot-gun union of Dutch and British colonies imposed by the South Africa Act of 1909, but it grew into a semi-secret society whose influence spread through osmosis into the highest echelons of the country's political, educational, judicial and bureaucratic structures, particularly in the police and the armed forces (Serfontein, 1979). One result of its omnipresence was that in the course of the 1930s Nazi Aryan racism and anti-Semitism were blended with two indigenous ideological idioms: a form of religious politics based on a bastardized form of Dutch Reformed Church protestantism and an epic 'myth of origins' which located the kernel of the future Afrikaner nation in the migrations of Boer settlers that had culminated in the Great Trek of 1838 (see Muller, 1981, ch.9). The result was a unique form of palingenetic politics: 'Christian Nationalism' (Bloomberg, 1981). It was symptomatic of how successful the *Broederbond* had been in combating the hegemony of Anglo-centric thinking that even Hertzog, prime minister from 1925 till 1939, became increasingly convinced as the war approached that Nazism was 'suited to the moral and religious outlook of the Afrikaner' and that 'a new world order was on the way' (Bunting, 1969, p.58).

In terms of what it reveals about the ideological dynamics of fascism, the most significant group to surface in inter-war South Africa was thus not the largely mimetic Greyshirts but the *Ossewa Brandwag* (OB), or Ox-wagon Sentinel, which drew heavily on indigenous ultra-nationalism. Its name evoked the neap-tide of populist Afrikaner consciousness unleashed by the centenary celebrations of the 'Great Trek' which, as chance or fate would have it, took place just when perennial tensions between the British and Dutch communities were reaching fever pitch in the wake of events in Europe. Fired by a palingenetic myth summed up in the slogan 'One God – One Faith – One People', the OB, or rather its para-military wing, the *Stormjaers* (Storm-troopers), took up the pro-Nazi interventionist cause when, at the outbreak of war, party politics were split between pro-British interventionists like Smuts and 'neutralists' like Hertzog and Malan, bitterly opposed to fighting on the British side. The defeat of the Third Reich sealed the fate of the OB's Operation Weissdorn to seize state power through a military coup, and also put paid to parallel campaigns fought by two smaller fascist groups, New Order and the *Boerenasie* (though the 'Boer Nation' was still active in 1967, see Eisenberg, 1967, pp.304–5).

As it turned out the Afrikaner equivalent of *völkisch* nationalism was to be incorporated into the state's basic law not by a fascist regime but by a political party, the (first 'Purified' then 'Reunited') National Party, which had increasingly shifted to the right both under the influence of the *Broederbond* and the *Ossewa Brandwag* – it is no coincidence that two future Nationalist prime ministers, Vorster and Botha, cut their ideological molars as members of both, or that the Greyshirts merged with the Nationalist Party after the war. Yet to hard-line 'Christian Socialists' and other white supremacists of fundamentalist persuasion even such pluralism as the Nationalist regime tolerated has been dangerous, opening the door to 'subversive' liberal, Jewish and communist influence and only fuelling the revolutionary aspirations of the disenfranchised black majority. Their worst fears seem justified now that the *verkrampte* (sound) policies of Verwoerd, Vorster and Botha have given way to de Klerk's new course of liberalization, and even the *Broederbond* has adopted a *verligte* ('enlightened') stance by discussing the possibility of an eventual transition to universal suffrage, though with a special status granted for the white minority.

On two occasions the extreme right's reaction to earlier liberalizing initiatives within the ruling Nationalist Party has been to form a new one: the Herstigte Nasionale Party or (Reconstituted National Party) in 1969, and the Conservative Party in 1982, whose leader, Treurnicht, was former chairman of *Broederbond*. Meanwhile, the ultra-right response has been to intensify its campaign for a post-liberal South Africa. Its purest expression in the build-up to a genuinely democratic South Africa has been the proposal of various schemes for a separatist homeland whether for the Whites, the Afrikaner, or the Boerevolk, the logical conclusion of all white supremacism when colonization, exploitation or *apartheid* by whites is ended. By 1989 no less than seven of such chimeric projects were in circulation. The most extreme reaction to the prospect of an integrated multi-racial society, however, was bound to come from the only true heir of the *OssewaBrandwag*, the *Afrikaner Weerstandsbeweging* (Afrikaner Resistance Movement) or AWB, which was founded in 1973 by the synchronistically named Terbanche (now Terre'Blanche) and can at present boast a membership of well over 50,000 and rising.

The AWB's ideological premises derive from fundamentalist Christian Socialism (much is made of the *Voortrekker* myth) laced with mimetic Nazism, especially its anti-Semitism and ritual. The resulting cocktail is symbolized in the AWB logo: the 777 of Good which will triumph over 666, the number of the Beast in the Book of Revelation, has been deliberately arranged so as to suggest the Swastika when placed on an armband or a banner. The AWB's *raison d'être* is to form the nucleus of a force capable of crushing the feared black uprising, thereupon clearing the way for the creation of the *Boerevolkstaat*, in which the Afrikaners will finally live as a true national community (and unlike the Orandians retain a black work-force). The first part of the programme is no empty rhetoric, for it wields a violent paramilitary arm, the Storm Falcons, and also controls *Brandwag*, a racist vigilante network, to mete out rough justice against 'trouble-makers'. Its interest in 'legal' routes to power was demonstrated in 1986 by a well-attended rally held jointly with the CPSA and HNP. Since Mandela's release the AWB has been in the vanguard of the organized backlash against de Klerk.

But the AWB is only the best known product of South Africa's post-war fascist culture, whose intensity and range even today bears comparison with that of Romania of the 1930s (when the centre of 'liberal' politics was also on the far right). It can boast guerrilla groups (the *Witkommando*), a youth movement (the *Voortrekker*), an organization for spreading the 'facts' about race (National Forum) and history (*Volkswag*), as well as a vast publicistic industry disseminating imported and home-produced literature in every conceivable dialect of ultra-right thought. It is a natural habitat for migrating members from such groups as the Ku Klux Klan or the British National Front and more obscure groups bent on saving the West against decadence and racial decay such as UNIDO (see Hill, 1988, ch.2). No wonder South Africa is seen by fascists and racists the world over as the front-line of the conflict between healthy nationalism and the forces undermining it, that is the detested 'One-World ideology' put forward by Marxists and Liberals alike (see, for example, the neo-fascist magazine *Nation Europa* for May/June 1989, an issue entirely dedicated to South Africa).

Unless racist theories about the Afrikaner national character are going to be invoked to explain why 1945 did not mark the effective end of fascism as a significant force in South African politics, then the answer must lie in the persistence and, recently, the intensification, of the same structural contradictions, economic, social, cultural and political, which nourished it in the inter-war period. De Klerk's bid to remove these contradictions could yet turn South Africa's fascisms into a mass movement on a par with, say, Salgado's AIB, though it is as doomed to fail in achieving its long-term goals as any of its inter-war forebears.

Post-war European Fascisms

Unlike South Africa, conditions in post-war Europe have precluded the formation of a micro-climate in which fascism could thrive as a significant oppositional force. In those countries pressganged into the Russian Empire, ultra-nationalism was smothered as effectively as any other indigenous political initiatives. Meanwhile, in Western nations the unprecedented scale of suffering caused by both the Third Reich and the war fought to defeat it soon gave way to a liberal–capitalist era of unprecedented stability and prosperity with the result that mainstream populist energies have stubbornly refused to flow along the channels carved out for it by fascist ideologies. As a revolutionary force, then, European fascism has been a dead letter since 1945. As a political sub-culture, however, it has shown a tenacious capacity not merely for survival but for adapting to the transformed environment in which it finds itself.

The first problem facing the student of contemporary European fascism, then, is not to find any signs of it but to disentangle its countless manifestations from the extraordinary proliferation of ultra-right phenomena which, paradoxically, only a society committed to pluralism can engender, and which have had nearly half a century to evolve since 1945 instead of the mere twenty years allotted to it by the inter-war period. The resulting taxonomic headache is vividly illustrated by the entries for European countries in Ó Maoláin's 'world directory' of the radical right (1987), which includes some fifty-five entries for the United Kingdom alone, not to mention over sixty defunct organizations. (The directory is invaluable for an appreciation of the profusion of post-war fascist organizations and their global sphere of operation, though they have to be carefully winkled out from non-fascist ones.) To flesh out the bare bones of the following overview, it can be supplemented with other sources which concentrate specifically on Europe: for example Beyme, 1988; Ford, 1990; Harris, 1990; Hainsworth 1992; Larsen, 1993. But by wielding our ideal type somewhat like secateurs (some would say a machete) to cut away varieties of politics not germane to our investigation, the topic is at least reduced to manageable proportions. In particular it precludes:

(i) reactionary military or dictatorial regimes (those of Franco and Salazar which survived from the 1930s or the Greek 'colonels' regime' of 1967–73, also a throwback to pre-war forms of authoritarianism);
(ii) extreme right-wing political parties whose illiberalism on issues of race, immigration and nationalism is 'reformist' rather than 'revolutionary', criteria which disqualify Le Pen's *Front National*, though they may well accommodate neo-fascist elements in both policies and support, a point to be developed below (see Harris, 1990, ch.3; Vaughan, 1991);
(iii) anti-socialist, anti-etatist, elitist forms of conservatism which remain on the cusp between the extreme right of liberal democracy and the 'ultra-right' which calls its institutions and principles into question (for example the British *The Salisbury Review* group or the Monday Club);
(iv) groupings whose publicistic or activist campaigns are single-target, for

example anti-socialist, anti-immigrant, anti-Semitic, without a blueprint for the new order, thus acting as extreme right-wing pressure groups on the status quo (for example in Britain the anti-immigration WISE, or the anti-communist Freedom Association);

(v) separatist or irredentist nationalists, even if they use highly palingenetic rhetoric and resort to terroristic, and thus highly undemocratic means, as long as they are fighting for democratic *ends* (that is a liberated or reunited national community living within its own liberal (or democratic socialist) state, and are thus not *ultra*-nationalists, for example some factions within the IRA, as well as Basque or Turkish Cypriot nationalists.

The most famous historical example of this hybrid of predominantly liberal ends and illiberal means is Zionism, a highly heterogeneous movement which originated in late nineteenth-century Europe inspired by an elaborate palingenetic scheme of Jewish history. Significantly, one of the many factions within it, the 'revisionists', rejected democratic institutions in the future Jewish state and thus exhibit close affinities with fascism as we have defined it (see Avineri, 1981, ch.15; Shavit, 1988). The modern descendants of this strain of Jewish ultra-nationalism are several minute groupings in contemporary Israel, such as *Tzomet*, the Renewed Zionism Party, which pursues radical anti-Palestinian and expansionist aims (see Mergui and Simonnot, 1987);

(vi) fundamentalist religious politics of the type associated with the ultra-Catholic National Restoration in France or the Islamic Party of Great Britain, which in 1990 declared the United Kingdom a 'non-territorial Muslim state'. (The Jewish equivalent is the National Religious Party.)

These exclusions still leave many hundreds of activist and publicistic organizations in post-war Europe whose core political myth can be shown to be a permutation of palingenetic ultra-nationalism, but which, because of the unique conjunctural and historical factors at work in each European country, compounded by the volatility intrinsic to all utopian politics, have manifested extreme heterogeneity in their surface ideology. As a result a complex taxonomic grid would be necessary to be able to pigeon-hole them even approximately according to basic doctrine, goals and tactics (as shown by the sub-divisions used by Ó Maoláin, 1987), while this information would have to be supplemented by indications of their geographical range of influence, longevity (or, more usually, ephemerality), size and social base of recruitment, leadership, funding and network of national or international affiliations before some sort of comprehensive overview could emerge. Though such a task goes way beyond the scope of this book, I must offer my own highly tentative set of sub-divisions to be made within post-war fascism so that the subsequent observations about its salient characteristics are not made in a vacuum.

Nostalgic Fascism/Neo-Nazism

This refers to formations which take up the basic world-view and struggle of inter-war fascist movements, albeit with programmes and tactics adapted to the transformed circumstances of post-1945 Europe:

(i) Highly marginalized and unsuccessful attempts to resuscitate inter-war movements, such as the Norwegian *Nasjonal Samling* (active in the seventies), the neo-Rexist *Rex National* and *Mouvement Social Belge*; in Britain, the Union Movement (1948–78), the Action Society (1978–) and the League of St. George (1974–), now an umbrella organization for the ultra-right, all of which originated as vehicles for the political ambitions of Oswald Mosley and Mosleyites. French fascists made efforts to regroup in the immediate post-war period, producing a cluster of ephemeral formations (see Algazy, 1984, ch.2), and a revived *Action Française* was active again in Paris student circles by the late 1980s. By 1976 four Spanish parties were disputing the right to wear the mantle of the Falange, one of them anonymous (see Ellwood, 1991, p.149). Mention should be made too of expatriate nostalgic parties such as the Hungarist Movement, direct descendant of Szálasi's Arrow Cross and the Legion of St. Michael, which recruited anti-communist Hungarians and Romanians living in Australia.

(ii) Italy's *Movimento Sociale Italiano* (MSI), the unique example of the resuscitation of an inter-war movement in an electoral party sufficiently durable (though consistently marginalized and now declining) to become a permanent fixture in national political life. Founded and led till his death in 1988 by Almirante, former head of propaganda in Mussolini's Salò Republic, the MSI has gradually outgrown its 'nostalgic' origins as a neo-Fascist party to become a fully fledged neo-fascist one (for the distinction see below) with well over a quarter of a million members, seats in the national and the European parliament, and links with neo-fascist activists, including three terrorist groups, *Nuclei Armati Rivoluzionari*, *Terza Posizione* and *Ordine Nuovo* (see Rosenbaum, 1975; Chiarini, 1991; Cheles, 1991).

(iii) The countless groupings which originated as attempts to perpetuate the Nazi struggle for a new order in the very different conditions of economic growth and political stability prevailing in the Federal Republic (sometimes affiliated with sister organizations in Austria). This 'nostalgic Nazism', and with mimetic Nazism outside Germany together comprise 'neo-Nazism' (though the term can be used with a more specialist meaning: see Husbands, 1991, pp.86–9). Neo-Nazism has never coalesced into a single force, creating instead a highly factionalized and 'fissiparous' political sub-culture which has shades of the *Los-von-Weimar* movement before the NSDAP succeeded in broadly uniting it (see Benz, 1989, chs. 1–3,5–7,9,14). This *Los-von-der-Bundesrepublik* movement originally recruited unreconstructed Nazis who had served the Third Reich, but the process of natural wastage has been partially compensated for by a continuous trickle of recruits to the cause from younger generations.

Organizationally, nostalgic Nazism includes ex-servicemen's associations, notably the still active Mutual Assistance Society Soldiers of the Former Waffen SS (HIAG); publishing houses (for example Christophersen's *Kritik Verlag*) and magazines (for example *Der neue Beobachter*); and terrorist groups (responsible for over 1,500 acts of violence in 1987 alone), ranging from notorious groups such as the Hoffmann Military Sports Group (WSG-Hoffmann), active from 1974 to 1980 when it was banned, to the Nagold Shock Troop (highly active in 1985) or even more obscure formations such as the People's Front for National Uprising which claimed responsibility for a bomb attack on the Berlin Wall in 1986 (Benz, 1989, ch.16; Husbands, 1991). There have been continuous attempts since 1945 to create a neo-Nazi movement on NSDAP lines, the better known of recent years being the People's Socialist League of Germany–Party of Labour (VSBD–PdA, 1971–82), the Action Front of National Socialists–National Activists (AFNS–NA) outlawed in 1983, *Die Bewegung* (the Movement) and the Free German Workers' Party (1984–). All such groups tend to spawn youth groups, magazines and prolific propagandistic literature which belie their minimal impact on society (Childs, 1991).

Mimetic Fascism/Neo-Nazism

A direct result of the cataclysmic 'success' which for a time crowned the Nazi bid to fulfil its racist–imperial goals is that it has established itself ever since 1945 as the dominant role model for fascists outside Germany, not just in Europe but all over the world, totally eclipsing in this respect Fascism, which had been so important in the inter-war period up to 1933. As a source of ultra-nationalism and racism, it resembles user-friendly ideological software placed in the public domain to be appropriated by anyone distressed by contemporary 'decadence' or just feeling 'bad'. This makes it important to distinguish the cosmetic use of Nazi trappings (insignia, slogans, SS- and Hitler-worship etc.) simply as a uniform for racial hatred, gratuitous vandalism and provocative 'anti-social' street theatre from a real commitment to National Socialism's underlying palingenetic vision. The persistence of non-cosmetic Nazism has led to:

(i) The foundation of crudely mimetic (and often highly ephemeral) Nazi parties which turn their back on any indigenous fascism, for example Belgium's *Mouvement Social Nationaliste*; the UK's British Movement and the British National Party, the group with the highest public profile in the early 1990s; Finland's National Democratic Party; France's 'Eurofascist' *Devenir Européen*, to name but a few.

(ii) The Nazification of indigenous neo-fascist groups, such as the francophone *Mouvement Social Belge* or Flemish separatist *Vlaams Blok* in Belgium, and most groups with paramilitary or terrorist leanings in Northern Europe such as the ODAL group in Belgium or Column 88 (referring to the eighth letter of the alphabet, 'H', that is 'Heil Hitler') which exists in France and the United Kingdom.

(iii) The assimilation of Nazism into all forms of 'white supremacist' ideology, with the result that neo-Nazi groups have sprung up in such far-flung places as Canada, Rhodesia (before it became Zimbabwe), Australia, Peru and Switzerland.

Special mention should be made of the United States, whose deep-rooted sub-culture of indigenous political Christianity and racism until 1945 generally lacked a fully fledged palingenetic vision. The subsequent Nazification of large parts of this diffuse subculture since then has turned parts of the country into hot-houses for overtly fascist versions of religious and secular white supremacism. Moreover, the legacy of the Vietnamese War has contributed a new strand to fascist activism, namely 'survivalism', which lends itself all too well to being fused with anti-communist and racist terrorism and has influenced some fascists in Britain (for example McClaughlin, who in the late 1980s was running a neo-fascist survivalist shop called Rucksack n'Rifle in North Wales). As a result the United States now has scores of defunct or active neo-Nazi organizations to its 'credit' with such evocative names as the National Socialist Liberation Movement, the Christian (Patriot) Defense League and Christian Vikings of America.

In the early 1980s one of them, The Order, attempted to enact the plot of a Nazi utopian novel, William Pierce's *The Turner Diaries*, by waging a private guerrilla war against ZOG (Zionist Occupation Government, in this case the United States), the violent and ultimately suicidal results of which were the basis of the 1987 Costa-Gavras film, *Betrayed*. This film also evokes the congresses of 1984 and 1986 held by Aryan Nation and attended by delegates representing the nation-wide 'Christian Identity' movement, the Ku Klux Klan and particular mimetic Nazi groupings, an ecumenicism made possible by shared (and extensively Nazified) premises about the degeneracy of liberalism, communism and 'inferior' races, that is blacks and Jews (see Ebels-Dolanová, 1985; Hainsworth, 1991).

(iv) The existence of an extensive web of linkages between Nazi groups on both a Europe-wide and a world-wide basis, maintained through personal contacts (for example on the occasion of the yearly Iron Pilgrimage to Diksmuide in Belgium), but in particular through a number of organizations set up to form the basis of a Nazi International to ensure the continuous dissemination and circulation of Nazi books and periodicals. Important examples are CEDADE (Spanish Circle of Friends of Europe) based in Spain; the NSDAP–AO (*Auslands-Organisation*, or Overseas Organization), and WUNS (World Union of National Socialists), both of which have their headquarters in the United States (Lincoln, Nebraska and Milwaukee respectively). There is also an international Nazi youth organization, Viking Youth, whose headquarters are in Germany.

(v) The conversion of a significant section of the international 'skinhead' sub-culture to Nazi-style racism, which then become liable to be recruited by such groups as the British National Front, the German Progressive Workers' Party (FAP), the Dutch Jongeren-Front and the American White Aryan Resistance (see Ford, 1990, pp.41–3).

Neo-fascism

One of the most significant developments in the post-war European ultra-right has been the emergence of groupings which, though pursuing ideological goals based on a core of palingenetic ultra-nationalist myth, have either introduced original themes or cultural idioms into major inter-war permutations, or reject them altogether in the name of entirely new rationales. These I would term generically 'neo-fascism', using the prefix with the connotations of 'offering something new with respect to inter-war phenomena' (and not those of 'attempting to resuscitate an earlier movement' as in 'neo-Nazism'). Used in this way the concept 'neo-fascism' is less all-embracing than 'post-war fascism', but is still a generic term, which like its parent concept, embraces a wide range of disparate, and, in principle at least, mutually contradictory phenomena. The main ideal-typical sub-divisions I would suggest are:

(i)   *Revolutionary Nationalism*. Following its incorporation into the name of some neo-fascist movements, this term, which originally designated the inter-war sub-culture of German fascism with which Ernst Jünger was associated, is appropriate to cover groupings which renounce all inter-war regimes as role models, including Fascism and Nazism, and instead find inspiration in more marginal movements. Thus the Nationalist Front–League of Social Revolutionary Nationalists drew on the examples of a 'leftist' (that is anti-capitalist but not socialist) fascism set by the Strasser brothers, while the Portuguese National Revolutionary Front set store by José Antonio and Codreanu.

   This form of palingenetic ultra-nationalism is in fact often referred to 'in the trade' as Strasserism, even though this is an intrinsically vague term, since Gregor Strasser remained faithful to Nazism while his brother Otto was its bitter critic (especially after his brother was assassinated in the Night of the Long Knives). Modern Strasserism has little to do with historic fascism but much more to do with the politics of the 'Third Position' (a name used by a racist group, in France, a faction within the German NPD, an Italian terrorist group and a splinter of a faction within the new National Front in Britain) dedicated to finding a 'third way' between communism and liberalism, or, as Sternhell would put it, 'beyond right and left'. The French student movement *Groupe Union Défense*, and its successor *Renouveau Français* (French Renewal) are also examples of this kind of neo-fascism.

(ii) *Crypto-fascism*. By this I refer to the latent ultra-nationalism contained within a number of pressure groups and political parties which, though they officially claim to be committed to liberal democracy and may explicitly dissociate themselves from inter-war fascist regimes, especially the Third Reich, recruit their former functionaries into executive positions, attract fascist members and funding, and through their publicistic activities and affiliations, act as bridges between the far right and the ultra-right. Examples of such pressure groups have been the British League of Rights (BLR), the Focus Policy Group set up by British freelance historian David Irving as the nucleus of a new ultra-right movement, the National Action for People and Homeland (NA–AN) in Switzerland and, in Germany, the Society for Free Publicism (GFP) and German Citizens' Initiative (DB), to name but two.

The hallmark of an apparently democratic political party with a crypto-fascist tendency is that its policies on such topical issues as immigration, Europe, ecology, AIDS, Russia and (in West Germany till November 1989) German reunification, contain an agenda which is not merely hidden but fascist. An illuminating case-study on the convoluted ideological and organizational dimensions of crypto-fascism is provided by Frey's *Deutsche-Volksunion* which started life as a 'national liberal' nation-wide organization for co-ordinating a number of 'action communities' associated with his vast ultra-right press and publishing empire. However, in 1987 it spawned a party, the DVU/Liste D (that is *Deutschland*), thus becoming the latest of several high-profile political parties in post-war Germany with thinly disguised neo-Nazi or neo-fascist tendencies, notably the *Deutsche Reichspartei* (1946–65) and *Nationaldemokratische Partei* (1964–). The most successful such party in recent years is Schönhuber's Republican Party, which after the 1989 elections boasted six members in the European Parliament (see Childs, 1991, pp.78–81; Benz, 1989, ch.15). Other such parties are Austria's National Democratic Party and *Freiheitliche Partei Österreichs*, a 'liberal', 'progressive' or 'freedom' party (all words which have been turned into euphemisms for ultra-right thinking) which under Jörg Haider has adopted increasingly crypto-fascist racist policies. European citizens with neo-fascist leanings are sometimes drawn to parties with a strong anti-immigrant platform such as Le Pen's *Front National*, the Dutch Centre Party or the Progress parties in Denmark and Norway.

(iii) *Revisionism* is arguably the most insidious form taken by crypto-fascism as a publicistic phenomenon, for it not only plays a crucial role in the ecumenicalization of post-war fascism but provides common ground and channels of communication between nostalgic, mimetic, (especially neo-Nazi) and neo-fascists of many persuasions. In view of the body blow dealt to the credibility and 'image' of fascism in general by the crimes against humanity perpetrated in the name of the Nazi New Order, the conscious minimalization, relativization or juggling away of those crimes plays a crucial role in the rehabilitation of palingenetic ultra-nationalism in general. Taking advantage of the more poorly educated strata of post-1945 generations concerning the realities of the Second World War, 'vulgar' revisionism boils down to a point-blank denial that six million Jews died as victims of the Nazis' genocidal anti-Semitic campaign, dismissing the idea as a hysterical myth put about by the Jews themselves or their backers (for example the Allies).

Sophisticated revisionism is produced by a cottage industry of self-appointed international 'experts' (of whom David Irving is a prime British example, rewarded for his efforts in the 1980s with a prize funded by the crypto-fascist Frey) who are at pains to go less far and therefore further than their 'vulgar' associates. By using sophistry and bad faith to exploit genuine problems involved in social science methodology as well as empirical gaps in the historical record, these 'para-historians' mimic orthodox academic research, publication and dissemination techniques to imply the benign or misunderstood nature of the Nazi project for a new European order, and the 'hysteria' of references to organized genocide and death camps (see Ebels-Dolanová, 1984, ch.2; Seidel, 1986; Eatwell, 1991). The revisionist cause has been, doubtless unwittingly, aided and abetted by more orthodox historians such as those who argue the unplanned nature of both the war and the Final Solution (for example A.J.P. Taylor, 1961) or stress the continuity between the aspects of the 'Blood and Soil' strand of Nazism and the contemporary ecological movement (see Bramwell, 1985). It is particularly served by some contributions to the recent debate among German academics over the most appropriate conceptual framework within which to interpret Nazism (the 'Historikerstreit'), especially by an explanation of it as synergetically engendered by Stalinism in a European 'civil war' (see Nolte, 1988).

(iv) *Conservative revolution.* I am using this term in a sense sometimes adopted, under the influence of Mohler, by neo-fascists who genuinely dissociate themselves from all inter-war movements, especially Nazism, and see the ultra-nationalist values they are fighting for as the healthy version of a revolutionary process rather than a perversion of it (an 'ultra-right Trotskyism' as opposed to its 'Stalinism': see Mohler, 1972, pp.4–5). It exists in two distinct forms, both called New Right (and certainly not to be confused with the monetarist evangelism of some British Conservatives and American Republicans in the 1980s). The most famous is the self-styled post-Nietzschean 'nominalism' identified with the French think-tank GRECE, which uses its magazine *Eléments* and the Copernic publishing house to disseminate the learned disquisitions on history and culture of a number of self-styled philosophers and cultural critics, the most famous of whom is Alain de Benoist. Since the late 1960s this 'Nouvelle Droite' – a tag which it was initially reluctant to accept because of the gulf that divides it from the traditional Right – has concentrated on the need to develop cultural hegemony for a philosophy of history which exposes the 'lies' of egalitarian humanism in its socialist and liberal permutations. By implication it calls for a civilization based on ethnic/national distinctivenss and excellence. Only in this way can the age of decadence be overcome and history 'regenerated' (see, for example, de Benoist, 1980).

The other form arrives at similar conclusions via the utterly different permutations of metaphysical, neo-idealist world-view associated chiefly with the Italian 'radical right' (see Ferraresi, 1984). One version of this based on a cult of the type of alternative consciousness embodied in epic fantasy literature (for example Tolkien) and in the ritual or sacred time of festivals (see Galli, 1983; Revelli, 1984), and there is even a French permutation of it in a Christian–occultist key (see Cologne, 1978). By far the most important current of it is known as Traditionalism, by which is meant the radically 'alternative' cosmology and philosophy of history elaborated in a monumental act of syncretism carried out by the Italian Julius Evola from the 1920s till his death in 1974. The stream of works he wrote in that period forge from occultist (for example Guénon), mythological (for example the Hindu cyclic theory of history) and fascist (for example the late Spengler) sources a 'revolt against the modern world' and its levelling demo-liberalism as well as a blueprint for a new one founded once more on the hierarchical Tradition. After his death many of these books became set texts within Italian neo-fascist culture: as one of its spokesmen put it, Evola was 'our Marcuse, only better'. He was also for a time Mussolini's favourite theorist of Fascism's version of Aryan racism (see Jellamo, 1984; Griffin, 1985).

It should be stressed that, though worlds apart in terms of their metaphysical premises, what both Evola and de Benoist have in common is that both offer total world-views which diagnose the alleged decadence of the present age and offer the prospect of supra-individual salvation in a new age where excellence, national uniqueness and cultural distinctiveness are paramount. This indirectly provides convoluted rationales for the mentality which breeds *apartheid*, anti-liberalism and anti-communism, leading (especially in Italy) to acts of terrorist violence against alleged sources of decay (see Sheehan, 1981). In other words the old wine of palingenetic ultra-nationalist myth has been poured into new bottles, the label originally marked 'Aryan' being covered with one marked 'Indo-European' or 'Traditional'. It is thus not surprising to learn that both Evola and some of the founders of GRECE were deeply embroiled with pro-Nazi strands of Italian and French fascism respectively in the 1930s or that both New Rights are deeply bound up with revisionism. They also play a major role in the internationalization of fascism: Evola's works have been translated into numerous languages, and inspire study centres in Italy, France and Mexico. Meanwhile, GRECE literature and articles are avidly translated into English, Portuguese and Italian by ultra-right presses, and are disseminated by study circles in Luxemburg and in Switzerland (by the resuscitated *Cercle Proudhon*). The outlet for GRECE ideas in Germany is the Thule Seminar, a great nephew of the Thule Society which had such a formative influence on the infant (NS)DAP (see Benz, 1989, ch.12).

A Synoptic View of Post-war European Fascism: Two Main Features

This makeshift scheme for classifying diverse manifestations of post-war European fascism hopefully evokes something of the labyrinthine complexity of the situation facing its would-be historian (and might account for why many works purporting to be on generic fascism have chosen to give the entire topic a wide berth!). However, a bald list of taxonomic sub-categories obscures rather than highlights two basic features which have a direct bearing on 'the nature' of post-war fascism in Europe. Summarized baldly the first is: *organizational complexity and ideological heterogeneity*.

It is implicit in the examples given of the sub-divisions I have suggested that post-war Euro–American fascism involves the entire gamut of organizational forms which political activity can assume in the modern world, ranging across pseudo-democratic political parties, pressure groups, international and national umbrella organizations, pseudo-academic institutes, publishing houses, magazines, mailing lists, local discussion groups, semi-initiatic societies and terrorist cells. Equally implicit in the above is the vital role played by a private army of individuals who, over and above any formal affiliations to such organizations, take it upon themselves to furnish some of the vast quantities of ideological fuel of a scientistic, publicistic and propagandistic nature which such a gargantuan sub-culture must continually consume, not to mention the other secret army of patrons who supply the equally indispensable financial fuel. But a point disguised by a simple list of categories is the extraordinary volatility and instability that this sub-culture exhibits when viewed diachronically, with formations and alliances continually appearing and dissolving alongside more stable formations.

The conspicuous absence of any single movement at either a national or an international level capable of forging a new *lingua franca* out of the old and new dialects of palingenetic ultra-nationalism and its organizations in the way that Fascism and Nazism managed to do within their own societies is clearly a symptom of chronic structural weakness. This point is borne out by the pathetically small membership of the majority of its formations, some of the most impressively titled of which can count on a mere dozen or so fractious fanatics and the systematic failure of even the largest neo-fascist parties to become movements with a constituency sizeable enough to be able seriously to threaten a Western democracy, let alone emulate the NSDAP (which goes even for Le Pen's basically non-fascist *Front National*).

The second main feature is *ideological and organizational innovation*. While very much a paper tiger as a national revolutionary force, fascism's potency as a political force is revealed in its remarkable capacity to adapt to shifting post-war realities, reminiscent of a 'super-virus' evolving anew into a variety of relatively innocuous but highly resistent strains. A technological aspect of this is the creation of a nation-wide PC-accessible data base to link up fascists in the United States, the spread of computer games such as 'Concentration Camp Manager II' to be played at home by German teenagers (Benz, 1989, ch.13), and the dissemination in Britain of 'vulgar' revisionist anti-Semitic tracts cheaply prepared on PCs using desk-top publishing software.

The readiness to keep fascism in step with the times has also brought about significant modifications to its surface ideology. Fascism old and new sometimes takes up 'contemporary' issues such as AIDS or feminism, so that a quadri-lingual pamphlet entitled *Feminine European Thought* in the series called 'Erika' turns out to be a piece of thinly disguised neo-Nazi propaganda. Similarly, the unification of Germany was a permanent issue for German groups up to 1989. Ecology has been particularly targeted as an ideological Trojan Horse to carry fascist ideas into the citadel of orthodox political debate, with attempts to infiltrate democratic Green groups in Germany, Britain, Italy, Spain and France, (see Ford, 1990), a move paralleled by some non-fascist ultra-right parties such as the Liberal Ecologist Party of Switzerland. The main ideological innovation, however, is the direct corollary of fascism's organizational internationalization, namely an internationalist or universalist interpretation of fascism as fighting for principles which should provide the basis of socio-political arrangements in every country, much as socialists and liberals hold their values to be 'self-evident'. There were important internationalist currents in the personal fascist visions of Mosley and Szálasi, within Fascism (see above p.70) and even under Nazism (see above p.109), but all were condemned by events to remain particularly utopian varieties of an already highly utopian political myth. But now the idea of fascism as the basis of (to coin a phrase!) 'a new world order' has moved centre-stage.

One symptom of this is the existence of a number of groupings, neo-Nazi (for example CEDADE) and neo-fascist (for example the Zurich-based New European Order), set up specifically to co-ordinate international activities of a propagandistic or terroristic nature, and there is a dense web of interconnections between individual organizations (again, see Ó Maoláin, 1987). Some of the links cultivated by such 'European-minded' groups extend to non-European terrorist groupings, such as the Grey Wolves in Turkey and the PLO. There have even been negotiations between Spanish neo-fascists and the Socialist People's Libyan Jamahiriya of Colonel Qadhafi (see Ellwood, 1991, pp.157–8).

An important ideological corollary of this development has been the confederate vision of a 'Europe of nations', according to which the active collaboration between all countries which had their own fascist revolution would enable Europe itself not only to stem the process of decadence and decline but to recover its birthright as the powerhouse of a superior civilization. This vision is preached by numerous publications, such as *Nouvel Europe Magazine*, *Notre Europe Combattant*, *Tribune Nationaliste* in France, and *Nation Europa* in Germany. Significantly, ultra-right Euro-MPs cultivate their own version of a European community within a grouping called (since 1989) The Technical Group of the European Right (see Harris, 1990, p.viii). The common denominator of all pan-Europeans is a pronounced anti-Russianism (which is doubtless being revised since the Soviet Empire started going into semi-voluntary liquidation), anti-Americanism (in the name of values shared, of course, by American neo-

Nazis), anti-egalitarianism and an *apartheid* form of racism which envisages strong nations each living in their own homeland. This nebulous vision commonly extends to the Croats, the Welsh and the Bretons, and it is no coincidence if Breton separatists formed their own pan-European fascist group, GNAR, which uses the menhir to symbolize eternal values (see *Droite Extrême*, 1989, p.62). In the 1980s the National Front even tried unsuccessfully to infiltrate Welsh nationalism (a generally liberal force).

The Neo-fascist Minimum: 'Palingenetic Ultra-nationalism'

Readers may rightly feel that they have been asked to take a lot on trust when such quite diverse forms of post-war politics are all treated as different permutations of the same generic ideology, fascism, and hence as cognate with the 'classic' inter-war fascisms treated in the standard non-Marxist texts on the subject. Misgivings, and even hackles, are bound to be raised when this label is applied equally to fully fledged parties such as the German NDP and publicistic 'schools of thought' such as the French New Right, both of which go out of their way to dissociate themselves from Nazism and Fascism. Certainly it is possible to demonstrate the continuity at the level of personal biography, for example by looking at the career of ex-Fascist ideologue Evola, or of Adolf von Thadden, former Hitler supporter then leader of the overtly nostalgic Nazi *Reichspartei* before founding the NDP.

It is also grist to our mill when in his classic *Qu'est-ce que le fascisme?* Maurice Bardèche, described by one expert as 'the most dangerous ideologue of French and European neo-fascism' (Algazy, 1984, p.221), characterized the structural relationship which links inter-war and post-war variants of fascism in terms which substantially confirm our own analysis (and incidentally the key taxonomic distinctions we put forward in Chapter 5 between fascist and para-fascist regimes). The reason that the two accounts tally is that Bardèche employs a remarkably similar ideal type of fascism to my own, with the important difference that he is trying to explain (and promote) the forces of palingenetic ultra-nationalism as an insider, while I am using it heuristically as an ideal type to understand (and implicitly condemn) the same phenomena as an outsider. Writing more than a decade into the post-war era, Bardèche's reply to his own question 'what is fascism' still centres on the mobilization of the whole nation in a fight to the death against the fetid decadence of liberal democracy. He points out that fascism's outer form will naturally differ from movement to movement because 'each nation has its own way of saving itself', but what each fascist has in common is that he is the harbinger of a new heroic type of man who will be the backbone of a 'Third Order' capable of rescuing the civilized world from the ravages of Americanization and Bolshevization. Fascism is 'by its essence' nationalist, and while it originates as the reaction to a crisis, 'all fascist reaction is resurrection'. Either the West will go under 'like a drowning old man' or 'the order of Sparta' will be reborn in a totally new form, the last bastion of 'freedom and the good life' (Bardèche, 1961, pp.173–195).

To those left hungry for more empirical evidence for the structural affinity which I am claiming exists, I can at least offer three independent morsels of corroboration. The first is provided by *Nation Europa*, described by Ó Maoláin as a 'neo-Nazi' magazine, whose book service (*Büchersuchlicht*) No. 35 of 1988 invites its readers to order from a list which clearly for the editor, Peter Dehoust, are all ideologically compatible. The 250 odd titles cover (i) *nostalgic Nazism* (for example books on Hitler, Hess, Göring, the Todt Organization and the Austrian SS); (ii) *neo-Nazism* in the form of three different dialects of Aryan racism in its occultist (for example books on Lanz von Liebenfels), anthropological (for example on Thule, primordial Germany and the Indo-Europeans), and biological (for example by Günther) strains; (iii) *revolutionary nationalism* (for example a book by Niekisch); (iv) *crypto-fascism* (for example by Frey); (v) *revisionism* (for example by Irving, Nolte and on the 'Historikerstreit'); (vi) *conservative revolution* in its nominalist, or *Nouvelle Droite* aspect (for example Mohler, Eysenck and the key text for the Thule Seminar – the German chapter of GRECE – Krebs's *Mut zur Identität*, The Courage to Have an Identity). For good measure there are several books celebrating the heroic stand against liberalism, communists, Jews and Blacks in pre-de-Klerkian South Africa. In other words *Nation Europa*, itself in the vanguard of the 'Europe of nations' movement, registers the structural kinship which I have postulated.

The only major lacunae in *Nation Europa* in terms of the taxonomy we have suggested are amply filled in our second piece of material evidence, the 'essential bibliography for an understanding of the Italian New Right' drawn up by two (non-fascist) experts on Italian ultra-right culture, Guerra and Revelli (1983). The exhaustive book-list contains abundant (and different) works representing all the earlier categories except *crypto-fascism* (which at a party-level is absent in Italy given that the MSI is an overtly neo-fascist party). Instead it supplements the earlier inventory with (i) classics of literary fascism by Céline, Benn, Jünger, Hamsun, Drieu la Rochelle, and (certainly fascist in ethos, if not technically speaking in ideology) Mishima; (ii) classics of Italian proto-fascism (for example Papini, Pareto); (iii) key works of the Traditionalist New Right (including all of Evola); (iv) fantasy literature, especially Tolkien and Meyrink; (v) works which provide a theoretical underpinning for the importance of the last two categories, most of them by Mircea Eliade (also associated with de Benoist's 'nominalist' New Right). In other words, while the compilers of both book-lists have made no attempt to cast light on generic fascism, they do indirectly point to the centrality of palingenetic ultra-nationalism as its definitional minimum, since a preoccupation with an aspect of national rebirth is the *only* common denominator which can be found between the world-views of all the very different writers cited. There are no references to other forms of right (for example conservative, authoritarian, political Catholic, militarist, fundamentalist).

The third witness I would like to call is Britain's National Front (NF). This organization has undergone two major metamorphoses. It was founded in 1967 by a number of nostalgic fascists who had been active in minute groupings before the war but was then hi-jacked by neo-Nazis. From 1971 onwards these exploited the rise of racism in areas of high immigration to win the NF considerable notoriety from a series of flash-in-the pan election results which seemed promising/alarming at the time. Once the Conservatives came to power and the mirage of achieving power through the ballot box evaporated, the party entered a prolonged period of schisms over tactics, ideology, leadership and style. The significance of this latest phase (1985–) for an understanding of the 'nature' of contemporary fascism is that out of the mainstream National Front have flowed a number of rivulets, some of which have dried up almost immediately while others are tributaries to powerful currents of fascism abroad. They have included (i) a neo-Nazi 'Flag' group whipping up crude nationalist and racist sentiments; (ii) a 'Third Way' faction blending anti-Zionism, white supremacism and native ultra-right thought (for example A.K. Chesterton and Hillaire Belloc) and socialist (for example William Morris) utopianism; (iii) a highly eclectic 'national democrat' faction peddling a pretentious mish-mash of New Right cultural criticism in its theoretically incompatible 'nominalist' (GRECE) and 'Traditionalist' (Evola) forms in the pages of *Scorpion* (it is no coincidence that this insect has many of the symbolic connotations of the phoenix); (iv) a paramilitary faction of self-styled political soldiers (modern Italian terrorist groups and The Order in America) which has run training camps for its cadres in remote farms in Britain and has exploited punk rock to foment racial hatred among skinheads; (v) a faction which put up a number of NF candidates at the 1992 General Election, thus operating as a crypto-fascist 'party'.

Most of the factions which loosely constitute the NF strand of British fascism have had a prolific publicistic output, much of it produced on the same presses which turn out much of Europe's revisionist literature (see Thurlow, 1987, ch.12; Gable, 1990). Meanwhile the commitment of its terroristic wings to the 'Europe of nations' principle is shown by their close collaboration in Britain with known neo-fascist Italian terrorists, with a number of pan-European fascist cells abroad (in France, South Africa, the United States) and with contacts with Ulster nationalists and Qadhafi (see Hill, 1988, which provides a mole's eye view of the intricate world of international fascism). The ideological counterpart to this was the conference co-hosted by *Scorpion* at a London hotel in 1986 on 'A Third Way for Europe' and attended by delegates from several European countries and fascist tendencies (see *Scorpion*, 1986, No.9). The NF has also tried to infiltrate the Green movement (Wall, 1989). The only demonstrable common denominator which can be found between so many disparate and desperate forms of political activism is that they pursue the chimera of an order in which a radical nationalism would replace liberalism as the matrix of society. As Ray Hill commented in a documentary on the National Front shown in 1988 in Channel Four's *Dispatches* series, its strategy is to throw liberal democracy into chaos so that 'out of the ashes the phoenix will rise.'

The Resilience of Fascism

It should by now be obvious that, far from being 'on its way out', the European fascist sub-culture is very much 'here to stay'. It is guaranteed a self-replenishing supply of new recruits because it has become an established cultural idiom within the Europeanized 'North' within which extreme racism, a gut reaction against 'the system' and a diffuse sense of *anomie* can articulate themselves. As such, it is available to infuse with meaning and purpose the lives of that small minority which will be instinctively and viscerally opposed to what they see as the nexus of decadent forces summed up in the single expression 'One World'. In fact, Euro–American society (along with its outposts in Canada and Australia) seems to be entering a historical conjuncture where the unstable sub-culture created by this minority is set to grow stronger rather than weaker, despite the best efforts of humanistic activists of every complexion to monitor and combat it. The escalating demographic, political and environmental crises in the Third World can only intensify the pressures on the First to accept more immigrants. Moreover, fundamentalist and ethnic ultra-nationalisms, especially Islamic ones, are likely to grow more strident among the communities they form at a time when ethnic minorities and the peoples of submerged nations all over the world are becoming more aware of their cultural identities in a way which makes them passionately resist assimilation by 'occupying' nations or 'alien' governments. Cultural polarization is liable to combine with structural unemployment, probably a permanent feature of all developed economies, to produce profound social tensions and collective crises of identity which are likely to be exacerbated rather than placated by mounting economic and ecological dysfunctions and irreversible deteriorations in the supplies of raw materials, especially fossil fuels.

Ominous signs of the times can be read into the swelling tide of organized racism, whether terrorist or party-political, in some West European countries (see Ford, 1990; Harris, 1990), of which a symptom is the sudden emergence in Italy of regional 'Leagues', notably the (non-fascist) Lombard League, to mobilize anti-state and anti-south sentiments and attacks on immigrant (Muslim) workers and gypsies. Meanwhile, the Great Thaw precipitated by *perestroika* has not only caused the Soviet Empire to start melting away, causing unreconstructed Stalinists and militarists to induce worrying cold snaps, but has released a muddy deluge of those separatist passions and ethnic tensions cryogenically suspended by the imposition of Soviet rule in 1945. It said much about the latent utopianism and Eurocentrism of Western intellectual and media culture that there was a wide-spread sense that the *annus mirabilis* 1989 had ushered in the 'end of history' in the sense of the final triumph of ('non-ideological') Liberalism–Capitalism. But given the dramatic breakdown of old certainties (and even a monolithic system based on terror can, as long as it appears a stable monolith, generate a paradoxical sense of security), it was naïve even for rationalists to expect that the social anxieties and *anomie* suddenly unleashed would be resolved through mass conversions to liberal nationalism and pluralistic democracy, especially when the old economic and social order had collapsed without a new one to replace it.

No wonder, then, that the 1989 revolutions immediately led to a renaissance of ultra-nationalism, xenophobia and anti-Semitism in the former East bloc, offering considerable potential markets for Western ideological salesmen. An example was the discovery that a professor of sociology at Poland's Radom University had been circulating to his students propaganda material emanating from the American neo-Nazi group Third Way. Meanwhile, in what had been East Berlin and in cities such as Rostock, Weimar, Leipzig and Dresden crypto-fascist groups such as the *Republikaner* of Schönhuber and the *Deutsche Alternative* of neo-Nazi impresario Michael Kühnen sprang up to fan smouldering anti-Semitic, anti-Slav and anti-immigrant resentments and exploit a potentially huge reservoir of undrained and untapped nostalgic and mimetic Nazism, especially among their burgeoning 'skinhead' population. Further south the Hungarian Arrow Cross has been resuscitated, and an organization calling itself *Vatra Romanesca* has emerged to take up the torch of the Iron Guard. The decaying Soviet Union also saw the sudden blossoming of a variegated movement of resistance to Gorbachevian reforms which can be seen as an indigenous equivalent to (strange to say) the opposition to de Klerk's liberal revolution to remove *apartheid*.

Alongside the military diehards and professional Stalinists resisting change (cf. the armed and security forces and the ultra-conservatives in South Africa), there has recently emerged a native Russian equivalent of the AWB. This is *Pamyat* (memory, heritage), a movement formed in 1987 with epicentres in Moscow and Leningrad and a total membership at present of over 70,000 members deployed in an intensive campaign of publicist, propagandist and terrorist activities (mostly against Jews) on behalf of a post-*perestroikan* New Order. The central myth in its ideology is (as implied by its name) an ultra-reactionary cult of medieval Mother Russia and her people which leads it to devise an iconography based on the twelfth-century prince who founded Russia, the Orthodox Church and the tsar; in fact *Pamyat* is tactically aligned to groups campaigning for his restoration. Into this has been injected a virulent anti-Semitism which blames Jews not only for the assassination of the Messiah, but for the overthrow and murder of the tzar in 1917 ('Marx was a Jew'), the horrors of Stalinism ('Stalin's advisers were Jews'), the chaos of *perestroika* ('Gorbachev's advisers were Jewish') and the food shortages ('the black market is run by Jews'). The 'Programme for National and Popular Revival' which results from this mixture is a direct analogue of the fusion of nostalgic monarchism, Catholicism and ultra-nationalism in Maurras's *Action Française*, and, like it, hovers on the cusp between renovationist conservatism (cf. the emperor cult of Kita Ikki) and an original form of fascism synthesizing mimetic and conservative revolutionary elements.

Certainly *Pamyat* has recently *behaved* increasingly like contemporary neo-fascisms in the West by infiltrating the country's main Green organization, Volga, cultivating links with ultra-right circles abroad and legally registering itself in Leningrad as the Republican People's Party of Russia. It has also attempted to widen its base by alliances with ultra-conservative and ultra-nationalist groups, notably the elitist and equally anti-Semitic *Fatherland Movement*, co-ordinated from Leningrad by university professor Vyacheslav Riobov and which has a para-military arm called the White Guards. Riobov openly admits looking forward to the failure of *perestroika* and the ensuing chaos as the opportunity for the ultra-right to take over power (Ford, 1990; on the rise of the extreme right in Europe generally see the magazine *Europ*, for example No. 57, April–June 1990).

The Resilience of Ultra-right Palingenetic Myth

Thus even if fascism (for reasons to be explored in Chapter 8) will always be successfully marginalized by mainstream politics and never again able to emulate Fascism or Nazism in seizing power, there is every indication that it will remain a permanent component of the ultra-right in democratized or democratizing societies, providing an inexhaustible well of organized xenophobia and ultra-nationalism. As in the case of *Pamyat*, it may even flare up briefly in spectacular new forms as a reminder that the particular set of psychological and socio-historical forces whose coupling begat the first generation of fascisms have lost none of their potency if ever they meet up again. Meanwhile, on the periphery of what the Euro-centric mind thinks of as the modern world, palingenetic forms of ultra-nationalist myth continue to produce capricious displays of its formidable power to mobilize populist energies in fundamentalist politics, as in the Indian sacred city of Ayodhya when in the autumn of 1990 the question of rebuilding the Temple rallied the forces of Hindu separatism powerfully enough to threaten India's secular democracy.

Nearer home, the 1980s saw the Provisional IRA adopt a fusion of ultra-nationalism, socialism and palingenetic myth as a rationale for its irredentist war to complete Ireland's *risorgimento*, an amalgam called 'republican socialism'. This is the latest of several flirtations with such an ideological hybrid of ideas closely akin to what we have defined as fascism (cf. the National Bolshevik wing of the *Los-von-Weimar* movement), except that it leads to a vanguard concept of revolution which effectively dispenses with the populist ground-swell provided by a mass party or 'people power' (see Patterson, 1989). Palingenetic fervour has also combined with other indigenous brands of national socialism to become the official rationale of regimes which resemble the para-fascist ones of inter-war Europe (for example in Greece, Austria) in that the resulting new order is imposed from above, and any subsequent populist support for the visionary leader is solely the product of intense social engineering. It was only after a military coup in 1969 that Qadhafi could set about creating the new Libya whose blueprint is expounded in his *Green Book* (1988), and the resulting state has been 'socialist' enough in the democratic-centralist sense to stop short of degenerating into a totalitarian one. In stark contrast the attempt by a para-military movement to create a new Cambodian national community inspired by the twelfth-century Angkor Empire led to atrocities on a scale worthy of Hitler and turned Angka, the Pol Pot 'system', into a euphemism for death. The Khmer Rouge came to power as a cadre move-ment with no backing from a genuine mass movement, like an SA without the NSDAP and hence no significant populist support. Its onslaught on the 'New People' allegedly contaminated by Western materialism, urban living and intellectual decadence inevitably led not to a ruralist utopia but the 'Killing Fields': the 'Year Zero' marked not recreation but annihilation (Ponchaud, 1978; Ngor, 1987; Evans and Rowley, 1990). An eloquent testimony to the power the regime's palingenetic myth could exert even over a Western intellectual is provided by the former wife of the Foreign Minister of Democratic Kampuchea, Laurence Picq (Picq, 1989).

Long before the Khmer Rouge were committing genocide against their own people conveniently remote from the global village, a second coup by the nationalist faction of the Iraqi Ba'ath Party in 1968 had enabled Saddam Hussein to start his rise from secretary general of the party to personal dictator. He thus took over the reins of a state whose entire apparatus was geared to enacting yet another palingenetic version of ultra-nationalism. This one culled elements from radical Islam, pan-Arabism, Third Worldism and socialism but was also infused with an elaborate philosophy of history and the state, as well as an obsession with building a new society and creating a national renaissance (*ba'ath*). The result is an official ideology far removed from Islamic fundamentalism but uncannily akin to Nazism in some ideological aspects (for example the emphasis on youth, the leader mystique, the critique of bourgeois mentality, the obsessive anti-Westernism and anti-Semitism, and the stress on the elusive 'Arab spirit', a direct analog to *nordischer Gedanke* or 'Nordic thought'). However, the ba'athism on which Saddam Hussein's Iraq was based rejects the notion of mass politics from below and represses genuine populism in a way quite unlike Nazism, so that, as with the Pol Pot regime, the analogies with fascism break down (see Al-Kahlil, 1989). Though not fascist, both regimes serve as baleful warnings that threats to the Western/liberal/capitalist scheme of things come not only from collective inertia in the face of potentially disastrous processes at work in the Third World and the ecosystem, but also from fresh epi-demics of systematized and technologized barbarism.

Such epidemics by definition defy accurate prediction, but at least appro-priate measures to limit the damage they might wreak on political and human life can be taken by the international community once they are understood as the product, at least in part, of new viruses of palingenetic myth immune to rational discourse or 'common sense'. In particular, move-ments and regimes which pursue goals infected with such a virus cannot be 'appeased', nor should they be treated by democratic countries as a legiti-mate custodian of a nation's interest, a tactical ally against a common foe or a suitable customer for arms supplies. As the third millennium hurtles towards us some humanists nurture fragile hopes that the prospect of a 'New World Order' – based, not on Anglo-American hegemony, but on the rule of an international law laid down and enforced by a United Nations committed to pluralism and tolerance – can act as a benign palingenetic myth. Clearly it could only bring about the necessary structural changes if it ultimately proves as contagious in its appeal as the anti-humanist visions which continue to inspire self-appointed elites to attempt to found a brave new world fashioned in their own image. What prevents fascism from being a closed chapter in twentieth-century history, though it has been reduced in its practical impact to little more than a footnote, is that there is no shortage of political visionaries in the world still obsessed in one way or other with national decadence. Lost in a world of abstractions they feel cold towards the flesh and blood of living human beings tormented or sacrificed in pursuit of their dream. Instead they would warm to the rhetorical images which Büchner places in the mouth of Saint Juste to justify the Terror before the National Assembly in his extraordinarily 'modern' drama, *Danton's Death* (1835).

> The Revolution resembles the daughter of Pelias: it tears mankind to pieces in order to rejuvenate it. Like the earth which emerged from the waters of the Flood, mankind will arise out of the blood cauldron, its limbs surging with primordial strength, as if it had been created for the first time.

References

Alexander, R.J., 1973. *Latin American Political Parties*, Praeger, New York and London.

Algazy, J., 1984. *La Tentation néo-fasciste en France 1944–1965*, Fayard, Paris.

Al-Kahlil, S., 1989. *Republic of Fear*, Hutchinson Radius, London.

Avineri, S., 1981. *The Making of Modern Zionism*, Weidenfeld and Nicolson.

Bardèche, M., 1961. *Qu'est-ce que le fascisme?*, Les Sept Couleurs, Paris.

Barrington Moore, Jr., S.D., 1969. *Dictatorship and Democracy*, Penguin, Harmondsworth.

Benoist, A. de, 1980. *Les idées à l'endroit*, Albin Michel, Paris.

Benz, W., 1989. *Rechtsextremismus in der Bundesrepublik*, Fischer, Frankfurt-on-Main.

Beyme, K. von, 1988. Right-wing extremism in post-war Europe, *West European Politics*, Vol.11, No.2.

Bloomberg, C., 1981. *Christian-Nationalism and the Rise of the Afrikaner Broederbond in South Africa, 1918–48*, Macmillan, New York.

Bramwell, A., 1985. *Blood and Soil: Walther Darré and Hitler's Green Party*, The Kensal Press, Buckinghamshire.

Brown, D.M., 1955. *Nationalism in Japan*, Cambridge University Press, Cambridge.

Bunting, B., 1969. *The Rise of the South African Reich*, Penguin, Harmondsworth.

Cheles, L., 1991. 'Nostalgia dell'avvenire'. The new propaganda of the MSI between tradition and innovation, in L. Cheles, *et al.* (eds), (op. cit.).

Cheles, L., Ferguson, R. and Vaughan, M. (eds), 1991. *Neo-fascism in Europe*, Longman, London.

Chiarini, R., 1991. The 'Movimento Sociale Italiano': A historical profile, in L. Cheles, *et al.* (eds), (op. cit.).

Cologne, D., 1978. *Julius Evola, René Guénon et le Christianisme*, Editions Eric Vatré, Paris.

Crowley, J.B., 1971. Intellectuals as Visionaries of the new Asian Order, in J.M. Morley, *Dilemmas of Growth in Pre-war Japan*, Princeton University Press, Princeton and London.

Davies, R., O'Meara, D. and Dlamini, S., 1988. *The Struggle for South Africa. A Reference Guide*, Zed Books, London.

Droite extrême et extrême droite en milieu universitaire, supplément à la lettre de

PSA, no. 52, 1989, Pour un Syndicalisme Autogestionnaire, Paris.

Eatwell, R., 1991. The Holocaust denial: a study in propaganda technique, in L. Cheles, *et al.* (eds), (op. cit.).

Ebels-Dolanová, V. (ed.), 1985. *The Extreme Right in Europe and the United States*, Anne Frank Foundation, Amsterdam.

Eisenberg, D., 1967. *The Re-emergence of Fascism*, Trinity Press, London.

Ellwood, S., 1991. The extreme right in Spain: a dying species?, in L. Cheles *et al.* (eds), (op. cit.).

Evans, G. and Rowley, K., 1990. *Red Brotherhood at War*, Verso, London.

Ferraresi, F., 1984. *La destra radicale*, Feltrinelli, Milan.

Ferraresi, F., 1988. The radical right in postwar Italy, *Politics and Society*, Vol.16, No.1.

Fletcher, W.M., 1982. *The Search for a New Order: Intellectuals and Fascism in Pre-war Japan*, University of North Carolina Press, Chapel Hill.

Ford, G. (ed.), 1990. *Report on the Committee of Enquiry into Racism and Xenophobia*, European Parliament Session Documents, Series A, No. A3–195/90.

Galli, G., 1983. *La destra in Italia*, Gammalibri, Milan.

Gable, G., 1991. The far right in contemporary Britain, in L. Cheles *et al.* (eds), (op. cit.).

Gilbhard, H. and Goblirsch, H., 1990. Rückkehr des Rassenwahns? Die ideologie des Neuen Rechtes, in W. Benz, (ed.), *Rechtsextremismus in der Bundesrepublik*, Fischer, Frankfurt-on-Main.

Gregor, A.J., 1969. *The Ideology of Fascism. The Rationale of Totalitarianism*, Free Press, New York.

Gregor, A.J., 1974. *The Fascist Persuasion in Radical Politics*, Princeton University Press, Princeton.

Gluck, C., 1985. *Japan's Modern Myths*, Princeton University Press, Princeton.

Griffin, R.D., 1985. Revolts against the modern world: the blend of literary and historical fantasy in the Italian New Right, *Literature and History*, Vol.11, No.1.

Guerra, P. and Revelli, M., 1983. Bibliografia essenziale per la conosscenza della nuova destra, in P. Bologna and E. Mana (eds), *Nuova destra e cultura reazionaria negli anni ottanta*, Notizario dell'Istituto storico della Resistenza in Cuneo e Provincia, No.23.

Hainsworth, P. (ed.), 1992. *The Extreme Right in Europe and America*, Pinter Press, London.

Harris, G., 1990. *The Dark Side of Europe. The Extreme Right Today*, Edinburgh University Press, Edinburgh.

Havens, T.R.H., 1974. *Farm and Nation in Japan, 1931–1941*, Princeton University Press, Princeton and London.

Hennessy, A., 1979. Fascism and Populism in Latin America, in W. Laqueur (ed.), *Fascism. A Reader's Guide*, Penguin, Harmondsworth.

Hill, R., 1988. *The Other Face of Terror*, Grafton, London.

Hilton, S., 1972. *Ação Integralista Brasileira*: fascism in Brazil, 1932–1938, *Luso-Brazilian Review*, Vol.9, No.2.

Husbands, C.T., 1991. Militant neo-nazism in the Federal Republic of Germany in the 1980s, in L. Cheles, *et al.* (eds), *Neo-Fascism in Europe*, Longman, London.

Jellamo, A., 1984. *J. Evola, il pensatore della tradizione*, in F. Ferraresi, (ed.) *La destra radicale*, Feltrinelli, Milan.

Kasza, G.L., 1984. Fascism from below? A comparative perspective on the Japanese right, 1931–1936, *Journal of Contemporary History*, Vol.19, No.4.

Larsen, S., 1993. *Modern Europe after Fascism*, Universitetforlaget, Bergen.

Levine, R., 1970. *The Vargas Regime: The Critical Years, 1934–38*, Columbia University Press, New York.

Mergui, R. and Simonnot, P., 1987. *Israel's Ayatollahs. Meir Kahane and the Far Right in Israel*, Saqi Books, London.

Mohler, A., 1972. *Die Konservative Revolution in Deutschland 1918–1932*, Wissenschaftliche Buchgesellschaft, Darmstadt.

Morley, J.M., 1971. *Dilemmas of Growth in Pre-war Japan*, Princeton University Press, Princeton.

Morris I.I.E., 1960. *Nationalism and the Right Wing in Japan. A Study of Post-war Trends*, Oxford University Press, London.

Muller, C.F.G., 1981. *500 Years. A History of South Africa*, Academia, Pretoria.

Najita, T., 1971. Nakano Seigō and the spirit of the Meiji Restoration in twentieth-century Japan, in J.W. Morley, (ed.), *Dilemmas of Growth in Prewar Japan*, Princeton University Press, Princeton.

Ngor, H., 1987. *A Cambodian Odyssey*, Macmillan, New York.

Nolte, E., 1969. *Three Faces of Fascism: Action Française, Italian Fascism, National Socialism*, Holt Rhinehart & Winston, New York.

Nolte, E., 1988. *Der europäische Bürgerkrieg. Nazionalsozialismus und Bolschewismus*, Propyläen, Berlin.

Ó Maoláin, C, 1987. *The Radical Right: A World Directory*, Longman, London.

Patterson, H., 1989. *The Politics of Illusion. Republicanism and Socialism in Modern Ireland*, Hutchinson, London.

Payne, S.G., 1980. *Fascism. Comparison and Definition*, University of Wisconsin Press, Madison, Wisconsin.

Payne, S.G., 1984. Fascism, Nazism, and Japanism, *The International History Review*, Vol.6, No.2.

Picq, L., 1989. *Beyond the Horizon: Five Years with the Khmer Rouge*, St. Martin's Press, New York.

Pinkney, R., 1990. *Right-wing Military Government*, Pinter, London.

Ponchaud, F., 1978. *Cambodia Year Zero*, Penguin, Harmondsworth.

Qadhafi, M., 1988. *The Green Book*, H.W. Christman (ed.), Prometheus, New York.

Revelli, M., 1984. *La nuova destra*, in F. Ferraresi, *La destra radicale*, Feltrinelli, Milan.

Rosenbaum, P., 1975. *Il nuovo fascismo. Da Salò ad Almirante. Storia del MSI*, Feltrinelli, Milan.

Seidel, G., 1986. *The Holocaust Denial*, Beyond the Pale Collective, Leeds.

Serfontein, 1979. *Brotherhood of Power – An Exposé of the Secret Afrikaner Broederbond*, Indiana University Press, Bloomington, Indiana.

Shavit, Y., 1988. *Jabotinsky and the Revisionist Movement 1925–1948*, Cass, London.

Sheehan, T., 1981. Myth and violence: the fascism of Julius Evola and Alain de Benoist, *Social Research*, Vol.48, No.1.

Shillony, B., 1973. *Revolt in Japan and the February 26, 1936 Incident*, Princeton University Press, Princeton.

Shillony, B., 1981. *Politics and Culture in War-time Japan*, Oxford University Press.

Sims, R., 1982. Japanese fascism, *History Today*, Vol.32.

Taylor, A.J.P., 1961. *The Origins of the Second World War*, Hamish Hamilton, London.

Trindade, H.H., 1974. *Integralismo: o fascismo brasileiro na decada de 30*, Difusão Européia do Livro, São Paolo.

Vaughan, M., 1991. The extreme right in France: 'Lepenisme' or the politics of fear, in L. Cheles *et al.* (eds), (op. cit.).

Wall, D., 1989. The Green Shirt effect, *Searchlight*, No.168.

Wilson, G.M., 1969. *Radical Nationalist in Japan: Kita Ikki 1883–1937*, Harvard University Press, Oxford.

7 The Psycho-historical Bases of Generic Fascism

The Contemporary Relevance of Understanding the Dynamics of Fascism

As we have seen, the genus 'fascism' shows no sign of becoming extinct. Like some wounded hydra, it continues to sprout new progeny which, though condemned to remain pathetically stunted compared with the anaconda-like protuberance it produced in Weimar Germany, still require careful monitoring by the upholders of human rights in many parts of the world. The minute groupings of fanatics who actively pursue the fascist chimera of national rebirth may never again be able to mount a credible challenge to state power, liberal or authoritarian. However, the international affiliations which many have cultivated at a publicistic and terroristic level and the respectable front behind which some camouflage their activities enabled them to act as a permanent fifth column in most liberal democracies where they continue to foment racial intolerance.

The ongoing need to keep fascism in any of its permutations, old and new, under surveillance means that it is still a matter of contemporary relevance to establish as far as possible the factors which produce it. Moreover, the central role played by its mythic component and the potential for extreme violence associated with it pose fundamental questions about the dynamics of modern political and social behaviour in general and how these can be reconciled with existing models of historical change and human nature. By addressing such questions and suggesting approaches to their resolution, fascist studies can contribute to an understanding of wider issues which concern political scientists, contemporary historians and analysts of current affairs, especially in that crucial area of 'ideology' where individual consciousness interacts with supra-personal structures to produce mass-mobilizing causes to fight for, however irrational they seem to an outsider. Indeed, as I suggested at the end of the last chapter, the raw ingredients of some of the most virulent political energies at work today in radical populist movements (and even in some particularly revolutionary authoritarian regimes) are close cousins of palingenetic ultra-nationalism as I have defined it, and important aspects of the internal logic of their ideology can at least be partially illuminated by cautious analogies with fascism.

There are, however, less pragmatic reasons for dwelling on such 'aetiological' issues. These have to do with the sheer scale of inhumanity caused directly or indirectly by Fascism, and particularly by Nazism. It would be a perversely myopic work on generic fascism that offered a definition of it without trying to make that inhumanity more comprehensible. A half-century on there are untold numbers of people still alive who suffered directly at the hands of the Nazis or whose immediate kith and kin died atrocious deaths in the name of a new European order. To ask in a spirit of open-ended enquiry how such a thing was possible forms part, no matter how insignificant, of the humanistic tradition which all fascisms were bent on destroying and at the same time indirectly keeps alive the memory of that suffering 'lest we forget'. Optimists might argue that the vitality of this tradition also helps forestall the possibility that such atrocities might ever again be deliberately carried out by a state which has been exposed to the influence of Western civilization.

Obviously the issues involved here are of immense complexity. The detailed historiographical research of an idiographic nature already carried out into several fascisms, especially Nazism and Fascism, has clarified a major aspect of their 'causes' by reconstructing the immediate background to their rise and hence the dense concatenation of particular social, economic, political and diplomatic events in which they consisted and were enmeshed. There is also a considerable body of information on the social base of a number of inter-war fascist movements and some major attempts to illuminate specific aspects of the dynamics of fascism 'as a whole' (for important examples of both see the monographs in Larsen *et al.*, 1980). Given the synoptic nature of this book, I can do no more than indicate at a high level of generality how, in the light of the ideal type it uses, certain existing lines of theorizing and levels of causal explanation might be fruit-fully combined both to explain the appearance of generic fascism and make the particular form it assumes and the fate which befalls it in a given context more intelligible. In doing so I will be building on and elaborating a number of points made in the course of constructing the new ideal type in Chapter 2.

The 'Whys' of Fascism

A matter to be clarified at the outset is precisely what problems are being addressed when there is talk of the dynamics or 'why' of fascism. In practice this is, like so many other basic questions in the human sciences, not a single issue but breaks down into a number of inter-related yet discrete ones. Some of the more important include (expressed in non-specialist language):

(1) What is the psychological basis of fascism?
(2) Why did fascism first emerge when it did?
(3) What enables a fascist movement to 'take off'?

(4) Why was there a 'fascist epoch'?
(5) Why did fascism break through autonomously in Italy and Germany but not in other countries?
(6) Why was Nazism so much more destructive than any other fascism?

The rest of this chapter will be dedicated to addressing the first two questions, concentrating particularly on fundamental psycho-historical issues often skimmed over in orthodox fascist studies but which can be seen in a fresh light using the ideal type I have proposed. The premises which emerge then inform answers to the remaining questions, which will be considered in the final chapter. These can be approached in a less discursive and speculative manner since they involve more immediate structural factors on which much excellent scholarship already exists. To avoid misunderstandings, it is worth spelling out a number of premises implicit in my attempted answers. They all have to do with the fundamental complexity of fascism which qualifies the 'neatness' and adequacy of explanations of any of its aspects:

(i)   The emergence of any fascist movement depends partly on the ideological commitment and ambitions of its nucleus of original founders which are rooted in their individual psychological predispositions, but also in a nexus of transpersonal social, economic, political and cultural factors which condition the decision to found the movement and the content, however nebulous, of its programme.

(ii) The subsequent strength or weakness of the movement will depend partly on intrinsic factors (qualities of leadership, tactics, organization etc.), but will be decisively affected by the socio-political space in which it operates and by the course taken by the many national and international processes and events on which its activities impinge.

(iii) It is important to distinguish between at least three types of support for a *movement* (that is before a party gains power): (a) the commitment of the leadership, ideologues, hard-core activists and fanatical converts; (b) the genuine but more passive and fickle commitment of rank-and-file supporters in the public at large who might be swayed by the stand it takes on a single issue (for example immigration, communism); and (c) the tactical support of those who traditionally belong to another political constituency but who see in it a force capable of combating common enemies (for example the 'left'). All three levels of support will be tend to be motivated by different considerations.

(iv) Once fascism takes power and forms a *regime*, factors other than ideological zeal (for example fear, opportunism, conformism, cynicism, gullibility, sadism, the effectiveness of social control or the absence of practical alternatives) will motivate many to support or become activists in official organizations and to collude with the new regime without any intense affective commitment to its ideology or policies (cf. the so-called *Märzgefallene* who flocked to join the NSDAP after March 1933).

(v)   Accounts of the psychological motivation for supporting fascism are only meaningful as part of an investigation into its nature if they concentrate on the most committed group of activists and converts in its movement phase because shallowness, cynicism and opportunism contribute to the support for all ideologies, especially in their orthodox aspect as the basis of a system.

(vi) It should not be assumed that even 'genuine fascists' understand or endorse everything contained in a fascist political programme or myth. Like all carriers of an ideology they will embody it partially and idiosyncratically, giving emphasis to different strands or potentials within it in a way which reflects their unique personality and circumstances.

(vii) The leadership, members, voters and tactical allies will not be drawn from a single social group (for example the 'petty bourgeoisie'), for, as Sternhell put it, 'fascism has no sound and obvious footing in any particular class' (1979, p.325). Similarly, the motivation to support the movement will be too heterogeneous to be reduced to a single factor, personality type or neurosis. Weinstein's observation about Nazi activists holds for all fascists: they 'participated in the movement for their personal idiosyncratic reasons: there was no homogeneity of motives' (quoted in Platt, 1980, p.69).

(viii) Attempts to illuminate the dynamics of generic fascism must refrain from assuming that it is essentially the product of inter-war Europe and especially from taking Nazism as the paradigm of all structurally related movements.

In other words, what makes it hazardous to generalize about the 'dynamics' of fascism is that each variant of it has its own story and is an irreducibly complex product of unique conditions and different levels of causation which require a multi-level and multi-disciplinary approach to be even partially illuminated. Once the full range of twentieth-century fascism glimpsed in Chapters 5 and 6 is taken into account, it becomes apparent that any generic explanatory model must accommodate the extremely varied types of societies and historical circumstances in which it has arisen and the considerable sociological and ideological diversity it has displayed. The literature which has a bearing on such a model is not merely vast but spans a wide range of approaches and disciplines, many of which contradict each other when taken to their logical conclusion as exclusive (that is holistic instead of heuristic, and thus unscientific) keys to truth. To establish one congruent with the ideal type I have constructed, I propose to draw on a number of disparate theories which illuminate the dynamics of the sort of ideology it suggests fascism to be, deliberately ignoring the areas which conflict. The result will be a consciously eclectic and synthetic 'conceptual framework' with which to discuss the causes of fascism. I am well aware that the psycho-historians, social anthropologists, semioticians, structuralists and post-structuralists have elaborated a number of specialized perspectives and vocabularies ('discourses'), with which to talk about the processes of cultural production and reproduction and that many points I make below might be translated into the 'idioglossia', or private and arcane language, of their individual specialisms. However, I have chosen to remain within a more exploratory, essayistic, and hopefully accessible, register which emphasizes the lack of any single authority on these complex matters, and the essentially tentative, speculative nature of my own approach to them.

1   What is the Psychological Basis of Fascism?

The Human Need for Self-transcendence

My approach to the question of fascism's psychological preconditions focuses on the inner motivation of those who show a strong ideological commitment to fascism rather than on its more opportunistic or passive fellow-travellers. I will not try to build on the pioneering psychoanalytical theories of Bataille (1985) which date from 1933 or Fromm (1960) and Reich (1970), both of which were first published in English in the 1940s, because, apart from the debatable status of Freudian categories of psychoanalysis when applied to collective or historical phenomena, all three naturally tended to reduce fascism to Nazism and to assume naïvely that this was a middle-class movement, thus perpetuating some of the fallacies alluded to above. Our starting point instead is provided by the analysis of the 'human condition' carried out by a twentieth-century equivalent of the Enlightenment *philosophe*, Arthur Koestler. In *The Ghost in the Machine* (1970) he offers a comprehensive theory of the physiological substrata of human psychology which places special emphasis on the poor neurological co-ordination between the neocortex/mesocortex in which the higher functions of the brain are located and the phylogenetically older 'animal' brain constituted by the limbic system. It is this 'archicortex' which is responsible not only for the body's basic regulatory mechanisms, but also for our instinctive, visceral (that is 'gut') emotions. The direct results of imperfect 'wiring' between the three brains are the major dysfunctions which can arise in human relationships with external reality and bring about what he calls 'the predicament of man'.

To simplify crudely Koestler's subtly argued and extensively documented contention, human beings are endowed with two basic drives, that of self-assertiveness and the opposite one of self-transcendence, which enable them to be both autonomous individuals and members of a social hierarchy such as the family or the tribe. A healthy relationship with the world in all its aspects, that is one based on harmony and creative symbiosis with it rather than possessive or destructive urges towards it, depends on a delicate balance of the two drives which allows people to experience themselves simultaneously as unique, independent personalities *and* as integral parts of larger social entities, both equally vital for the continued dynamism and cohesion of all human societies. However, because of the 'paranoid', 'delusional' streak in the human make-up, both the self-assertive and self-transcendent drives can assume a pathological aspect when they take on an obsessive, nihilistic form inconsistent with the demands of survival and irrespective of the damage they inflict on fellow creatures. Ironically, it is the perversion of *self-transcendent* emotions, not self-assertive ones, which has been largely responsible for the chronicle of atrocities which human beings have inflicted on each other down through the ages: they allow the perpetrators of 'inhuman' deeds to act not on their own behalf but as subordinate parts of a hierarchy, whether human or metaphysical, which absolves them of personal responsibility and invests their actions with the sense of fulfilling a 'higher' purpose or mission.

As a symptom of how the capacity for self-transcendence can be perverted, Koestler cites the wide-spread use of human sacrifice in traditional cultures, a notorious example being that of the Aztecs, who annually sacrificed between twenty and fifty thousand young men, virgins and children so that the sun would not die. The basic mechanism at work in such a culture (fortunately, the majority of societies in history have not been the product of this kind of institutionalized paranoia) is that individual self-transcendent emotions are no longer sublimated through ritual and tradition into mature, humane *integration* with the external world. Instead, they express themselves via a culturally reinforced collective regression to an infantile type of projection which abolishes the all-important affective distinction between part and whole, thus producing a potentially destructive *identification* with the supra-personal entity (in this case Aztec culture). In such circumstances the human urge to belong and the thirst for meaning is channelled into a sense of unquestioning oneness with a depersonalized social myth which deprives individuals of a creative, 'human' relationship with the world. This turns them into tools of ritual violence in the name of an abstract cause or delusory collective purpose.

It is this line of argument which leads Koestler to consider two phenomena which are crucial to our investigation of fascism: the emergence of political ideologies and of crowd psychology. Because the structural defects in the neurology of the brain and its affective apparatus have not repaired themselves through evolution, the decay of religions and the rise of science have not resulted in a general trend towards human beings enjoying a more rational, integrated relationship with society. If anything their predicament has deepened:

> Religious wars were superseded by patriotic, then by ideological, wars, fought with the same self-immolating loyalty and fervour. The opium of revealed religions was replaced by the heroin of secular religions, which commanded the same bemused surrender of the individuality to their doctrines, and the same worshipful love offered by their prophets. The devils and succubi were replaced by a new demonology: sub-human Jews plotting world dominions; bourgeois capitalists promoting starvation . . . (Koestler, 1970, p.273)

The secularization and fragmentation of modern society has generated periodic waves of collective commitment to ideologies in which some individuals become caught up in the type of group mentality which often goes by the name 'crowd psychology', even if, as a result of the uncanny strength of the human mythopoeic faculty which allows the monk alone in his cell to still feel embraced by the love of God, an individual does not need to commingle physically with a crowd to be part of a mass movement. By the twentieth century conditions in Europe were right for the enlistment of millions of ordinary citizens in the battle for 'the Classless Society' or the 'Millennial Reich', lured not by their egotism but by their unselfishness, their idealism, their urge to place their lives in the service of a higher cause: 'Both the Fascist and the Soviet myths were not syncretic constructions, but revivals of archetypes, both capable of absorbing not only the cerebral component but the total man; both provided emotional saturation' (ibid., p.293).

Applied to modern political ideologies in general, Koestler's theory implies that genuine affective commitment to any of them is an act of self-transcendence. What distinguishes the content and consequences of that commitment is first, whether the ideology encourages *integration* (the retention of individuality, critical distance, humanity) or *identification* (blind obedience, fanaticism, suppression of individual conscience) and second, what the precise mythic object of integration/identification is. Liberalism is an integrative ideology, as is communism in principle, though since Stalin all communist regimes have tended to operate as an identificatory 'state religion' in practice, despite the stress on a universal classless and stateless society as the ultimate goal of humanity. In the case of fascism, its core myth of the regenerated national community led by a revolutionary elite calls *a priori* for an act of identification, a neurologically based mischannelling of the human drive for self-transcendence. This engenders a paranoid, dualistic mind-set conducive to boundless idealism and fanatical devotion towards the embryonic new nation, coupled with ruthless violence directed at its alleged enemies. Fascism is not 'resistance to transcendence' (*pace* Nolte, 1965) but the result of succumbing to a perverted and peculiarly modern form of it.

A Syncretic Amplification of Koestler's Theory

I have quoted Koestler at length, not as an objective authority on the human condition (which cannot exist), nor because his ideas are based on 'hard' facts (for I am sure many scientific objections could be raised to aspects of his thesis). I cite him because his theory has so many points of correspondence with themes explored by more 'academic' representatives of several different disciplines in the human sciences who have investigated some of the basic psycho-historical forces shaping modern society. For instance, the susceptibility of 'modern man', despite 'his' alleged rationality, to archaic private and collective mythic forces was also a theme which dominated the life's work of C.G. Jung. On the basis of extensive experience as a psychoanalyst combined with research into religious iconography and mythical imagery the world over, he postulated the existence of a Collective Unconscious, the repository of archetypal symbols which he believed held the key to the generation and channelling of deep affective energies (for which he sometimes used the anthropological term 'mana'). Jung saw a harmonious relationship between Consciousness, the Personal Unconscious and the Collective Unconscious as an essential precondition for human beings to enjoy a creative psychic life and to form integral parts of a healthy society. In the West the Reformation, the Enlightenment and the Industrial Revolution progressively destroyed the relative equilibrium in spiritual (or rather, mythopoeic) life assured by the Christian Church, giving rise to a 'mass man', the product of the 'isolation and atomization of individuals' which accompanied 'the neglect and repression of the instincts of the unconscious'. A concomitant of this has been the emergence of a 'mass psyche' particularly susceptible to what Jung calls 'psychic inflation' (Odaj-nyk, 1976, pp.36–44).

In this process the Archetypal Unconscious, badly co-ordinated within a personality in which the delicate process of individuation has been impaired, is fired into life by exposure to events pregnant with symbolic significance because of their archetypal resonance. It then grows out of all proportion so as to overwhelm both the personal unconscious and consciousness. The Crusades and millenarian movements of medieval and early modern Europe can both be seen as episodes of psychic inflation. With its overemphasis on rationalism and individualism, secular culture has made 'modern man' par-ticularly vulnerable to epidemics of psychic energy channelled no longer into religions but into any number of secular cults based on cultural and political ideologies or what Jung calls simply 'isms'. 'Our fearsome gods have only changed their names; now they rhyme with "ism" ' (Jung, 1988, p.81). It is especially when the mass psyche feels threatened that psychic inflation takes place 'which is why mana-movements and mana-personalities arise frequently under new or distressing circumstances, whether environ-mental or psychological' (Odajnyk, 1976, p.25). Though using a different model of the psyche from Koestler, Jung also explained the rise of Nazism specifically in terms of the mobilization of irrational drives that had once been channelled into religion, but which have been dangerously repressed by the forces of rationalism and individualism (see especially the essay *The Fight with the Shadow* in Jung, 1988): we would still insist on not referring to it as a 'political' or 'secular' religion, however, but a form of political rather than religious myth.

It is worth adding that Campbell (1968, 1990) corroborates many of Jung's insights, particularly the distinction between a 'healthy' mysticism which 'goes beyond the whole field of separation' (1990., p.162), namely world-views which breed dualisms and divisions. The 'concretization of symbols' into historical facts and into political goals, to be realized at all costs, turns a cosmology promoting a healthy transcendence into one which breeds violence and hate: 'The Promised Land . . . has to do with what you're doing inside yourself, not whom you've got your weapons pointed at to kill. The shift is dramatic. And so you can say that history is simply a function of misunderstood mythology' (ibid., p.166).

Another example of a major theorist whose ideas are congruent with aspects of Koestler's analysis is Mircea Eliade, who, as we have seen (above, p. 31), resembles Arnim Mohler in that he has not only contributed to an academic understanding of the fascist world-view, but by allowing himself to be associated with the French New Right think-tank, GRECE, has actively contributed to legitimating one its more influential modern permutations. Eliade's extensive study of the role played by ritual and cosmological myth in traditional societies in perpetuating a metaphysical sense of the world's meaning and purpose led him to diagnose the threat to 'modern man' posed by the erosion of his ability to escape the 'terror of history' (that is achieve transcendence) through the repeated experience of sacred time and space afforded by an all-embracing cosmology and social ritual. He is thus forced to take refuge in the fragile pockets of space in which linear, personal time can be abolished and transcendence achieved which are generated haphazardly and inadequately in secular, pluralistic society (Eliade, 1959, 1964, 1971). Some of the most relevant sections in Eliade's works are those which dwell on the crucial role played by myths of the cyclic decay, destruction and rebirth of the cosmos, in keeping at bay a sense of absurdity and despair in times of calamity. Pre-modern societies which had some notion of irreversible, linear and hence historical time (for example the Egyptians, Aztecs) all cultivated myths which located major events inside their culture within a vast scheme of decadence and renewal (either infinitely repeatable or as a 'one way' sequence). Even catastrophes could be accommodated by being interpreted as signs that the phase of decline was reaching its nadir and a new cycle was beginning. Human beings living through ages of destruction and chaos were thus 'able to bear the burden of being contemporary with a disastrous period by becoming conscious of the position it occupies in the descending trajectory of the cosmic cycle' (Eliade, 1971, p.118).

For example, a constant theme of political thought throughout Roman history was the span of time which had been allotted by fate to the city before it would finally be destroyed and whether it could be regenerated in a process of *renovatio*. Thus every socio-political crisis, whether external or internal, sparked off a wave of speculation about Rome's decadence, imminent collapse and potential for rebirth in a 'new Rome' (ibid., pp.118–20, 133–7). Eliade sees the 'swarm of gnosticisms, sects, mysteries, and philosophies that overran the Mediterranean–Oriental world during the centuries of historical tension' as prompted by the same urge which underlay the myth of Rome's regeneration. Their proliferation was a sign that the cultural energies produced by this urge were no longer being effectively channelled into cohesive ritual culture because of the erosion of a traditional centre by secularization, syncretism and pluralism.

The implication for modern political science is that the physical hardships and psychic distress experienced by those living through 'bad times' is able to be borne by the mass of human beings as long as it is not *meaningless* distress. The perennial human craving to find release from pain and despair through mythopoeia and ritual makes it inevitable that 'modern man' too will continue to create havens from the terror of history in cyclic myths of renewal and in their corresponding ceremonials, both of which have the function of abolishing profane time. Each new crisis will thus release currents of energy potentially available for channelling into palingenetic myths. But in stark contrast to traditional society, the secularization and pluralism which define the modern age lead to the appearance of new myths. Moreover these myths often take the form of socio-political ideologies: namely, revolutionary theories of how *renovatio* is to be brought about and which claim to have an empirical basis in historical events. No longer supported by an all-pervasive cosmology and ritual, these modern myths necessarily fail to capture the minds of the whole of society and will generate for those they do capture mythic expectations that cannot be fulfilled in reality.

Working on quite different methodological principles from Eliade, Erich Fromm came to conclusions which also reinforce elements of Koestler's argument by focusing, not on the 'terror of history', but the 'fear of freedom' (Fromm, 1960). Central to his theory is the premise that human beings have a built-in dread of isolation and a corresponding need for a sense of belonging. The 'natural' sense of being part of a greater whole created in traditional societies has been progressively sapped by the rise of individualism, a concomitant of the Renaissance, the Reformation, industrialization and capitalism. The result is that, while some are able to take advantage of the freedom to pursue personal paths of individuation, others are driven by a fear of loneliness and freedom to form sado-masochistic relations with the outside world in which they are absolved from personal responsibility for their acts. This forms the basis of the identification between an authoritarian leadership and its compliant subjects, only too eager to 'obey orders'. Fromm also explores the notion that periods of crisis make it psychologically vital for most people to take refuge in the illusion of a higher order of reality in which they are relieved of the pain of being themselves in a mythless, private time.

Koestler, Jung, Campbell, Eliade, Fromm: these may seem a rather dubious set of 'expert witnesses' to call on in order to corroborate a certain line of causal explanation for the motivation of fascism. But two of the founding fathers of modern socio-political thought came to conclusions about the dominant processes at work in modern society which also have points of congruity with all of them. A major focus of Emile Durkheim's study of modern society was the unsustainability of individual human existence without collective myths and goals. The function of religion was to create a sense of solidarity and social cohesion, forces which he ultimately came to see as a purely subjective (that is mythic) phenomenon (see Hughes, 1958, pp.282–3; Pickering, 1984). A concomitant of the decay of Christianity was the growth of *anomie*, creating in individuals a sense of rootlessness and isolation which could drive them to despair and suicide. The problem of 'civilized' man was that he still had the psychological needs of social man.

> Social man necessarily presupposes a society which he expresses and serves. If this dissolves, if we no longer feel it in existence and action about and above us, whatever is social in us is deprived of all objective foundation. All that remains is an artificial combination of illusory images, a phantasmagoria vanishing at the least reflection; that is, nothing which can be a goal for our action. (Durkheim, 1951, p.213)

Underlying much of Max Weber's investigation of the forces shaping industrial society was a deep concern that the long-term consequences of the world's progressive 'disenchantment' (*Entzauberung*) through the rise of rationalism would lead to a passionless 'iron cage' of reason suspended in

a void of absurdity. The political vacuum created by the erosion of traditional politics with their metaphysical foundations would continue to be filled
in the twentieth century by the 'legal/rational' (that is liberal) systems which
could only exercise a weak affective hold on the citizens subject to them.
This created the conditions for sporadic outbursts of 'charismatic' energy in
which movements headed by leaders endowed by their followers with quasi-
magical properties would temporarily replace them on the basis of spontaneous popular consensus (Weber, 1948).

There are a number of other similarly 'orthodox' tacks from which
components of Koestler's hypothesis could be elaborated. Cohn (1970)
extensively documented the proliferation of millenaristic cults, both elitist
and egalitarian, puritanical and hedonist, which sprang up in the extended
period of socio-psychological dislocation that marked the transition from
feudalism to the 'modern age' in Europe. Drawing on a variety of Christian
eschatological traditions, both Biblical and apocryphal, the various sects can
be seen as spontaneous mythic communities united by a fanatical devotion
to their leader's idiosyncratic interpretation of his mission to forge from
them the nucleus of God's new dispensation, the post-apocalyptic new
order. Complementary work exists on the Renaissance witch craze, fruit-
fully exploring its parallels as a 'psychic epidemic' with the 'Hippy' counter-
culture (Harris, 1975), a line of enquiry corroborated by evidence that it was
complex forces of social *dysfunction* which also gave rise to the creative
achievements of the Renaissance and Reformation (see Kinsman, 1975). As
mentioned in Chapter 2, another relevant area of research has concentrated
on the way modern political ideologies which succeed in generating a
fanatical mass following operate as *ersatz* religions with their own creeds,
icons and rituals (for example Voegelin, 1968; Talmon, 1980; Sironneau,
1982: an extensive exploration of this theme with respect to Soviet Russia is
offered in Lane, 1981). This in turn ties in with works exploring the utopian
aspect of political myth (for example Goodwin and Taylor, 1982; Reszler,
1981), a notable example of which is Lasky's (1976) investigation of how the
quasi-religious dimension of revolutionary utopianism is expressed in the
visionary metaphors used by its major ideologues such as Marx and
Bakunin.

But the specialists referred to here are just a handful of the scores of
academics, famous or obscure, whose research in one way or another
converges on the notion that ancient psychological mechanisms of mythopoeia and self-transcendence, whether healthy or unhealthy, continue to
operate just under the surface of modern consciousness to supply the
affective vitality and dynamics of all political cultures, however rational or
'progressive' they might seem. To cite another almost at random, the
American academic, Platt, has drawn attention to a basic mechanism involved in revolutionary processes: namely the way individuals who live
through the dramatic breakdown of the social order and of their familiar
position within it experience the chaotic events involved as a 'sense-making
crisis'. The urge to ward off the psychic distress they suffer when their
world-view is no longer able to accommodate what is happening to them
leads to 'the search for new methods for cognizing and experiencing the

world and making sense of the emotional arousal'. This results in 'alternate world views' which 'harness emotional arousal and . . . guide persons to a renewed sense of meaning in the world', one based on 'both an explanation of the failure and a reason for hope'. If the 'sense-making crisis' leads to personal conversions to a new form of *sense-making myth* in sufficiently large numbers, this myth will produce its own political movement, leadership and ideology, and may even become the basis of a regime which will attempt to implement it. Yet, though converts to the new revolutionary ideology imagine themselves to be members of a unified party or force for change, 'each adherent constructs from his circumscribed commitment to and conception of the ideology his particular conception of the movement'. Indeed, the strength of the new world-view is precisely that it can mean so many things to so many people that it creates an *illusory* socio-political community which is still capable in the right circumstances of achieving real power (Platt, 1980, pp.79–87). Platt's essay, like several in the volume in which it appears (Albin, 1980), underlines how far psycho-history has advanced in subtlety and in compatibility with 'mainstream' human science since the pioneering works on fascism by Bataille, Fromm or Reich.

Platt's observations about the relationship of ideology to what I would like to call 'nomic' crises in modern society are corroborated by research into political myth. Tudor, for example, explores how myth functions as a way of allowing individuals to make sense of history, especially when society is undergoing a crisis:

> Any sudden disintegration of the established order, whether through revolution or economic collapse, breeds the need for a new understanding of man's place in the world and for new ways of going about the ordinary business of life, and this need is satisfied by the introduction of new myths and new rituals. In the myths, the nation's past is dramatized in such a way to make its future destiny apparent; and, in the rituals, obsolete customs are replaced by gestures which sustain the solidarity of the people and illustrate their new-found conception of what they are about. (Tudor, 1972, p.30)

Sewell (1985) has indirectly corroborated this approach to the dynamics of political revolutions but also added an important dimension by demonstrating that palingenetic impulses and myths are vital not only to such overtly irrational forces as ultra-nationalism and fascism, but to liberalism as well, often assumed to be their polar opposite. His reflections on the structural nature of ideologies leads him to highlight the crucial role myth of renewal played in the French Revolution, an event associated with the triumph not of 'charismatic' politics but of 'legal/rational' ones. For example, the members of the National Assembly at its crucial meeting on the 4 August 1789 were 'participating in what seemed to them to be the regeneration of the world' (ibid., p.70). Against the background of the acute political, economic and social dysfunction of the *ancien régime*, the revolutionaries had forged a new 'ideological structure' derived from a number of 'cultural idioms' of the day, principally Anglo–American liberalism and various strands of native Enlightenment thought, without which they could not have created a new constitution and so laid the basis of a new type of state.

Hunt (1981) has (again unwittingly) woven together themes explored by all of the writers we have mentioned by investigating the mythic dimension of the French Revolution expressed in the special discourse, ritual and festivals that spontaneously grew up to legitimate the overthrow of absolutism. She argues that they conspired to conjure up in the minds of the revolutionaries a 'mythic present' inaugurated in 'the instant creation of the new community, the sacred moment of the new consensus'.

> The ritual oaths of loyalty taken around a liberty tree or sworn *en masse* during the many revolutionary festivals commemorated and recreated the moment of the social contract, the ritual words made the myths present, come alive, again and again . . . The festivals reminded participants that they were the mythic heroes of their own revolutionary epic. (ibid., pp.27–32)

Like Sewell, Hunt independently stresses the palingenetic aspect of this myth when she observes that the sense of 'national regeneration' induced the 'exhilaration of a new era' (ibid.), and goes on to refer to the wide-spread assumption among the revolutionaries that the 'national regeneration required nothing less than a new man and new habits' (ibid., p.56), and that these could somehow be created by new symbols. The events in the East bloc in the bicentenary of the French Revolution provide eloquent testimony to the fact that liberalism in its extra-systemic, utopian aspect is still as capable of acting as a populist form of palingenetic myth as fascism was in its day. The crucial difference between the two is that in principle liberalism's embrace of pluralism means that it celebrates the psychic principle, not of 'pathological' identification, but of 'healthy' integration. However, the zeal of the Jacobins for the 'purging' effects of Terror show that even an ideology whose content and goals imply integration may induce delusional, fanatical (that is identificatory) forms of self-transcendence in the revolutionaries, convinced they are fighting its 'enemies' who stand in the way of the 'new age' which we saw so eloquently evoked by Büchner (see above p.179).

We might add that Sorel's analysis of history as being driven not by reason but by 'myths' which mobilize collective movements of structural change is one which dovetails neatly with this way of conceptualizing the dynamics of revolutionary social movements. The important difference is that, unlike all the scholars referred to, he did not set out to understand the historical power of myth but to act as the catalyst to new collective outbursts of it, deliberately fomented psychic epidemics which would, in Eliade's (and de Benoist's) phrase, 'regenerate history'. In other words he was not content to analyze the West's decadence but was consumed by a passionate desire to find a remedy for it, to inaugurate a cultural rebirth. He was driven by his own palingenetic myth, rather than that of the disinterested, pacifistic quest to render the world more intelligible which motivates most human scientists.

The Psychological Dynamics of Fascism

What this rampant syncretism boils down to in relation to the psychological foundations of fascism is that the affective basis of all ideologies can be located in a perennial neuro-psychological human drive to find a sense of belonging. This drive is fulfilled through the medium of myths capable of providing a powerful experience of self-transcendence which immunizes people from the sense of isolation, impotence and absurdity which might otherwise engulf them. It is this drive which underlies the complex cosmologies which have been a defining feature of the countless cultures created by human communities since time immemorial, as well as the elaborate metaphysical legends and rituals which have always underpinned them. In modern (that is partially secularized and pluralistic) culture there is no longer any central all-pervasive source of transcendent myth. Since, as T.S. Eliot observed, 'human beings cannot bear too much reality', the need for transcendence has come to express itself in contemporary society through myriad personal and communal forms of cultic behaviour, including the conversion to one of the scores of belief systems, religious and non-religious, now on offer.

In *Equus* Peter Shaffer explored the way individuals can even be driven by the need for self-transcendence to create a personal religion. In it he dramatized the story of a psychologist, Dysart, who is called upon to 'cure' Alan Strang of the private horse cult he has evolved. Dysart comes to recognize its psychic source to be the same mythic energy that had created the Greek legend of the centaurs and permeated the civilization whose greatness he vainly attempts to recapture through the experiences of the tourist on summer holiday in the Aegean. The sessions with Strang leave him tormented by the impoverishment of his own experience of the numinous and anguished at the ambiguity of the bland, magic-less (or to use Weber's term, 'disenchanted') normality into which his professional skill is meant to seduce those living in a painful but intensely real delusional world of their own. The implication is that the countless idiosyncratic complexes and fixations known to abnormal psychology as forms of madness are fuelled by the same archaic psychic energy that, channelled through a communal cosmology and ritual, guarantees the cohesion of all so-called 'primitive' societies. At the same time the play suggests that a rational existence bereft of the direct experience of that energy is the world of greyness punctuated by the *Angst* explored by existentialist philosophers and artists.

In modern anomic or 'centre-less' society the communal aspect of myth is by its very nature more conspicuous, though not necessarily more prevalent than the private one, providing the raw material of a mass culture and a media age dominated by fashion, consumerism, spectator sports, and soap operas, and susceptible to the latest equivalents of the seventeenth century tulip craze in Holland such as skate-boarding, aerobics or Madonna-mania. The continuous 'manufacture of myth' is as important to the cohesion and stability of modern society as the 'manufacture of consensus'. With mythic energies no longer securely invested in a cohesive religious or ethnic culture, they move freely around social space like petro-dollars, available to fund new sub-cultures such as the student and Hippy movements of the sixties, and the 'skinhead' or 'new age' movements of the eighties. It is in political ideologies, however, that mythic energies have the greatest power for effecting social and historical change, and where the distinction between integration and identification with the community of fellow-believers becomes crucial in the potential for inhumanity and destruction they unleash.

It follows from this analysis that the psychological precondition for the ideology of fascism to be espoused with a degree of genuine affective commitment is *an individual's need for self-transcendent myth which, in the 'right' historical circumstances, is satisfied by one centred on the reborn nation.* We will consider more closely what constitutes such circumstances in the next chapter. For now it is enough to say that this particular form of identification can only take place in a society where secularization, populist nationalism and a plurality of values and ideologies are already well established and where the life of the nation can be subjectively perceived as undergoing a profound crisis. In a minority of cases the individual's sense of external social or historical crisis may be practically autogenic (self-induced), the externalization of a defective capacity for individuation and integration with few apparent objective triggers. But clearly for the experience of dysfunction to trigger the rise of a mass movement it needs to be concretized in major upheavals in contemporary history which affect society as a whole (for example a power vacuum, civil war, economic breakdown). This then constitutes the 'situationally produced chaos' (Platt, 1980, p.83) which may undermine a person's material and psychological security, and hence sense of self, to a point where he (for it is a predominantly masculine syndrome: see Milfull, 1990) becomes inwardly available to an ideology of national regeneration which offers 'both an explanation of the failure and a reason for hope' and hence 'a renewed sense of meaning in the world' (Platt, 1980, p.83). This cannot occur if he is already 'booked by', or predisposed to take refuge in, another mythic scheme, whether this is a religious or ethical value-system or a competing ideology, or if he is sufficiently tough-minded (integrated, individuated, in existentialist terms 'authentic') to cope with the nomic crisis and the distress it causes without resorting to such a mythic panacea.

The committed fascist is thus someone who has resolved his 'sense-making crisis', whether objective or subjective, by projecting the experience of chaos and longing for a feeling of wholeness and meaning on to external reality so that it is the nation which he experiences as sick and the nation which is to be healed. Were he psychically healthy he would surmount the crisis by creating a new *psychological* order for himself in which he would become the hero of his inner life and achieve spiritual self-control, self-knowledge and freedom, whatever the physical and material privations he is exposed to. Instead, he wants to play a heroic role in public life by participating in the foundation of a new *social and political* order under the aegis of a national leader-figure, one who has total certainty of the mission history has assigned 'his' people. In this way he seeks to be fully relieved of the burden of individualism and freedom altogether (that is if he does not, like Mussolini and Hitler, arrogate the historic role of leader to himself and thus find an even more radical solution to his crisis of identity). Rather than search for a new level of consciousness, for mystic reawakening, for a personal 'Buddha experience' (in Sanskrit Buddha connotes being 'awoken') to rise above the vicissitudes of material and temporal existence, the fascist craves for 'the people' to be stirred from 'their' sleeping sickness, a hope embodied in the Nazi slogan *Deutschland erwache*, Germany Awake!

The psycho-historical dynamics of this situation as it manifested itself in the early Weimar Republic were explored with remarkable lucidity by Broch in his novel, *The Sleepwalkers*. Published in 1932 this trilogy portrays the life of three contrasting characters, the romantic Pasenow, the anarchist Esch and the realist Hugenau, each one emblematic of the reactions of a different generation to the progressive 'decay of values' which, as Broch argues in a lengthy excursus of that name interpolated into the narrative, set in with the Renaissance but which reached crisis point (in Europe) between 1888 and 1918. Broch's central theme is the way the inexorable break-down of the absolute system of meaning, the erosion of the mythopoeic centre, once provided by the Christian church, has produced in the mass of ordinary citizens of the modern age a profound sense of isolation, 'for the speech of the old community life has failed them'.

The acute personal disorientation which this causes makes them strive continually 'to find a haven in some partial system' of values, each one of which fuses its own logical premises with irrational energies and aspires to become a total, absolute truth to provide a bulwark against the definitive disintegration of nomic principles. The distressing experience of the 'icy breath sweeping over the world, freezing it to rigidity and withering all meaning out of the things of the world', has turned the individual into a sleepwalker groping his way through a reality which is becoming increasingly unintelligible, and has made him 'defenceless before the invasion of the irrational', or the 'irruption from below' in the form of spontaneous conversion to one of these partial (mythic) systems. It was this peculiar cultural climate of nomic crisis, radicalized by the cataclysm of the First World War, which bred in Weimar Germany the conditions for revolution, revolution which represents 'that act of self-elimination and self-renewal, the last and greatest ethical achievement of the old disintegrating system and the first achievement of the new, the moment when time is annulled and history radically formed in the heightened emotional climate of absolute zero!' (Broch, 1964, pp.631–48).

These conditions of acute psychological and epistemological crisis arouse in the man 'who becomes aware of his isolation' a 'doubly strong yearning for a Leader to take him tenderly and lightly by the hand, to set things in order and show him the way . . . the Leader who will build the house anew that the dead may come to life again . . . the Healer who by his actions will give meaning to the incomprehensible events of the Age, so that Time can begin again' (ibid., p.647). With the subtlety and emotional intensity that can only be communicated in art, Broch thus suggests that the psychological bases of Nazism (and hence of generic fascism) lie in an intense longing for rebirth projected on to a revolutionary nationalist movement.

The same conclusion has been arrived at on the basis of entirely different methodological premises and in a quite different register by Theweleit's case study of several individuals who played an active part in German proto-fascism (1987, 1989). Theweleit documents his highly individual investigation of the fascist mentality with the *mémoires*, diaries and letters of several members of the *Freikorps* (one of whom, Höss, later became commandant of Auschwitz) and supplements these with the literary expressions of 'soldierly nationalism' bequeathed by Ernst Jünger, Franz Schauwecker and Ernst von Salomon, as well as with Goebbels' novel *Michael*. Using a highly syncretic psychoanalytical model of the mechanisms which allow individuals to form a dynamic relationship with external reality, Theweleit explores the inner compulsions which motivated his sample of proto-fascist and future fascist activists to volunteer in the aftermath of 1918, thereby taking the nationalists' battle against communism into their own hands. He argues that in each case there is evidence that a particular syndrome was at work: the process of 'separation-individuation' had been disrupted in childhood, leaving the person trapped in a state of consciousness which precluded a healthy relationship between a 'whole ego and a whole other', so that, psychologically speaking, they were 'not-yet-fully-born'. This induced not only an urge to turn their body into a (military) machine so as to tame the chaotic inner world of instincts and emotions but a radical misogyny or flight from the feminine, manifesting itself in a pathological fear of being engulfed by anything in external reality associated with softness, with dissolution, with the uncontrollable.

The result of this syndrome is the 'soldier-male', driven by a longing to transcend the hell of his private self in a collective struggle against an inner chaos which has been projected on to society. At this point the mainstream of the fascist's affective energy becomes channelled into the fight for victory over the perceived agents of the nation's dissolution which would represent the final completion of his birth into the world:

> The texts of the soldier males perpetually revolve around the same axes: the communality of the male society, nonfemale creation, rebirth, the rise upward to hardness and tension . . . The man is released from a world that is rotten and sinking (from the morass of femaleness): he finally dissolves in battle. (Theweleit, 1989, p.361)

According to Theweleit it is this drive which promoted the violent reaction of *Freikorps* members to the undisciplined masses, to communists, to Jews, to any forces which could be perceived as enemies of the national community, for it is with this mythic entity that the craving for wholeness had led them to identify. Obsessed by a permanent sense of the imminent decomposition of inner and outer reality, the aim of all those who are 'not-yet-fully-born' is to 'annihilate what they perceive as absolute falsity and evil, in order to regenerate their ego in a better world' (ibid., p.253), in fact to become 'new men' (ibid., pp.161–2). This leads Theweleit to conclude that 'fascism's most significant achievement was to organize the resurrection and rebirth of dead life in the masses', by assembling it 'into blocks of human totality-machines, knitted into interlocking networks of order' (ibid., p.189). Nazism's success as an ideology can thus be ascribed to its capacity to transmute the repressed drives and fantasies of thousands of 'not-yet-fully-born' males into fanatical commitment to a political programme of national rebirth. (Interestingly enough, the most articulate representatives of the minority of women who became Nazi activists before 1933 saw in a Third Reich based on Aryan principles the chance, not to return to the passive roles imposed by the 'bourgeois' Second Reich, but to be reborn as a *'new woman'*. Not only would she be emancipated from emancipation, that is from the 'perversions' of her natural and biological functions advocated by feminists under Weimar, but through her maternal qualities and ethical integrity play a key role in the racial and social regeneration of the Germans. See Kaplan and Adams, 1990.)

Thus whether we approach the question from the point of view of comparative religion, the history of ideas, sociology, political science or psychoanalysis, there is no shortage of theories which can be adduced to suggest that the convinced fascist is to be seen as someone whose flight from inner chaos has found expression in a powerful elective affinity with an intensely mythic ideology of national regeneration. This ideology, though objectively representing just one partial system of values among so many others, he (and even on occasions she) experiences affectively as an absolute vehicle of personal salvation. By promising to redeem the nation from the quagmire of 'demo-liberalism', fascism offers its converts the prospect of a renewed sense of meaning, of transcendence, of ritual time, of imminent rebirth in a world otherwise threatened with inexorable decadence, a decadence which, however real the objective factors of social dysfunction at the time, at bottom was no more than their inner world of anxiety and chaos projected on to contemporary history.

Having made this pronouncement, though, we must never lose sight of the fact that only a small percentage of the population, and then only in special historical circumstances, will fall prey to this particular elective affinity, and that, no matter how much they share the same structural core in terms of psychological predisposition, even they will have their own idiosyncratic motivations and rationalizations for investing their yearning for rebirth in an actual fascist movement. This point, though made powerfully by Platt (1980) and Weinstein (1980), is blurred by several others among the more psychoanalytically inclined theorists we have cited, including Fromm, Jung and Theweleit (for example, the *Freikorps* cannot stand for *all* fascists, let alone *all* males, even if they certainly provide a valuable case study of one way the predisposition to one current within one form of fascism could manifest itself). Ultimately the mechanisms of the psyche and its interactions with external reality are simply too complex to be comprehensively modelled or fully unravelled. As Theweleit's study confirms, writers provide the psycho-historian in their novels and poems unusually articulate guides to the labyrinth of their personality. Yet it is still impossible to establish precisely why Barrès, Drieu la Rochelle, Pound, Johst and Hamsun succumbed to the lure of ultra-nationalist and fascist political myth, while figures such as Gide, Hesse, Huxley, Wyndham Lewis and Yeats, who shared so many of their preoccupations with the crisis and decadence of modern culture, remained (the latter two only just) within the fold of a relativist humanism (see for example Soucy, 1972, p.92; Leal, 1985; Cadwallader, 1981). Definitive answers to such questions are simply beyond the explanatory powers of the human sciences. In this respect the theoretician who sets out to lay bare the psychological dynamics of fascism is in the same dilemma as Dysart when he tries to get to the bottom of Strang's 'case'. Left alone to wrestle with Equus he muses:

> I can hear the creature's voice. It's calling me out of the black cave of the Psyche. I shove in my dim little torch, and there he stands – waiting for me. He raises his matted head. He opens his great square teeth, and says – (*Mocking*) '*Why?* . . . Why me? . . . Why – ultimately – *Me?* . . . do you really think you can account for Me? Totally, infallibly, inevitably account for Me? . . . Poor Doctor Dysart!' . . . A child is born into the world of phenomena all equal in the power to enslave. It sniffs – it sucks – it strokes its eyes over the whole uncountable range. Suddenly one strikes. *Why?* Moments snap together like magnets, forging a chain of shackles. *Why?* I can trace them. I can even, with time, pull them apart again. But why at the start they were ever magnetized at all – just those particular moments of experience and no others – I don't know. *And nor does anyone else.* (Shaffer, 1973, p.44)

The psychological dynamics of fascism are thus destined to remain in the last analysis shrouded in mystery and speculation. Nevertheless, using the psycho-historical model we have devised it is possible to identify some of the *external* factors that are conducive to the establishment of the particular ideological structure it represents, the objective situation in which it is likely to attract a mass following as a refuge from the pervasive *anomie* of modern society or the sensation of being overtaken by the collapse of society. In doing so we will be addressing the problem of answering our second question concerning the dynamics of fascism – why it first surfaced as a new form of 'total identification' myth in the early twentieth century, and then only in certain areas of Western and Central Europe.

Why Did Fascism First Emerge When It Did?

A Speculative 'Philosophy of History'

The central premise of our tailor- or home-made explanatory schema is that the slow breakdown of Christianity and of the associated feudal and absolutist systems in Europe released the mythic but, (*pace* Voegelin *et al.*: see above pp.29–32) not religious, energies locked within them. These were free to be invested in the secular or the quasi-religious social and political myths which have continued to proliferate wherever a European style of secularization, pluralism and nationalism has gained ascendancy (that is initially in North America and thereafter in any part of the world where an indigenous *ancien régime* or traditional society has been eroded by Western imperialism, military, economic or cultural). This would explain why nineteenth-century Europe, even more than the eighteenth, became an age awash with new overarching philosophies, cosmologies and ideologies personified in the likes of Saint-Simon, Marx, Darwin, Hegel, Nietzsche and Freud, to name but a very few. On one level fascism is but one of a number of partial systems of values produced by the 'modern age' which have aspired to provide a total explanation of contemporary history and become the basis of a new absolutist (and, when enforced, a tendentially 'totalitarian') socio-political system. It surfaced in Europe in the early twentieth century because it was there and then that the secularization and pluralization of human society first became sufficiently 'modern' or 'advanced' to make the formation of absolutizing political ideologies possible.

Our ideal type of fascism allows us to be more precise about its historical preconditions than this, however, for it suggests that it is made up of three mythic components, one of which is archetypal, the other two sufficiently culture-specific to make palingenetic ultra-nationalism the product of a unique conjuncture of ideological factors. These components are (i) the rebirth myth, (ii) populist ultra-nationalism and (iii) the myth of decadence. As we argued in Chapter 2 (pp.32–36) the rebirth myth has always been available to serve as an ingredient of cosmologies and value-systems, since it seems to constitute a constant of human mythopoeic thinking: an 'archetype', in fact. Ultra-nationalism in its populist sense is clearly of far more recent origin and is also far more culture-specific. It presupposes both the decay of feudal (in Weberian terms 'traditional') notions of power, the emergence of the nation-state, pre-Romantic and Romantic concepts of the uniqueness of national culture, a growing awareness of shared history, ethnicity, and language, the rise of mass politics as well as various other factors investigated by experts on the subject (for example Kedourie, 1966; Smith, 1979; Alter, 1989; Hobsbawm, 1990). Despite the complexity of nationalism's dynamics, the elusiveness of its definition and its many discernible sub-varieties (for it is an ideal type hardly less protean than fascism), there is a degree of consensus on the notion that populist nationalism of a tendentially illiberal or anti-liberal complexion emerged to fill the nomic vacuum left in the lives of millions of 'ordinary' citizens by the decay of traditional religion and community. Implicit in this insight is the recognition that the nation which forms the focal point of all populist nationalisms is a mythical construct, or as Anderson puts it, an 'imagined community' (Anderson, 1983, pp.12–13; cf. also Talmon, 1980; Hobsbawm, 1990).

Once populist nationalism focusing on an imagined community was (to use the terminology of Sewell, 1985) firmly established in a number of ideological idioms or an entire ideological structure, then the stage was set for it to produce a new variant of itself through synthesis with the perennial human propensity for rebirth myth and so assume a specific anti-conservative, revolutionary and illiberal character in the form of *palingenetic* ultra-nationalism, or what has come to be known as 'fascism' after the first movement to put it on the historical map as a new type of politics. The catalyst to such a synthesis taking place was the currency of a myth of *national decadence* conceived in such a way that it could be reversed by a radical process of *national regeneration*. In other words, our ideal type suggests that from the moment populist nationalism coincided with a climate of palingenetic expectancy fascism was 'bound' to appear. Yet it also suggests that it was only likely to gain any sort of mass following in conditions of objective structural dysfunction profound enough to create a wide-spread sense-making crisis. This seems to be borne out when we consider the cultural situation in Europe before 1914 in which groupings of (proto-)fascism first made a localized appearance, even if they were doomed to be still-born or remain stunted in the absence of the complex set of structural crises which would be unleashed by the First World War.

The Incubation of Fascism

It was in late nineteenth-century Europe that the two historical variables first came together which created the conditions in which ultra-nationalist permutations of palingenetic myth could appear. It was Europe that was first affected (albeit highly unevenly) by secularization and the subsequent decay of absolutist (traditional) political systems, and which experienced the concomitant rise of scientific rationalism, the nation-state, of liberal (legal/rational) politics and populist nationalism both liberal and illiberal, as well as of a wide spectrum of alternative political visions, both socialist and ultra-conservative. Clearly this was not only an ideological process, for it was accelerated by the decay of feudalism, the rise of capitalism, urbanization, industrialization, social mobility and other components of the nexus of forces often collectively referred to as 'modernization'. Elsewhere in the world traditional cultures with their non-nationalist varieties of political religions or myths still held sway. (The important exception to this generalization, of course, were many of Europe's colonies and former colonies, in which Western world-views had achieved hegemony over indigenous ones, a point to which we will turn shortly.)

It was also in Europe that towards the end of the nineteenth-century there grew up in intellectual and cultural circles a generalized sense of the failure of Western civilization, in other words diffuse cultural idioms of the myth of *decadence*. This myth was far from mobilizing a homogeneous social, let alone political, movement, for it was cultivated in geographically dispersed circles in a number of diverse non-political or apolitical 'discourses', namely religion, spirituality, morality and culture (see Swart, 1964; Weber, 1982), aesthetics (see Praz, 1970; Julien 1971), theories concerning the evolution of human society (see Pick, 1989), or race (see Poliakov, 1974) and literature (see Kermode, 1967). A disturbing symptom of its prevalence was the way a preoccupation with physical degeneration informed the thought of so many social scientists and commentators after 1850 (Pick, 1989). Equally disturbing (in retrospect) were the dualistic conceptions of health and decadence which shaped common-sense (that is mythic) male assumptions about the 'opposite sex', manifesting themselves in countless paintings and tracts which point to a veritable 'psychic epidemic' of pathological impulses towards women in the period 1850 to 1914 (Dijkstra, 1989).

In this cultural climate it was only natural that the preoccupation with decadence would cause some to indulge in palingenetic mythopoeia, leading to schemes to reverse decay and bring about regeneration in every sphere in which it was perceived to be at work: the occultism of Eliphas Lévi (McIntosh, 1972), the Catholic revivalism of Péguy (Griffiths, 1966), Péladan's hopes that the Slavs would rejuvenate the moribund Europeans (Swart, 1964), the aesthetics of Wagner, Picasso and Kandinsky (Hughes, 1980), the philosophy of Bergson, the social theories of Tönnies, Durkheim, Pareto and Sorel (Hughes, 1958), the criminological theories of Lombroso (Pick, 1989), the eugenics of Häckel and the racial theory of H.S. Chamberlain (Poliakov, 1974) are just individual ripples in a tide of disparate personal and collective initiatives to bring about the regeneration of a Western civilization perceived in one way or another as locked into a phase of dissolution and degeneration, but still just redeemable.

Symptomatic of the countless idiosyncratic ways in which cultural pessimism could be transformed through the alchemy of palingenetic temperament into manic cultural optimism is Max Nordau. Established by *Entartung* (Degeneration), first published in 1892, as one of the foremost spokesmen of the sense of engulfing decadence, he became after 1895 a passionate convert to Zionism, which not only provided a sense of purpose for his own life, but which he believed was a remedy for the 'black plague of degeneration and hysteria' whose symptoms he saw all around him (Baldwin, 1980). It was in an age saturated with such deeply personal visions of decadence and palingenesis that regenerationist idioms of social darwinism, racist imperialism and anti-Semitism started to make deep inroads into European culture at a number of levels and that Nietzsche enjoyed such extraordinary success as a cultural prophet after 1890.

Against this background it was predictable (or rather it is now 'retrodictable') that some would project the myth of decadence and rebirth even more narrowly on to the sphere of politics than Nordau, so that capitalism, liberalism, the *ancien régime* (where it still survived), or traditional conservative elites were blamed for the loss of essential values such as equality, freedom, racial strength, heroism, law and order, the human spirit, which had allegedly once prevailed. Such assumptions gave an intensified palingenetic thrust to the many varieties of socialism, in particular Marxism, anarchism and revolutionary syndicalism which proliferated in the latter part of the nineteenth-century, as well as to the new forms of dynamic 'regenerationist' conservatism that started to make their presence felt.

It was then only a matter of time before ideologues diagnosing the malaise of modern society in countries where populist nationalism and the myth of decadence were particularly rife (as in France after the traumas of military defeat and the Commune in 1870–1) came to create personal brands of palingenetic nationalism which point the way forward to fully fledged fascism: in France, Barrès, Maurras, and Sorel (once he was drawn to the *Action Française* rather than the syndicalists); in Italy, Papini, Marinetti and Federzoni; in Germany, Langbehn, Fritsch and Lagarde; in Austria, von Schönerer. These individuals were not lonely voices crying in the wilderness, but symptomatic of the diffuse currents of embryonic fascism which were affecting the political subcultures of these countries by drawing on varieties of Nietzscheanism, left or right (Sternhell, 1987; Aschheim, 1988), fusions of syndicalism with nationalism (Mazgaj, 1982), or speculations about the regeneration of the race (Mosse, 1966), indigenous versions of which appeared even in a country such as Britain, where liberalism seemed so securely anchored (Kennedy and Nicolls, 1981).

The structural precondition for proto-fascism emerging in Europe before 1914 was thus the coexistence of both populist nationalism and a myth of decadence as idioms within the same culture which could be fused into a new political ideology through the agency of the perennial human propensity to palingenetic myth. It is in this sense that Sternhell is perfectly correct to see in the *fin-de-siècle* sense of the crisis of civilization the 'incubation years of fascism' (Sternhell, 1979, p.333). It should be noted, however, that although those who experienced this crisis could rationalize it by reference to events and processes in contemporary history, no nation had as yet undergone socio-political and economic collapse on a large enough scale for a longing for national rebirth to be generalized and radicalized into a full-scale 'psychic epidemic'. Therefore no mass movement emerged bent on creating a new type of society. Clearly historical factors (for example the 'humiliation' of France in 1870, the incomplete *risorgimento* of Italy and Germany, the decline of Habsburg absolutism) must have played a part in fostering the circumscribed and muted political revolt against decadence in those particular countries. Yet such factors were probably less significant than the nebulous social anxieties and *anomie* induced by the extraordinary rapidity of modernization in a continent dominated by a sense of continuous history reaching back over two thousand years and therefore ripe for secular theories of decay and rebirth.

Indirect corroboration of this diagnosis is provided by the fact that a country like Britain also hosted degenerationist and regenerationist speculations before 1914, despite the relative absence of crisis symptoms to compare with those manifested by France or Italy (Pick, 1989). On the other hand, until the inter-war period little in the way of indigenous political myths of decadence and rebirth seem to have taken root in Europe's former colonies undergoing their own processes of modernization such as Australia, Canada, the United States, Mexico and Brazil. This is presumably because their intelligentsias were still dominated by the collective sense of being new nations or part of the 'New World' which acted as a prophylactic against a mood of cultural pessimism (though certainly not against racism or chauvinism), and hence against the palingenetic myths necessary to transform it into optimism.

Our rudimentary 'psycho-historical' scheme has been able to account for the first appearance of fascism, at least in its embryonic pre-1914 forms, primarily in terms of perennial psychological predispositions in conjunction with a particular cultural climate. To explain why fascism was able to hatch and quickly mature into a major historical force after 1918 means that the objective structural forces which combined to spread and radicalize a 'sense-making crisis' must move to the foreground of our analysis. In other words for fascism to 'take off', let alone 'break through', it must be the product of an interaction of psychological, cultural and ideological factors with social, political and economic ones, a point rightly stressed by Fromm (1960, p.4). It is the internal dynamics of this interaction which condition fascism's success or failure, its impotence or destructiveness as a political force and which form the subject of the final chapter.

References

Albin, M. (ed.), 1980. *New Directions in Psychohistory*, Lexington Books, Lexington, Massachusetts.

Alter, P., 1989. *Nationalism*, Edward Arnold, London.

Anderson, A., 1983. *Imagined Communities – Reflections on the Origins and Spread of Nationalism*, Verso Editions, London.

Aschheim, S.E., 1988. Nietzschean socialism – left and right, 1890–1933, *Journal of Contemporary History*, Vol.23, No.2.

Baldwin, P.M., 1980. Liberalism, nationalism and degeneration. The case of Max Nordau, *Central European History*, Vol.13, No.2.

Bataille, G., 1985. The psychological structure of fascism, in A. Stoeckl (ed.), *Georges Bataille. Visions of Excess. Selected Writings, 1927–1939*, University of Minnesota Press, Minneapolis.

Broch, H., 1964. *The Sleepwalkers*, Grosset and Dunlap, New York.

Cadwallader, B., 1981. *Crisis of European Mind: A Study of André Malraux and Drieu la Rochelle*, University of Wales Press, Cardiff.

Campbell, J., 1968. *The Hero with a Thousand Faces*, Princeton University Press, Princeton.

Campbell, J., 1990. *The Hero's Journey*, Harper and Row, New York.

Cohn, N., 1970. *The Pursuit of the Millennium*, Paladin, London.

Dijkstra, B., 1989. *Idols of Perversity. Fantasies of Feminine Evil in Fin-de-Siècle Culture*, Oxford University Press, Oxford.

Durkheim, E., 1951. *Suicide: A Study in Sociology*, The Free Press of Glencoe, New York.

Eliade, M., 1959. *The Sacred and the Profane*, Harcourt, New York.

Eliade, M., 1964. *Myth and Reality*, George Allen and Unwin, London.

Eliade, M., 1971. *The Myth of the Eternal Return, or Cosmos and History*, Princeton University Press, Princeton.

Frazer, J.G., 1957. *The Golden Bough*, Macmillan, London.

Fromm, E., 1955. *The Sane Society*, Rinehart & Winston, New York.

Fromm, E., 1960. *The Fear of Freedom*, Routledge & Kegan Paul, London (1st edition 1942).

Goodwin, B. and Taylor, K., 1982. *The Politics of Utopia*, Hutchinson, London.

Griffiths, R., 1966. *The Reactionary Revolution. The Catholic Revival in French Literature 1870–1914*, Constable, London.

Harris, M., 1975. *Cows, Pigs, Wars & Witches*, Fontana, London.

Hobsbawm, E.J., 1990. *Nations and Nationalism since 1780*, Cambridge University Press, Cambridge.

Hughes, H.S., 1958. *Consciousness and Society*, McGibbon and Kee, London.

Hughes, R., 1980. *The Shock of the New*, BBC Books, London.

Hunt, L., 1981. *Politics, Culture and Class in the French Revolution*, University of California Press, Berkeley and Los Angeles.

Joll, J., 1978. *Europe since 1870*, The Penguin Press, Harmondsworth.

Julien, P., 1971. *Dreamers of Decadence*, Phaidon, London.

Jung, C.G., 1964. *Man and his Symbols*, Aldus Books, London.

Jung, C.G., 1988. *Essays on Contemporary Events – Reflections on Nazi Germany*, Ark Paperbacks/RKP, London.

Kaplan, G.T. and Adams, C.E., 1990. Early women supporters of national socialism, in J. Milfull (ed.), *The Attractions of Fascism*, Berg, New York.

Kedourie, E., 1966. *Nationalism*, Hutchinson, London.

Kennedy, P. and Nicolls, A., 1981. *Nationalist and Racist Movements in Britain and Germany before 1914*, Macmillan, London.

Kermode, J.F., 1967. *The Sense of an Ending*, Oxford University Press, Oxford.

Kinsman, R., 1975. *The Darker Vision of the Renaissance*, Cornell University Press, Ithaca.

Koestler, A., 1970. *The Ghost in the Machine*, Pan, London.

Lane, C., 1981. *The Rites of Rulers*, Cambridge University Press, Cambridge.

Larsen, S.U., Hagtvet, B. and Myklebust, J.P. (eds), 1980. *Who Were the Fascists?: Social Roots of European Fascism*, Universitetsforlaget, Bergen.

Lasky, M.J., 1976. *Utopia and Revolution*, Macmillan, London.

Leal, R.B., 1985. Drieu la Rochelle and Huxley: cross channel perspectives on decadence, *Journal of European Studies*, Vol.15.

Lyttleton, A., 1973. *Italian Fascisms from Pareto to Gentile*, Jonathan Cape, London.

McIntosh, C., 1972. *Eliphas Lévi and the French Occult Revivial*, Rider, London.

Mannheim, K., 1960. *Ideology and Utopia*, Routledge & Kegan Paul, London.

Mazgaj, P., 1982. The young Sorelians and decadence, *Journal of Contemporary History*, Vol.17, No.1.

Milfull, J., 1990. 'My Sex the Revolver': fascism as a theatre for the compensation of male inadequacies, in J. Milfull (ed.), *The Attractions of Fascism*, Berg, New York.

Mosse, G.L., 1966. *The Crisis of German Ideology*, Weidenfeld & Nicolson, London.

Mühlberger, D., 1988. Germany in *The Social Basis of European Fascist Movements*, Croom Helm, London.

Nolte, E., 1969. *Three Faces of Fascism: Action Française, Italian Fascism, National Socialism*, Holt Reinhart & Winston, New York.

Odajnyk, V.W., 1976. *Jung and Politics; The Political and Social Ideas of C.G. Jung*, New York University Press, New York.

Pick, D., 1989. *Faces of Degeneration: A European Disorder, c.1848–c.1918*, Cambridge University Press, Cambridge.

Pickering, W.S.F., 1984. *Durkheim's Sociology of Religion*, Routledge & Kegan Paul, London.

Platt, G.M., 1980. Thoughts on a theory of collective action: language, affect, and ideology in revolution, in M. Albin (ed.), *New Directions in Psychohistory*, Lexington Books, Lexington, Massachusetts.

Poliakov, L., 1974. *The Aryan Myth*, Chatto and Windus, London.

Popper, K., 1957. *Poverty of Historicism*, Routledge & Kegan Paul, London.

Praz, M., 1970. *The Romantic Agony*, Oxford University Press, Oxford.

Reich, W., 1970. *The Mass Psychology of Fascism*, Simon and Schuster, New York, (1st German edition 1933).

Reszler, A., 1981. *Mythes Politiques*, Presses Universitaires de France, Paris.

Roberts, D.D., 1980. Petty bourgeois Fascism in Italy: form and content, in Larsen *et al.* (op. cit.).

Shaffer, P., 1973. *Equus*, Samuel French, London.

Schnapper, E.B., 1965. *The Inward Odyssey*, George Allen & Unwin, London.

Sewell, W.H., 1985. Ideologies and social revolutions: reflections on the French case, *Journal of Modern History*, Vol.57, No.1.

Sironneau, J.-P., 1982. *Sécularisation et religions politiques*, Mouton, The Hague.

Smith, A., 1979. *Nationalism in the Twentieth Century*, Martin Robertson, Oxford.

Soucy, R., 1972. *Fascism in France. The Case of Maurice Barrès*, University of Los Angeles Press, Berkeley and Los Angeles.

Sternhell, Z., 1979. Fascist ideology, in W. Laqueur (ed.), *Fascism: A Reader's Guide*, Pelican, Harmondsworth.

Sternhell, Z., 1987. The anti-materialist revision of Marxism as an aspect of the rise of fascist ideology, *Journal of Contemporary History*, Vol.22, No.3.

Swart, K.W., 1964. *The Sense of Decadence in Nineteenth-century France*, International Archives of the History of Ideas, The Hague.

Talmon, J.L., 1980. *The Myth of the Nation and the Vision of Revolution*, Secker and Warburg, London.

Theweleit, K., 1989. *Male Fantasies*. Vol.1 (1987): *Women, Floods, Bodies, History*; Vol.2 (1989); *Male Bodies: Psychoanalyzing the White Terror*, Polity Press, Cambridge.

Tudor, H., 1972. *Political Myth*, Pall Mall, London.

Voegelin, E., 1968. *Science, Politics and Gnosticism*, Gateway Editions, South Bend, Indiana.

Weber, E., 1964. *Varieties of Fascism*, D. Van Nostrand, New York.

Weber, E., 1982. Decadence on a private income, *Journal of Contemporary History*, Vol.17, No.1.

Weber, M., 1948. *From Max Weber*, Routledge & Kegan Paul, London.

Weinstein, F., 1980. *The Dynamics of Nazism: Leadership, Ideology and the Holocaust*, Academic Press, New York.

8 Socio-political Determinants of Fascism's Success

What Enables a Fascist Movement to 'Take Off'?

In the last chapter the causes of fascism were explored at a high level of generality in terms of psycho-history and the history of ideas to establish both the mythopoeic needs which fascism satisfies and the circumstances which would enable embryonic forms of it to surface first in pre-1914 Europe. However, it is possible to translate some of the premises and insights thus arrived at into a theoretical schema of how ideological factors interact with other necessary (but not sufficient) historical conditions to make fascism seem, to a significant political constituency, a viable alternative to the existing system, thus amplifying some tentative observations on this issue made *en passant* in Chapter 6. The result is a cluster of four preconditions for fascism's emergence which can be expressed in the perhaps more familiar register of socio-political analysis.

The Presence Either of Native Currents of Ultra-nationalism, or of Fascist 'Role Models' to Build on

Fascist political myth is unable to become a nucleus of extra-systemic political energies in a particular country unless the forces of secularism and pluralism have already taken root there, and given rise to either (i) currents of non-fascist ultra-nationalism which palingenetic mythopoeia can turn into components of a revolutionary ideology, or (ii) indigenous or foreign examples of fascism to draw on.

Negative corroboration of this principle is provided by inter-war Japan. Here secularization had been inadequate to allow a *radically* palingenetic myth to emerge, with the result that the powerful currents of ultra-right myth which surfaced as a result of the nation's profound structural crisis generally flowed in neo-conservative channels. Further negative corroboration is implied in twentieth-century Latin America, demonstrating how rare it is for populist right-wing energies, even when abundant, to take an outright fascist form, unless elaborate schemes of decadence and rebirth have become as well established as an integral part of the cultural and intellectual tradition as they were in *fin-de-siècle* Europe. For example, in Paraguay, which lacked a proto-fascist sub-culture, such energies found an outlet in the political Catholicism of the *Febreristas* rather than in fascism proper, while the Peruvian *Apristas* never aspired consistently to become the kernel of a 'new order'. Brazil, however, had seemingly been through enough of its own 'revolt against positivism' to lay the socio-cultural foundations necessary for Salgado's Integralism to take off.

Positive confirmation of this pattern can be seen in the fact that all the most significant examples of original fascist movements which we have encountered (for example in Italy, Germany, Romania, Finland, Brazil, South Africa) emerged when genuinely palingenetic political aspirations were able to legitimate themselves by invoking components of indigenous populist ultra-nationalism, so that with hindsight the latter can be seen to have prepared the ground for the fascist formulations.

An important basis on which some inter-war fascists could build was the presence of a native tradition of pre-1914 proto-fascism, for example national syndicalism in Italy, currents of *völkisch* thought in Germany, the revolutionary syndicalist wing of the *Action Française* in France, Afrikaner nationalism in South Africa. In the same way, post-war fascists were able to draw on any national variants of fascism which flourished before 1945 ('nostalgic fascism'). Another important potential source of fascist mytho-poeia has been the existence of 'ready-made' foreign examples on which to model the ideological programme, organization, style and tactics of a local variant. In the inter-war period up to 1933 these were predominantly Fascism (for example in Britain, Brazil) and thereafter Nazism (for example in South Africa, Norway).

Since 1945, while such inter-war movements as the Iron Guard, *Rex* and the Falange have sometimes been lionized in fascist publicism, it is Nazism which has proved to be the most important source of mimetic fascism. As stressed in Chapter 6, what results in such cases can vary considerably from slavish imitation to creative adaptation. The post-war period has also demonstrated that ideologues are far from being trapped in the past and have been able to create new variants of palingenetic ultra-nationalism. At the same time it has underlined the fact that the mere existence of a nucleus of fervent fascist ideologues and activists is far from sufficient to create a revolutionary movement of any significance.

Adequate Political Space in a 'Modern' Society Undergoing a Structural Crisis

Because fascism is literally unthinkable where what (from a Euro-centric point of view) are seen as 'modern' forces of populist politics and nationa-lism are weak, it cannot emerge wherever 'pre-modern' political systems are largely intact (for example traditional or absolutist societies unaffected by liberalization). Even in societies where secularization and democratization have had an impact, and pockets of fascist myth have formed, they can only become the nuclei of significant political forces when the myth can evoke a credible and desirable alternative order to sectors of the general public at large. A precondition for this is a major structural dysfunction at the heart of the existing system, whether owing to the complex strains of 'modernization' (as in inter-war Brazil), or to the acute socio-economic and political tensions arising from war (as in Europe after 1918), or economic collapse (for example in Europe after 1929). A negative corroboration of this is the numerical insignificance and marginal impact of those theorists and activists who make up fascism's natural constituency in stable pluralistic (or 'Westernized') societies.

However, even such a conjuncture of factors will not be enough to generate a powerful fascist *movement* if it is precluded adequate space by other political forces. This is illustrated by the case of inter-war Bulgaria, which in the early 1920s hosted a mass agrarian movement under Stamboliisky and a potent military and monarchical ultra-right, while IMRO, the Macedonian separatist movement, developed a powerful Bulgarian irredentist faction. Hence, although the country was undergoing a severe structural crisis and had a vigorous *völkisch* subculture (two vital preconditions for the emergence of a native fascism) potential recruits for fascism either as a populist or a cadre force tended to be already 'catered for', and such a force was in any case denied room in which to thrive. As a result native fascist movements, such as the mimetic Nazi group led by Tzankov, got nowhere, especially after Boris III tightened his grip on power in the early 1930s by installing an authoritarian (and superficially fascistized) regime from above (see Fischer-Galati, 1980; Groueff, 1990). The imposition of state commu-nism in 1944 completed the picture: fascism had been systematically denied political *Lebensraum*. Authoritarian regimes based on military, monarchical, personal or presidential dictatorship have all proved equally lethal to fascism's micro-climate (as would be one based on religious fundamentalism).

On the other hand, there were a number of structurally weak liberal democracies in the inter-war period (for example in Spain, Romania, Brazil, Hungary, Latvia, Estonia) where a contest for hegemony took place between the palingenetic and non-palingenetic ultra-right. In these cases fascism had the space to develop a substantial following, but lost out to anti-fascist authoritarianism, even if the fundamental antagonism between them was camouflaged to the untrained eye because the regimes which eventually took over adopted fascist trappings (thereby becoming what we have called 'para-fascist'), and in the case of Spain and, temporarily, in Romania, cynically co-opted the most powerful fascist movement into the state apparatus. There is no precedent for fascism prevailing over non-fascist authoritarian forces, a pattern confirmed by the fate of Japan's own prolific ultra-right under Imperial government.

In principle, then, fascism's *only* chance to take off without being crushed is in a relatively advanced liberal democracy undergoing a structural crisis without a strong non-fascist ultra-right poised to take over. Not only does the pluralism of such a society guarantee considerable political space in which competing ideological movements can develop, but liberalism's commitment to such values as materialism, internationalism, party politics and racial tolerance means that it can more easily be equated by ultra-nationalists with a corrupt, decadent system needing to be destroyed and replaced. However, even when a liberal democracy of this sort is riven by major structural tensions (as was generally the case in inter-war Europe), this will only become a nomic crisis on a scale necessary for fascism to mount a serious assault on state power if another condition is fulfilled.

An Inadequate Consensus on Liberal Values

So far we have argued that Fascism can only break out of its marginalized position as part of the 'lunatic' right if it operates in a secularizing and pluralist society struck by crisis. It will only stand a chance of carrying out a successful revolution in a liberal democracy caught in a particularly delicate stage of its evolution: mature enough institutionally to preclude the threat of a direct military or monarchical coup, yet too immature to be able to rely on a substantial consensus in the general population that liberal political procedures and the values which underpin them are the sole valid basis for a healthy society.

Latin America, Africa and the Far East provide abundant examples of fragile democracies being snuffed out by military dictatorships incapable of pursuing anything as sophisticated as a new order, and this pattern obtained in the inter-war period in the Iberian peninsula and much of Eastern Europe. By contrast those European countries in the inter-war period in which civic and political culture had over time become extensively humanized and liberalized (for example Britain, France, Sweden) were not seriously challenged by fascism because parliamentary government remained generally, though of course not universally, assumed to be the only legitimate force which could take the action necessary to deal with structural crises, no matter how severe.

Arguably there have only been four countries where fascism briefly grew into a significant opposition movement within a liberal democracy in this vulnerable transitional state: Italy (1918–22), Germany (1918–23, 1929–33), Finland (1929–33), and South Africa (1939–43). The examples of Finland and South Africa underline the fact that, to make matters worse for those who hanker after neat 'nomothetic' generalizations to apply to fascism, a conjuncture of the three preconditions which we have identified as necessary for it to become a credible revolutionary force is by no means 'sufficient' to ensure that it finally seizes power. It is here that a final factor comes into play.

Favourable Contingency

Clearly chance or (from the fascist point of view) 'destiny' plays a crucial role in enabling fascism to 'take off' in the first place and develop momentum as a revolutionary movement thereafter. A number of contingent factors relating to the internal dynamics of the fascist movement itself condition how credibly it is able to present itself as an alternative to the prevailing 'system' to potential followers such as the personal qualities of its leadership (especially the 'charismatic' appeal of any undisputed leader who emerges), the energy which it invests in attracting a popular following and its flair for propaganda and self-advertisement. Underlying all these factors, course, is the most contingent factor of all: human psychology. The 'elective affinity' with fascism experienced by every individual involved in it, from the leader to the most luke-warm fellow traveller, is the product of unique psychological predispositions which are reducible to tendencies, patterns and types only at a high level of generality and tentativeness.

As for the external forces acting on fascist movements, the fate of the handful which have been strong enough to mount a direct challenge to state power ultimately depended on the way the state reacted to the threat it posed. As we have stressed, authoritarian regimes were ideally placed to crush or absorb the challenge. In the case of the four liberal democracies which we have identified as the most vulnerable to the fascist revolution, the outcome was decided by a host of chance factors, ranging from crucial decisions taken by key individuals to the vagaries of the electoral system. In the event both internal and external contingent factors conspired to close the door on fascism in Finland and South Africa, while in Italy and Germany they worked in conjunction with the other three preconditions which I have identified to allow it into the citadel of power. Though scores of other fascist movements have arisen where the first precondition was fulfilled, none of them have got as far because the others were not. These highly schematic points should become more concrete as we consider the next question.

Why was there 'a Fascist Epoch'?

The Incubation Period of Fascism, 1880–1914

By approaching the question of fascism's success in terms of its structural preconditions, we can now be more precise about the reasons why proto-fascism (as well as the populist racist nationalism and revolutionary forms of neo-conservativism which helped incubate it) first appeared where and when it did than when we treated the question principally from the point of view of 'the history of ideas'. It was only in German-speaking Austria–Hungary, Germany, France and Italy at the turn of the century that the conjuncture of structural forces which we identified above as conducive to (proto-)fascism first materialized in history. In all these countries (and *only* in these countries): (i) the state had undergone a sufficient process of liberalization for the hegemony of traditional conservatism to have been irreparably broken; (ii) the legitimacy of liberalism (and the internationalist socialist alternative) was being widely called into question; (iii) the cultural climate in which liberalism was being challenged was rife with currents of palingenetic speculation and ultra-nationalism. However, in France the compound disasters of 1870–1 (defeat in the Franco–Prussian war, the loss of Alsace and Lorraine, the collapse of the Second Empire, the Paris Commune) took place in a country with tangled but deep liberal roots, and the country recovered quickly enough from the crisis to preclude the various forms of palingenetic political myth which it engendered from developing into mass movements. German proto-fascisms had to wait till 1918 before a major state crisis provided them with the right climate in which to thrive. Austria was until 1918 a nation submerged within a multi-racial empire still based theoretically on legitimist principles.

Significantly, proto-fascism first demonstrated its potential to become the focal point for populist mythic energies when between 1910 and 1915 Italy was hit by a compound crisis: (minority) currents of populist nationalist fervour aroused by the Libyan war (partially fulfilling the first precondition) coincided with revolutionary action taken by Italian 'maximalist' socialists and the perceived incompetence of the Giolittian administration to achieve economic and political stability (partially fulfilling the second precondition). The interventionist crisis which ensued in 1914–15 whipped up a degree of populist chauvinism while simultaneously exacerbating the country's socio-political tensions. This provided the ideal environment for disparate forces of proto-fascism to join forces, especially since the conjuncture materialized in a country with a relatively mature but highly impaired liberal tradition and system (partially fulfilling the third precondition). The result was a partial paralysis of the liberal 'system' which was only artificially resolved by the Italian state going on to a war-footing.

The Impact of the First World War and its Aftermath

The First World War itself was not only to undermine further the Giolittian system but severely test the liberal democratic system of any nation directly involved by creating conditions in which the mass politicization of society coincided with acute socio-economic problems, the polarization of the radical left and the radical right and the weakening of the parliamentary centre. States with weak parliamentary traditions were thus liable to experience a power vacuum which new integrating populist forces would arise to fill, unless, that is, it was artificially sealed by the imposition of authoritarian government from above (for example Hungary, Spain, Portugal). One of the ideological forces which attempted to fill the space suddenly evacuated in the centre-right of several European countries in this period with its own crusade of social renewal was political Catholicism (see Conway and Buchanan, 1993/4). But the most significant new populist force to muscle its way to the centre of the political stage was what we have come to know as fascism, its mythic appeal fostered by the climate of extreme chauvinism and palingenetic fervour which gripped many combatants and 'victory watchers' of the younger generation all over Europe. These would therefore be among the most dedicated activists of its 'first hour' (Stromberg, 1982; Wanrooj, 1987; Mosse, 1986; Hüppauf, 1990).

It was the long-term structural changes brought about by the war which ensured that this fledgling ideology did not just burn out once the immediate problems of completing the transition to a peace-time regime had been solved. A profound political consequence of the war had been to destroy the constellation of great powers which had dominated European politics throughout the nineteenth century, leaving in their place a mixed assortment of nation-states in highly uneven stages of development towards mature liberal economic and political systems. The exception to this generalization, of course, was Russia where the tsar had been overthrown in 1917 and replaced by a Bolshevik government convinced that their revolution was the harbinger of the end of capitalism throughout the industrial world. The authoritarian system of 'democratic centralism' or 'state capitalism' that arose precluded the emergence of an ideologically sophisticated ultra-right in Russia itself. Nevertheless, the symbolic importance of the revolution itself within the palingenetic myth of history elaborated by Marxism, and the official policy of the new regime to propagate it through cellular action abroad, acted as an important catalyst to the rise of fascism in the rest of Europe.

Paradoxically, the more effective the strategy of Bolsheviks to bring about the dictatorship of the proletariat in a particular country, the more powerful the political and para-military forces which arose there, determined that communists would not destroy the nation however ineffectual liberalism was in stopping them. The communist seizure of power in newly independent Finland in 1918 was only thwarted by civil war, while in the following year Leninist revolutionaries temporarily took over in Munich and Budapest, and for a time threatened to do the same in Vienna, in each case provoking an intense reactionary backlash which outlasted the immediate crisis. But the mythic consequences of Bolshevism went far beyond its actual achievements in destabilizing regimes, for even when it posed no serious challenge to the state, if it existed in a country where militant socialism had been strong before the war (for example France, Italy, Austria), or which bordered on Soviet Russia (for example Latvia, Estonia, Hungary), radical ultra-nationalist groupings were 'structurally' bound to form. Some of these would not be reactionary but associated with rival palingenetic myths about the imminence of liberalism's collapse and the new order which would replace it.

The Russian Revolution was only one of the seismic upheavals which resulted from the First World War, and the wave of international Bolshevism and rise of Stalinist violence which followed in its wake never had the pivotal role in precipitating the ascendancy of fascist violence argued in some quarters (see Nolte, 1988). The consequences for the Habsburg Empire and Second Reich which had lost the war had been equally far-reaching. Austria–Hungary was broken up into separate nation states with liberal constitutions on the basis of ethnic majorities, so that Austria was suddenly transformed from being the heart of a multi-racial empire with a millennial tradition of European power to a small, economically impoverished rump state based on unfamiliar republican institutions. In Germany, the closing phase of the war had precipitated an internal political crisis which was only resolved by the abdication of the monarchy and the creation of a radical form of liberal democracy in a situation of considerable confusion. The Weimar Republic which eventually emerged had to cope with changed frontiers, a devastated economy and an acute polarization between communist and nationalist forces. Thus in Germany and Austria, both of which faced the immediate problem of reintegrating millions of demobilized soldiers, not to mention overcoming the deep psychological trauma of national humiliation, conditions were rife for the diffusion of a sense of revanchist nationalism and for the emergence of radical forms of anti-communism and anti-liberalism.

They were not the only countries compelled by circumstances to operate unfamiliar liberal constitutions which could easily seem an alien importation. This was also the case of the states which had regained their autonomy in the wake of the Russian Revolution – Finland, Estonia, Latvia and Lithuania – as well as of the three new nations brought into being by the Versailles Treaty: Yugoslavia, Czechoslovakia (both of which in addition had major ethnic and separatist tensions to deal with) and Hungary, which was suffering the consequences both of defeat and of the violent suppression of Béla Kun's short-lived communist regime. A potent tradition of ultra-nationalism and anti-Semitism existed in all three, as well as in Poland and Romania, which, though on the winning side, had democratic traditions too shallow to act as a bulwark against ultra-nationalism, militarism and authoritarianism. These two countries also had to adjust to major frontier changes which, in the case of Romania, though almost doubling the national territory, had also led to the incorporation of significant proportions of Hungarians and Jews.

Even in victorious countries where liberalism had deep roots, the destabilizing effects of the war could be felt. Its human and material cost had been enormous for France, and both communism and socialism emerged from it invigorated and radicalized. Both here and in Belgium, where tensions between the ethnic communities had never been resolved, the war generation, especially the veterans themselves, would prove particularly susceptible to mobilization for ultra-nationalist causes. Italy was an even greater casualty of peace, for, though technically on the winning side, its treatment at Versailles unleashed a wide-spread sense of frustrated territorial ambitions and wounded national pride (the 'mutilated victory'), fanned by acute socio-economic and political problems.

The New Climate

In short, the war had directly or indirectly given rise to unique sets of structural problems in a number of European countries, not all of whose liberal systems were sufficiently sound, or whose legitimacy was adequately underpinned by subjective public consensus, to preclude indigenous fascisms from taking off. What considerably reinforced the impact of these problems was the way the war had affected the whole ideological climate of

Western society. If before 1914 the 'cultural pessimism' and 'palingenetic expectancy' which had prevailed in Western intellectual circles were little more than a question of mentalities and moods (see above, pp.202–4), the 'spiritual' crisis at the heart of such speculation now seemed to have given irrefutable objective proof of its existence by the cataclysmic course taken by contemporary history. Thus it was that the exponents of expressionism, constructivism, suprematism, dada and surrealism – the pioneers of new movements in architecture such as Gropius, Taut and Le Corbusier, novelists such as James Joyce, Italo Svevo, Thomas Mann, T.E. Lawrence, D.H. Lawrence, Hermann Hesse, Aldous Huxley, André Malraux, poets such as T.S. Eliot and William Butler Yeats – all produced major works which bear witness to the profound sense of disorientation and to the different varieties of longing for a new reality which the crisis had precipitated. It was against this background that Spengler's *Decline of the West*, with its epic evocation of the terminal phase European civilization had reached in the cycle of cultural birth and death became an international best-seller, many readers abroad apparently failing to spot the work's cryptic message, namely that Germany was destined to inaugurate a heroic new cycle under a new race of 'Caesars'.

Deep cultural pessimism and manic historical optimism were now no longer just avant-garde phenomena. Even inhabitants of countries which had kept aloof from the conflict, especially those of the younger generation, could be forgiven for feeling that a shattering blow had just been dealt to Western civilization, refuting once and for all the scheme of unlimited progress embodied in science, liberalism and capitalism which had seemed to mark out its destiny before 1914. Subjectively, contemporary reality was in flux, pregnant with unforeseen potential for both disaster and regeneration. It was in this climate that militarism and authoritarianism, modernized forms of conservatism, experiments with totally new types of political and economic systems, unprecedented forms of populism and community life could now seem viable, even necessary alternatives. The authoritarian systems set up within months of the war ending in Hungary and Spain no longer seemed as aberrant as they would have done before 1914, and even more radical projects for centralized states, planned economies and revitalized national communities could be placed on the agenda as realistic alternatives to a moribund liberal world.

The Establishment of Fascism as a New Ideological Structure

Thus in the immediate aftermath of the war the necessary structural conditions for the rise of potent fascist movements, namely defective liberal democracies undergoing major dysfunctions in a climate of crisis and palingenetic expectation, now existed in an arabesque patchwork across the Westernized world. In countries which were marginally affected by the war (for example Scandinavia, Switzerland), or which had suffered extensively but were still dominated by countervailing myths of liberal hegemony bound up with a strong national sense of tradition (Britain), or with being heroic, youthful nations, (Britain's dominions, the United States), the pre-conditions for fascism were practically non-existent. But in Germany, Austria and German-speaking parts of Czechoslovakia, as well as in Hungary, Romania and Finland, all areas where unique combinations of all the first three structural preconditions for fascism which we have identified were particularly in evidence, groupings pursuing goals shaped by indigen-ous varieties of palingenetic ultra-nationalism soon surfaced. It was in Italy, however, where the conjuncture of factors, including the fourth one of contingency, was particularly ideal, that fascism not only became a truly mass movement (albeit on an uneven regional, local and class basis) but where its leader's direct challenge to government authority culminated in his appointment as head of government.

Even before Mussolini established himself as dictator of a new type of populist authoritarian state in 1925, the dramatic capitulation to a violent movement of the ultra-right of a country generally considered a junior but reliable member of the exclusive club of progressive liberal nation-states crystallized the aspirations of the political activists and theorists all over Europe and beyond who believed that a Third Way could be found be-tween liberalism and communism. The fact that we are still struggling with the definition and analysis of the word 'fascism' seven decades later, bears testimony to the powerful sense generated by the March on Rome and the subsequent metamorphosis of the Giolittian system that a new force had arrived to break the mould of modern politics. As a result minute groupings directly modelled on Fascism were formed in various countries, including France (*Le Faisceau*), Britain (the British 'Fascisti'), Sweden (the Swedish Fascist People's Party), and in Romania (National Romanian Fasces). In Nordic countries it was Nazism which was more likely to create a sense of affinity than Fascism, and as early as 1924 a mimetic National Socialist Party was founded in Sweden. However, the recovery of the European economy and the stabilization of political systems, whether under liberal or authoritarian government, did much to quell this first fascist wave (by removing the second precondition of fascist success which we have ident-ified, namely 'structural crisis'). Though the NSDAP and the Legionaries of the Archangel Michael continued to grow in strength as para-military cadre parties as late as 1928, there was as yet little sign that fascism would become a mass movement outside Italy, let alone form a regime.

Fascism: the Second Wave

After 1928 the situation changed rapidly as a new structural crisis hit the Western world. The Great Depression triggered off, not just a major socio-economic upheaval which had considerable impact on all industrialized countries but a renewed nomic crisis, conjuring up once more the spectres of the breakdown of liberal civilization created by the Great War, and creating the local conditions for Nazism's spectacular rise in electoral strength. The apparent success of Mussolini's totalitarian state in solving Italy's endemic problems of economic backwardness and political instability now combined with the growing impact of the 'national reawakening' led by Hitler to enhance the impression of revolutionary potency which fascism could make on those susceptible to ultra-nationalist myth. Policies such as corporatism, eugenic racism and anti-Semitism, but above all the apparently irresistible dynamism of a movement of populist nationalism led by a charismatic leader, could seem viable solutions to the ills of the nation. Indeed, they could seem to those with ultra-right propensities the only way of giving first aid to a senescent Western civilization which was visibly crumbling and drastically needed enforced rejuvenation. As we saw in Chapter 5, almost every liberal democracy, and every authoritarian regime in which pockets of pluralism remained, now experienced a unique conjuncture of the first two preconditions for fascism to take off: ultra-nationalism plus adequate political space for extra-systemic movements combined with a profound structural crisis. The new ideological structure represented by fascism now moved to the fore as an alternative path of 'modernization' on a par with Marxism and political Catholicism.

The result in democracies where the third precondition did not obtain (that is which were stable) and with no strong indigenous proto-fascist or fascist tradition (for example Iceland, Denmark, The Netherlands, Switzerland) was some generally insignificant attempts to copy Fascism or Nazism directly. Bucard's *Francisme* was also an example of this mimesis. But in a number of unseasoned democracies in Eastern Europe (namely, Estonia, Slovakia, Latvia, Bulgaria and Yugoslavia), fascism, especially in its Mussolinian variety, now came to exert considerable influence on more sizable constituencies of populist and autocratic ultra-nationalists (see Borejsza, 1980). In other countries, both liberal and authoritarian, original syntheses of foreign and native elements emerged but without gaining significant support, for example in Sweden (The New Sweden, National Socialist Workers' Party, the Swedish Socialist Unity), Norway (*Nasjonal Samling*), England (the BUF), Portugal (the National Syndicalists) and Spain (the Falange).

A more significant manifestation of fascism's 'second wave' in the crisis-ridden thirties was the growth of popular support for embryonic or fully fledged forms of it which owed little or nothing to foreign models, as in Romania (Iron Guard), Belgium (*Verdinaso*, the VNV and the later *Rex*), Finland (*Lapua* and the IKL), Estonia (*Vaps*), Hungary (Arrow Cross), Latvia (*Perkonkrust*), France (PPF). Other signs of the times were the *Heimwehr*'s espousal of explicitly fascist policies, the incorporation of Nazi elements into the *Falanga* in Poland and the adoptions of fascist trappings by authoritarian regimes in Portugal, Spain, Greece, Austria, Estonia, Latvia, Lithuania, Hungary and Yugoslavia. The collaborationist regimes installed by the Nazis in France (Vichy), Hlinka's Slovakia and Croatia (*Ustasha*), though essentially neo-conservative in the first instance and ethnic separatist in the other two, were also extensively fascistized or rather, Nazified.

As we saw in Chapter 6, the second fascist wave also had repercussions in (at least partially) Westernized societies outside Europe. Some populist ultra-right movements in Latin America consciously adopted external elements from Fascism, Nazism or the Falange, while Salgado's Integralist movement fused components of all three with a palingenetic philosophy of history of his own devising. In the main, Japan developed its own neo-conservative palingenetic right, but Nakano Seigō was deeply impressed by the regimes of Mussolini and Hitler as fulfilments of the political salvation which he yearned to provide for Japan with his Society of the East and he modelled its ritual aspects (but not its ideology) on them. South Africa hosted clones of Nazi political formations, but its most powerful proto-fascist movement, the *Broederbond*, injected Ayran racism into its own special brew. In the United States on the other hand, at least for the time being, the powerful racist ultra-right which had grown up especially in the southern states remained free of alien influence, and it was the New Deal which captured populist energies for national regeneration, not the New Order. By the time the war broke out in September 1939, though it was only in Italy and Germany that fascism had broken through, there was no shortage of fascists in other countries who thought that their time had come much as Marxists the world over had thought by the end of 1917.

The Impotence of Fascism Since 1945

If in 1942 it might seem to both liberals and socialists as if the tradition to which they belonged might be extinguished by the Nazis' New European Order, by 1945 the tempest of fascism had passed. To use phrases which Shakespeare created in the context of a very different tempest, its 'insubstantial pageant' had 'faded' revealing 'the baseless fabric of its vision'. The superficial impact which fascism had on the bulk of the populations of Europe who had lived under it was underlined by the rapid liberalization or (enforced) communization, not just of those exposed to it in puppet regimes or occupied countries, but even in Italy, Austria and what were soon to be the two Germanies. Obviously as an ideology fascism did not die with Mussolini and Hitler. As we showed in Chapter 6, pockets of 'nostalgic' and 'mimetic' fascism have persisted since 1945, predictably sizable ones in the case of West Germany and Italy. Moreover, new generations of fascists have appeared in every Westernized country to challenge consumerism, pluralism and hedonism, either by imitating or modifying versions of inter-war models or experimenting with completely new formulations of the vision of national rebirth, some of which envisage a pan-European or even a global movement of regeneration.

Thus palingenetic ultra-nationalism can be assumed to be a permanent (that is for the foreseeable future) ideological structure among the many which together constitute Western socio-political culture. As long as virulent forms of anti-socialism and racism exist and there are aspects of modern society that can be perceived by radical nationalists as symptoms of decadence, it is difficult to see how this structure will ever lose its potential appeal to a small minority of individuals temperamentally predisposed to experience a spontaneous elective affinity with it. Yet, apart from South Africa, where the first three preconditions of fascism's vitality still obtained in the early 1990s sufficiently to give the AWB an active, though peripheral, role in shaping national politics, fascism has remained a paper tiger. This is not through any lack of commitment or ingenuity on the part of its supporters, but because the structural factors that turned Fascism and Nazism into successful revolutions have simply disappeared. In the countries of Eastern Europe which became part of the Soviet Empire, space for its growth was automatically denied by the imposition of a regime based on 'democratic centralism', that is authoritarian single-party rule, (though significantly minute fascist groups have sprung up since 1989 wherever the apparatus of oppression has been removed). As for Western Europe, its post-war liberal democracies have suffered no internal structural crisis on the scale of the inter-war period.

The rapid reconstruction of Western Europe, especially of Germany, the almost uninterrupted rise of living standards for the vast majority, the growing impact of technology in the spheres of consumerism, private transport, television, hi-fi, travel (which have created a public which compared to the 1930s is generally 'informed' but depoliticized) contrasts sharply with the two phases of economic crisis in 1918–20 and 1929–33. In addition, the overwhelming consensus for the adoption of universal suffrage and social liberal principles in the spheres of politics, economics and welfare policy has forestalled crises of popular confidence in democratic and capitalist principles. Finally, the governments of parliamentary democracies have learnt vital lessons from the inter-war period about what strategies, economic measures and constitutional mechanisms are necessary to cope with unforeseen national and international emergencies which might threaten the liberal fabric of society. The responses of the 'Free World' to the 1973 oil crisis, to the 1987 'Black Monday' stock market crash and to Iraq's invasion of Kuwait bear witness to the way liberalism and capitalism have matured and an international resolve is growing to nip imperial aggression in the bud.

These factors are indissociable from the radically different mythic climate which prevailed after 1945. The war may have been fought by Britain and America partly, as in Russia, for reasons of national self-defence and survival, but it was also for the idealistic motive of destroying inhuman systems imposed on a number of countries by the Third Reich and Imperial Japan. When the full scale of the atrocities committed by them came to light after the war this reinforced the mythic sense (but not the myth) that humanistic values had prevailed over barbarism. The result was a liberal renaissance in 'the West' inconceivable between the wars. At least in part because the lessons of Versailles had been learnt, the defeated 'enemy' nations under Allied control – West Germany, Austria, Italy and Japan – were treated as countries which had been occupied by fascism rather than ones whose inhabitants had been collectively responsible for it and soon became integral partners in the 'free' (that is liberal and capitalist) world. In different ways, the EC and the United Nations were both products of the wide-spread sense of urgency among liberal nations about the need to build an international community united on liberal (and capitalist) principles.

Whatever crises liberal nation-states face in the future, there is every reason to assume that fascism will continue to be denied the political space and ultra-nationalist climate in which to thrive as a co-ordinated political force. Even attempts by neo-fascists in the 1970s to provoke artificially (with the so-called 'strategy of tension') the crisis conditions of the inter-war period in Italy, a country with a chronically unstable liberal govern-ment, failed totally to create any public swing towards fascism or against liberalism. Certainly every effort should be made to monitor fascism's evolution and its role in promoting racism and xenophobia (which look set to become increasingly virulent). But it seems that a much greater threat to humanity is posed by palingenetic movements based on combinations of nationalism and socialism but which lack a genuine populist dimension, as the very different examples provided by modern Cambodia and Iraq have demonstrated.

Why did Fascism Seize State Power Autonomously in Italy and Germany but not in Other Countries?

If we apply our explanatory schema to the special cases of Fascism and Nazism, what becomes apparent is that they grew into mass movements because of an exceptionally ideal conjuncture of fascistizing structural forces but succeeded in conquering state power only as a result of con-tingent factors. By 1918 liberalism and modernization had advanced far enough to have destroyed irremediably the *ancien régime* and weakened traditional conservatism in both Italy and Germany. It had also generated pluralistic economic, social and ideological forces well entrenched enough to make it impossible for a purely conservative personal or military dicta-torship to establish itself as the guarantee of (reactionary) law and order. On the other hand, the liberal systems in both countries were profoundly flawed. In very different ways both had failed in the crucial formative period between national unification and the First World War to create stable and efficient structures of parliamentary representation able to accommodate the deeply antagonistic constituencies within their respective political cultures and mediate among their conflicting interests. Moreover, their ability to cope smoothly with the pressures imposed by the rise of the new industrial working and middle classes was severely impaired by the absence of a broadly based civil society affectively committed to parliamen-tary institutions and *laissez-faire* capitalism as the foundations of the national and international order. Instead, both countries contained, even before 1914, sub-cultures committed to ultra-left and ultra-right visions of a post-liberal society.

These two highly defective liberal democracies then underwent in the period immediately following the First World War a profound multi-level and multi-factorial socio-economic and political crisis. Furthermore, they did so in conditions where neither the Giolittian system in Italy nor the newly created Weimar system in Germany was able to prevent the rise of deeply polarized and rapidly maturing factions of the ultra-left and ultra-right, both opposed for different ideological reasons to the overthrow of existing parliamentary institutions. These two political sub-cultures thrived in a cultural climate supercharged with currents of palingenetic myth released by the war, the ultra-left given cohesion by Marxism–Leninism, the ultra-right initially highly fragmented but nourished by robust pre-1914 roots. No other European countries had emerged from the war with a fully-formed but structurally imperfect liberal tradition beset with such a welter of interacting socio-economic and ideological tensions of revolutionary intensity.

The fascist breakthrough occurred in Italy in 1922 and in Germany a decade later, but in both cases the crucial factor which enabled a fascist regime to be established was the powerful appeal which fascism had come to exert far beyond the immediate nuclei of veterans, political outsiders and educated youth of the war generation who provided the original hard core of its activists in the 'first wave'. The key to the transition of fascism in both countries from a cadre party to a mass movement was that the prospect of national integration and regeneration captured the minds of many who in the new age of mass politics and universal suffrage would in 'normal' circumstances have formed the backbone of populist middle- and even working-class parliamentary parties. In the midst of an acute and quite unprecedented socio-economic crisis aggravated by a perceived threat from the left and a genuine government paralysis, these had in significant numbers come to despair of the liberal system and the prevailing forces of order. This created a legitimacy crisis and a corresponding political vacuum which could be filled by a dynamically led mass movement waiting in the wings to seize the first opportunity to take power. They seemed to offer a real possibility of creating a new trans-class or trans-sectional political constituency to replace the parties which previously assured the stability of the state and so overcome the current political fragmentation and inertia. Since the left was too split between reformists and Bolsheviks to form a common front, the only realistic candidate for such a movement was an ultra-right one with a trans-class appeal.

That Fascism and Nazism actually managed to exploit the exceptional opportunities to enact their vision of a post-liberal order was ultimately determined by contingent factors (our fourth precondition of success). However, they were only able to do so because, well in advance of the state crises which brought them to power, both had already become associated with indigenous versions of palingenetic ultra-nationalism and had become genuine mass movements headed by charismatic leaders who astutely combined legal tactics with the ruthless deployment of extra-parliamentary force. This meant that when a deep-seated state crisis (which they themselves had done so much to create) came to a head, both were in an ideal position to take advantage of the situation. Wherever else fascism developed a mass base (for example Finland, France, pre-*Anschluss* Austria, Brazil), one or more of these vital ingredients was always missing.

The Appeal of a Trans-class Version of Nationalist Myth in Italy and Germany

Obviously such a highly condensed summary of how quite different manifestations of the same genus of political movement came to power in two

European nations which were dissimilar in practically every aspect of their cultural, economic and social development rides roughshod over intricate empirical details and tangled academic debate. In particular, it fudges the deep differences which emerged in Chapters 3 and 4 between the ideological contents of the mobilizing myths they embodied and between the political cultures in which they operated. It also blurs major distinctions in the process by which they conquered state power, not the least of which is that the Fascist revolution took place in two stages, the first in the wake of the immediate post-war crisis, the second in the aftermath of Matteotti's assassination, whereas Nazism had to wait for the Depression to hit Germany before it could finally break through the crumbling republican defences. Nevertheless, for all its generality, the thrust of the argument I have sketched out is not only consistent with my abstract explanatory schema of the dynamics of generic fascism, but, more important, it is broadly in line with main-stream scholarship on both Fascism and Nazism.

In Chapters 3 and 4 I have already pointed out that detailed research exists concerning the powerful indigenous currents of palingenetic ultra-nationalism on which both Fascism (for example Gentile, 1975, 1982; cf. Anderson, 1989) and Nazism (for example Mosse, 1966; 1980) could build. Considerable work has been carried out, too, confirming that both were highly defective liberal democracies which underwent severe structural crises and generated generous pockets of space for a 'late-comer' movement of the ultra-right (for example for Italy, see Vivarelli, 1967; Lyttleton, 1973; Baglieri, 1980; for Germany, see Kühnl, 1980; Abraham, 1981; Kershaw, 1990). The appeal of the trans-class images of national solidarity and integration which they promoted as an 'extra-systemic' solution to the political vacuum thus created has been focused on in Italy by Roberts (1979), in Germany by Hagtvet (1980) and in both countries by Allen (1975). This complements the scholarship which amply documents the sociological heterogeneity and shifting make-up of their support (Revelli, 1987; Mühlberger, 1987, 1991), hopefully laying to rest any simplistic preconceptions of their (petty-)bourgeois nature once and for all.

Independent corroboration of the approach I have adopted here is also provided by Eley (1983), who argues that the success of Fascism and Nazism is attributable to the way 'deep historical or long-term structures' undermining liberalism and an 'immediate crisis' combined to generate wide popular support for the 'self-confident, optimistic, and affirming . . . vision of the future' [that is to say palingenetic myth] based on an 'aggressive belief in the authenticity of the German/Italian national mission' [i.e. ultra-nationalism] (ibid., p.71). In each case the movement was able to present itself as 'a radical populist solution' to the paralysis and bankruptcy of parliamentary institutions in the context of 'thwarted imperialist ambitions' and 'unprecedented gains of the left'. He extrapolates from his two case studies the conclusion that generic fascism 'prospered under conditions of general political crisis, in societies that were dynamically capitalist (or at least, that had a dynamic capitalist sector) but where the state was incapable of organizing for the maintenance of social cohesion' (ibid., p.78).

Translated into Platt's psycho-historical model of revolution introduced earlier (pp.192–3), the theses put forward by such experts are consistent with the hypothesis that Fascism and Nazism solved the profound 'sense-making crises' experienced by 'diverse sociological and psychological populations' in inter-war Italy and Germany by offering them the 'illusion of welding [their] heterogeneous members together for a single purpose' (Platt, 1980, p.87). They did so through the promise of radical action to deal with specific symptoms of political instability, national weakness and social crisis. Their solutions were presented, not as discrete policies to be debated, but as emanations from a single, coherent, 'total' world-view; not as the pragmatic measures formulated by professional party politicians but as the result of an irresistible national movement of rejuvenation; not as decisions taken by committees and cabinets but the inspirations of a natural leader who embodied the will of the people. In the absence of concerted action taken to repel their assault on power by the forces of liberalism, their myth became a self-fulfilling prophecy.

Contingent Factors behind the Seizure of Power

Despite the exceptionally ideal conditions in which Mussolini and Hitler made their bid for power, nothing made the installation of the Fascist or Nazi regimes 'inevitable'. This emerges clearly in detailed reconstructions of the rise both of Fascism (see Lyttleton, 1973) and Nazism (see Bracher, 1978). Key areas of contingency were decisions and actions, not just of Mussolini and Hitler, but of other individuals at crucial points in the rise of the movements. King Victor Emmanuel III and Hindenburg could, for example, have thwarted the fascist challenge rather than aided and abetted it had they responded differently to the state crises in 1922 and 1933 respectively. Meanwhile secondary figures such as Farinacci and Gregor Strasser played important roles in building up the movements' strength in their formative period. Equally contingent was the readiness to collude with fascism of potentially hostile forces, such as (in Italy) the monarchy, Catholic church and key liberals, and in both countries the bulk of the army, conservatives, the civil service and the aristocracy. Equally crucial was the failure of the left to form a common front against fascism in either country, largely owing to the mutual antagonism of reformist and revolutionary factions.

The timing of national and international events over which neither party leadership had any control also played its part. Examples in Italy are the complex conjuncture of factors which fed *squadrismo* and hence the dramatic rise of agrarian Fascism in 1922 (see Baglieri, 1980), or the Matteotti crisis of late 1924–5 which was directly of Mussolini's making and which created a considerable amount of room for manoeuvre by parliamentary forces that might have forestalled the creation of the Fascist state. Parallel instances of contingency in the rise of Nazism are the occurrence of the Great Depression when the movement still showed no sign of breaking through, and the timing of the death of Hindenburg in 1934 which enabled Hitler to merge 'legally' the Chancellorship and the Presidency, a crucial stage in the dismantling of the constitutional constraints which Weimar had placed on the aggregation of despotic power by individuals. As Bracher puts it, 'Mishaps and errors, consequence and accident, became an almost inextricable mass of causes of the National Socialist seizure of power' (1978, p.256; cf. p.70).

The factors and episodes to which I have alluded are doubtless susceptible to further analysis, revealing hidden patterns and structures which reduce the role played by 'blind' chance. For example, Mayer (1990) has brought out structural and causal analogies between the apparently gratuitous anti-Semitism of the Nazis which culminated in the Holocaust and earlier episodes in the long history of anti-Semitic violence in Europe. But I believe in the last analysis that perpetuators of the humanist tradition are condemned always to be in the position of 'poor Dr Dysart' in Equus's cave when trying to account for the Fascist and Nazi seizure of power (p.200). Even if we bring in teams of speleologists with halogen arc lamps we will still be left with the question: why, *ultimately* did it happen? The title of Mayer's book still contains a note of anguish which cannot be exorcized by rational inquiry: Why Did the Heavens not Darken? By applying our general explanatory framework to Nazism we can at least attempt to illuminate this dark era in European history in way which makes it, not a uniquely German phenomenon, but an integral part of the history of generic fascism.

Why was Nazism so much more Destructive than any Other Fascism?

If in contrast to conservatism fascism is 'simply more extreme in every way' (Eley, 1990, p.52), then Nazism is more extreme in every way than all other types of fascism. The atrocities committed by the Fascist secret police (OVRA) in Italy or by Black Shirts in Ethiopia and the Balkans pale into insignificance in terms of sheer scale of organized barbarism when compared with those of the Gestapo and SS at home and abroad. Nor was there any other 'failed' permutation of fascism which contained such a potential for organized inhumanity. For example, even if the Romanian Iron Guard had created an autonomous state which somehow managed to institutionalize on a grander scale the murder of political and racial enemies carried out randomly by its Legionaries, there was no call in its ideology for territorial expansion. Moreover, their virulent anti-Semitism was of a macabre ritualistic variety to which the techniques of mass production could not have been applied to increase the 'output' of death. Though it is sobering to remember that the contemporary Japanese and Stalinist regimes applied modern technology and logistics to mass murder in the pursuit of their ends, the Third Reich differed from both in implementing the policies of what had been the country's largest political party, the NSDAP, albeit with a ruthlessness and destructiveness never made explicit in its electoral programmes before the semi-constitutional seizure of power. In addition, both regimes arose in countries which, unlike Germany, had never had an experience of liberal democracy nor made major contributions to Renaissance humanism, the Reformation, the Enlightenment and every branch of the human and natural sciences.

Of course, the determining factor which allowed Nazism to start implementing its racist and genocidal fantasies in the first place was Hitler's seizure of power in 1933, an event which was, as we have stressed, far from inevitable, even if it was enormously facilitated by a freak conjuncture of structural preconditions. This fact alone shatters any deterministic equations between German history or national character and the atrocities committed by Nazism. We now propose to concentrate on a number of other factors consistent with the explanatory model used so far which make the extreme degree of potential and actual destructiveness intrinsic to Nazism more intelligible. Clearly each factor would require considerable scholarly analysis and elaboration before a fuller, more intellectually satisfying picture could emerge, but in the present context a brief annotation of each must suffice.

It should be stated yet again that the search for 'factors' in the explanation of Nazi atrocities in no way implies the intention to juggle away the role of personal human responsibility or guilt in specific instances of cruelty or to discount the importance of non-ideological ingredients such as fear, survival instinct or pathological personality disorders (for example sadism) in motivating them in individual cases. It is also to be borne in mind that, whatever cause is being fought for, even 'just' wars lead to the destruction of enemy lives to achieve what are perceived by the high command and the politicians to be 'strategic ends' and may trigger bouts of gratuitous cruelty and wanton violence by soldiers owing to the stress conditions of battle. Here we are interested exclusively in the structural factors which imparted Nazism such an enormous intrinsic potential for violence if it was ever to be in a position to implement its policies. These factors made personal motivations or complexes superfluous for atrocities to be carried out on a gargantuan scale in the service of the regime, for they ensured that, as long as everybody simply 'did their job' as efficiently as possible and the chains of command and execution functioned tolerably well at all levels of the state apparatus, Nazism was bound 'automatically' to mass produce inhumanity simply through the pursuit of official objectives – a Boschian nightmare painted by numbers.

Factors Contributing to the Destructiveness of Nazism

The Intensity of the Weimar Crises

One group of factors relates to the particularly acute nature of the socio-political crisis to which Nazism presented itself as the solution. Seen synchronically these were:

(i)   The deep degree of national humiliation inflicted by the defeat at the hands of the Allies combined with the simultaneous collapse of the Second Reich and the loss of the monarchy. The compound trauma which resulted was exacerbated by the strength of imperialist and nationalist fervour existing before the war, the (artificially) sustained belief in imminent German victory till the bitter end and the huge casualties and social hardships caused by the four years of fighting.

(ii)   The general sense of injustice and indignation at the punitive terms of the Versailles treaty which imposed substantial territorial losses, the decimation of the country's armed forces, the denial of her European super-power status, foreign occupation, crippling reparations and the infamous 'guilt clause'.

(iii) The alarm created by the attempted Communist revolution in Berlin and the temporarily successful one in Munich within months of the armistice, compounded by the commitment of the Communist Party (KPD) to Bolshevik revolution and alignment with Moscow.

(iv)   The wide-spread material and psychological distress caused by the demobilization of hundreds of thousands of troops, the transition from a war-time to a peace-time economy, the acute food and material shortages caused by the war and exacerbated by the Allied embargo and a crisis in the economy which culminated in the hyperinflation of 1923.

(v)   The massive socio-economic impact of the Great Depression followed by the renewed growth in the extra-parliamentary agitation and parliamentary strength of the Socialists and Communists, which, coming after only five years of a period of relative stability and recovery (1923–9), combined to reopen the wounds of distress and fear inflicted in the immediate aftermath of the war.

(vi)   A common, though not universal, sense that the republican form of liberalism on which the Weimar system was based was contaminated by its identification with the *Zusammenbruch* and in any case alien to German history and society, sentiments encouraged by the prolific publicistic output of the various factions within the diffuse *Los-von-Weimar* movement.

(vii) The apparent impotence of official government in the face of the post-war and post-Depression crises combined with the extensive fragmentation of political culture into increasingly inward-looking sub-communities. This created a wide-spread sense that society desperately lacked a legitimate state power and trans-sectional basis for national solidarity.

The acute nomic crisis created by this combination of factors peaked in two phases, 1921–3 and 1930–3, the second creating a socio-political climate in which for millions of 'ordinary' citizens even the most 'irrational' diagnoses of what had gone wrong could become plausible. As a result the most Draconian remedies for recovery could seem palatable.

The Destructive Potential of the Component Myths of Nazism

The pattern that suggests itself from our earlier observations on revolutionary ideologies is that in a secularized culture the more profound the objective crisis and the deeper the subjective climate of cultural despair, the more likely it will be for there to be a 'common-sense' but irrational assumption that history has reached a turning point. In these conditions an enormous mythic appeal will be exerted by radical palingenetic visions of contemporary events which promise the 'regeneration of history', thereby protecting individuals from the awful realization that catastrophic contemporary events are not only distressing but chaotic and *meaningless*. That such radical myths surfaced in Weimar was guaranteed by the variegated ultra-right political (*völkisch*) sub-culture that had formed in Wilhelmine Germany, well before the First World War. As we saw in Chapter 4, some of its outstanding features were (i) symptoms of a profound degree of alienation from the Judeo–Christian liberal and Enlightenment tradition within some intellectual and artistic circles, encouraged by a powerful Romantic tradition of apolitical spirituality and the cult of 'inwardness' among the educated classes; (ii) the openness in such circles to forms of philosophy of history and cultural speculation which called into question egalitarian, pacifistic and humanitarian values and celebrated openly pagan, anti-rational, elitist, vitalistic and ultra-nationalist ones (for example in vulgarized and travestied forms of Nietzschean or Wagnerian thought); (iii) powerful currents of pan-Germanism and imperialism (both in the form of demands for a colonial empire and for *Lebensraum*, or vital space, in the East); (iv) a wide-spread popular belief that a strong state is weakened by excessive democracy and is at its most dynamic when in the hands of inspired statesmen, emperors or leaders, who alone can guarantee internal cohesion and national greatness; (v) the prevalence, both within academic circles and as part of educated 'common sense', of various discourses of scientistic (biological) racism informed by vulgarized Darwinism and materialistic determinism which drew attention to the alleged symptoms of social pathologies, stressed the danger of degeneration and decadence and promoted eugenic social and physical measures to stem the decline or inaugurate regeneration; (vi) ubiquitous (though by no means universal) anti-Semitism rationalized through a wide range of historical, religious, cultural, scientistic, occultistic, and populist discourses.

The violent imperialist and racist (especially anti-Semitic) contents of all these pre-war nationalist myths in Germany contrasts strongly with the ideas being promoted by the Futurists, revolutionary syndicalists and even the Papinian or Corradinian ultra-nationalists in pre-1914 Italy. In the supercharged mythic climate of an unpopular Weimar Republic apparently threatened by economic collapse, political bankruptcy and left-wing revolution in the aftermath of the war, leading Nazis had little difficulty in forging cognate forms of a syncretic *Weltanschauung* out of these pre-1914 currents of political myth and eventually establishing itself as the *lingua franca* of the *Los-von-Weimar* movement. Once the spectres of another national collapse haunted the public imagination in the wake of the Wall Street Crash of 1929, Nazism found itself able to reap the harvest it had sown in the preceeding lean years and won an affective consensus far broader and far less perfunctory than that enjoyed by Fascism even at the height of its popularity (that is on the foundation of the 'East African Empire' with the defeat of Abyssinia in 1936). In contrast to the support for Fascism in its formative years, the enthusiasm for Nazism before its seizure of power sanctioned a political programme which, even if shrouded in euphemisms and ambiguities about the scale of mass murder and destruction it implied, left no doubt about the need to remove from circulation the country's 'internal enemies' and to conquer territories abroad in order for the New Order to be constructed.

It is a particularly grotesque and tragic example of the operation of 'Murphy's Law' in the historical process that of the only two forms of fascism that managed, against the odds, to seize state power, one of them was informed by an ideology of unparalleled destructive (though not 'nihilistic') potential. The Mazzinian, *squadrista* or Roman Empire myths invoked by Fascist Italy, Mosley's vision of a Greater Britain, the dream of a new Burgundy nurtured by Degrelle's more fanatical Rexists or the notion of a Finnish super race cultivated by the Academic Karelia Society cannot compare with the sheer scale of military aggression and racial persecution implied by the Nazi dream of a Jew-free racial empire. Once war had broken out both of these were radicalized to involve the subjugation of Russia and the physical liquidation of the world's Jewry, at which point the Third Reich overshadowed even Imperial Japan in imperial ambition and systematic barbarity. Tragically for untold millions, when the NSDAP finally seized power in 1933 it was under a leader who would unswervingly pursue the self-ordained mission which he had inscribed into its programme of social change, and who would soon have at his disposal sufficient military–industrial might and fanatical support to undertake its realization.

The Personality of Hitler and the Style of his Leadership

A crucial factor in assuring both the ideological radicalness of Nazi anti-Semitic and imperialist policies, and the relentlessness of its implementation once the NSDAP had seized power was, of course, the personality of Hitler himself. Both Nazism and Fascism reflected much of the personality of their leader. Mussolini's vagueness about the content of the Fascist revolution, while an asset in the early years, allowed unresolved tensions to grow up between rival interpretations of it, leading to the extensive factionalization of Fascism, as well as extraordinary U-turns in official doctrine and policy. After 1926 he seems to have fallen victim to his own personality cult, and was more intent on removing rivals who might outshine him than recruiting efficient cadres, suggesting that narcissism and megalomania were more important character structures in him than sadism, necrophilia or other forms of psycho-pathologies.

Hitler was driven by markedly different complexes and neuroses from his Italian counterpart, making him fanatically committed to policies to create a vast 'Jew-free' European empire as an integral phase of his programme for a regenerated empire, irrespective of the human cost. The tight control which he exercized over the party leadership ensured that the main thrust of Nazi ideology and policy remained a remarkably faithful reflection of his own fanaticism, despite the inevitably polycratic nature of the Third Reich. Consistent with this was his ruthless suppression or marginalization of rival versions of Nazism which did not suit his tactical purposes (for example the suppression of Dinter, the physical liquidation of the Strasserite and Röhm factions, the downgrading of Darré and Rosenberg). After he seized power his personality did not degenerate into vanity and solipsism, nor was he subject to paralysing bouts of indecision and withdrawal from responsibility like Mussolini. Instead the same pragmatism, tactical ability and capacity for ruthless action which he had used to build up the party after 1925 were now applied to creating out of the abundant raw materials at his disposal a state sufficiently powerful, efficient and 'totalitarian' (even if nowhere near as much as the propaganda suggested) to enable his vision to be realized to a terrifying degree (see Kershaw, 1991).

The Absence of Moderating Compromise and Inefficiency

That Nazism was able to make a serious attempt to realize its revolutionary programme was partly owing to the fact that it had not had to contend with a number of forces which had conspired to blunt the ideological and executive edge of Fascism. As we saw in Chapters 3 and 4, whereas Fascism had been a loose alliance of distinct versions of palingenetic myth (syndicalism, *squadrismo* etc.), Nazism became an effective synthesis of more closely cognate ultra-nationalisms (*völkisch* thought, Conservative Revolution, Revolutionary Nationalism etc.). Moreover, unlike Fascism, it did not have to make significant concessions to liberalism (for example in the retention of considerable pockets of freedom of speech), Catholicism (in the Lateran Pacts), monarchism (in allowing the king to remain head of state and the army), nor did it allow a constitutional situation to arise where the leader could be voted out of office by his own ministers, which was the fate that eventually befell Mussolini. It was also able to restructure or 'co-ordinate' state institutions (civil service, army, judiciary) and the economy much more extensively than Fascism, which for pragmatic reasons was forced to graft the new state on to existing socio-economic relations rather than carrying through a major structural reform of them. As a result the Fascistization of the new Italy was even more uneven, superficial and cosmetic than Germany's far from complete process of *Gleichschaltung* and Nazification.

The ruthlessness and efficiency with which Nazism pursued its ends when compared to Fascism had other causes as well. After the March on Rome Mussolini became head of an Italian state whose social and economic backwardness, state incompetence and corruption, level of illiteracy and poverty, and poor degree of national integration, though varying considerably from region to region, created massive problems for any government to operate effectively or manufacture a consensus. In particular the south was an area especially resistant to integration into a modern nation-state. A significant part of Fascism's palingenetic appeal derived from the prospect it held out to educated people that it would complete the unification of Italy and finally transform it into a modern nation-state on a par with its North European neighbours. In the event, Fascism's proclaimed totalitarian co-ordination of the hearts, creative energies and productive capacities of the whole nation remained the hollow rhetoric of a regime extensively based on illusion and self-deception, as the rapid collapse of the war effort and then of the regime itself after 1939 dramatically demonstrated. Even if

Fascism had the ideological goals rivalling those of Nazism in potential destructiveness, it could never have carried them through because the necessary technical and institutional tools were missing.

Nazism, however, inherited a modernized agricultural sector, a technologically advanced industry, an efficient state apparatus and a highly educated, socialized population most of whom were already fully integrated within a collective sense of loyalty to a German nation, even if many felt instinctively alienated from the ephemeral republican form taken by the state since 1918. Once Nazism became identified with both the nation and the state for millions of its inhabitants, and once all forms of potential opposition had been crushed or muted, the programme of *Gleichschaltung* allowed it to create within a few years a new industrial–military–state complex of extraordinary power and efficiency compared to the one over which Mussolini presided. Considerable pluralism, overlap or duplication of departmental functions, corruption, inter-sectional rivalries, tensions between incompatible policies and sheer incompetence still existed at the heart of the Third Reich. However, the organization, discipline, training and equipment of the armed forces and SS, and the cohesion of the party and state apparatus, were still sufficiently high to enable them to become devastatingly effective instruments of terror, conquest, occupation and genocide.

It should be added that an important factor which contributed to the destructiveness of Nazism was the autonomous executive momentum which is developed by all hierarchical structures, and hence of the programmes they adopt, once they have been properly set up. One macabre case study in this phenomenon is provided by the perversely-brilliant organization of a concentration camp system which manipulated the fanatical obedience and racial hatred of the few, and the human survival instinct of the many, to ensure the smooth, practically automatic, operation of the terror and execution machine at every level of the hierarchy right down to that of victims themselves (see Phillips, 1969, ch.4). Clearly there was a considerable degree of contingency in both the timing and scale of the escalation of the imperialist and anti-Semitic programmes, but once the crucial decisions had been made in high places, the efficiency of the Nazi state machinery was such that both the arms industry and the extermination factories created for the Final Solution maintained their lethal productive efficiency till the bitter end, even when the demands of the genocidal programme and of the war effort came into direct conflict, and long after defeat was inevitable. Similarly, the armed forces did not desert in massive numbers when the chips were down as did their Fascist counterparts. Indeed, to extirpate the Nazi high command, Berlin finally had to be taken street by street and the lives of well over one and a half million soldiers and citizens were 'sacrificed' in the process.

The Role of National Character

By raising the issue of national character we are clearly touching on an subject fraught with the danger of relapsing into racial stereotypes, and certainly we are dealing with complex socio-cultural tendencies rather than genetically determined traits. Nevertheless, it is *a* factor in explaining the violence of Nazism which has received serious scholarly attention in Jonathan Steinberg's *All or Nothing* (1990). His starting point is to ask why, in marked contrast to officers and men of the German army, their Fascist counterparts and allies overwhelmingly refused to comply with official policies and specific orders which would have made them direct accomplices of the Nazi genocidal campaign against the Jews. As a professional historian Steinberg does not answer this question in simplistic terms, but gives due weight to the much greater number of Jews in German society and their disproportionate penetration into the mass media and the 'modern' professional and commercial sectors of the economy when compared with Italy. He also stresses the wave of collective paranoia unleashed by the *Zusammenbruch* of 1918 and the psychotic anti-Semitism of Hitler himself. Yet his central argument is that cultural history was a major determinant in conditioning the practically universal collusion of the German *Wehrmacht* in the Holocaust and equally the almost systematic refusal of Italian soldiers and commanders to obey the orders to follow suit.

Shaped by the absence of a central state, a strong regional culture, poverty, internal political strife and an almost continuous history of foreign occupation in many regions, Italy failed to develop a mature civic culture. Public life, at least by the advent of Fascism, was dominated by a string of 'anti-social' behaviourial reflexes to authority and responsibility such as disorder, disobedience, casualness and slovenliness (*menefreghismo*), corruption, nepotism and bureaucratic inefficiency. However, Steinberg argues that these 'secondary vices' coexisted and facilitated the persistence in Italy of a 'primary virtue', namely humanity. In the context of Fascism this combination of traits in the national character (or what Fromm, 1960, pp.239–53, called 'social character') meant not only that the regime encountered major obstacles in carrying out its schemes to make the state apparatus, agriculture, industry and the armed forces more efficient, but that the *stato totalitario* was 'internalized' only by a minority of fanatics. Most went along with the regime opportunistically while the going was good but rebelled instinctively against the orders which implied the senseless sacrifice of their own lives or the massacre of innocent victims. The anti-Semitic campaign simply made no intuitive sense to most Italians and as a result, Mussolini's express orders to collaborate with the SS in Croatia, southern France and Italy were almost universally disobeyed: the social 'vices' developed to circumvent rules and regulations down the ages were now employed both by the army and ordinary citizens to protect the Jews who fell into their hands instead of handing them over to the traditionally detested 'authorities'.

The situation which prevailed in Germany was very different. There, Prussian military, educational and civil service traditions had inculcated a deeply engrained respect for the authority of the state and the validity of 'higher orders'. This trait was reinforced by habits of thought (epitomized in Hegel and absorbed as part and parcel of 'culture') which reified abstractions and reinforced dualistic thinking. Such a trait encouraged an instinctive subservience to authority and created a dichotomy in most educated

German thinking between on the one hand duty, objectivity, facts, areas of human life which can be legislated for and formulated in rules, and, on the other, spontaneity, subjectivity, emotions, the unquantifiable. A puritan instinct ensured that the former was regarded as the realm of the 'tidy' and 'healthy', and the latter as that of the 'messy' and 'degenerate' (the link with the dichotomous psychological universe inhabited by the 'soldier–males' studied in Theweleit, 1987–9 is obvious: see above pp.197–8).

The result was that the German national character acquired a range of 'secondary virtues' such as efficiency, obedience, sense of duty, incorruptibility, but at the expense of the primary virtue of humanity. This is why 'messy' ethical considerations did not arise for most Germans when carrying out genocidal orders, a task substantially aided by the use of bureaucratic abstractions such as 'supplies' for human beings, or euphemisms such as 'special treatment' for execution which helped depersonalize the whole process of mass extermination. The Fascist, even in uniform, retained a deep link with his 'private', off-duty, human personality. By contrast, not just the Nazi, but most members of the German army who had never been converted to Nazism, tended to suppress their individuality when the validity of state policies and doctrine were involved, even when not on duty. Instead of *menefreghismo* there was *Pflicht* (duty).

Steinberg's theory about the 'Germans' may be essentially speculative and heuristically 'one-sided' perhaps to the point of caricature, (for example when he uses such phrases as 'The First World War drove Germany mad', p.236). Yet if it contained only a kernel of truth, it would indeed help account for the glaring contrast which he extensively documents between the countless acts of humanity shown to Jews by Fascists, some of whom 'privately' had anti-Semitic prejudices and the dispassionate participation in the attempted genocide of the Jews by Germans, some of whom were 'personally' neither fanatically Nazi or anti-Semitic. If such 'secondary virtues' were indeed prevalent in the German population as a whole, then it would also count as an important factor in explaining the far deeper degree of their Nazification than the Fascistization of the Italians – and the readiness of the countless bureaucratic and military henchmen of the Nazi regime to carry through its ideologically and juridically carefully legitimated programme of systematic barbarism in Europe with such 'exemplary' thoroughness.

The Dynamics of Nazi Destructiveness

The pictures of thousands of frozen corpses littering Russian Steppes or of the contorted, skeletal remains of what had once been human beings frozen in their death agony in the pits of Belsen still boggle the human imagination and chill the heart. But if we take into account the clusters of factors identified in this chapter, the historical and sociological imagination can at least start to formulate partial but coherent answers to the question 'why?' The abstract register we have used should not be confused with the dehumanizing objectivity in which leading Nazis cloaked their heinous moral crimes to their accusers at Nuremberg, and even to themselves, but as an integral part of humanistic enquiry, the urge to probe beyond 'common sense' answers, the impulse to understand the world rather than to change it.

When applied to Nazism, our approach to the definition of generic fascism and the explanatory model it incorporates suggests that the serious structural difficulties to which Weimar was exposed after 1929, opening deep socio-political wounds left by the *Zusammenbruch* a decade earlier, created conditions in which millions of Germans came in their own way to experience a powerful elective affinity with components of Nazism, which, in the diagnosis and remedies it proposed for the current situation, drew on and reformulated myths whose roots extended deep into pre-war and even pre-unification culture. Moreover, the way it reduced contemporary history to the crude categories of chaos and order, decay and health, German or Jew appealed to the dualistic, rule-bound mentality which many Germans had acquired through secondary socialization, encouraging millions of them (though always a minority) to identify their own fate and that of Germany with the NSDAP and its absolute leader, Adolf Hitler, at a deep affective level. This relieved them of the acute psychic distress they were going through at a time of unprecedented sense-making crisis by locating its ultimate causes firmly within a historical turning point from national decadence to national rebirth, thus transmuting private despair into collective hope.

Once the Nazis had seized power, systematic propaganda, indoctrination and terror at every level of society reinforced the wave of genuine conversions to their cause which helped bring them to power. Even when the war started going against the Third Reich, the Hitler myth (as opposed to belief in the NSDAP and its leadership) proved remarkably tenacious, and the commitment of many hard-core Nazis to the official utopia even survived the suicide of their leader. It should never be forgotten that many thousands of Germans courageously fought Nazism despite the atrocious deaths they faced if found out, while millions more may have understandably emigrated from Nazism 'inwardly'. But millions of others also colluded with it, while hundreds of thousands willingly carried out orders which would result directly in mass destruction and murder being committed on a vast scale. I would argue that most did so neither out of nihilism, nor out of automaton-like obedience, but because at some level of their consciousness they had persuaded themselves that this destruction had a cathartic, hygienic purpose. It was but the prelude to a new Germany, an era of vitality and creativity, a reborn nation.

In Nazism the full potential for inhumanity latent in a political ideology based on palingenetic ultra-nationalism had been revealed. It placed Germans before drastic alternatives: to be sick or to be reborn, to die or to live. On occasion the horrific human implications of this dualism were spelt out eloquently by Nazi leaders themselves, as when they made an appeal to the instinct for self-transcendence and 'creative nihilism' in their listeners so as to enlist them as incarnations of the New Man, the *homo fascistus*. A notorious example is the morale-boosting speech which Himmler delivered to SS leaders at Posen on 6 October 1943. He assured those among them who knew what it was like to see a thousand corpses lying side by side, that 'to have stuck it out and at the same time remained decent fellows' was a 'page of glory in our history which has never been written and must never be written'. After all the destruction of the Jews was not a matter of personal hatred or gain:

> We had the moral right, we had the duty to our own people, to destroy this people which wanted to destroy us. But we have not the right to enrich ourselves with so much as a fur, a watch, a mark, a cigarette or anything else. We have exterminated a bacterium because we do not want in the end to be infected by the bacterium and die of it. I will not see so much as a small area of sepsis appear here or gain a hold. Wherever it may form, we will cauterize it. All in all, we can say that we have fulfilled this most difficult duty for the love of our people. And our spirit, our soul, our character has not suffered injury from it. (Noakes and Pridham, 1971, pp.493)

In passages such as these the 'nature of fascism' is revealed in its purest form: a sense of heroic self-sacrifice to an ideal unadulterated by the 'decadent' spirit of compassion, but inspired instead by the knowledge that, in order for the national phoenix to arise, everything and everyone that stands in its way first has to be burnt to ashes, literally if necessary.

References

Abraham, D., 1981. *The Collapse of the Weimar Republic*, Princeton University Press, Princeton.

Allen, W.S., 1975. The appeal of fascism and the problem of national disintegration, in H.A. Turner Jr. (ed.), *Reappraisals of Fascism*, Franklin Watts, New York.

Anderson, W.L., 1989. Fascism and culture: avant-gardes and secular religion in the Italian case, *Journal of Contemporary History*, Vol.24, No.3.

Baglieri, J., 1980. Italian Fascism and the crisis of liberal hegemony: 1901–1922, in Larsen *et al.* (op. cit.).

Barbu, Z., 1980. Psycho-historical and sociological perspectives on the Iron Guard, the fascist movement of Romania, in Larsen *et al.* (op. cit.).

Borejsza, J.W., 1980. East European perceptions of Italian Fascism, in Larsen *et al.* (op. cit.).

Bracher, K.D., 1978. *The German Dictatorship. The Origins, Structure and Effects of National Socialism*, Penguin, Harmondsworth.

Conway, M. and Buchanan, T. (eds), 1993/4. *Political Catholicism in Europe, 1918–1960*, Oxford University Press, Oxford.

Eley, G., 1983. What produces fascism: preindustrial traditions or the crisis of the capitalist state, *Politics and Society*, Vol.12, No.1.

Eley, G., 1990. Conservative and radical nationalists in Germany: the production of potentials, in M. Blinkhorn (ed.), *Fascists and Conservatives*, Unwin Hyman, London.

Fischer-Galati, S., 1980. Introduction to Part 4, in Larsen *et al.* (op. cit.).

Fromm, E., 1960. *The Fear of Freedom*, Routledge and Kegan Paul, London.

Gentile, E., 1975. *Le origini dell'ideologia fascista*, Cremona Nuova, Cremona.

Gentile, E., 1982. *Il mito dello stato nuovo*, Laterza, Bari.

Groueff, S., 1987. *The Crown of Thorns. The Reign of King Boris III of Bulgaria 1918–43*, Madison, New York.

Hagtvet, B., 1980. *The Theory of Mass Society and the Collapse of the Weimar Republic*, in Larsen *et al.* (op. cit.).

Hüppauf, B., 1990. The birth of fascist man from the spirit of the front: from

Langemarck to Verdun, in J. Milfull (ed.), *The Attractions of Fascism*, Berg, New York etc.

Kershaw, I. (ed.), 1990. *Weimar: Why Did German Democracy Fail?*, Weidenfeld and Nicolson, London.

Kershaw, I., 1991. *Hitler*, Longman, London.

Kühnl, R., 1980. Pre-conditions for the rise of and victory of fascism in Germany, in Larsen *et al.* (op. cit.).

Larsen, S.U., Hagtvet, B., Myklebust, J.P. (eds), 1980. *Who Were the Fascists: Social Roots of European Fascism*, Universitetsforlaget, Bergen.

Larsen, S.U. Hagtvet, B., Myklebust, J.P. (eds), 1980. *Who Were the Fascists: Social Roots of European Fascism*, Universitetsforlaget, Bergen.

Linz, J.L., 1979. Some notes towards a comparative study of fascism in sociological historical perspective, in W. Laqueur (ed.), *Fascism: A Reader's Guide*, Pelican, Harmondsworth.

Linz, J.L., 1980. Political space and fascism as a late-comer, in Larsen *et al.* (op. cit.).

Lyttleton, A., 1973. *The Seizure of Power: Fascism in Italy 1919–29*, Jonathan Cape, London.

Mayer, A.J., 1990. *Why Did the Heavens Not Darken?*, Verso, London.

Merkl, P.H., 1980. The Nazis of the Abel collection: why they joined the NSDAP, in Larsen *et al.* (op. cit.).

Mosse, G.L., 1966. *The Crisis of German Ideology*, Weidenfeld & Nicolson, London.

Mosse, G.L., 1980. *Nationalization of the Masses*, New York.

Mosse, G.L., 1986. Two world wars and the myth of the war experience, *Journal of Contemporary History*, Vol.24, No.4.

Mühlberger, D., 1987. Germany, in D. Mühlberger (ed.), *The Social Basis of European Fascism*, Croom Helm, London.

Mühlberger, D., 1991. *Hitler's Followers*, Routledge, London.

Noakes, J. and Pridham, G., 1971. *Documents on Nazism 1919–1945*, Jonathan Cape, London.

Nolte, E., 1988. *Der europäische BürgerKrieg Nazionalsozialismus und Bolschewismus*, Propyläen, Berlin.

Passchier, N., 1980. The electoral geography of the Nazi landslide, in Larsen *et al.* (op. cit.).

Phillips, P., 1969. *The Tragedy of Nazi Germany*, Routledge and Kegan Paul, London.

Platt, G.M., 1980. Thoughts on a theory of collective action: language, affect and ideology in revolution, in M. Albin (ed.), *New Directions in Psychohistory*, Lexington Books, Lexington, Massachusetts.

Revelli, M., 1987. Italy, in D. Mühlberger (ed.), *The Social Basis of European Fascism*, Croom Helm, London.

Roberts, D.D., 1979. *The Syndicalist Tradition in Italian Fascism*, Manchester University Press, Manchester.

Sontag, R.J., 1971. *A Broken World, 1919–1939*. Harper and Row, New York.

Steinberg, J., 1990. *All or Nothing*, Routledge, London.

Stromberg, R.N., 1982. *Redemption by War*, The Regents Press of Kansas, Lawrence.

Theweleit, K., 1989. *Male Fantasies*. Vol.1 (1987): Women, floods, bodies, history; Vol.2 (1989): Male bodies: psychoanalyzing the white terror, Polity Press, Cambridge.

Vivarelli, R., 1967. *Il dopoguerra in Italia e l'avvento del fascismo (1981–22)*, Vol.1, *Dalla fine della guerra all'impresa di Fiume*, Istituto Italiano per gli Studi Storici, Naples.

Wanrooij, B., 1987. The rise and fall of Italian Fascism as a generational revolt, *Journal of Contemporary History*, Vol.22, No.3.

Weinstein, F., 1980. *Germany's Discontent. Hitler's Vision: The Claims of Leadership and Ideology in the National Socialist Movement*, Academic Press, New York.

Postscript

Though as an effective revolutionary force fascism has long since burnt itself out, there is no prospect that ideologies drawing on the raw materials of the phoenix myth will ever be a thing of the past. The world political arena is dominated by the complex tensions between egotistic or radical nationalisms and a spirit of international co-operation. Cassandras cross verbal swords with self-appointed prophets of a new dawn, while a continuous flow of speeches and news articles announce conflicting visions of the historical turning point at which humanity stands. Meanwhile, beneath the torrent of words, the fragile balance of the ecosystem on which our species depends is eroded a little more with every day that passes. This is no mythological 'Twilight of the Gods', no 'immanentized *eschaton*' (see above p.31), but the real thing.

This book has ascribed the horrific human consequences of fascism, when put into practice, to its mythic core of a palingenetic vision, a vision which encourages, not a creative interaction and healthy integration with the external world, but a total and perverse identification with only a narrow part of it. Perhaps there is still time for the course of history to be changed by the force of a healthy palingenetic movement, a supra-national movement of ecological humanism working from below and above which centres its hopes, not on 'one people, one empire, one leader', but on 'one humanity, one life, one world'.

In this sense the closing words of the chorus in Seamus Heaney's play *Cure at Troy* (1990) are timely:

History says don't hope on this side of the grave,
but then once in a life-time the longed for tidal wave of justice can rise up,
and *hope and history rhyme*,
So hope for a great sea-change on the far side of revenge.
Believe that a further shore is reachable from here.
Believe in miracles and cures and healing wells.

Glossary

The explanations given here are not dictionary definitions, but simply aim to make comprehensible in their context within the book specialist terms which might be unfamiliar to the reader and act as a barrier to understanding a particular passage.

aetiology – the study of the causes of illnesses and diseases

anarcho-syndicalism – a form of revolutionary socialism influenced by anarchism and the theories of Georges Sorel

anomie – an acute sense of meaningless and loss of identity precipitated by socio-political upheavals (see p.191)

archetype – a symbol or myth whose affective power lies in the resonance it has within the universal, supra-individual level of the psyche whose existence was postulated by the psychologist C.G. Jung

Ariadne (in Greek myth) – the woman who helped Theseus out of the labyrinth by means of a thread

autarky – the goal of the nation's economic self-sufficiency pursued through eliminating the need for imports

binomial – description of a single concept in the combination of two terms (e.g. nation state, liberal democracy)

biocidal – tending to the destruction of all life-forms, human or non-human

charisma – the magnetism and authority emanated by someone perceived as the embodiment of higher powers

chiliastic – expressing beliefs associated with **millenarianism**

corporatism – a socio-political system based on the organization of the economy into discrete sectors in which the interests of workers, managers, state and nation are supposedly reconciled

cosmology – a total world-view explaining the main features of perceived reality and creating the basis of meaningful existence

demo-liberalism – a Fascist term which lumps together the 'enemy' movements of (proletarian) socialism and (bourgeois) liberalism

diachronic – analysing phenomena in a way which respects their chronological development and historical particularity (opposite: synchronic)

dialectical materialism – the Marxist concept of history as an evolutionary process ultimately driven by the impact of economic forms and modes of production on human society

dirigiste – the description of a state which is highly interventionist, especially in matters of socio-economic policy

dysfunction – a structural malfunction

eclectic – drawing on or synthesizing a variety of (tendentially incompatible) sources of influences

ecumenicism – the principle that all the factions and groups within a movement should form a common front in the pursuit of certain shared goals

elective affinity – a deep-seated attraction towards or fascination with something experienced as a natural kinship with it

entropy – the principle that all systems tend towards loss of energy and the breakdown of internal cohesion

epiphenomenon – the side product of a more fundamental reality

ersatz – substitute, bogus, pseudo-

eschatology – a body of knowledge relating to the Last Days of the present era which will culminate in the millennium

ethnocentrism – placing one's own race or kind at the centre of all value judgements and policies

eugenics – a scientific (and frequently pseudo-scientific) discipline concerned with the 'laws' determining the racial purity, degeneration and progress of the human species

exegesis – the interpretation of a sacred text

extra-systemic – operating from outside the dominant socio-political system in a way which disrupts or transforms it

Faustian – expressing the myth of Faust who was driven to make a pact with the devil in order to transcend ordinary human experience

fin-de-siècle – a term describing the peculiar cultural and intellectual climate which prevailed in Europe at the 'end of the (19th) century' in which many rival visions of decadence and rebirth were proposed (see pp.202–5)

fissiparous – tending constantly to divide up into smaller groups

francophone – French-speaking

fundamentalism – a dogmatic form of belief based on revealed religious truth

gerontocracy – a political system in which power is exercised by the oldest generation

gnostic – relating to gnosticism, the ancient Greek cult of an initiatic type of knowledge which acts as a source of mystic enlightenment and of ecstasy

hegemony – the preeminence or domination of a particular socio-political system over all rivals

heterogeneous – belonging to discrete and unrelated kinds or groups

heuristic – relating to a conceptual device or model designed to help in the investigation of a subject or problem

historiography – the discipline in the human sciences concerned with the accurate reconstruction of historical events and their underlying causes

homogeneous – belonging to the same kind or group on the basis of shared defining characteristics

hydra – a monster in Greek mythology whose head sprouted snakes which grew back immediately they were cut off

ideal type – a consciously constructed definitional concept or model used in the scientific investigation of human realities

idealizing abstraction – the human faculty of discerning regular patterns in phenomena and processes which are ultimately particular and unique

idiographic – concerned to reconstruct particular events without reference to general principles or generic phenomena (i.e. a basic quality of historiography)

immanentization – making something into an intrinsic part of historical time (as opposed to treating it as a supernatural reality)

Kraken – a mythological sea-monster which reawakens after centuries of lying dormant

limbic – pertaining to the oldest or 'animal' part of the human brain immediately connected to the body's central nervous system

lingua franca – common language, a force which rallies a number of different elements into a single movement

menhir – a large stone sacred to the Celts

millenarianism – a religious world-view which sees the symptoms of crisis in contemporary history as the sign that the reign of Christ is about to begin

mimetic – purely imitative

mythic – unleashing irrational psychological and social energies through a world-view which reduces the world into simplified beliefs and images on which to act

mythopoiea – the faculty of human beings which creates myths and visions

neutralist – relating to a form of fascism which does not aspire to incorporating 'unredeemed' territories or to imperial expansion (see p.49)

nihilism – an absence of beliefs and values which leads to the will to destroy those of others

nomic crisis – a generalized breakdown of meaning, values and purpose (see p.193)

nominalism – a philosophical doctrine which holds that general or universal nouns do not stand for an object but are merely names

nomothetic – concerned to formulate general principles, patterns or laws operating in human society and history (opposite: **idiographic**)

nosology – the comprehensive classification of types of illness

osmosis – a process by which one substance absorbs another, as when sugar takes up water

palingenetic – expressing the myth of rebirth, regeneration. In a political context, embodying the aspiration to create a new order following a period of perceived decline or decadence (see pp.32–6)

para-fascism – a form of authoritarian and ultra-nationalist conservatism which adopts the external trappings of fascism while rejecting its call for genuine social and ethical revolution (see pp.120–4)

paradigm – a set of concepts, theories and value judgements which dominate the way an academic discipline or society operates at a given time in its development

phallocrat – male chauvinist, sexist

phenomenology – a philosophical and sociological approach based on the attempt to describe existence in terms of how it appears or is experienced without reference to essences or abstractions

philo-(Fascist) – predisposed to become a fellow-traveller or supporter of (Fascism)

pogrom – a terrorist campaign of violence and murder calculated to drive out political (e.g. Communist) or ethnic (e.g. Jewish) groups perceived as a threat to society

polycentric – having several centres of power and influence

protean – assuming many different guises or aspects

proto-fascism – a form of palingenetic ultra-nationalism which lacks the tactical or populist radicalism to be considered a fully fledged form of fascism (see pp.50–1)

putschist – striving to seize power through a military or para-military *coup d'état*

Scylla and **Charybdis** in Greek myth – the steep cliffs and enormous whirlpool between which Ulysses had to navigate his ship to avoid destruction

semiotic – relating to the power of signs and symbols, whether verbal or non-verbal, to convey meaning and condition behaviour

Sonderweg (German) – special path of historical development

subliminal – operating just beneath the threshold of consciousness

supra-historical – operating in a sphere above or beyond 'ordinary' time or history

syncretic – fusing several potentially incompatible theories into a single synthesis

synergetic – relating to two or more systems operating in dynamic interdependence and interaction with each other

systemic – operating within and accommodated by the existing sociopolitical system

tautology – an explanation which is circular because it involves the central term it is seeking to clarify

taxonomy – a scientific system of classification and categorization

teleological – a view of history which attributes to it a definite shape and purpose

topos – a recurrent theme or image

triadic – relating to a scheme of historical development which falls into three distinct phases

trichotomy – a theoretical division into three separate and mutually exclusive categories

typology – a system of classification based on significant characteristics

ultra-nationalism – a form of nationalism incompatible with liberal democratic notions of the basic equality in civil rights and political autonomy of other nation-states or nationalities

universalist – relating to a form of fascism open to alliances with other fascist movements or regimes on the basis of common goals and enemies (see p.49)

vulgar Marxism – the application of Marxist precepts in a simplistic and deterministic spirit

zoón politikon (Greek) – political animal

Index

NB: This does not include all cited sources, but only those whose authors have been referred to in the main body of the text. The individual chapter bibliographies could be used to confirm whether a particular book or author has been taken into account in the course of the analysis, while Chapter 1 could be consulted as a starting point to further reading and alludes to several 'readers' guides' available for new-comers to fascist studies.

Academic Karelia Society (AKS) 140, 229
Acão Integralista Brasileira (AIB) 150-2, 209
Acción Española 118
Acción Revolucionaria Mexicana 149
Action Française 30, 118, 133, 163, 209
Afirmación de una Nueva Argentina (ADUNA) 149
Africa, fascism in 156-60, 165
Afrikaner Weerstandsbeweging (AWB) 160, 176, 220
Allen, William S. 223
Allende, Salvador 152
Allardyce, Gilbert 7
anomie 175, 189, 191, 192, 193, 195-6, 200, 201, 204, 215-6, 227-8
anti-Semitism 48, 73-4, 87-9, 94, 98, 103, 107, 109, 111, 117-8, 119, 120, 122, 129, 130-1, 134, 140, 149, 151, 160, 161, 165, 167, 170, 174, 175, 176-7, 183, 203, 204, 218, 225, 228-9, 231-3
Antonescu, General Ion 126-7, 152
Apra 149, 209
Arditi 63, 65
ARENA (Brazil) 152
Argentina, putative fascism in 149, 152
Arrow Cross 30, 127-8, 130, 163
Aryan myth 87, 101, 105, 169, 199, 219
  see also anti-Semitism
Associazione Nazionale Italiana (ANI) 57-8, 60, 61, 64, 76, 85
Auschwitz 104
Australia, expatriate fascism in 163
Austria, fascism and para-fascism in 124-6, 167, 177, 218, 222

Ba'ath Party (Iraqi) 178-9
Bakunin, Mikhail 192
Balbo, Italo 68, 72
Ballanche, Pierre Simon 33
Bardèche, Maurice 172
Barnes, Major James Strachey 70
Barraso, Gustavo 151
Barrès, Maurice 6, 118, 199, 203
Bataille, Georges 186, 193
Bauer, Otto 3
Belgium, fascism in 132-3, 141, 163, 164, 165, 218
Belli, Carlo 70
Belloc, Hilaire 174
Beltramelli, Antonio 75
Benn, Gottfried 105
Benoist, Alain de 51, 147, 168-9, 194
Beran, Rudolf 131
Bergson, Henri 138
Bethlen, Count István 124
biennio rosso 3, 66, 68
Blue Shirts (Ireland) 119
Blunck, Hans Friedrich 87
Boccioni, Umberto 59
Bolivia, putative fascism in 150, 152
Bontempelli, Massimo 70, 71
Boris III, King of Bulgaria 121, 210
Böszörményi, Zoltán 127
Botha, Pieter W. 159
Bottai, Giuseppe 69, 79
Bracher, Karl D. 225
Brasillach, Robert 142
Brazil, fascism and para-fascism in 148, 150-52, 209, 210, 222
Brecht, Bertolt 147

Breton nationalism and neo-fascism 172
British Union of Fascists (BUF) 1, 8, 129-30, 137-8, 139, 163, 218
Broch, Hermann 197
Broederbond 158-9, 219
Brzezinski, Zbigniev 44
Bucard, Marcel 134, 218
Büchner, Georg 179, 194
Bulgaria, failure of fascism in 121, 210, 218
Burger, Thomas 9
Burte, Hermann 87

Cagoule 119
Campbell, Joseph 33, 189, 191
Canada, neo-Nazism in 165
Carella, Domenico 70
Carmona, Marshal António 122
Carnaro, Charter of, 65, 77
Carol II, King of Romania, 126, 151
Cartel of the Productive Estates (Germany) 89
Ceaușescu, Nicolae, 33, 37, 110
CEDA (Spanish Confederation of Autonomous Rightist Groups) 118
CEDADE (Spanish Circle of Friends of Europe) 152, 165, 171
Céline, Louis-Ferdinand, 173
Central Association of German Industrialists 89
Chamberlain, Houston Stewart 87, 203
charisma 30, 37, 42-3, 62, 111, 192, 193
Chesterton, Gilbert K. 174
Chile, fascism in 150, 152
Christian Social Party 118
Christian Socialism 159-60
Class, Heinrich 89
Clausen, Frits 131
Codreanu, Corneliu Z. 42, 126, 139, 166
Cohn, Norman 31, 33, 192
Communión Tradicionalista 118
Communist International 2, 3
'conservative revolution' 91, 92, 168-9
Corradini, Enrico 58, 76, 228
Corridoni, Filippo 58-9
Costa-Gavras, Constantine 165
'creative nihilism' 47, 93, 104, 110-11
Croatia 120, 172
Croce, Benedetto 79, 82
'crypto-fascism' 166-7, 173
cultural pessimism 47, 204, 215-6
Cuza, Alexander 140
Czechoslovakia, fascism and para-fascism in 130-131, 215

Dahn, Felix 87
D'Annunzio, Gabriele 59, 61, 62, 65-66, 68, 70, 75, 77
Darré, Walter 98, 99, 108, 111, 230
Darwin, Charles 201
Davanzati, Roberto F. 68
De Ambris, Alceste 58, 65, 77
De Clerq, Staf 132
De Felice, Renzo 5
de Klerk, Fredrik W. 158, 159
de Maistre, Joseph 4, 49
Déat, Marcel 136
decadence, myth of 201-4, 208-9, 211
  see also palingenetic myth

Degrelle, Léon 132-3, 136, 141, 229
Dehoust, Peter 173
Denmark, fascism in 131, 167, 218
Déroulède, Paul 117
Deutsche-Volksunion 167
Deutschnationale Volkspartei (DNVP) 91, 99
Diedrichs, Eugen 88
Dimitroff, Georgi 3
Dinter, Arthur 32, 87, 99, 229
Dollfuss, Engelbert 125
dopolavoro 72, 105
Dorados (Gold Shirts) 149
Doriot, Jacques 134, 136, 139
Dostoevsky, Fëdor M. 33
Douglas, Clifford H. 138
Drieu la Rochelle, Pierre 51, 142, 173, 199
Drumont, Edouard 117
ducismo 74-5, 77, 80
Durkheim, Emile 191

East bloc (former), neo-fascism in 176-7, 219-20
Ebert, Friedrich 90, 95
Eckhart, Dietrich 94
ecology vii, 2, 34, 167, 168, 171, 174, 175, 176, 178, 237
Ecuador, neo-fascism in 152
El Salvador, neo-fascism in 152
Eley, Geoff 36, 223
Eliade, Mircea 31, 33, 173, 189-91, 194
Eliot, Thomas S. 216
Enciclopedia Italiana 68, 72
Estado Novo (Portugal) 122, 135, 141
Estonia, proto-fascism in 119, 210, 218
Ethiopia, colonization of 73, 74, 76-7, 80, 81, 103, 225, 228
'Europe of Nations', neo-fascist vision of 76, 109, 137, 164, 171, 173, 174 *see also* fascism, universalist
European Economic Community (EEC) 8, 34, 37, 171, 220
Evola, Julius 47, 51, 69, 147, 152, 169, 172

Faisceau, Le 1, 133
Falanga (Polish) 119, 120, 218
Falange (Spanish) 7, 123-4, 141, 151, 163, 209, 218
Falange Española (FE) 123
Falange Española Tradicionalista (Mexican) 149
Falange Socialista Boliviana 150
Farinacci, Roberto 68, 70, 75, 79, 224
Fasci di azione rivoluzionaria 58-9, 61
Fasci di combattimento 56
fascism (generic)
  'age of' 5, 147
  abortive fascisms in inter-war Europe 116-45
  and anti-decadence 47, 201
  and anti-modernism viii, 47
  and anti-Semitism, *see* anti-Semitism
  and chiliasm 30
  and conservatism 49, 50, 78
  and contingency 211
  and counter-revolution 48
  and cultural despair 47
  and cultural pessimism 47, 204, 215-6
  and idealism 46
  and imperialism 48, 138

and leader-cult 42, 197
and liberal democracy 211, 213-7, 220-1
and millenarianism 30, 46, 138, 147, 187-8, 189,
    192
and modernization vii, 20, 47
and nationalism 36-8, 41-3, 201-2
and nihilism 46–7, 93, 100, 104, 110–11, 234 *see
    also* cultural pessimism
and racism, *see* Aryan myth, anti-Semitism
and (radical) right 49-50, 117-20, 161-2, 177-9
and reaction 47-8
and 'revolt against positivism' 86, 202-5
and revolution 47-8
and separatist nationalism 120
and territorial expansion 133, 137, 138, 139, 140
and (threat of) Marxist revolution 147, 111,
    214-5
and transcendence 186-8, 194-7
and war veterans 63, 66, 92, 164
and women 73, 77, 199, 202
anti-dimension of 5-6, 7, 14, 46
as charismatic force 42-3, 62, 111
as generic term 1, 21
as political ideology 26-32
as Third Force 38, 166
as Third Way 50, 71, 166, 174
causal complexity 184-6
concise definition of 26
debate over 1-8, 11-12
discursive definition of 44-5
elitism of 41-3
factiousness of 78
fascist minimum viii, 13, 38-9, 110
fascist negations, *see* fascism, anti-dimension of
first emergence of 200-5
fundamentalism 50
generic ideological features of 26-7
heterogeneity/homogeneity of 27, 44, 78, 79, 81,
    99–100, 111, 136-43
ideology of 5, 13-15, 26-39
impotence since 1945 219-221
in democracies occupied by Nazis 130-33
incubation period of 202-5, 212-13
irreducible complexity of 225, 226
leftist 58-9, 61, 64, 68, 95, 96, 100, 166, 203
Marxist interpretations of 2-4, 38, 48, 148
mimetic 164-6
myth of national community in 39-40, 79, 140,
    see also Fascism, National Socialism
'nature of' 18-21
need to understand 182-83
neo-fascism 163-4, 166-9
nomothetic versus idiographic explanations of
    18, 19, 211
non-Marxist definitions of 4-8
'nostalgic' 163-5, 209, 219
palingenetic ultra-nationalism in 38-45, 79, 136-
    44, 172-4
paradigms of 5
populism of 41-3
post-war 21, 147, 161-77
psycho-historical dynamics of 182-207
psychology of 5, 194-200
relationship with para-fascism 120-8
resilience of 175-7
'revisionist' 167-8, 173

ritual in 13-4, 111, 190-91, 193-4, *see also*
    charisma
self-destructiveness of 42-3, 81
skinhead fascism 165, 174
social base of 5, 20, 99, 185, 222-4
socio-political determinants of 208-36
structural preconditions of 156-7, 182-235
structural weaknesses of 39-44, 78-81
'style' of 13-14 *see also* charisma, ritual
tendency to entropy of 40, 80
'totalitarian' myth of 39-40, 43-4, 45, 79-80,
    107-110
under liberal regimes 128-30
universalist 49, 69-70, 74, 76, 108-9, 134, 137,
    138, 147, 171
youth movements associated with 72, 74, 77, 88,
    102, 121, 122, 123, 130, 135, 165
'whys' of 183-6, 223
see also individual countries
Fascism (Italy) 1, 5, 40, 45, 51-2, 56-84, 86, 150
and *trincerismo* 64, 66
anti-Semitism in 73-4, 231-3
art and architecture 70-1
as 'parenthesis' 82
compromise with conservatism 77
contingency in success of 224-5
contrasted with Nazism 110, 228-35
co-ordination of society by 71-6
corporativism 71-2, 76-7
demographic campaign 76
economics of 71-2
educational policy in 77
exceptionalness of 40, 45, 116, 143, 157, 170,
    221-5
exoteric ideology of 71-6
ideological heterogeneity of 78, 79, 81, 147
imperialism of 73-4, 76-7, 80, 81
influence of 120, 128, 150, 155, 209, 217, 218
last stage of 76, 81
modernizing thrust of 81
'mystic' 69
palingenetic myth in, *see* palingenetic myth
polycentrism of 79
proto-fascist stage of 56-63, 204
racism of 73-4
relationship to Catholicism 69-70, 79, 103
role of Mussolini's personality in 229-30
role of national character in 231-3
Sansepolcro Fascism 64,
secret police in 80
structural reasons for success of 221-5
'totalitarian' state of 71, 76, 80
trans-class appeal of 222-4
transition to authoritarian regime 67
Universal 69-70, 134
unsustainability of 76-2
women under 73, 77
youth cult 74
fascismo 1, 64
Febreristas 149, 209
Feder, Gottfried 100
Federzoni, Luigi 57, 68, 203
Ferri, Enrico 70
fin de siècle 6, 86, 204, 209
Final Solution (Holocaust) 103-4, 111, 225, 231
    see also anti-Semitism

Finland, fascism in 129-30, 140, 143, 164, 218, 222
First World War vii, 34, 63-4, 92-3, 117, 135, 202, 213-6, 221-2
Flora, Joachim of 32
Flower Power 34
France, fascism and para-fascism in 6, 7, 133-6, 141-3, 164, 166, 174, 218, 222
Francisme 134
Franco, General Francisco 2, 7, 104, 123-4, 148, 161
Frank, Walter 99
Franquism, *see* Franco
Frazer, Sir James G. 33
Free Corps (*Freikorps*) 93
French Revolution 34, 74, 179, 194
Freud, Sigmund 186, 198, 201
Frey, Dr. Gerhard 167, 173
Friedrich, Carl J. 44
Fritsch, Theodor 88, 98, 203
Fromm, Erich 186, 191, 193, 199, 205
Front National 161, 167
Futurism 59, 60, 61, 64, 70, 86

Gajda, General Radola 131
Gentile, Emilio 31
Gentile, Giovanni 68, 69, 75, 77, 79
George, Stefan 87
'German nihilism' 93, 104
German *Völkisch* Defensive and Offensive League (DVSuTB) 94
German Workers' Party (DAP) in Bohemia 118
German Workers' Party (DAP) in Germany 94
German Workers' Party (DAP, DNSAP, NSDAP) in Austria 125-7
Germany, fascism in, 85-115, 166-8, 170, 173 *see also* National Socialism
Giddens, Anthony 15
Gide, André 200
Goebbels, Joseph 96, 100, 138, 198
Goethe, Johann Wolfgang von 142
Göring, Hermann 108, 173
González von Mareés, Jorge 150
Gömbös, Captain Gyula 127
Gramsci, Antonio 3
Grandi, Dino 69
Gravelli, Asvero 70
Graziani, Rodolfo 75
Great Britain, fascism in 129, 163, 164, 166, 167, 218
GRECE (Groupement de recherche et d'étude pour la civilisation européenne) 168-9, 173, 174, 189
Greece, para-fascism in 122, 161, 177, 218
Green movement, *see* ecology
Grey Wolves (Turkey) 171
Greyshirts (South Africa) 159
Gropius, Walther 216
Guénon, René 169
Günther, Hans F.K. 100, 105, 173
Guerra, Patrizia 173

Häckel, Ernst Heinrich 88, 203
Hagtvet, Bernt 223
Hall, Stuart 15
Hamsun, Knut 173, 1999
Harrer, Karl 94

Haushofer, Karl 88
Hayashi, Fusao 156
Hegel, George W.F. 201, 232
Heidegger, Martin 105
Heimwehr 124-6, 218
Henlein, Konrad 130
Hertzog, General James 158
Hess, Rudolf 99, 173
Hesse, Hermann 200, 216
Hill, Ray 174
Himmler, Heinrich 102, 108, 234-5
Hindenburg, Paul 102, 135, 224
Hindu separatism 177
Hirohito, Emperor of Japan 155-6, 218
'Historikerstreit' 168, 173
Hitler, Adolf 1, 42, 43, 45, 94-102, 111, 124,125, 134, 138, 139, 146, 173, 176, 218, 219, 224, 234
    and Final Solution 103-4
    as charismatic leader 110
    as new man 106
    as 'weak dictator' 107
    change of revolutionary strategy 95
    contribution to success of Nazism 229-30
    palingenetic vision 100-1, 107, 112
    personality cult of 106, 110
Hlinka, Msgr. Andrej 130-1, 218
Höss, Rudolf 198
Holocaust denial 167-8
homo fascistus, see New Man
Hoornaert, Paul 132
Horkheimer, Max 4
Horthy de Nagybanya, Admiral Nicolas 128
Hungarism 138-9, 163
Hungary, fascism and para-fascism in 127-8, 139-40, 143, 210, 218
Hunt, Lynn 194
Hussein, Saddam, 35, 37, 110, 178
Huxley, Aldous 200, 216

Iceland, fascism in 128, 218
ideal type,
    fascism as 11-12, 136
    ideology as 14
    premises of the new ideal type of fascism 12-14
    theory of 8-12
ideological 'core' 17, 19
    see also mythic core
ideology,
    definition of 17
    generic 17
    ideal type of 15-18
    Marxist theories of 15
    political ideologies 27-30
Ikki, Kita 155, 176
Iliesco, Ion 2
Imperial German Middle Class League 89
IMRO (Internal Macedonian Revolutionary Organization) 120, 210
Integralismo Lusitano 118, 123
International Centre of Fascist Studies (CINEF) 70
interventionism (Italy) 56, 61, 62
Iorga, Nicolae 140
Ireland, fascism in 119, 128, 164, 177
Iron Guard 30, 42, 126-7, 139-40, 151, 209, 218, 225

Irving, David 167, 168, 173
Isänmaallinen kansanliike (IKL) (People's Patriotic Movement) 129-30, 140, 218
Italian Social Republic (Salò Republic) 75-6, 81, 163
Italy, fascism in 163, 166, 169, 219
   see also Fascism

Jacobinism 110
Japan, putative fascism in 5, 76, 147, 153-6, 208, 210, 225, 229
Joachim of Flora 32, 147
Joan of Arc 134
Johst, Hanns 199
Joyce, James 216
Jünger, Ernst vii, 51, 92, 98, 166, 173, 198
Jung, Carl Gustav 33, 188-9, 191, 199
Jung, Edgar 92, 98, 99
Juntas de Ofensiva Nacional-Sindicalista (JONS) 123

Kandinsky, Vassily 203
Kennedy, Paul 109
Keynes, John Maynard 138
Khmer Rouge 178
Koestler, Arthur 186-8, 191
Ku Klux Klan 37, 160, 165

Lagarde, Paul de 87, 203
Landvolkbewegung 93, 98
Langbehn, August Julius 87, 203
Lanz von Liebenfels, Jörg 87, 173
Lanzillo, Agostino 58, 63, 68
Lapua 119, 130, 140, 218
Lasierra, Raymond 119
Lasky, Melvin J. 192
Lateran Pacts 66
Latin America, putative fascism in 5, 146, 148-52, 153, 156, 208
Latvia, fascism in 122, 210, 218
Lawrence, David Herbert 34, 216
Lawrence, Thomas Edward 216
Le Corbusier, Charles E.G. 216
Ledeen, Michael 5, 70
Legion of the Archangel Michael 126-7, 139-40, 163
Lehmann, Julius Friedrich 91
Lenin, (V.I. Ulyanov) 3
Le Pen, Jean-Marie 161, 167, 174
Lévi, Eliphas 203
Levi, Primo 19
Lewis, Wyndham 200
Lietz, Hermann 88
Libya 171, 177
List, Guido (von) 87
Lithuania, para-fascism in 121, 218
Ljotić, Dimitrije 120
Ludendorff, General Erich F.W. von 90, 100
Lueger, Karl 118, 124
Luxembourg, neo-fascism in 167, 169

McClelland, John S. 49
McLaughlin, Michael 165
Malaparte, Curzio 69, 70
Malraux, André 216
Mandela, Nelson 160

Mann, Thomas 216
March on Rome 67, 68, 69
Marcos, Ferdinand 37
Marinetti, Filippo Tommaso 59, 62, 65, 70, 71, 75, 203
Marx, Heinrich Karl 39, 192, 201
Matteotti, Giacomo 67, 223
Maulnier, Jacques L.T. 142
Maurras, Charles 118, 132, 133, 176, 203
Mazzini, Giuseppe 28, 33, 74, 229
Mayer, Arno J. 225
Mein Kampf 95, 96
Meskó, Zoltan 127
Metaxas, General Ionnis 122
Meyrink, Gustav 173
Mexico, putative fascism in 149, 152
Michels, Robert 6, 63
Middle East, proto-fascism in 157
Mihai I (Michael), King of Romania 126
Mishima, Yukio 156, 173
Moeller van den Bruck, Arthur 51, 91, 93
Mohler, Arnim 91, 93, 104, 168, 189
Morris, William 174
Mosca, Gaetano 63, 147
Mosley, Sir Oswald 1, 7, 129, 137-8, 139, 163, 171, 229
Mosse, George L. 38, 77
Moța, Ion 139
movement as concept 86
Movimento Sociale Italiano (MSI) 163
Movimiento Nacional Socialista 150
Mussert, Anton 131
Mussolini, Benito 1, 4, 43, 45, 60, 61, 62, 66, 67, 70, 74, 78, 79, 80, 82, 124, 134, 138, 146, 151, 197, 218, 219, 224
   as centre of leader cult 74-5
   as ideologue 60, 74, 75, 77
   as new man 75
   contrasted with Hitler 101, 107, 229-30
Mussolini, Vito 69
Mussolini, Vittorio 69
myth,
   integrative versus identificatory 186-8, 237
   'mythic core' 27-9
   mythic core of fascism 39-44, 45, 46, 116
   political and religious myth 30-2
   political myth 27-30
   Sorelian concept of 28, 194
   see also palingenetic myth

Nakano, Seigō 147, 155-6, 157, 219
Namier, Sir Lewis B. 27-8
Nasjonal Samling (NS) 131, 137, 163, 218
National Bloc (Spain) 118
National Front (Britain) 166, 172, 173-4
National Socialism 5, 6, 18-19, 40, 42, 45, 52, 94-112
   agricultural policy of 108
   and charisma 111
   and cultural despair 111
   and millenarianism 111, 187-8, 9
   and Vichy 135-6
   anti-modernity' of 111
   anti-Semitic policy 98, 101, 104, 108, 109-10, 111, 225-6, 227-8, 231-3
   architecture under 105

art under 103, 105
attempted genocide of gypsies 104, 120
as basis of New Order 101, 109
as creator of the *Volksgemeinschaft* 85, 87, 89, 94, 98, 106, 110, 111
Christianity under 103
compared to ba'athism 178
contingency in success of 86, 224-5
contrasted to Fascism 110, 225-33
cosmetic Nazism 164
economic structures of 108
efficiency of 230-31
dependency on socio-political crisis 106
exceptionalness of 40, 45, 116, 143, 157, 170, 221-5, 225-35
failure of 107-110
Gleichschaltung (co-ordination) of Germany by 102-4
ideological heterogeneity of 99-100, 111, 147
intentionalist' and 'structural' explanations of 104
imperialism 101, 108-9
influence of 120, 128, 150, 151, 155, 158, 209, 217-8
institutional anarchy of 107
Marxist theories of 111
mimetic Nazism 164-66, 219
modernizing effect of 107
myth of total state 107-110
need to understand 182-3
'nihilism' of *see* fascism and nihilism
nostalgic Nazism 163-4, 173
occult basis of 19, 87
palingenetic core of 98-101, 104-6, 111
polycratic nature of 107
propaganda 108
racial policy of 101, 107, 111
regimentation of leisure by 105
relationship to Bolshevism 111, 168, 214-5
relationship to fascism 6, 106-110, 130
relationship to *völkisch* movement 86, 99-100, 101, 103, 111
role of national character in 231-3
schemes for New Europe 108-9, 183, 219
secret police (Gestapo) under 102
social base of 99, 221-4
structural inviability of 110
structural reasons for success of 221-5
structural reasons for violence of 225-35
'totalitarianism' of 107-10, 231
trans-class appeal of 221-4
uniqueness of 110-1, 225-35
women under 199
see also neo-Nazism
National Socialist Party (Czech) 118
national syndicalism (Italy) 60, 133
National Syndicalists (Portugal) 123, 141, 152, 218
nationalism viii, 36-8, 201, 203
integral 37, 85
radical 37, 85
see also ultra-nationalism
Nationalsozialistische Deutsche Arbeiterpartei (NSDAP) 129, 170, 225, 229
foundation of 94
transformation of 96
mission of 97

see also National Socialism
Nazism, *see* National Socialism
neo-fascism 166-9, 219
see also post-war fascism
neo-Nazism 163-66, 167, 173, 174, 176, 219
internationalization of neo-Nazism 165-6
neo-syndicalism 58-9, 61, 64, 68, 203
see also national syndicalism
Netherlands, fascism in, 131-2, 166, 167, 210
New Deal, The 33, 219
New Man 35
fascist 38, 42, 43, 49, 74, 75, 77, 106, 139, 234
New Order, *see* palingenetic myth
New Right 49, 168
in France and Italy 168-9, 173
in Weimar Germany 91
'new woman' 199
'New World Order' vii, 34, 178
Niekisch, Ernst 92, 173
Nietzsche, Friedrich W. 6, 42, 59, 60, 87, 138, 201, 204, 228
Nolte, Ernst 6, 111, 118, 173, 187
nomic crisis, *see* anomie
Nordau, Max 203
Norway, fascism in 131, 137, 163, 167, 218
Nouvelle Droite 168-9, 173
Novismo 69
Nuova Destra 169, 173

O'Duffy, Eoin 119, 128
Ojetti, Ugo 71
Ó Maoláin, Ciarán 161, 162, 173
One World 175, 237
Orandia 159
Orwell, George 43
Ossewa Brandwag (OB) 159

Palestine Liberation Organization (PLO) 171
palingenetic myth viii, 32-6, 38, 112, 116, 177-9, 187, 188, 190-1, 194, 196-200, 202-3, 208, 215-6
contemporary need for 237
see also palingenetic ultra-nationalism
palingenetic ultra-nationalism 32-6, 38-9, 74-5, 79, 93, 98, 201, 217
definition of 38
in abortive inter-war fascism 136-43
in Fascism 68-71
in Nazism 98-106
in neo-fascism 172-4
resilience of 177-9
Pamyat 176-7
Pan-German League (*Alldeutscher Verband*) in Austria 118
Pan-German League in Germany 89, 102
Panunzio, Sergio 58, 68
Papen, Franz von 93
Papini, Giovanni 51, 56-7, 59, 60, 70, 173, 203, 228
para-fascism 120-28, 130, 177
definition of 121
Paraguay, putative fascism in 149
paramilitary leagues 93, 102, 119, 132, 133, 135, 149, 158-9, 160, 164, 198, 199
see also squadrismo
Pareto, Vilfredo, 28, 42, 63, 147, 173
Parti Populaire Français (PPF) 134, 139, 142

Parti Social Français 134
Partito Nazionale Fascista (PNF) 67
patriotic leagues 118-9
   in France 118-9
   in Hungary 127
   in Wilhelmine Germany 88
Päts, Konstantin 119
Pavelić, Dr. Ante 120
Pavolini, Alessandro 75
Payne, Stanley 5, 6, 7, 38, 147
Péguy, Charles 203
Péladan, Joséphin 203
'people power' 41, 152
perestroika 34, 175, 177
Perkonkrust (Thundercross) 122, 218
Perón, Evita 148
Perón, Juan 37, 148
Perónism 148
Peru, putative fascism in 149, 152
Pétain, Marshal Henri Philippe 134, 135, 148
Petzold, Joachim 4
Pfrimer, Dr. Walter 124
Piacenti, Marcello 74
Picasso, Pablo 203
Pierce, William 165
Picq, Laurence 178
Piłsudki, Josef 121
Pinochet, Augusto 37
Plamenatz, John 15
Platt, Gerald M. 192-3, 199, 223
Plumyène, Jean 119
Pol Pot 110, 177-8
Poland, para-fascism in 121
political Catholicism 6, 30, 69, 118, 120, 123, 124,
   132, 135, 141, 148, 150, 151, 209, 213
political religion 29-32, 33, 46, 186-8
political space 209-11
Political Futurism 59, 60, 61, 64
populism 36, 41-3
Portugal, fascism in 122-3, 141, 148, 156, 166, 169
post-war fascism
   impotence of 219-21
   innovation in 170-2
   main features of 170-4
   manifestations of 161-77
Preto, Rolão 123, 141
Preziosi, Giovanni 75
Prezzolini, Giuseppe 57, 60, 70
Primo de Rivera, José Antonio 123, 141, 150, 151,
   166
Primo de Rivera, Miguel 121, 122
proto-fascism 50-1, 202-5, 212-5
   in Germany 85-94
   in Italy 56-60, 61-3
Proust, Marcel 9
publicistic fascism 167, 172-3, 174, 209

Qadhafi, Muammar Al 37, 171, 177
Quisling, Vidkun A.L. 131, 136, 137

racism 203, 219
   see also anti-Semitism
Rapallo, (First) Treaty of 65
Rassemblement National Populaire (RNP) 136
Rauschning, Hermann 5, 101
regenerationist movements (Spain) 118

Reich, Wilhelm 186, 193
religious politics 30, 36, 125, 132-3, 134, 137, 138,
   139, 141, 162, 192
   see also political Catholicism, political religion
Republikaner, Die 167
Revelli, Marco 173
'revisionism' 167-8, 173
'revolutionary nationalism' 166, 173
Rex 30, 132-3, 141, 163, 209, 229
Ricci, Renato 70, 75
Riobov, Vyacheslav 177
Rocco, Alfredo 58, 68
Röhm, Ernst 100, 102, 229
Rogger, Hans 49
Romania, fascism and para-fascism in 126-7, 139,
   143, 160, 210
Romanità 73, 74, 151, 229
Rosenberg, Alfred 95, 108, 11
Rossi-Landi, Ferruccio 15
Rossoni, Edmondo 58, 68,
Russia 76, 118, 176-7, 214-5, 219-20
Russian Revolution 214-5

Saigō, Takamori 155-6
Saint-Simon, Comte de 39, 201
Salandra, Antonio 56
Salazar, Dr. Antonio de Oliveira 104, 122-3, 135,
   148, 161
Salgado, Plinio 147, 150-2, 157, 209
Salomon, Ernst von 92, 100, 198
Sarfatti-Grassini, Margherita 71
Schauwecker, Franz 92, 198
Schemann, Ludwig 87
Schmitt, Carl 105
Schnapper, Edith B. 33
Schönerer, Georg Ritter von 118, 124, 203
Schönhuber, Franz 167
Schröter, Manfred 105
Schuler, Alfred 87
Schuschnigg, Kurt von 126
Seekt, Hans von 95
Sewell, William H. Jr 193
Seyss-Inquart, Arthur 125
Shaffer, Peter 195-6, 200
Shaw, George Bernard 138
Sima, Horia 126
Sinarquistas 149
Sironneau, Jean-Pierre 29, 30
Slovakia, para-fascism in 130-1, 218
Smetona, Antanas 121
Smith, Anthony D. 38
Society of Orange Workers 159
Soffici, Ardegno 57, 59, 70
Sombart, Werner 88
Sonnino, Sidney 56
Sorel, Georges 6, 28, 42, 194, 203
Sotelo, Calvo 118
Soucy, Robert J. 119
South Africa, fascism in 45, 146, 156-61, 173, 174,
   209, 219, 219
Spain, fascism and para-fascism in 7, 118, 121, 123-
   4, 156, 210, 218
Spanish Civil War 2, 73, 139
Spengler, Oswald 92, 98, 138, 169, 216
Spinetti, Gastone 70, 75
squadrismo 65-7, 68, 70, 73, 75, 80, 92, 118, 224

Stalinism 46, 110, 111, 120, 168, 175, 176, 225
Stamboliisky, Alexander 210
Starace, Achille 68, 75
Steinberg, Jonathan 231-3
Sternhell, Zeev 6, 38, 133, 141, 166, 204
Stojadinović, Dr. Milan 121
strapaese 70, 72
Strasser, Gregor 95, 96, 100, 166, 224, 229
Strasser, Otto 166
'Strasserism' 166, 174
Sturmabteilung (SA) 96, 118, 119, 149, 177
Sudeten German Party 130
Swastika 87, 99, 105, 128, 160
Sweden, fascism in 128, 218
Switzerland, fascism in 129, 167, 169, 171, 218
Szálasi, Ferencz 127-8, 136, 138-9, 163, 171

Tasca, Angelo 20–21
Taut, Bruno 216
Terboven, Josef 131
Terre'Blanche (Terblanche), Eugene 160
terrorism, neo-fascist 163, 166, 174
Thadden, August von 172
Thalheimer, August 3
Theweleit, Klaus 198-9, 233
Third Reich 32, 92,
   as fascist regime 101-6
   see National Socialism
Thulegesellschaft (Thule Society) 94, 95,
Thule Seminar 169, 173
Thundercross (*Perkonkrust*) 122
Tiso, Msgr. Jósef 130-1
Tōjō, General Hideki 154
Tohokai (Society of the East) 155
Tolkien, John R.R. 169, 173
Traditionalist fascism 169, 173, 174
transcendence 186-8, 194-7, 234, 237
Treitschke, Heinrich von 88
Trevor-Roper, Hugh 5,
Tudor, Henry 27, 193

Ugunkrust (Fiery Cross) 122
Ulmanis, Kārlis, 122
ultra-nationalism viii, 36-8, 201, 208
   imperialist 49, 74
   neutralist 49, 79
   renaissance of 175, 176
   universalist *see* fascism, universalist
ultra-right, fascism's relationship to 49-50
Unión Nacional Sinarquista 149
Unión Patriotica 118
United States of America, fascism in, 45, 165, 170, 219
uomo fascista 74, 75

see also New Man
Ustasha 30, 120, 218
utopias (political) 28, 104, 111, 192, 194
   see also palingenetic myth

Valois, Georges 1 133
van Severen, Joris 132
van Tonningen, Rost 131
van Zeeland, Paul M. 132
Vaps (*Vabadussöjalaste Liit*) 119, 218
Vargas, Getulio 37, 148, 151
Vaterlandspartei (Fatherland Party) 89
Vecchi, Ferruccio 64, 65
Vega, Unzaga de la 150
Versailles, Treaty of 63, 90, 97, 215, 220, 226
Verwoerd, Dr. Hendrik F. 159
Vichy 134-6, 218
Victor Emmanuel III, King of Italy 66, 67, 224
Vittorio Veneto 63
Vocian ultra-nationalism 57-8, 60, 61
Voegelin, Eric 29, 30, 31, 35
Volk concept of 85
völkisch nationalism in Germany 85-90
   non-German equivalents of 120, 122, 124, 137, 153, 158-9, 209, 210
   relationship to Nazism 86, 99-100, 101, 103, 111
Volksgemeinschaft myth of 85, 87, 89, 94, 98, 106, 110, 111
Vorster, Balthazar J. 159

Wagner, Richard 87, 203
Wandervogel 88
Weber, Eugen 20, 40, 49, 140
Weber, Max 9, 37, 38, 43, 191-2
Weinstein, Fred 199
Welsh nationalism and neo-fascism 172
white supremacism 165, 173
Wilkinson, Paul 6
William II, Emperor of Germany 90
Wilson, Woodrow 34
Woltmann, Ludwig 87
Wulle, Rheinhold 91
WUNS (World Union of National Socialists) 152

Yeats, William Butler 200, 216
Yugoslavia, putative fascism in 120, 121, 215, 218

Zehrer, Hans 93
Zionism 162
Zunino, Piergiorgio 75